GRAPHIC DESIGN IN AMERICA

GRAPHIC DESIGN IN AMERICA

A VISUAL LANGUAGE HISTORY

Foreword

Caroline Hightower

Introduction

Mildred Friedman

Essays

Joseph Giovannini
Neil Harris
Estelle Jussim
David Kunzle
Maud Lavin
Ellen Lupton and J. Abbott Miller
Lorraine Wild

Interviews

Steven Heller

Walker Art Center, Minneapolis
Harry N. Abrams, Inc., New York

This book is published on the occasion of the inauguration of the exhibition *Graphic Design in America: A Visual Language History*, organized by Walker Art Center in collaboration with the American Institute of Graphic Arts. Following its premiere at the Walker Art Center, the exhibition will be shown at the IBM Gallery of Science and Art, New York; the Phoenix Art Museum, Phoenix, Arizona; and the Design Museum, Butlers Wharf, London.

Graphic Design in America: a visual language history/essays by
Mildred Friedman . . . [et al.]; interviews by
Steven Heller.
p. cm.
Catalog of an exhibition opening at Walker Art Center in Nov. 1989.
    Bibliography: p. 256
    Includes index
    ISBN 0–8109–1036–5 (Abrams). —
    ISBN 0–935640–31–2 (pbk.)
    1. Commercial art — United States —
Exhibitions. 2. Graphic arts — United States —
Exhibitions. I. Friedman, Mildred S. II. Walker
Art Center.
NC998.5.A1G65 1989
741.6'0973'074 — dc19   89–445 CIP

First edition

Printed and bound in the United States

Edited by Mildred Friedman and Phil Freshman

Designed by Glenn Suokko

Dimensions are in inches; height precedes width precedes depth. Except where noted, the works illustrated in this book are offset lithographs.

Graphic Design in America: A Visual Language History is made possible by a generous grant from Champion International Corporation. Additional support is provided by the National Endowment for the Arts.

Major support for the Walker Art Center exhibition program is provided by The Bush Foundation. Additional support is given by the Dayton Hudson Foundation for Dayton's and Target Stores, the First Bank System Foundation, the General Mills Foundation, the Honeywell Foundation, The McKnight Foundation, The Pillsbury Company Foundation, and the Minnesota State Arts Board, through an appropriation by the Minnesota State Legislature.

This book has been made possible by the Walker Art Center publication fund, established with generous support from The Andrew W. Mellon Foundation.

Contents

Foreword

Graphic design is a ubiquitous presence in our daily lives that can engage and inform us or simply add to the visual morass of contemporary culture. Important and unimportant messages are graphically communicated throughout the day. From the face of the clock that wakes us, the morning newspaper, and the subway or expressway signs on our way to work to the weather map on the evening news and the preparation of dinner, graphics are a constant in the lives of a captive audience unaware that the profession of graphic design exists and that quality can be of consequence.

Founded in 1914, the American Institute of Graphic Arts has provided an ongoing forum on graphic design in America through exhibitions, publications, seminars, and projects in the public interest — primarily aimed at an audience of practitioners. We were therefore especially pleased to cooperate with the Walker Art Center in the development of the exhibition *Graphic Design in America: A Visual Language History*, which presents graphic design from the nineteenth century to the present in a cultural context. This book, which complements the exhibition, investigates and challenges a field that has only recently become the subject of critical analysis.

Our hope is that this major undertaking will bring a relatively new profession under public scrutiny, where it can be evaluated by an audience increasingly aware of that profession's contributions. The time has come for the capacity of graphic designers to enhance our lives to be recognized as a source of pleasure, not simply through exhibitions of work collected as an art form but as a continuing contemporary presence that, at its best, is worthy of informed appreciation.

Caroline Hightower
Director, American Institute of Graphic Arts

"Information" is a pictogram from *Symbol Signs Repro Art* (1974–1979), a publication by the American Institute of Graphic Arts for the United States Department of Transportation. This study by a committee of designers, chaired by Thomas Geismar and including Seymour Chwast, Rudolph de Harak, John Lees, and Massimo Vignelli, was an effort to bring order to the use of graphic symbols in the public realm by providing the international community with a series of visual symbols that could be universally adopted, understood, and replicated in a diversity of materials and in various dimensions.

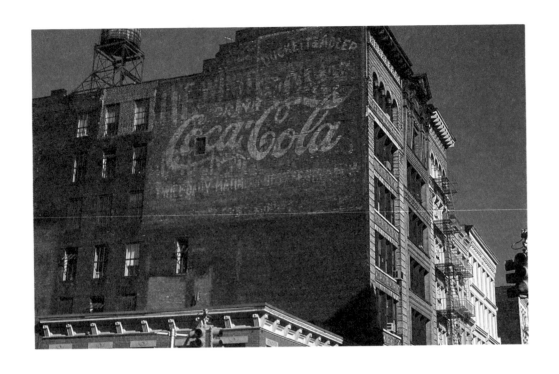

The function of the designer is to increase the legibility of the world.
— Abraham Moles

Opening a History

Mildred Friedman

In July 1988 *The New York Times* ran an editorial bemoaning the current corporate practice of converting familiar logotypes into characterless abstractions — or, as the editorial writer put it, "lifeless blobs."[1] Understanding the desire of ever larger conglomerates to create universal, nonspecific identities, *The Times*, nevertheless, makes a convincing case for a return to the old Prudential rock and for the continuing use of such long-standing trademarks as the fat and friendly Pillsbury Doughboy. The editorial, both witty and profound, recognizes the power of the words and images that constitute America's most pervasive, least understood public art form, an art form that depends for its efficacy on the degree to which those words and images communicate a coherent message.

The gradual shift in the United States from production to consumption in the early part of the twentieth century stimulated the development of a graphic design (né commercial art) profession, a discipline initially geared to maintaining the essential advertising revenues of the growing number of North American newspapers and magazines. By the late 1920s American graphics had, to a large extent, moved out of the print shop into the studio. While the printer had used typography in a perfunctory way to convey a message directly, the designer sought more complex relationships among text, typography, and image, creating ever more expressive means of communication. In the 1930s a depressed market led American business to the drawing board, not to celebrate its prosperity but to rejuvenate a lagging economy: industrial and graphic designers were given that charge by the resting industrial giants.

Since that time, graphic design has played a key role in the appearance of almost all print, film, and electronic media, as well as architectural and

The Coca-Cola trademark has changed very little since its earliest appearances in the 1880s. Fading from one New York City wall, it is reasserted in vivid night lights on another.

1. *The New York Times* (20 July 1988): 26.

9

urban signage. Today it literally dominates our visual environment. Yet even as the century draws to a close, there is only nominal acknowledgment of the significance of this least recognized visual art form. Why this is so has more to do with cultural mores and economics than with art, for a variety of reasons. First, the taint of commerce has relegated graphic design to the status of "second class" discipline in the academic realm, where it has historically been viewed as unworthy alongside the traditions of painting and sculpture. Second, graphic design is a collaborative, interpretive form. As a musician interprets musical composition, a designer interprets verbal and visual information; consequently, the designer has a less heroic image than that of the composer's opposite number, the painter. Third, graphic design is an art of unlimited reproduction, and so its mass-produced images are seen as less "valuable" than the unique ones of the "hand-made" arts. Today graphic design faces a new conundrum. The production of many print materials has moved from the design studio back into the office or shop, where it is no longer in the hands of trained designers but with non-designers empowered by the computer. A graphic cottage industry is emerging that returns graphics to the printer (now the office worker), one that has already impinged on the designer's territory. Despite these provisos, it is fair to say that this omnipresent art form, and those who create it, are worthy of critical attention.

Because graphic design is a verbal-visual expression, the designer's ideas must be accessible on several levels. In *Objects of Desire* (1986), the English critic Adrian Forty wrote of industrial design, "No design works unless it embodies ideas that are held in common by the people for whom the object is intended." Similarly, the visual language employed by the graphic designer must, to be effective, have a recognizable formal vocabulary, as frame of reference is all in communications.

The preeminent American designer Paul Rand has characterized the history of the typographic arts in America as "the history of a struggle between the craftsman and the creative artist, between common sense and sentimentality." These two strains continue to vie for attention on the American scene, for graphic design reflects the realities of contemporary life, and those realities include everything from the blatant imagery of McDonald's golden arches to the controlled sophistication of the Borzoi Books of Alfred A. Knopf.

Many questions arise in exploring the totality of American graphic design: What have been its derivations and influences? How have the communication arts contributed to American cultural life? How have technological innovations affected design? How have social and political changes emerged in graphic design? And what is inherently American about American graphic design?

As the breadth and depth of graphic material is daunting, the contributors to this book attempt to address these questions by concentrating on exemplary works, while at the same time providing a comprehensive view of the field. Those areas in which the graphic designer has made positive contributions to the ways in which we see and understand the world are examined; but deficiencies are also recognized, and the authors attempt to indicate where design might play a more significant, broader role.

In order to find a way into the extraordinary number and variety of designs of which we should be aware, a time line, using the terms of American Presidents as a framework, has been developed for this volume by Ellen Lupton and J. Abbott Miller. In each four-year segment, from 1829 to 1989, the coauthors have elected to include for discussion a single development in graphic design, always pointing out the ways in which the developments relate to their social, political, and cultural environments, and thus providing a historical context for the material that follows.

One area that has had little attention in design discourse is that of graphic art for the public good — or design as a social force. Neil Harris concentrates his discussion of this little-known genre in the so-called Progressive Era, the period from about 1900 to the end of World War I, during which the recognition of poverty and health problems in the United States came under serious scrutiny by such institutions as New York's Charity Organization Society and its sister association in Washington, D.C., Jane Addams's Hull House in Chicago, and the Russell Sage Foundation in New York, which provided support for a remarkable series of studies of urban life. Harris also discusses the innumerable American city plans that were beautifully described in maps and diagrams between 1900 and 1920, and he touches on the public concerns expressed in a number of publications of American companies such as New York Edison and Metropolitan Life Insurance. He points out that in the ensuing decades the American graphic designer has played an active, visible role in the education of a broad public in health, welfare, planning, and ecological concerns through such governmental bodies as the Works Progress Administration, the Smithsonian museums, and through privately funded efforts by health organizations, hospitals, and social agencies.

Related to design for public cause is the genre called "information graphics," which includes travel guides, maps, charts, and diagrams. Although the genre is not new, the proliferation of data in this information age has generated a wide spectrum of work, and an awareness of this diverse, fascinating area is essential to an understanding of contemporary graphic design.

While the impetus for design comes from many directions, the metamorphosis of the design process can be directly traced through the evolution of its tools and technologies. Changing technologies and the affect of those changes on design are the subjects of Estelle Jussim's essay; she places the practice of design within the larger frame of reference of the typographic, printing, and motion-graphics industries.

While she emphasizes the fact that technological progress does not ipso facto make design better, she points out that certain inventions have had enormous impact on graphic design, opening up new ways of seeing, producing, and combining images. Photography, film, television, and the computer have all radically altered the way graphics are conceived and the way they appear when realized.

Advertising design has been the most visible of the graphic arts. Maud Lavin approaches advertising in a radical manner. She examines the paternalistic image of the American corporation and illustrates how that characterization is abetted by design. In her essay she traces the ways in which advertisers promote products, target audiences, and control the structure of commercial communications. She raises a number of knotty questions about the designer's role vis-à-vis the client and the message the client wants to convey. She points out that the power of commercial design lies not in its formal resolutions but in the fact that it consists of images that are recycled many, many times and shared by a broadly based public. Lavin also demonstrates that designers can co-opt the methods of advertising, becoming the instigators and producers of projects that deal with serious societal needs, addressing these in much the same way that advertising addresses commerce. These are issue-oriented rather than client-oriented works; some recent examples of this innovative genre are described.

Although the field of view in this book is focused on the evolution of graphic design in America, European influences on American design are examined, particularly effects of the immigration to the United States in the late 1930s of a number of brilliant designers, many of whom came here to escape political repression. Now for the most part gone, that renowned generation (which included Herbert Bayer, Will Burtin, Ladislav Sutnar, and Herbert Matter) brought with it the modernist tradition that was the product of the visual, social, and scientific revolution of the early part of the century. Steeped in the intellectual traditions of Cubism, De Stijl, the Bauhaus, Dada, and the political movements that arose between the world wars, those émigrés looked to this country for the political and artistic freedom they had lost. They were, for the most part, experienced designers, known to American publishing and academic circles. So most of them found rewarding work quite rapidly after their arrival. (A few, like Mehemed Fehmy Agha, recruited in 1929 by Condé Nast, the American publisher of *Vanity Fair* who was familiar with European art and design, simply came to greener pastures.) There is little doubt that much of what we term American in American design today is actually an interpretation, or transformation, of those ideas that were in the remarkably fruitful minds of that group of transplanted Europeans. Lorraine Wild takes us through this history, pointing out the ways in which the aesthetics and the ideology of Modernism merged with an American vernacular. Wild believes that it was in the realm of advertising design that the separation of modernist ideas from pragmatism occurred. The two major

American design movements emerged, and parted ways, at that juncture — advertising design going in one direction and graphic design in the other. The personal expression that becomes a primary element in postwar American design moves, for the most part, out of commerce into the institutional and cultural arenas that include most of the design genres outside advertising.

The influence of European painting on American graphic design has been apparent since the turn of the century in such works as Will Bradley's posters for the little magazine *The Chap-Book*, in which the flat two-dimensionality of his overlapping figures is reminiscent of the Postimpressionist works of Toulouse-Lautrec and Vuillard. The influence from painting persists well into the century in, for example, Paul Rand's 1955 book jacket for Alan Harrington's novel *The Revelations of Dr. Modesto*, which reflects the designer's admiration of works by the artists Joan Miró and Jean Arp. Many of today's designers have looked even farther afield, and the arts of revolutionary Russia and postwar Japan have had an impact comparable to that felt earlier from Western Europe. Yet, as designers have become more self-assured, and new printing and photographic technologies have opened the door to prodigious design invention, the formal and expressive means of the designer have been less dependent on outside influences. The interaction between painting and design in America has become, to a degree, reciprocal. In commenting on popular culture, Roy Lichtenstein's comics, Andy Warhol's soup cans, James Rosenquist's billboards, Claes Oldenburg's hamburgers, Jasper Johns's flags, and Jenny Holzer's prose have used graphic design to take "high art" in new directions.

One of the directions taken by the graphic artist has been into the political arena. David Kunzle traces the course of that genre in the 1980s, comparing the protest works of the Vietnam era with the recent flurry of imagery that comes, for the most part, out of the continuing crisis in Central America and concerns that stem from the South African situation. Current domestic issues that have elicited graphic responses are associated with women's rights, gay rights, poverty and the lack of adequate affordable housing, and the scourge of AIDS. These posters of the so-called radical left are often spontaneous and "undesigned." But there is a growing category of professional work, dubbed the "poster of liberation" by Kunzle, which deals with current societal questions. Just as the Vietnam protest was slow to become a meaningful issue for the majority of Americans, many of today's painfully difficult problems, unacknowledged by many, may become central issues tomorrow, in part through the influence of the graphic image.

The attitudes analyzed in Kunzle's essay are at the far end of the design spectrum from those essentially formal and aesthetic issues addressed by Joseph Giovannini. Alarmed at what he calls the hyperactive appearance of many current periodicals and books, in which illustrations and typographic design often overwhelm the word, Giovannini makes a case for careful analysis of what is and is not appropriate in the design of the printed page. He contends that the intermixing of editorial content and advertising in many magazines is both confusing and distracting to the reader and that much of current design discourages reading, leaving something akin to the television "sound bite" on the printed page. Giovannini writes a cautionary tale, reminding us that the designer has a dual responsibility: one to the content of the material to be communicated and one to himself. The danger lies in the potential for the first to be obscured by the overwrought enthusiasm of the second. He also points to several publications that he believes maintain a balance between word and image. For the most part the examples he cites employ a very conservative design vocabulary. Somewhere between these and free rein perfection must lie.

Because designers are critically analyzed throughout this volume, it seems only just to provide an opportunity for them to speak in their own words and images. Steven Heller's interviews with a number of America's most illustrious designers, dispersed throughout the book, provide direct insights into the minds and hearts of our protagonists.

Finally, a number of designs from the exhibition this book accompanies are illustrated. The organization of the exhibition, by genre, divides the material into three primary sections: environmental graphics, including signs and symbols, guides and maps, posters and billboards, and public events such as the 1939 New York World's Fair; design for the mass media, including newspapers, magazines, books, and graphics in motion in film, television, and digitized imagery; and lastly, design for institutions, including works for government, business, and the design professions.

This art form, widely seen but rarely noted, is ripe for serious analysis and study. This book is an effort to open the way toward a deeper awareness and understanding of the history and theory of graphic design in America.

Starring James Stewart/Lee Remick/Ben Gazzara/Arthur O'Connell/Eve Arden/Kathryn Grant and
Joseph N. Welch as Judge Weaver/With George C. Scott/Orson Bean/Murray Hamilton/Brooks West.
Screenplay by Wendell Mayes/Photography by Sam Leavitt/Production designed by Boris Leven
Music by Duke Ellington/Produced and Directed by Otto Preminger/A Columbia release

FRANK SINATRA · ELEANOR PARKER · KIM NOVAK

THE
MAN
WITH
THE GOLDEN
ARM

A FILM BY OTTO PREMINGER · FROM THE NOVEL BY NELSON ALGREN · MUSIC BY ELMER BERNSTEIN · PRODUCED & DIRECTED BY OTTO PREMINGER

Saul Bass

[born 1920]

There were film titles before Saul Bass came along, but few were as graphic or as imaginative as his. There were also many alluring movie posters going back to the days of silent films, but most of these were overly rendered pictorial narratives. When in 1949 Saul Bass premiered his minimalist full-page newspaper ad for *Champion*, he skirted the star-studded, text-laden ads for the more symbolic gesture. His distilled graphic images for *Anatomy of a Murder*, *The Man with the Golden Arm*, and *Exodus* became arresting, animated film titles as well as posters. Not content with animation alone, Bass later turned to directing live-action film titles, which, rather than simply identifying the film, introduced the plot by making the titles the first scene. Bass's titles were collaborations between the designer and visionary directors and represent a golden age that lasted for more than a decade.

My first real job was working in the art department of the New York office of Warner Bros., in the late 1930s. Movie ads in those days covered all the bases. The idea of committing to a point of view in a campaign and saying, "This is the essence of what the picture is," was not considered. You showed all the ingredients of a picture: the dancing girls, the romance, the clinch, the hoopla, some action — whatever it might be. There was something for everybody. My tendency was to be reductionist. Gyorgy Kepes had just written a book called *Language of Vision* [1944], which really excited me. He had an embracing point of view about art, which I had not encountered before. But I could only carry it so far, because the other ingredients had to be there. I played with scale. I tried to push one idea and subordinate the others.

Finally, I said "enough." I quit my job and found one in an agency that did non-movie advertising. Soon after, I moved to Los Angeles and went to work for Buchanan & Co., the agency that handled Paramount Pictures. In the late 1940s *Life* was the big media buy, and I did an ad for *Champion* — the Kirk Douglas picture — that ran in the magazine. It was a totally black page with a tiny little halftone and a little scrawl, the whole thing taking up about an inch-and-a-half in the center of the page. It was dramatic. Even then, the name of

Film symbol for *Anatomy of a Murder*
various formats
© United Artists 1959, Los Angeles

Film symbol for *The Man with the Golden Arm*
various formats
© 1956 Bass/Yager and Associates, Los Angeles

17

OTTO PREMINGER PRESENTS PAUL NEWMAN, EVA MARIE SAINT, RALPH RICHARDSON, PETER LAWFORD, LEE J. COBB, SAL MINEO, JOHN DEREK, HUGH GRIFFITH, GREGORY RATOFF, JILL HAWORTH IN "EXODUS." SCREENPLAY BY DALTON TRUMBO, BASED ON THE NOVEL BY LEON URIS. MUSIC BY ERNEST GOLD. PHOTOGRAPHED IN SUPER PANAVISION 70, TECHNICOLOR® BY SAM LEAVITT. TODD AO STEREOPHONIC SOUND. A U.A. RELEASE. PRODUCED AND DIRECTED BY OTTO PREMINGER.

ALL WRAPPED UP

TODAY OTTO PREMINGER COMPLETED THE FILMING OF 'EXODUS.' ALL THE SHOOTING TOOK PLACE IN ACTUAL LOCALES AT HAIFA, ACRE, NAZARETH, CAESAREA, KAFR KANA, ATLIT AND JERUSALEM IN ISRAEL AND FAMAGUSTA, NICOSIA AND CARAOLOS ON THE ISLE OF CYPRUS. NOW 'EXODUS' ENTERS THE FINAL STAGES OF MUSICAL SCORING AND EDITING.

'EXODUS' STARS PAUL NEWMAN, EVA MARIE SAINT, RALPH RICHARDSON, PETER LAWFORD, LEE J. COBB, SAL MINEO, JOHN DEREK, HUGH GRIFFITH, GREGORY RATOFF, FELIX AYLMER, DAVID OPATOSHU & JILL HAWORTH. SCREENPLAY BY DALTON TRUMBO FROM THE BEST SELLING NOVEL BY LEON URIS. PRODUCED AND DIRECTED BY OTTO PREMINGER IN NEW PANAVISION 70 AND TECHNICOLOR® — A UNITED ARTISTS RELEASE.

'EXODUS' WILL OPEN AT THE WARNER THEATRE IN NEW YORK ON DECEMBER 15, 1960, THE CINE STAGE THEATRE IN CHICAGO ON DECEMBER 16, THE FOX WILSHIRE THEATRE IN BEVERLY HILLS ON DECEMBER 21, AND AT THE SHERIDAN THEATRE IN MIAMI BEACH ON DECEMBER 21.

CONTAINER CORPORATION OF AMERICA

the game was how do you separate yourself?

After I left Buchanan I went to Foote, Cone & Belding and worked for about a year with Howard Hughes, who ran RKO in those days. It was a fascinating experience. But he had a dead hand on things, a very boilerplate point of view.

Then I quit and began to free-lance. That's when I met Otto Preminger, which kicked off what became my most familiar work at Paramount. One incident tells the whole story: I remember walking into Preminger's office once, after the ads for *The Man with the Golden Arm* [1955] were done and out. He was sitting with his back to me — he didn't know I was there — talking on the phone, obviously to an exhibitor somewhere in Texas. The exhibitor was complaining about the ads and saying that he wanted to have a picture of Frank Sinatra in the ad. And I heard Otto say to him, "Those ads are to be used precisely as they are. If you change them one iota, I will pull the picture from your theater." And he hung up on him. I know that almost everybody hated those ads. They broke all the rules of what a campaign should do, because they only told one thing — they didn't provide

the normal stew, with potatoes, meat, and carrots. My ads were so reductive, they became metaphors. The trick, of course, with that approach was how do you get the essence of the film and yet present it in a sufficiently provocative way to excite the audience to go to the film?

The print advertising quickly evolved into motion picture titles. There was a time when titles were very interesting, going back to the early 1930s or even the late 1920s. Then it bogged down, and became bad lettering produced by firms that ground out titles. What I did was reinvent the whole notion of using a title to create a little atmosphere. For *The Man with the Golden Arm*, I made a series of moving white bars on a black screen, then a sort of abstract ballet — erratic and strident. Then, finally, the bars were transformed into the arm as symbol.

The early titles I made were essentially mood-setting. They started as animation and then evolved into live action. Animation is fun, but I feel closer to live action. I was dealing with metaphorical live action. For instance, in *Walk on the Wild Side* [1962] I filmed a cat fight. A black cat and a white cat meet, have a fight, and then part. That was a metaphor for New Orleans street life. Next the titles became a prologue. With *Grand Prix* [1966] I dealt with the preparation for the Monte Carlo race. What you saw was a montage of drivers, cars, the pack, the preliminaries, the warm-ups, the revving, then setting off the race. The viewer was into the picture when the race began.

Film symbol for *Exodus*
various formats
© 1960 Bass/Yager and Associates, Los Angeles

Trade advertisement for the film *Exodus*
various formats
© 1960 Bass/Yager and Associates, Los Angeles

John Stuart Mill on the Pursuit of Truth 1958
Advertisement for Container Corporation of America from the series Great Ideas of Western Man
13 x 10 1/2
Published by Container Corporation of America, Chicago

typo
graphy

by
Aaron Burns

HHHHHHHHHHHHHHHHHHHHHHHHHHHHHHHHHHHHHHHHHHHHHHHHHHHHHHHHHHHHHHHHHHHHHHHHHHHHHHHHH
HHHHHHHHHHHHHHHHHHHHHHHHHHHHHHHHHHHHHHHHHHHHHHHHHHHHHHHHHHHHHHHHHHHHHHHHHHHHHHHHH
HHHHHHHHHHHHHHHHHHHHHHHHHHHHHHHHHHHHHHHHHHHHHHHHHHHHHHHHHHHHHHHHHHHHHHHHHHHHHHHHH
HHHHHHHHHHHHHHHHHHHHHHHHHHHHHHHHHHHHHHHHHHHHHHHHHHHHHHHHHHHHHHHHHHHHHHHHHHHHHHHHH
HHHHHHHHHHHHHHHHHHHHHHHHHHHHHHHHHHHHHHHHHHHHHHHHHHHHHHHHHHHHHHHHHHHHHHHHHHHHHHHHH
HHHHHHHHHHHHHHHHHHHHHHHHHHHHHHHHHHHHHHHHHHHHHHHHHHHHHHHHHHHHHHHHHHHHHHHHHHHHHHHHH
HHHHHHHHHHHHHHHHHHHHHHHHHHHHHHHHHHHHHHHHHHHHHHHHHHHHHHHHHHHHHHHHHHHHHHHHHHHHHHHHH
HHHHHHHHHHHHHHHHHHHHHHHHHHHHHHHHHHHHHHHHHHHHHHHHHHHHHHHHHHHHHHHHHHHHHHHHHHHHHHHHH
HHHHHHHHHHHHHHHHHHHHHHHHHHHHHHHHHHHHHHHHHHHHHHHHHHHHHHHHHHHHHHHHHHHHHHHHHHHHHHHHH
HHHHHHHHHHHHHHHHHHHHHHHHHHHHHHHHHHHHHHHHHHHHHHHHHHHHHHHHHHHHHHHHHHHHHHHHHHHHHHHHH
HHHHHHHHHHHHHHHHHHHHHHHHHHHHHHHHHHHHHHHHHHHHHHHHHHHHHHHHHHHHHHHHHHHHHHHHHHHHHHHHH
HHHHHHHHHHHHHHHHHHHHHHHHHHHHHHHHHHHHHHHHHHHHHHHHHHHHHHHHHHHHHHHHHHHHHHHHHHHHHHHHH
HHHHHHHHHHHHHHHHHHHHHHHHHHHHHHHHHHHHHHHHHHHHHHHHHHHHHHHHHHHHHHHHHHHHHHHHHHHHHHHHH
HHHHHHHHHHHHHHHHHHHHHHHHHHHHHHHHHHHHHHHHHHHHHHHHHHHHHHHHHHHHHHHHHHHHHHHHHHHHHHHHH
HHHHHHHHHHHHHHHHHHHHHHHHHHHHHHHHHHHHHHHHHHHHHHHHHHHHHHHHHHHHHHHHHHHHHHHHHHHHHHHHH
HHHHHHHHHHHHHHHHHHHHHHHHHHHHHHHHHHHHHHHHHHHHHHHHHHHHHHHHHHHHHHHHHHHHHHHHHHHHHHHHH
HHHHHHHHHHHHHHHHHHHHHHHHHHHHHHHHHHHHHHHHHHHHHHHHHHHHHHHHHHHHHHHHHHHHHHHHHHHHHHHHH
HHHHHHHHHHHHHHHHHHHHHHHHHHHHHHHHHHHHHHHHHHHHHHHHHHHHHHHHHHHHHHHHHHHHHHHHHHHHHHHHH
HHHHHHHHHHHHHHHHHHHHHHHHHHHHHHHHHHHHHHHHHHHHHHHHHHHHHHHHHHHHHHHHHHHHHHHHHHHHHHHHH
HHHHHHHHHHHHHHHHHHHHHHHHHHHHHHHHHHHHHHHHHHHHHHHHHHHHHHHHHHHHHHHHHHHHHHHHHHHHHHHHH
HHHHHHHHHHHHHHHHHHHHHHHHHHHHHHHHHHHHHHHHHHHHHHHHHHHHHHHHHHHHHHHHHHHHHHHHHHHHHHHHH
HHHHHHHHHHHHHHHHHHHHHHHHHHHHHHHHHHHHHHHHHHHHHHHHHHHHHHHHHHHHHHHHHHHHHHHHHHHHHHHHH
HHHHHHHHHHHHHHHHHHHHHHHHHHHHHHHHHHHHHHHHHHHHHHHHHHHHHHHHHHHHHHHHHHHHHHHHHHHHHHHHH
HHHHHHHHHHHHHHHHHHHHHHHHHHHHHHHHHHHHHHHHHHHHHHHHHHHHHHHHHHHHHHHHHHHHHHHHHHHHHHHHH
HHHHHHHHHHHHHHHHHHHHHHHHHHHHHHHHHHHHHHHHHHHHHHHHHHHHHHHHHHHHHHHHHHHHHHHHHHHHHHHHH
HHHHHHHHHHHHHHHHHHHHHHHHHHHHHHHHHHHHHHHHHHHHHHHHHHHHHHHHHHHHHHHHHHHHHHHHHHHHHHHHH
HHHHHHHHHHHHHHHHHHHHHHHHHHHHHHHHHHHHHHHHHHHHHHHHHHHHHHHHHHHHHHHHHHHHHHHHHHHHHHHHH
HHHHHHHHHHHHHHHHHHHHHHHHHHHHHHHHHHHHHHHHHHHHHHHHHHHHHHHHHHHHHHHHHHHHHHHHHHHHHHHHH
HHHHHHHHHHHHHHHHHHHHHHHHHHHHHHHHHHHHHHHHHHHHHHHHHHHHHHHHHHHHHHHHHHHHHHHHHHHHHHHHH

Aaron Burns

[born 1922]

Aaron Burns cares passionately about typographic communication and has been a major participant in the recent revolutions, which, after four hundred years of adherence to Gutenberg's methods, occurred in quick succession beginning in the late 1940s. As director of The Composing Room (the legendary New York type house that not only set and sold type commercially but exhibited in its gallery the best practitioners in the world) he contributed to a qualitatively better environment for advertising typography through a union of technique and aesthetics. In *typography* (1961), the first of many "instructional guides" that marked major technological advancements, Burns was teaching designers about typographic expression and how to overcome the constraints of hot metal. He was an early proponent of the new phototypography. Pushing the technology that is taken for granted today was actually uphill all the way. As a founder, with Herb Lubalin, of International Typeface Corporation in 1970, he revitalized and modified for film many significant metal typefaces one thought lost because of the new technology. And today, with the digital revolution in full tilt, Burns is once again an evangelical typophile, working to provide personal computers with well-integrated typographic systems.

Aaron Burns's *typography* is about communicating with the printed word, using phototypesetting technologies that were state-of-the-art at the time it was written. The "color and texture" that can be created through the repetition of typographic forms is demonstrated in a design by the author.

typography 1961
14 1/4 x 10 1/8 format
Published by Reinhold, New York

Perfect communication is person-to-person. You see me, hear me, smell me, touch me. Television's the second form of communication; you can see me and hear me. Radio is the next; you hear me, but you don't see me. And then comes print. You can't see or hear me, so you must be able to interpret the kind of person I am from what is on the printed page. That's where typographic design comes in.

The designer's job is to present as clearly and succinctly as possible the message of the author. Anything that comes between the author and the clarity of the message is bad. I was the first graphic designer in New York City, to my knowledge, to work for a type shop. Before that, an art director, working for an advertising agency, would make a layout and then send it to a type shop and say, "Set to fit." Type selection was left in the hands of a non-designer. There were some exceptional designers who loved type, but the type shop as we know it was a typographic service. They set type and provided proofs. If you didn't know what a good setting was, you simply accepted whatever came back.

New technology made better, more expressive design possible. The specimen booklets that I developed at The Composing Room for metal type were an effort to create variety and color. They attempted to

We take pleasure in reprinting the accompanying appreciation of the Rover 3-Litre Sedan by the editors of Sports Cars Illustrated. We believe that it will help define, for the interested motorist, the unique qualities that have endeared the Rover to generations of owners.

ROVER

THE ROVER MOTOR COMPANY OF NORTH AMERICA LIMITED
36-12 37th Street, Long Island City 1, New York / 373 Shaw Road, South San Francisco, Calif. / Mobile Drive, Toronto, Ontario, Canada / 136 W. Second Ave., Vancouver, B.C., Canada

One of the last things a driver thinks about while threading through today's frenetic traffic is how long the manufacturer of his choice has been in business. This little nugget of information, on first thought, would seem to have little to do with how well the car goes. On reflection, however, and in connection with the Rover 3-Litre to be examined here, it has a great deal to do with the performance and appearance of an auto firm's end product.

Only two other U.S. car builders—Ford and Olds—can match the Rover Company's 56 continuous years of designing and fabricating automobiles. In many ways the newest Rover reflects traditional thinking—solid rear axle, chair-high seating, F-head engine—while in others—laminated torsion bar front suspension, monocoque chassis, disc brakes—it is abreast of, if not ahead of, contemporary engineering. A modern aspect of the 3-Litre is its body shape. Externally it owes much to the Italian school of design, suitably worked around in front to retain—though faintly—some flavor of the traditional Rover grille. This marriage of the Latin line and British conservatism has been tried on one or two other English luxury cars in the past. The results, unfortunately, have not produced a lasting union. The 3-Litre, however, seems to be a happy combination of both schools of thought, one that we think will wear well. Attaining a modern appearance that would not offend old-line Rover owners must have been one of the more difficult jobs faced by the engineering staff when they laid out the new car. Down through the years Rover cars have been adopted by some of Britain's better families. A new model in vulgar taste would be tantamount to having a young son sent down from Oxford for slovenly dress. This deference to the tastes of past Rover buyers gives a clue to the type of car that the company has been building for the past half century. Rovers have been solid, dependable, unostentatious automobiles that quietly inform driver and passengers alike that they are riding in a luxury car. This same impression is given onlookers as the Rover goes silently by.

The new 3-Litre in no way differs from this established approach. Entrance through the 36-inch wide front door opening can be accomplished without loss of dignity or breath. The first thing that strikes a neophyte Rover driver when he gets behind the wheel is that this is a big car. Its wheelbase is only 7.5 inches less than the latest Plymouth, yet overall length is 22.5 inches less than the same be-finned U.S. sedan. The next thing that one notices is the quality of workmanship displayed in the interior trim. For one attuned to the vagaries of production-line techniques employed on small economy sedans, the Rover interior impresses by its lack of sharp points, ragged edges, and short-measure head linings. Adding to this feeling of richness are the real leather upholstery and walnut-faced door fillets and glove compartment lids.

The pleasantly thick-rimmed steering wheel is set at just about the right angle and does not project into the driver's line of sight, while the instrument binnacle is positioned high enough to allow readings to be taken without consciously having to take one's eyes from the road. This instrument pod, cowled to eliminate reflections, contains dials for speed, water temperature, fuel and oil levels, switches for panel lights (with brightness control) main lights, oil level and key start ignition lock. Warning lights, placed between the two big dials, are used to indicate lack of oil pressure and sparks. With the exception of the cold start device—manual choke with an amber light that warns when it's in use, and the oil level gadget that utilizes the fuel gauge pointer when the right switch is flicked to give a rough estimate of the amount of oil in the sump—all of these instruments can be found on many other cars. What you don't find, however, is the quality of workmanship that makes everything on the Rover work with such a degree of smoothness that you find yourself clicking things on and off just to look and listen,

The seating position (our test car had the bench seat—bucket seats can be had as optional extras) is very comfortable with the emphasis on giving a driver of more than average size plenty of room. Distaff drivers (that most American women drive is a fact that has to be faced) might find the driving seat just a little too commodious. The fold-down arm rest cuts the 55-inch-wide front seat roughly in half, thus limiting the distance that the smaller driver will slide on the smooth leather, but it still leaves a generous space for the small-derriered to rattle around in. Gears are shifted in the four-speed box by a crooked lever that projects, after suitable bends, from under the car-wide parcel shelf. It is shaped so as not to discommode a central passenger. After getting the gear shift lever very neatly out of the way, it seems a shame that the rather large transmission tunnel does encroach on the foot room of the middle passenger. In use the gearbox fits the temperament of the Rover to a T. Strong, blocker-type synchromesh prevents ultra-fast shifts, while making normal shifts simple and silent. On our test car the detent spring that prevents accidental engagement of reverse when one is going for first gear was a little weak. This proved a minor embarrassment on one occasion. Rover drivers should never appear flustered to people in lesser vehicles.

With a twist of the ignition key the 182-cubic-inch six is ready to go. When cold there is just the slightest amount of valve noise. After the engine is warm you have to use the ignition warning light to find out whether or not you've stalled. (An aside on the amount of time it takes for the 3-Litre to warm up: Apparently Rover owners are not expected to

ride in cold cars. Within blocks the very comprehensive heating system is pouring out warm air.) Under way the Rover impresses by its silence. Up to 45 or 50 mph you can hear the electric clock ticking. At speeds over that, wind noise—right around the center door post—muffles the sound of the clock, but doesn't intrude on conversation carried on at a living room level of pitch and volume. On the open road the Rover reveals its reason for being. At speed the steering that seemed heavy in slow crawling traffic is light and precise, while the big, roomy seats allow plenty of fidgeting space. It is easy to visualize a captain of industry hurrying from one end of England to the other on important business in the comfort of his Rover. Ride is just a little firmer than on domestic sedans, which does away with that floating sensation you sometimes get in softly sprung cars at turnpike speeds. Bumps, with the softer suspension of the 3-Litre, are over and done with without the series of diminishing oscillations familiar to users of American-built luxury cars. Cornering—or just plain handling—is good for any situation that a Rover user might find himself in. Tires do howl on tight corners if recommended pressures are adhered to, and the car understeers to a greater and greater degree as speeds into turns are increased.

The Rover brakes are more than a little responsible for the car's ability to put up high averages. When first tried we thought they were a little puny to cope with the 3-Litre's 4,000-odd pounds of bulk. This, however, was a case of familiarity breeding satisfaction. It was also an interesting case of how preconditioned senses can mislead. In 90 percent of the automobiles being built today one sign of husky brakes doing their job is the sight of the nose of the car dipping violently. This is not what happens with the Rover, however. When the stop pedal is pushed the car simply stops—without dipping, swaying or swerving—it just stops. Few of the effects of deceleration are transmitted to the occupants. One simple way to achieve this non-dipping quality is by tipping the front wishbones up slightly, which is what the Rover people have done. All of the above commentary was based on the brakes of our test car, which were drum-type all around. Newer 3-Litre cars are equipped with Girling discs on the front which should make braking capabilities that much better.

The empathy between buyers and builder is nowhere better displayed than in the very comprehensive owner's manual that accompanies every Rover car. Its tone is that of two old friends having a chat over a good dinner. . . . If the unthinkable should happen and a Rover owner came to an unscheduled halt, ten well-made hand tools reside in a form-fitting sponge rubberlined tray that slides out from under the parcel shelf. If it's only a flat tire, however, a jack, lug wrench, tire pump and spare tire valve in a little lidded depression can be found in the trunk—all securely fastened to prevent rattles, of course. For a flat battery a crank is also clipped on the side of the trunk. All of these things, along with the very well-written owner's manual, should make a Rover driver fairly self-sufficient. A delivered price of about $5,000* makes the 3-Litre Rover an expensive car to buy. However, purchase of a Rover is the nearest an individual can come to buying a friend. —SCI May, 1960

**Prices of the Rover 3-Litre Sedan vary with ports of entry and equipment. It is available with Borg-Warner automatic transmission as well as four-speed gearbox with overdrive.*

AUTHORIZED ROVER SALES & SERVICE: CONNECTICUT: Imported Cars of Greenwich (a division of Greenwich Auto Repair Company), 240 Mason Street, Greenwich / D.C.: Flood Pontiac Company, 4221 Connecticut Avenue, Washington / MARYLAND: Motor Sales Company, Mt. Royal and Maryland Avenues, Baltimore / MASSACHUSETTS: Britannic Motors Ltd., 1033 Commonwealth Avenue, Boston / Concours Motors Inc., 15 Mill Street, Springfield / NEW JERSEY: Stillman & Hoag, 85 Van Nostrand Avenue, Englewood / Lloyd Buick Company, 300 St. Georges Avenue East, Linden / NEW YORK: Schumann-Van Atta Buick, Inc., 32 State Street, Binghamton / North Country Motors Ltd., 790 Northern Blvd., Great Neck / Surrey Motors Corporation, 49-21 Northern Blvd., Long Island City / Sidney-Elliot, 421 Columbia Street, Utica / Foreign Cars of Westchester, 25 Martine Avenue, White Plains / Autoland, Inc., 1065-1081 Main Street, Buffalo / Vintage Car Store, Inc., 93-45 South Broadway, Nyack / OHIO: Salter Automotive Imports Inc., 9009 Carnegie Avenue, Cleveland / PENNSYLVANIA: Nick Ciliberti of Cutztown, 601 East Main Street, Cutztown / Community Motors Inc., 588 Market Street, Kingston / Ascot Imported Cars, 604 Beaver Street, Sewickley / Berry Buick, Inc., 3908 North Broad Street, Philadelphia.

28

29

Aaron Burns

sleep

dear

In the wordplay above, typographers Lester Teich and Abraham Seltzer have attempted to make words look like what they mean. The droopy-eyed, inverted "e's," and the supine "d" are amusing attempts to personalize abstract letter forms.

In another example (opposite) from Burns's book *typography*, designer René Bittel has painstakingly organized type around the shape of the car — a difficult task in 1961; today this setting could be instantly realized with digitized typography.

show what one could do with the materials of the day. Many years later, when I was with a company called TGC, we were the first commercial type shop in New York City to advance phototypesetting successfully because we spent about a third of a million dollars each year to replace metal type. Film doesn't have to be replaced as quickly as metal, which was the reason we went to film. My job at TGC was to convince the city of New York that phototypesetting was going to be as good as metal.

We chose Mergenthaler because it was the Rolls Royce of typesetting equipment. But how was I going to prove that to New York designers? I asked Mergenthaler to give me specimen books, and the three they gave me were terrible. When I looked at the spacing between letters, I said, "I can't show this to a designer." So I designed my own booklet, *The TGC Handbook of Linofilm Typography*. The point was to educate people.

With metal type, each letter had a shoulder. Film had no shoulder, so you could put the letters closer together. We were creating a new texture, because the space between the characters made for poorer, harder-to-read typography. The eye could grasp a group of words, but if the spacing between the letters forced you to limit the number of words that you could grasp, that was poor typography. It was possible, with the new technology, to set a high quality of typography that had never existed before. It didn't take long for this to happen. Now we are in the midst of an even more significant revolution — digital typography.

I believe that eventually there will be a universal language. We're working at it right now. You know, if you can read musical notes, you can play Beethoven's Fifth Symphony in any language, in any country in the world. Why can't we create one universal typographic language that would mean the same thing all over the world?

Hermann Zapf and I are working to create a common language and publishing something called the "ABC Styles." We're working on a series of things that will make it possible for the uninitiated user of typography to produce reasonably well-set typographic communications. It takes nonprofessionals away from the typewriter's monotone look. It helps them to start thinking, "Shall I put this work in italic? Shall I put it in boldface?" It makes them think typographically. And we're putting in safeguards. We're creating defaults.

I believe that with the new technology and personal computers, typography will become like stepping into a new car and turning on the ignition. Everything will be automatic, and you won't have to learn how to shift.

23

A Time Line of American Graphic Design, 1829–1989

Ellen Lupton and J. Abbott Miller

As a genre of graphic design the time line occupies an intermediate zone between pictorial and textual composition. Typically written in a terse, telegraphic style that dispenses with punctuation, the time line substitutes the rhythm of chronological order for the cohesion of traditional writing. The time line visualizes history in a way that traditional prose does not, distributing words across a grid that regulates their placement.[1]

Yet often what the time line visualizes is merely the temporal proximity of one event to another. Time becomes an organizing principle that overwhelms all other criteria of analysis and interpretation. By its very structure, the time line adopts chronology as an explanatory model, conceiving of history as a ribbon whose sequence reveals its meaning.

The condensed and schematic quality of the time line arises from its ambition to distill the "fundamental" points of its subject. In the interest of brevity and clarity the time line masks the interpretive character of historical narrative — hence its emphasis on "facts" and "information." The "objective" language commonly used in time lines and the exclusion of interpretive commentary obscure the presence of an active decision-making "author." This is reinforced by the fact that time lines are rarely "written" but are more often compiled, researched, and designed. By masking the opinion and subjectivity that are part of any kind of writing and research, time lines tend to foster the notion that history is a matter of fact rather than a question of values. They de-politicize the writing of history, attributions of influence, and assigning of roles. The continuous linear model of the time line promotes an understanding of history as an organic "progression" toward contemporary values.

The following essay adopts the discontinuous, fragmentary character of the time line. But instead of trying to present a schematic picture of a monolithic, novelistically unified development, we have tried to show that "the history of graphic design" is diffused among a number of institutions and discourses. Rather than attempt to construct a spatial field for listing the "most important" events and names, we have used the time line format to create a chronological framework for a set of independent texts.

Whereas many time lines divide a historical span abstractly according to decades or centuries, we have used the four-year cycle of the American Presidential term as our unit of measure. While some of the case studies directly consider the Presidency, we have employed the "Presidential grid" primarily for its familiarity in American public life.

A number of these case studies are broken into two parts, reflecting an opposition within the text. This division exploits the graphic character of the time line genre, using typography to mark a shift in content. Each break indicates a polarity such as theory/practice, production/consumption, dominant/marginal, and artistic/anonymous; these divisions have allowed us to indicate contradictions, to bring together isolated discourses, or to present a topic from two different vantages. We have thus tried to use the time line as a critical matrix for representing history.

Ellen Lupton and J. Abbott Miller are graphic designers and writers and are partners in Design Writing Research, New York. Lupton teaches design history at The Cooper Union and is curator of the Herb Lubalin Study Center of Design and Typography there. Miller teaches design history at the New School for Social Research, New York.

This essay was researched and written in cooperation with the Herb Lubalin Study Center of Design and Typography at The Cooper Union for the Advancement of Science and Art, New York.

1. For a fuller discussion of the time line as a way of representing history, see J. Abbott Miller, "Tracking the Elusive Time Line," *Journal of Graphic Design* 6, 2 (1988): 7.

Creating National Culture(s): Old Hickory and Sequoyah

Andrew Jackson's fierce campaign in 1828 against John Quincy Adams initiated the modern American system of political campaigning.[1]

Because of revisions in state voting laws, the election of 1828 was the first in which nearly all white male adults could vote. Candidates now had to appeal to a mass electorate. The decorum and propriety circumscribing earlier Presidential contests gave way to an aggressive use of slogans and electioneering that was supported by an array of posters, pamphlets, bandanas, buttons, mugs, plates, snuff-boxes, and rallies. What had been a contest of statesmen turned into an aggressive battle of public personalities vying for office by discrediting one another and using mass-produced propaganda to make visible their popular support. Jackson's campaign workers, called "hurrah boys," distributed hickory sprigs, hickory sticks, hickory brooms, and planted hickory poles, playing upon the "Old Hickory" nickname that Jackson earned when he gave his horse to an injured soldier, completing the long journey back to camp on foot with a walking stick he made from a hickory branch.

Jackson's landslide victory was due in part to the failure of the Adams campaign to compete with the imaginative and extensive publicity produced by Jackson's supporters. Much of this promotional material capitalized on imagery of Jackson as a uniformed general, invoking his earlier notoriety as a war hero in the 1815 Battle of New Orleans. His war record included the massacre of many Indian populations, earning him a reputation, commendable to those untroubled by genocide, as a ruthless and efficient military leader. The era of Jacksonian democracy was ushered in by a media campaign that attacked the aristocratic residue of the American Presidency while fashioning a larger-than-life Everyman.

While white Americans were forging a "national" culture aided by the military and political campaigns of Andrew Jackson, so too were the Cherokee Indians constructing a formal "nation" with written laws and elected leaders. Although many Cherokees could read English, the native Cherokee language had no written form until, between 1809 and 1828, an Indian named Sequoyah designed an alphabet that would transform his native culture.[2]

Although Sequoyah could neither speak nor read English, during his contact with white

Americans he became curious about their books, or "talking leaves." Some Cherokees believed that writing was a gift mystically bestowed on Europeans. But Sequoyah believed that writing was a mere human invention, and he set out to design a similar system for the Cherokee language. He began by trying to match every word with a separate character, but when this proved too cumbersome he began to analyze the language into syllables, which could be recombined into words. Initially he represented each of

1833 Andrew Jackson

his eighty-five syllables with a picture but later turned to arbitrary signs. Many of these, borrowed from the Roman alphabet, were given new meanings; the rest were designed with flourishes, geometric shapes, and fragments of other letters.

The Cherokee Phoenix, established in 1828 as the first Indian newspaper, was printed in English and Cherokee, with castings of Sequoyah's alphabet. Although its syllabary became a politically powerful tool for the Cherokees, it inevitably changed their culture. Missionaries used it to teach Christianity and to promote European customs;

members of the Cherokee middle- and ruling classes used it to advocate and publicize the "civilization" of "savages." Beginning with the "discovery" of the New World in the fifteenth century and the colonization that followed, Indian societies were confronted with new customs and technologies, provoking change in societies that had been stable for centuries. The Cherokee alphabet became an important tool for the dynamic Cherokee society of the nineteenth century, helping to preserve tribal culture by spreading political news, transmitting information between communities in eastern and western America, and extending literacy to the non-English-speaking population; at the same time it participated, unavoidably, in the destruction of the old way of life.

Newspapers Become a Mass Medium

Although printed news sheets and handwritten "news letters" were circulated in colonial America, the newspaper did not become a mass medium until the 1830s with the emergence of the penny press. (The first penny paper was founded by Ben Day in Manhattan, 1833.) The penny papers, hawked on the street, challenged the established "six-penny" papers, sold by subscription to an elite business class. Whereas most six-penny papers were backed by political parties, the new cheap press was run by independent entrepreneurs; politicians were now represented through an aggressive medium that chose its own candidates. The "news" as we know it today emerged in this period: an ongoing, immediate narrative with no beginning or end, serving as both disposable entertainment and an ethically bound historical record.

As the historian Michael Schudson has pointed out, the names of most six-penny papers included terms such as "advertiser," "mercantile," or "commercial," which referred to the interests of business, while the titles of the new popular papers employed words such as "critic," "herald," "tribune," "star," or "sun," which suggest prophetic sources of enlightenment.[1]

Although the penny press was progressive as an economic and a literary institution, it was conservative visually: text ran in densely set columns of tiny type with minimal headlines. The need for a cheap, fast, and uninterrupted production routine discouraged editors from designing new typographic formats, and newspaper production solidified into a rigidly conservative trade, changing only in minor ways before the rise of the illustrated newspaper in the 1880s.[2]

1. Roger A. Fischer, *Tippecanoe and Trinkets Too: The Material Culture of American Presidential Campaigns, 1828–1984* (Urbana: University of Illinois Press, 1988). Fischer notes that the material culture of Presidential campaigns dates back to the founding of the Presidency, when such objects generally served as commemorative tokens. What his book — and this essay — is concerned with is the persuasive or propagandistic function of objects used in political campaigns. Considered from that vantage, the campaign of 1828 marks a turning point.
2. On Sequoyah, see Althea Bass, "Talking Stones: John Howard Payne's Story of Sequoya," *The Colophon* (pt. 9, 1932); reprint of an 1835 account of the life of Sequoyah. Theda Perdue's introduction to *Cherokee Editor: The Writings of Elias Boudinot* (Knoxville: University of Tennessee Press, 1983) includes an essay on Sequoyah by Elias Boudinot, "Invention of a New Alphabet," originally published in the *American Annals of Education*, 1 April 1832. On American Indian presses, see Daniel F. Littlefield, Jr., and James W. Parins, *American Indian and Alaska Native Newspapers and Periodicals, 1826–1924* (Westport, Conn.: Greenwood Press, 1984).

1. For the history of the American press, see Michael Schudson, *Discovering the News: A Social History of American Newspapers* (New York: Basic Books, 1967, 1973).
2. For a comprehensive history of newspaper design, see Allen Hutt, *The Changing Newspaper: Typographic Trends in Britain and America, 1622–1972* (London: Gordon Fraser, 1973).

Advertising Advertising

Unlike the established six-penny papers that were supported largely by subscription, the more mainstream penny press was dependent on advertising revenues. The subservience of advertisers to the newspapers they patronized was reflected in the restriction of ads to small "agate" type in a want-ad style, sometimes including a larger initial capital or a generic illustration. Such restrictions did not, however, carry over into editorial matters: for example, the penny press was the primary vehicle for the spurious claims of patent medicine advertising.[1]

The shift in the newspaper-advertiser hierarchy may be registered in the increase in size, imagery, and typographic variety of ads throughout the nineteenth century. When the *New York Herald*

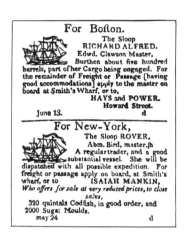

allowed advertisers to exceed the traditional one-column width in 1836, the severe reaction among competing advertisers forced the paper to ban display typography and to enforce size restrictions. Techniques for circumventing the "agate only" rule signaled the gradual erosion of these restrictions in the face of the powerful and profitable advertising industry.[2]

The Ad Man

In 1841 John L. Hooper was working as an advertising solicitor for the *New York Tribune*. Advertisers who submitted copy to Hooper often requested that he place their copy in other newspapers as well. Realizing that he could work in this capacity for a number of newspapers and advertisers, Hooper left the *Tribune* to form his own advertising office. At about the same time Volney Palmer announced that his Philadelphia real estate office would procure and administer space in newspapers on behalf of advertisers who wished to avoid the "trouble of perplexing and fruitless inquiries, the expense and labour of letter writing, the risk of making enclosures of money &c, &c."[1] For advertisers, Palmer and Hooper did not write or design ads but negotiated the complicated terrain of the newspaper trade.

For newspapers, which paid their commission, they acted as space salesmen, simplifying a process that would otherwise have involved hundreds of individual

requests. By the end of the 1840s Palmer was operating out of offices in Baltimore, Boston, Philadelphia, and New York and claimed to represent thirteen hundred newspapers. Newspapers were, however, unwilling to assign agents exclusive contracts, encouraging the proliferation of a highly competitive profession.

1. For the relationship between advertising in the "establishment" press and the penny press, see Schudson, *Discovering the News.*
2. The early development of advertising typography and illustration in relation to the penny press is discussed in Frank Presbrey, *The History and Development of Advertising* (New York: Doubleday, Doran, 1929).

1. For information on the development of the ad agency out of the newspaper industry, see Daniel Pope, *The Making of Modern Advertising* (New York: Basic Books, 1983), 119–129; and Presbrey, *The History and Development of Advertising.*

1845 James Polk

Abolition:
Idealism and Realism

A movement to abolish slavery in the United States had gathered force by 1840. Organized by white reformers in the North, the movement spoke through newspapers, pamphlets, posters, books, and almanacs, which aimed to instill moral outrage among whites against the institution of slavery. The publications of the American Anti-Slavery Society in New York, for example, included a magazine for children called *The Slave's Friend*, distributed to school libraries, and an illustrated *Almanac* which documented Southern atrocities. The practice, depicted in the *Almanac*, of branding slaves with their master's insignia was a violent typographic act emblematizing the conversion of human beings into private property.[1]

The white-dominated abolition movement identified slavery as a self-contained evil that could be cleanly cut away from America's moral conscience; black activists, on the other hand, saw slavery as only one aspect of a culture structured by racism. As the historians Jane and William Pease have noted, white abolitionists had little concern for the civil rights of free blacks in the North or the political and economic future of freed slaves.[2] The white abolitionist William Lloyd Garrison changed the character of the movement by including blacks among the writers, speakers, and audience of his crusade; his journal *The Liberator*, founded in 1831, was largely supported by blacks. Garrison's thought, however, remained directed at purging sin from white society: "freedom" served as an abstract ideal. *The New York Weekly Advocate*, a black newspaper, wrote in 1837, "Free indeed! ... when almost every honorable incentive to the pursuit of happiness, so largely and freely held by his fairer brother, is withheld from [the black man]."[3]

1849 Zachary Taylor, Millard Fillmore

Chromolithography

In the process of lithography an image is drawn with a grease crayon onto a lithographic stone or a metal plate; when the surface of the stone is bathed in water, ink adheres only to the crayoned areas. A chromolithograph combines several different stones, each carrying a separate color. The first American chromolithograph was printed in Boston in 1840. Printing companies marketed chromolithograph reproductions of oil paintings, bringing art to the middle classes; the technique was also used for advertisements, book illustrations, calendars, and other graphic ephemera. The industry peaked and then began to decline in the 1890s with the improvement of photomechanical reproduction.[1]

1853 Franklin Pierce

Photography and the Graphic Arts

Processes for recording an image on a light-sensitive surface — what we now call photography — were announced independently by several inventors in the 1830s and 1840s.[1] Whereas Louis-Jacques-Mandé Daguerre's daguerreotype was a unique image imprinted on a heavy plate, the method introduced by the English scientist William Henry Fox Talbot involved a paper negative, which had the potential to generate an infinity of positive prints. Talbot's book *The Pencil of Nature* (1844–1846) consisted of individually printed and mounted photographs: portraits, architectural views, reproductions of engravings, and cameraless silhouetted prints made by laying botanical specimens directly on light-sensitive paper.

One of the first photographic books published in the United States was Nathaniel Hawthorne's *Transformations; or, The Romance of Monte Beni*.[2] Like Talbot's *The Pencil of Nature*, Hawthorne's novel is illustrated with actual photographic prints, pasted by hand into a conventional typographic book. When Hawthorne's novel was reissued in 1890 it was illustrated by photogravure, a process in which a layer of fine powder is exposed to a

1. Dwight Lowell Dumond's book *Antislavery: The Crusade for Freedom in America* (Ann Arbor: University of Michigan Press, 1961) includes reproductions of antislavery propaganda.
2. Jane H. Pease and William H. Pease, *They Who Would Be Free: Blacks' Search for Freedom, 1830–1861* (New York: Atheneum, 1974).
3. Ibid., 9.

1. For an extensive history of chromolithographs, see Peter C. Marzio, *The Democratic Art: Chromolithography, 1840–1900*, exh. cat. (Fort Worth: Amon Carter Museum of Western Art, 1979), 99, 100.

1857 James Buchanan

The Railroad: Managing Nature and Business

photographic negative, and the resulting image is etched into a metal printing plate.

Photogravure offers richer, finer-grained images than process halftone engraving, invented by Frederick Ives in 1881 and commercially viable by 1893, which remains the standard method for reproducing photographs today. In this technique a screen translates tonal gradations into a fine pattern of black dots, perceived by the eye as continuous shades of gray. The major advantage of the halftone is that it can be printed on the same paper, with the same ink, and at the same time as metal type. The halftone revolutionized the graphic arts, allowing photographic images to be cheaply integrated into mass-media publishing.

During the nineteenth century the railroad transformed America's landscape, economy, and imagination: it was a vehicle for colonizing the unsettled wilderness and distributing industry, natural resources, and information across the continent; its rails were often the first permanent human path to be cut into a stretch of land.[1]

Although painters such as Thomas Cole and John Kensett often included railroads in their paintings during the 1850s, they usually showed the train as a tiny machine engulfed by its natural setting — the critic Leo Marx contends that because landscape painting in America at this time had an almost religious status, to monumentalize the details of the train would have debased the seriousness of the art.[2] Popular chromolithographs, on the other hand, often celebrated the smoke, speed, and mechanical details of the locomotive.

AMERICAN RAILWAY SCENE, AT HORNELLSVILLE, ERIE RAILWAY.

Behind the heroic image of the train as civilizer of the American wilderness lay a revolution of a different sort: a revolution in management. Unprecedented quantities of capital were needed to finance a vast range of enterprises, from the laying of tracks and the construction of engines to the control of traffic and the scheduling of trains. A new form of business emerged to direct these projects: the modern corporation.[3]

In a large corporation ownership is separate from management — there can be thousands of owners, most of whom have minimal influence on policy. (The New York Stock Exchange, where shares in businesses are bought and sold in the interest of speculation rather than entrepreneurship, was born in the 1840s in order to finance the railroads.) A large corporation consists of numerous independent units controlled by a hierarchy of salaried managers —

those at the top of a given unit report to officials at the next level, who may have little direct knowledge of the operations below. This division of bureaucratic labor was necessitated by the technical and geographic diversity of a railroad's activities, which made it impossible for any single individual to control — or even understand — every level of the system. David McCallum, an executive of the Erie Railroad, designed one of the first "corporate management charts" in 1856, made available

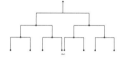

for one dollar per copy by the American Railroad Journal.[4] Today similar corporate management charts remain an important form of internal — rather than public — imagery, visualizing the position of each employee within a network of varying levels of accountability.

1. The main source here is Estelle Jussim, *Visual Communication and the Graphic Arts: Photographic Technologies in the Nineteenth Century* (New York: R.R. Bowker, 1974).
2. Nathaniel Hawthorne, *Transformations; or, The Romance of Monte Beni* (Boston: Houghton Mifflin, 1860). Hawthorne's novel was reissued under the title *The Marble Faun; or, The Romance of Monte Beni* (Boston: Houghton Mifflin, 1890).

1. On American railroad culture, see Susan Danly, "Introduction," Susan Danly and Leo Marx, eds., *The Railroad in American Art: Representations of Technological Change* (Cambridge, Mass.: MIT Press, 1988), 1–50.
2. On the meaning of small trains in big paintings, see Leo Marx, "The Railroad-in-the-Landscape: An Iconological Reading of a Theme in American Art," *The Railroad in American Art*, 183–206.
3. Material on the history of the railroad corporation comes from Alfred D. Chandler's *The Visible Hand: The Managerial Revolution in American Business* (Cambridge, Mass.: Belknap Press of Harvard University Press, 1977). Chandler details the growing independence and professionalization of the "managerial class" in nineteenth- and twentieth-century America.
4. Ibid., 95–105.

1861 Abraham Lincoln

Picturing the Civil War: Art and Documentation

The Civil War destroyed many American magazines by starving the Northern-focused press of its Southern readership and by cutting off supplies from the South. (Confederate papers were sometimes printed on wallpaper.)[1] Yet two magazines flourished as never before: *Harper's Weekly* (founded 1857) and *Frank Leslie's Illustrated Newspaper* (founded 1855), which represented the war from the vantage of the Union, with news reports and wood engravings.[2] Although photographs were extensively documenting war for the first time, they could not yet be mechanically translated into a type-compatible medium but had to be interpreted by hand into the linear codes of wood-engraving. Photography had other limitations as well: because the exposure time for film was very slow, photographs could not depict battle scenes but only landscapes, architecture, stiffly posed figures, and corpses.[3]

Winslow Homer had become popular before the Civil War as an illustrator of fashionable urban life for *Harper's Weekly* and other magazines. In the early 1860s he gained a reputation as a painter as well, which raised the prestige of his illustrations.[4] Most of Homer's war engravings represent "genre" scenes (such as *A Cavalry Charge*, published as a centerfold in *Harper's*, 1862) rather than concrete historical events. Other well-known "signature" illustrators, including Thomas Nast and A.R. Waud, produced similar centerfold designs; printed at the middle of the journal, such pictures could be removed easily in one piece and framed like paintings. Homer's *A Cavalry Charge*, detachable both from the physical binding of the magazine and from the verbal context of news reports, shares the autonomy of a work of "fine art," acting as a self-contained aesthetic object which aims to transcend its immediate situation.

While the work of well-known artists such as Homer and Nast maintained aspects of painting in the context of journalism, many engravings emulated the neutral, documentary function associated with photography, mapmaking, and newspaper prose. *Birds-Eye View of the City of Charleston, South Carolina, Showing the Approaches of Our Gun-Boats and Our Army*, ran in the same issue of *Harper's* as Homer's *A Cavalry Charge*. Whereas Homer's picture dramatizes the violence of war, this anonymous landscape dispassionately reports the positions of land, water, boats, and army camps, and it is keyed to a specific news story on a later page. The editor identifies neither the artist nor the source of the image — it could have been reconstructed in the engraver's studio from a map, or from a photograph of a landscape, or from a written report. Thus while *Birds-Eye View* appears to be more concretely "factual" than Homer's cavalry charge, it may be many steps removed from direct observation.

The rise of fast film and halftone reproduction at the end of the century forced hand-drawn pictorial journalism to surrender its dual function as art and information. Photojournalism made the ambiguity between hard fact and interpretation unacceptable, and magazine illustration was quarantined, for the most part, to the realm of fiction.[5]

1. An edition of *The Daily Citizen*, Vicksburg, Mississippi, 1863, printed on wallpaper is preserved at the National Museum of American History, Washington, D.C.
2. General histories of American magazines include Frank Luther Mott, *A History of American Magazines* (Cambridge, Mass.: Belknap Press of Harvard University Press, 1967).
3. For a general history of journalistic illustration, see Paul Hogarth, *The Artist as Reporter* (London: Gordon Fraser, 1986). Jussim discusses the technical relationship between wood-engraving and photography in *Visual Communication and the Graphic Arts*.
4. For a monograph on Homer's illustrations, see Phillip C. Beam, *Winslow Homer's Magazine Engravings* (New York: Harper and Row, 1979). John Wilmerding's *Winslow Homer* (New York: Praeger, 1972) relates Homer's illustrations to his painting career, arguing that he was influenced by the monumentality and flatness of contemporary photography. It is characteristic of these and other texts on Homer to devalue qualities typical of illustration, such as anecdotal detail, in favor of the severe "proto-Modernism" of the artist's later nature paintings.
5. Neil Harris discusses the importance of halftone reproduction on the value of images in his essay "Iconography and Intellectual History: The Half-Tone Effect," John Higham and Paul K. Conkin, eds., *New Directions in American Intellectual History* (Baltimore: Johns Hopkins University Press, 1979).

1865 Abraham Lincoln, Andrew Johnson

1869 Ulysses S. Grant

The Election and Assassination of Abraham Lincoln

At the beginning of his first campaign for the Presidency, in 1860, Abraham Lincoln's face was virtually unknown to the American public, creating an enormous demand for cheap likenesses.[1] Yet as the historian Harold Holzer has documented, the face of Lincoln was not considered pretty: Abraham Lincoln was seen as almost comically unattractive, even by his supporters. Walt Whitman wrote that Lincoln's face was "so awful ugly it becomes beautiful."[2]

Lincoln was legendary for his humble frontier origins but also for his cultured love of Shakespeare. An anti-Lincoln cartoon published during his second campaign, in 1864, evokes the grave-digging scene in *Hamlet*, subtitled with the line "I knew him, Horatio: A fellow of infinite jest.... Where be your gibes now?" The cartoon makes fun of Lincoln's sense of humor, which his critics believed he exercised inappropriately.

On Good Friday, 14 April 1865, Abraham Lincoln was mortally wounded by a well-known Shakespearean actor, John Wilkes Booth, a pro-South Northerner, while attending Ford's Theatre in Washington. The caption for an image depicting the assassination adapts lines from Shakespeare, with Lincoln as the good king murdered by the evil, ambitious Macbeth.

The Civil War had ended the week before with the surrender of Robert E. Lee at Appomattox Courthouse in Virginia. Lincoln had professed a conciliatory stance toward the restoration of the South, but his assassination resulted in renewed feelings of hatred toward the fallen Confederacy, which was wrongly blamed for plotting the assassination.[3]

Lincoln's death turned him into a political martyr, converting many of his former critics into regretful admirers. This murder, the first assassination of an American President, shocked the nation, and the face that had once been almost too ugly to elect entered the idealizing realm of myth, taking a place second only to that of George Washington.

THE MARTYR OF LIBERTY

1. See Harold Holzer, Gabor S. Boritt, and Mark E. Neely, Jr., *The Lincoln Image: Abraham Lincoln and the Popular Print* (New York: Scribner's, 1984).
2. Ibid., 89.
3. For material on public reaction to Lincoln's death, see Thomas Reed Turner, *Beware the People Weeping: Public Opinion and the Assassination of Abraham Lincoln* (Baton Rouge: Louisiana State University Press, 1982).

Thomas Nast and Muckraking Journalism

Thomas Nast contributed to the tradition of political cartooning in America with his visual campaign against the infamous Tweed Ring in New York City.[1] The series was published in *Harper's Weekly* from 1867 to 1876, concurrent with a journalistic exposé in *The New York Times*. The cartoons vividly publicized the situation, and J. Henry Harper later recalled that Tweed said, "Let's stop those damned pictures. I don't care much what the papers write about me — my constituents can't read; but damn it, they can see pictures!"[2] Tweed was so distressed by the cartoons that he offered Nast $200,000 to "study art abroad." Nast declined.

THE "BRAINS"

1. Sources on Thomas Nast include Morton Keller, *The Art and Politics of Thomas Nast* (New York: Oxford University Press, 1968); and Albert Bigelow Paine, *Thomas Nast: His Period and His Pictures* (New York: Macmillan, 1904).
2. Quoted in J. Henry Harper, *The House of Harper: A Century of Publishing in Franklin Square* (New York: Harper and Brothers, 1912), 292.

1873 Ulysses S. Grant

The Public Landscape

Before the 1870s outdoor posters and painted signs were a popular, although unorganized, advertising medium: spaces were not leased but *taken* by aggressive bill-posters. By the end of the Civil War there were 275 bill-posting companies with varying rates and business practices. The proliferation of signs accelerated with the perfection of web-fed printing presses in 1870 and the increasing flexibility of lithography. The anarchy of "guerrilla" bill-posting was a visible intrusion of advertising onto the American landscape: temporary fences, lampposts, and facades were buried in layers of typography. A formalization of the profession began in the early 1870s, when companies began to lease temporary fences on a standardized weekly or monthly basis, followed by the formation of professional associations of bill-posters, and billboard regulation.[1]

1. For information on the history of outdoor advertising, see John W. Houck, ed., *Outdoor Advertising: History and Regulation* (South Bend, Ind.: University of Notre Dame Press, 1969); and Presbrey, *The History and Development of Advertising*, 490–511.

1877 Rutherford B. Hayes

Display Lettering: Typographic and Lithographic

The growth of advertising throughout the nineteenth century encouraged the proliferation of new "display" letter styles. A technique was invented in 1828 in America for mass producing typefaces from wood, a material cheaper and more durable than the traditional lead; the process involved tracing over the lines of a drawing with a device linked to a mechanical wood-engraver. Whereas the "punches" (molds for lead type) were laboriously crafted in metal, the pattern for wood type was simply a drawing.[1]

The wood-type industry reached its creative and economic peak in the 1860s and 1870s, when it was in dynamic competition with the more graphically malleable technique of lithography. Whereas the material constraints of wood or metal typography encourage grouping separate elements into parallel rows, lithography, because it is a drawing-based medium, allows letters to be freely arranged in overlapping, interlacing, curving, and perspective patterns. And, unlike typography, lithographic lettering can be easily integrated with illustrations.

Compare the perspective illusion of a wood-type design

with a chromolithograph. Only by fighting the natural logic of the medium could the letterpress printer compete with the lithographer — by cutting the blocks of type to make them touch, for example, or by setting them into plaster beds to make them follow a curve. The typographic poster remained more economical than the lithograph, however, because the printer could reuse its elements again and again.

1. For a comprehensive study, see Rob Roy Kelly, *American Wood Type, 1828–1900* (New York: Van Nostrand Reinhold, 1969). For a more condensed essay by the same author, see "American Wood Type," *Design Quarterly* 56 (1963).

1881 James Garfield, Chester A. Arthur

Selling with Pictures and People

During the 1880s new production and distribution methods transformed American food culture. Advanced technology made some traditional goods, including flour and beef, more widely available, while it flooded the market with new products, such as cigarettes and oatmeal, for which there was minimal demand. As the historian Alfred Chandler has noted, the automatic factory for milling oatmeal forced the leading processors to "invent the modern breakfast cereal industry."[1]

When Henry P. Crowell opened the first automatic oatmeal factory, in 1882, the product had a tiny United States market. Breaking the custom of distributing grain in bulk, Crowell decided to ship his product in convenient, graphically appealing containers; he wrapped the oatmeal in its own advertising, enticing the consumer with contests and box-top premiums and enforcing brand-name recognition in store and pantry. Other companies, such as Procter & Gamble, Borden, Campbell Soup, and H.J. Heinz, employed packaging and brand names to create new habits of consumption in the 1880s and 1890s.[2]

In 1888 Crowell and his competitors merged into a giant oatmeal conglomerate, the American Cereal Company; one of the businesses the company absorbed had used a picture of a Quaker as its

trademark.[3] The conglomerate adopted the symbol and in 1901 changed its name to The Quaker Oats Company.

The symbol of the Quaker has remained constant throughout the product's history, but his graphic form has changed. The logo used in 1946, designed by Jim Nash, replaced the older full-figure Quaker; it was a well-established "household face" when the prominent graphic designer Saul Bass was asked to design a corporate mark for The Quaker Oats Company in 1970.[4] Bass, who has designed symbols for AT&T, United Airlines, Minolta, and other companies, created a schematic, shorthand, corporate Quaker. The modernized mark appears on contemporary packages with the company's address, but

the cereal's main image remains a full-color, realistic portrait. Until 1988 a graphic link was drawn between the abstract and the realistic Quaker, both of whom had a TV-shaped frame.

Familiar personalities such as the Quaker, Dr. Brown, Uncle Ben, and Old Grand-Dad came to replace the shopkeeper, traditionally responsible for measuring bulk foods for customers and acting as an advocate for products. Particularly after the rise of mass-distribution food chains such as the Great Atlantic and Pacific Tea Company in the early twentieth century, a nationwide vocabulary of brand names replaced the small local shopkeeper as the interface between consumer and product.[5]

Modern Advertising

The first advertising agencies of the 1840s acted as liaisons between advertiser and newspaper. Through the efforts of such agencies, the placing of ads was simplified and rates became more uniform. In 1869 the advertising agent George Rowell published his *American Newspaper Directory*, which made circulation and publication data — the guarded expertise of competing advertising agents — commercially available. Thus the function of the agency as a "space-broker" was being challenged by its own professionalization but also by the growing force of national media, which, sure of their power, could set and maintain rates without the help of intermediaries. Brand-name manufacturers developing national marketing strategies also needed advertising services that could maintain a consistent image throughout the national and local media. Thus the 1880s saw the development of the "full-service" ad agency, which, in addition to securing space and facilitating transactions, offered writing, design, illustration, and production to its clientele.[1]

Women as Consumers, Women as Producers

By the time *The Ladies' Journal* (which later became *The Ladies' Home Journal*) was founded, in 1883, innumerable goods previously manufactured at home were being mass produced, making shopping a central part of life.[1] Under the direction of editor Edward W. Bok and publisher Cyrus H.K. Curtis, *The Journal* became a profitable medium for advertising consumer goods. By 1900 *The Journal*'s back cover was the most expensive advertising position in American magazines.[2] Curtis and Bok believed that advertising, if closely monitored, could be a service to readers, a guide through the arduous task of shopping.

The magazine built up the trust of its readers by refusing to mention brand names in articles. Yet, while forbidding direct links between editorial and advertising, *The Journal* recognized the fruitfulness of juxtaposing relevant ideas; ads for flower seeds appeared beside the gardening column, and buttons and lace showed up in the fashion section. In the layout reproduced overleaf, the advertiser's image (right) strongly resembles the illustrated logo for the monthly "Practical Housekeeper" column. Both women wear white aprons and dark dresses, both have pinned-up hair,

1. Chandler, in *The Visible Hand*, analyzes The Quaker Oats Company in relation to the growth of modern mass production and mass distribution. Quote, 253.
2. Ibid., 295.
3. Hal Morgan's book *Symbols of America* (New York: Viking, 1986) provides brief illustrated histories of many trademarks, including that of Quaker Oats, 130.
4. Dates provided by The Quaker Oats Company.
5. For a brief history of supermarkets, see Chester H. Liebs, *Main Street to Miracle Mile: American Roadside Architecture* (Boston: Little Brown, 1985), 117–135.

1. For information on the full-service ad agency and Rowell's role in its development, see Pope, *The Making of Modern Advertising*, 117–140.

and both are cooking. These similarities between the two pictures give significance to their differences: the "Extract of Beef" cook is nearly four times as big as the Practical Housekeeper, and she is far more elegant. Her apron is pleated rather than plain, her dress is tailored, her hair is ornamented, and the utensils she works with are not homely pots and pans but a decorated tureen and some richly labeled tins of Extract of Beef. The advertiser used the Practical Housekeeper, an image familiar to *Journal* readers, as a modest counterpoint to a glamorous life enhanced by modern packaged goods.

The audience of *The Ladies' Home Journal* was presumed to be white, Anglo-Saxon, and middle class; its female readers were assumed to be mothers working in the home. Whereas this audience provided a mass of *consumers* for advertising, another group of women was engaged in graphic arts *production*. Many working-class women held wage-earning jobs, especially during early adulthood; and in the middle classes, a single, widowed, or abandoned woman had to choose between work and dependency on family members.[3]

In response to a growing number of women in need of employment, some reformers promoted the decorative arts as appropriate work for single women. While traditional academies taught painting, sculpture, and crafts as genteel avocations for middle-class "ladies," the Woman's Art School in New York, founded by Peter Cooper in 1852, aimed to give working-class women respectable professions in illustration, textile design, and teaching. One of the main skills taught at Peter Cooper's school was wood-engraving, a painstaking and usually anonymous task, in which the engraver translates a "design" produced by an illustrator into the codes of woodblock printing.[4]

Women by no means dominated the graphic arts work force, however. According to an 1883 account, women in the design industries were paid much less than men, and they would usually do piecework at home rather than earn salaries to avoid the "jealousy" of male employees.[5] A study conducted forty years later found that among 276 designers surveyed in advertising agencies, only five were women; out of 324 designers employed by independent studios, only eighteen were women.[6]

In 1986 roughly half the students enrolled in college-level art programs were women, but this is not evidence that opportunities after graduation are the same for both sexes.[7] More women are represented today in trade annuals than were thirty years ago, indicating an increased interest in, and perhaps opportunity for, professional self-promotion. Yet there has been little organized feminist activism within the field.[8] An exception is the work of Sheila Levrant de Bretteville, a designer working in California, who, since the 1970s, has helped women use graphic design as a political tool.

1. On women and work, see Christopher Clark, "Household Economy, Market Exchange and the Rise of Capitalism in the Connecticut Valley, 1800–1860," *Journal of Social History* 13, 2 (Winter 1979): 169–189.
2. For a detailed history of *The Ladies' Home Journal*, see Salme Harju Steinberg, *Reformer in the Marketplace: Edward W. Bok and* The Ladies' Home Journal (Baton Rouge: Louisiana State University Press, 1979).
3. See Leslie Woodcock Tentler, *Wage-Earning Women: Industrial Work and Family Life in the United States, 1900–1930* (New York: Oxford University Press, 1979).
4. On women's education and the industrial arts, see Thomas B. Woody, *A History of Women's Education in the United States*, vol. 2 (New York: Science Press, 1929), 75–80. Peter Cooper's Woman's Art School later became part of The Cooper Union for the Advancement of Science and Art, which is a full-scholarship, B.F.A.-granting college today, although The Cooper Union had a coeducational night school; the day art school did not admit men until 1933 (see *The Cooper Pioneer*, 8 March 1933).
5. Ibid.,79.
6. Charles R. Richards, *Art in Industry: Being the Report of an Industrial Art Survey Conducted under the Auspices of the National Society for Vocational Education and the Department of Education of the State of New York* (New York: Macmillan, 1929).
7. See *Peterson's Guide to Four-Year Colleges* (Princeton, N.J.: Peterson Guides, 1988).
8. In 1960 the *Annual* of the Art Directors Club of New York listed approximately 380 "art directors and designers," including about a dozen women, or three and two-tenths percent (New York: Farrar, Straus and Giroux, 1960). In 1982 the *Annual* listed about 1,120 "art directors," including about 165 women (15 percent) and around 900 "designers," including about 240 women (26 percent).

1893 Grover Cleveland

White City, Whited Sepulcher

The World's Columbian Exposition of 1893, held in Chicago, was housed in bright white neoclassical palaces dedicated to art, industry, and agriculture: the architectural setting itself, referred to as the "White City," was the fair's most spectacular exhibit and helped make Beaux-Arts neoclassicism the favored style for major civic projects at the turn of the century.[1]

In addition to nourishing an architectural style, the World's Columbian Exposition helped change the role of museums in American culture. Whereas early collections of artifacts were assembled primarily for scholarly study, scientific museums at the end of the nineteenth century turned to the education of the general public; as one historian proclaimed in 1888, "An efficient educational museum may be described as a collection of instructive labels each illustrated with a well-selected specimen."[2]

The Smithsonian Institution in Washington, D.C., prepared displays on American Indians for the exposition, in which artifacts were elucidated with charts, diagrams, photographs, and explanatory texts. The historian Robert Rydell has interpreted the racial message of the Columbian Exposition, showing how it presented Indian culture as a "primitive" one necessarily doomed to extinction.[3] A contemporary newspaper illustration depicts wax Indians encased in glass, and an exhibit devoted to "physical anthropology" quantified the proportions of individual racial types, explaining the results with charts and diagrams.

A book by the anthropologist F.W. Putnam, a lush photographic

folio of ethnic "types" in costume, combines the conventions of artistic portraiture with the scientific realism of photography.[4] As both Estelle Jussim and Peter Marzio have pointed out, the publications of the Columbian Exposition were distinguished from those of all previous fairs by the preponderance of

halftone photographs. The fair marked the death knell of chromolithography and the birth of the age of the photographic book.[5]

American Indians were not given the opportunity to produce their own exhibit for the exposition; they were treated only as objects of study. Petitions by black Americans to participate were denied, leading Frederick Douglass to write that "to the colored people of America ... the World's Fair ... [is] a whited sepulcher."[6] Nonwhite Americans, whether black, Indian, or Asian, appeared in the fair as anthropological specimens or menial servants but not as creative participants — for example, a black woman dressed as Aunt Jemima brought graphic design to life, serving pancakes in the food pavilion.[7]

1. Texts that analyze the style and influence of the White City include Mario Manieri, "Toward an 'Imperial City': Daniel H. Burnham and the City Beautiful Movement," *The American City: From the Civil War to the New Deal*, Giogi Ciucci et al., eds., Barbara Luigi La Penta, trans. (London: Granada, 1980), 1–142; and Richard Guy Wilson, "Architecture, Landscape and City Planning," *The American Renaissance, 1876–1917*, exh. cat. (New York: Brooklyn Museum, 1979), 74–109.
2. On the history of museums, see Kenneth Hudson, *A Social History of Museums: What the Visitors Thought* (Atlantic Highlands, N.J.: Humanities Press, 1975).
3. For an extensive reading of the racial message of the 1893 exposition, see Robert W. Rydell, *All the World's a Fair: Visions of Empire at American International Expositions, 1876–1916* (Chicago and London: University of Chicago Press, 1984).
4. See F.W. Putnam, *Oriental and Occidental Northern and Southern Types of the Midway Plaisance* (St. Louis, Mo.: N.D. Thompson, 1894).
5. Jussim, *Visual Communication and the Graphic Arts*, 288–295; and Marzio, *The Democratic Art*, 204.
6. Reid Badger, *The Great American Fair: The World's Columbian Exposition and American Culture* (Chicago: Nelson Hall, 1979), 106.
7. The presence of "Aunt Jemima" at the exposition is reported in Morgan, *Symbols of America*, 55.

1897 William McKinley

Poster Advertising: "Artistic" and Anonymous

A new kind of advertising emerged in America in the 1890s: the "artistic poster." The genre had originated in France, where posters for books and cultural events incorporated styles such as Art Nouveau and Postimpressionism. The new French posters functioned both as advertising and as art; during the 1880s books, magazines, and exhibitions devoted to the poster established it as a legitimate child of painting and inspired the interest of art collectors in Europe and New York.

The first American business to make extensive use of the artistic poster was *Harper's Monthly*, which assigned its in-house illustrator Edward Penfield to design monthly placards in 1893. Other magazines quickly followed *Harper's*, commissioning posters from Will Bradley, Maxfield Parrish, Ethel Read, and others. By the mid-1890s there was a collecting "craze" in American cities; booksellers sometimes sold the posters rather than display them — the prints proved more valuable as art than as advertising.

As the historian Victor Margolin has noted, the artistic poster helped establish graphic design as a respected profession by bringing American illustrators into contact with the European avant-garde, encouraging them to develop distinctive artistic styles and to compete in the international art community.[1]

Will Bradley, one of the most influential American poster artists, was also one of the first designers to be called an "art director." His work included typefaces, books, ads, and magazines as well as posters and illustrations.[2] In 1894–1896 Bradley worked for the progressive magazine *The Chap-Book*, which published European avant-garde literature and graphics by Toulouse-Lautrec, Aubrey Beardsley, and others.

The first American book devoted to the poster genre, entitled *The Modern Poster*, was published in 1895. In 1988, nearly a hundred years later, The Museum of Modern Art, New York, published an exhibition catalogue with the same title, and despite the historical span dividing the two books, they are remarkably similar. Both describe a history of "the modern poster" that begins with the French lithographer Jules Chéret and progresses toward the work of Toulouse-Lautrec and other avant-garde painters whom he influenced. Although some art historians consider Chéret stylistically frivolous, they name him the "father" of the modern poster because his work, featured in books, magazines, and art galleries, transcended its mundane advertising function to serve as a new kind of "fine art."[3]

Such genealogies of the poster value graphic design for its relevance to museums and collectors rather than for its role in popular commercial life. What these histories omit is "nonartistic" or anonymous posters, which constituted a powerful advertising medium by the 1890s and would continue to flourish after the poster craze ended at the turn of the century.[4]

Most advertising graphics were produced by anonymous

craftsmen uninterested in developing personal styles or challenging artistic conventions. Their descriptive tonal style contrasts with Bradley's flattened, decorative design.

1. See Victor Margolin, *American Poster Renaissance* (New York: Watson-Guptill, 1975).
2. For material on Will Bradley, see Roberta Wong, *Bradley: American Artist and Craftsman*, exh. cat. (New York: Metropolitan Museum of Art, 1972).
3. See Arsene Alexandre et al., *The Modern Poster* (New York: Scribner's, 1895); and Stuart Wrede, *The Modern Poster*, exh. cat. (New York: Museum of Modern Art, 1988).
4. For material on outdoor advertising, see Philip Tocker, "History of Outdoor Advertising: History, Economics, and Self-Regulation," in Houck, *Outdoor Advertising*.

Public Pickles and Private Enterprise

In 1869 Henry John Heinz began to sell processed horseradish in rural western Pennsylvania, and by 1890 he was manufacturing a nationally distributed line of preserved, packaged, ready-to-serve foods.[1] Heinz's advertising included ten-foot-high, cast-concrete renditions of the number 57, symbol of the company's range of products, installed on a dozen hillsides across the country. He built one of the first large electric signs in New York, a six-story billboard at the corner of Fifth Avenue and Twenty-third Street, where huge letters made of

light bulbs flashed below a forty-foot pickle.[2]

Environmental graphics like these promoted Heinz products; at the same time, the company worked to advertise the industrial procedure that made the pickles possible: the mass processing of food in factories. A pioneer of the corporate "image," Heinz used fine art and feminine beauty to proclaim the benefits of modern industry to the consumer, the employee, and the community.

Beneath the six-story electric sign in New York was a display room where attractive young women packed vegetables in clear glass jars; one could see hundreds more women workers when touring Heinz's plant in Pittsburgh, a model of enlightened labor relations. The centerpiece of the complex was the Time Office, a freestanding Beaux-Arts monument to wage labor; paintings and drawings were displayed in public spaces, an early use of fine art as a public relations tool.

Heinz provided his all-female labor force with sunroofs, classrooms, and a swimming pool, bringing contentment to his workers and goodwill from the community. Young women commonly worked in factories for several years before marrying, and they routinely were paid

less than men for comparable labor — it was assumed that women did not need wages for survival.[3] Heinz used this business custom not only for its obvious economic advantages but also for the image it gave his factory. As period photographs indicate, the women Heinz employed were not only young but also white and well groomed; each wore a freshly laundered uniform, sewn by herself with fabric purchased from Heinz, and every week she received a manicure. One might be pleased to have such women cook in one's own home. Heinz's model factory used labor itself as a form of advertising.

1. For a history of the first fifty years of the Heinz business, see Robert C. Alberts, *The Good Provider: H.J. Heinz and His 57 Varieties* (Boston: Houghton Mifflin, 1973).
2. For a cultural history of the electric light bulb, see Carolyn Marvin, "Dazzling the Multitude: Imagining the Electric Light as a Communications Medium," Joseph J. Corn, ed., *Imagining Tomorrow: History, Technology, and the American Future* (Cambridge, Mass.: MIT Press, 1987), 202–217.
3. For a discussion of women and work, see Leslie Woodcock Tentler, *Wage-Earning Women*.

Machines and Craft

The American type designer Frederic W. Goudy designed the font Village in 1903. By the end of his life, in 1947, he had designed more than one hundred typefaces, an achievement that would have been nearly impossible without the invention in 1884 of the "pantographic" punch-cutter, which produced molds for metal type. The new technology enabled any letterer to make designs for a typeface; in contrast, typographers traditionally had carved metal punches by hand — a slow, painstaking process.[1]

❧IT WAS THE TERRACE OF God's house
That she was standing on,—
By God built over the sheer depth
In which Space is begun;
So high, that looking downward

Although Goudy depended on modern technology, much of his work reflected a medievalizing trend in American design that emerged in the 1890s and continued through the 1920s and beyond.[2] Goudy, Will Bradley, Bruce Rogers, and others were inspired by the English socialist reformer William Morris, a founder of the Arts and Crafts movement.[3] Morris, reacting against the debased products and working conditions brought on by the Industrial Revolution, rejected contemporary styles and techniques and called for the unification of aesthetics and production that he believed had existed in the Middle Ages. The cost of his labor-intensive products, however, made them inaccessible to most consumers.

Morris modeled his typeface Golden (1891) after the

ILLIAM ✿✿ MORRIS items preserved at the University Press, Cambridge, include the punches, matrices and some cast type of the three Kelmscott founts, Golden (in which these pages are set), Troy, and Chaucer; two paper-making moulds; a page from the 'Chaucer', and the printer's copy for Ruskin's 'Nature of Gothic' including the manuscript of Morris's preface. ✿ ✿ This leaflet was printed for the William Morris Society's visit to Cambridge on 15 July 1961.

fifteenth-century Venetian font Jenson; his dark letters, with thick slab serifs and a relatively uniform line weight, opposed the spiky, airy, "modern" book faces that dominated Victorian printing. Morris's dense pages fueled a generation of American book and type designers.

Arts and Crafts-inspired typographers such as Goudy, Bradley, and Rogers were moved by the idea of joining aesthetics and technique, yet they worked in a period when devices like the pantographic punch-cutter and Linotype and Monotype machines were widening the gap between design and production. Bradley and Goudy both designed faces for Monotype; the longevity of their influence lies not in reunifying art and craft but in acting as modern "designers," whose plans are executed by technicians and machines.

1. A useful primary text on early twentieth-century typography is Frederic W. Goudy, *A Half-Century of Type Design and Typography, 1895–1945* (New York: The Typophiles, 1946). Secondary sources include Sebastian Carter, *Twentieth Century Type Designers* (New York: Taplinger, 1987).
2. "Literary" and "private" presses had operated in the 1890s, alongside the poster craze, but many failed economically by the turn of the century. Several enlightened trade publishers in the early twentieth century sustained the movement by opening fine-press subdivisions; Bruce Rogers, for example, designed sixty limited-edition books for Houghton Mifflin Company's Riverside Press between 1900 and 1912. In the 1920s Alfred A. Knopf commissioned innovative book designs from William Addison Dwiggins and Merle Armitage. See Joseph Blumenthal, *The Printed Book in America* (Boston: David R. Godine, 1977).
3. On the Arts and Crafts movement, see William Morris, *The Ideal Book: Essays and Lectures on the Arts of the Book*, William S. Peterson, ed. (Berkeley: University of California Press, 1982).

Analyzing the Market

"Legitimate advertising is simply calling people's attention to a good thing, and describing it."[1] This statement from an 1890 article called "Advertising from a Religious Standpoint" characterizes the way "legitimate" advertising professionals understood their practice. By 1900 the notion of advertising as a kind of benevolent information service gave way to more aggressive and sophisticated attitudes, informed by the emerging literature of psychology. Pamphlets, lectures, and articles on "advertising psychology" appeared as early as 1896, and the first book-length study, Walter Dill Scott's *The Theory of Advertising*, appeared in 1903, followed in 1908 by *The Psychology of Advertising*.[2] By 1910 a number of people were working in the field of "advertising psychology," and its ideas began to have, and continue to have, a discernible impact on the profession.[3]

Advertising psychology called into question the dominant understanding of the consumer as rationally motivated, and it consequently devalued "objective" or "reason-why" approaches to advertising.[4] The basis of Scott's "theory of advertising" was the concept of suggestion: "Every idea of a function tends to call that function into activity, and will do so, unless hindered by a competing idea or physical impediment."[5] According to Scott, purchases are made impulsively,

without methodical reasoning. Thus suggestion must be pleasurable and directed yet not strong enough to cause reflection and "lead the reader into a critical or questioning state of mind."[6] His practical advice was that, rather than describe a product, an ad should describe its pleasurable effects; negative imagery, even if intended humorously, should be avoided. He also advocated the use of the direct command ("Use Pears Soap") and the return coupon, comparing their effectiveness to the children's game of Simon Says.

Scott's theory and psychology of advertising, as well as the academic psychology he drew upon, made direct use of contemporary theories of hypnosis. Academic psychologists had turned from regarding hypnosis as an abnormality usually affecting hysterics to an understanding of it as a kind of sleep induced by suggestion and the elimination of conflicting ideas. His application of the concept followed the example of Boris Sidis, who in 1898 had used the concept of suggestion to explain crowd behavior, economic booms, revivalism, and other social phenomena.[7] Scott, however, used the concept not only for its explanatory force but also as a tool that would "replace the haphazard of rule of thumb procedures in advertising and effect great economies in time and money."[8]

1913 Woodrow Wilson

The Suffragette and the Suffragist

1. Quoted in Merle Curti, "The Changing Concept of 'Human Nature' in the Literature of American Advertising," *The Business History Review*, 41, 4 (Winter 1967): 339.
2. Walter Dill Scott, *The Theory of Advertising* (Boston: Small, Maynard, 1903); and idem, *The Psychology of Advertising* (Boston: Small, Maynard, 1908). The references here and below are to the 1931 edition of *The Psychology of Advertising*, published by Dodd, Mead, New York.
3. Merle Curti's article, supra, note 1, traces the way the rationalist school of advertising is succeeded by what he terms the "impressionist" school of advertising.
4. "Reason-why" advertising is credited to John E. Powers, described as the "father of modern advertising." It was distinctive in its time largely because it told the truth and did not exaggerate in the manner of patent medicine advertising. For Powers as the father of modern advertising, see Presbrey, *The History and Development of Advertising*, 302–309.
5. Scott, 195.
6. Ibid., 190.
7. For suggestion in advertising, see David P. Kuna, "The Concept of Suggestion in the Early History of Advertising Psychology," *Journal of the History of the Behavioral Sciences* 12 (1976): 347–353.
8. Scott, 1.

The struggle for women's voting rights entered a new phase in 1910 when the National American Woman Suffrage Association, having successfully campaigned in a number of states, began a concerted effort toward federal legislation. One of the tactics employed by suffrage activists was the picture poster, whose artistic status and novelty were primarily used for promoting commercial goods. As the historian Paula Hays Harper observes, these images mark some of the earliest uses of the political picture poster, predating the extensive use of such posters in World War I.[1] It has been noted that the posters and publicity produced during World War I served to consolidate and legitimize the advertising industry; less often noted is the fact that, prior to the war, suffragists had established the picture poster as a political forum, using commercial imagery for a political struggle.

The suffragist's use of commercial imagery was not, however, parodistic or subversive. Instead it used popular and conventional imagery of women as wives and mothers to assure the continuity of roles in spite of political change. Characteristic of this strategy is a poster that features a row of marching toddlers, stylistically reminiscent of children's books, who plead for daddies to "GIVE MOTHER THE VOTE." Such posters affirmed traditional social roles for women and thus acted as a buffer to the anti-

suffrage posters that represented suffragists as enraged, unfeminine, homely spinsters.

Perhaps the most revealing posters are those that directly invoke the high-culture tradition of the artistic poster, using the decorative style and Pre-Raphaelite imagery of the Art Nouveau posters that advertised cultural events and publications. As Harper notes when discussing this pictorial tradition, "They are 'feminine' styles not created by women but carrying connotations of what constitutes femininity from a masculine point of view." As women's enfranchisement

rested in the hands of a male legal system, so did their imagery: "they had no tradition of image making to draw upon except the masculine one in which they were embedded as second-class citizens."[2]

Thus the projection of a positive, traditional imagery was conservative in that it maintained existing, politically useful notions of the feminine. Yet it may also be seen as inevitable, since the earlier strategies of the nineteenth-century suffrage movement were often met with ridicule, hostility, and violence.[3] The historian Aileen Kraditor has noted that the early suffrage movement, influenced by its abolitionist origins, waged its campaign on the

1917 Woodrow Wilson

The War and the Masses

moral issue of equality. Early leaders, notably Elizabeth Cady Stanton, Lucy Stone, and Susan B. Anthony, encouraged a fundamental reevaluation of social roles and familial traditions, questioning values considered sacred to the middle class. When these pioneer activists died or retired, in the 1890s, their posts were filled by younger, more conservative women, who, in response to the intensified anti-suffrage movement, based their appeals on the political expediency and social benefits of suffrage rather than on the more confrontational issues of equality and justice. The broad critique initiated by the early women's movement was narrowed into a contest for the ballot: marching toddlers proved more effective than appeals to equality.

1. The material on suffrage posters relies heavily on Paula Hays Harper, "Votes for Women?: A Graphic Episode in the Battle of the Sexes," Henry A. Millon and Linda Nochlin, eds., *Art and Architecture in the Service of Politics* (Cambridge, Mass.: MIT Press, 1978), 150–161.
2. Ibid., 156, 157.
3. For strategy changes within the suffrage movement, see Aileen Kraditor, *Ideas of the Women's Suffrage Movement, 1890–1920* (New York: Columbia University Press, 1965).

Many Americans opposed United States entry into World War I because of commitments to pacifism, cultural ties to Europe, or belief in America's former policy of neutrality. President Wilson's statement that "It is not an army we must shape and train for war, it is a nation" aptly summarizes the government's interest in securing unified national support for the war. The principal means of mobilizing public sentiment was the Committee on Public Information (CPI), founded in 1917, which served in a threefold capacity as censor, information clearinghouse, and publicity organ.

A number of people advised Wilson against instituting an overtly censorial policy that might create, as it had in the French and British press, a militaristic and undemocratic atmosphere. George Creel, a journalist who chaired the CPI, was an early critic of any form of blatant, unreflective censorship.[1] The information and public relations aspects of the CPI were intended, as Creel noted, to overshadow its repressive, undemocratic activities of censorship: "suppressive features [will be] so overlaid by the publicity policy that they will go unregarded and unresented."[2]

The committee's twenty divisions each concentrated on particular forms of propaganda. Press releases, pamphlets, radio programs, photographs, films, books, cartoons, lectures, store displays, English classes, exhibitions, and posters were disseminated in America and in more than thirty countries. Described as a "war emergency national university," the CPI gave America and the rest of

The GREATEST MOTHER in the WORLD

the world a crash course in democracy, patriotism, and "Americanism."[3] Creel conceived of the committee as an educational agency that would provide a "simple, straightforward presentation of facts."[4]

Conflicts between the educative aims and manipulative tactics of the CPI are perhaps nowhere more visible and numerous than in the posters and graphics produced by the Division of Advertising and the Division of Pictorial Publicity. The Division of Advertising was formed to create ads, but also, as stated in the Presidential charter, to

administer the "generous offers of advertising forces of the Nation" by directing the use of donated space and services.[5] The "generosity" of the advertising community was not entirely altruistic, however, since the war represented an opportunity to demonstrate the power and skill of a profession held in low esteem by the public and the government. Thus, for the advertising industry, the war was good public relations.

Headed by the prominent illustrator Charles Dana Gibson, the Division of Pictorial Publicity worked in concert with the Division of Advertising to publicize, among other things, enlistment, volunteer work, and war bonds. Creel's ideals of "objectivity" and "facticity" were not shared by Gibson, whose belief that people are essentially irrational echoed contemporary advertising theory. The posters commonly make an emotional appeal by connecting domestic comfort and intimacy to the specter of modern war: "Every bond you buy fires point blank at Prussian Terrorism," "Don't Waste Bread! Save Two Slices Every Day and Defeat the U Boat." Less subtle threats to the sanctity of the home were the horrific illustrations of the atrocities in Belgium, which portrayed women being choked and children having their hands cut off.[6]

Despite the propaganda efforts of the CPI, many discerned in the war the corrupt interests of big business. Among the voices of antimilitarism and dissent was the socialist press, which was a growing vehicle for progressive and reform issues.[7] While socialist magazines and newspapers differed in their attitudes toward the war, they drew upon common sources in muckraking journalism and drawings of romanticized, allegorical figures symbolizing the class struggle.

"A Revolutionary and not a Reform Magazine" called *The Masses*, founded in 1911, rejected the notion of "official" left-wing imagery and journalism.[8] Irreverent, inconsistent, humorous, and pluralistic, *The Masses* transformed magazine design, illustration, and writing by creating a forum for radical writers and artists. Collectively owned, and edited through group meetings, the magazine avoided the demands of commercial publishing and the hierarchies of editorial censure.[9] Writers and artists received no pay and were not commissioned; thus the topic and editorial angle of a given piece were not predetermined. This was especially liberating to artists, who, when working for the commercial press, were expected to "illustrate" someone else's article. *The Masses* considered illustration equal, rather than subservient, to text. This parity was reinforced

by the design of the magazine, whose generous margins and quality reproduction techniques accorded an autonomy and importance to illustration.[10]

Writers and artists attracted to *The Masses* — Max Eastman, Emma Goldman, John Reed, John Sloan, Art Young, and Stuart Davis, among others — were part of the larger bohemian community of Greenwich Village. Thus the magazine's effectiveness in reaching "the masses" remains dubious, since the range of issues it covered — free love, Freud, contraception, feminism, homosexuality — placed it outside of mainstream America.[11]

In 1917, after America's entry into the war, Congress passed the Espionage Act, allowing the government to suppress activities and messages considered injurious to the United States or advantageous to enemy governments. When an issue of *The Masses* was declared "unmailable" the editors brought the case to court, forcing the government to specify the treasonable items, which included a drawing by Henry Glintenkamp entitled *Physically Fit*. The drawing darkly alludes to a contemporary newspaper account of the Army's plans to order coffins in bulk quantities.

The court eventually ruled

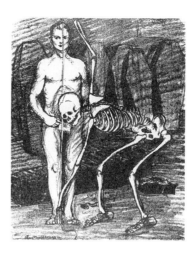

against the magazine. Drained of funds and without access to the postal service, *The Masses* closed in December 1917. Some of its original contributors reassembled in 1918 to form a magazine called *The Liberator* and again in 1926 to form *The New Masses*. Neither attempted to recreate the pluralistic and sometimes contradictory arena in which *The Masses* had so fruitfully questioned the traditions of, and relationships among, journalism, art, and politics.

1. Confident in the "absolute justice of America's cause, the absolute selflessness of America's aims," Creel saw his work for the CPI as a continuation of his earlier reformist activity. The CPI attracted a number of reformists and socialists and was even accused of employing "radicals" and "bolsheviki." See Stephen Vaughn, *Holding Fast the Inner Lines: Democracy, Nationalism and the Committee on Public Information* (Chapel Hill: University of North Carolina Press, 1980), 251.
2. Ibid., 17, 18.
3. Ibid., 37–39.
4. Ibid., 20.
5. *Creel Report: Complete Report of the Chairman of the Committee on Public Information, 1917; 1918; 1919.* (New York: Da Capo Press, 1972), 43. Reprint of first edition

published in Washington, D.C., 1920.
6. Creel stated that atrocity materials were used in instances not under his supervision. The poster referred to is *This Is Kultur*, reproduced in Vaughn, 165. For Creel's statements on atrocity images, see Vaughn, 156–158.
7. See Rebecca Zurier, *Art for* The Masses: *A Radical Magazine and Its Graphics, 1911–1917* (Philadelphia: Temple University Press, 1988), 85–91. An indication of the importance and range of socialist positions on the war is the fact that the CPI organized lecture tours for "patriotic American socialists" to represent our positions on the war to foreign leftists. Emily S. Rosenberg, *Spreading the American Dream: American Economic and Cultural Expansion, 1890–1945* (New York: Hill and Wang, 1982), 79.
8. *The Masses* began with a traditional socialist look and agenda. It was not until 1912, after economic and editorial reorganization, that it departed from those conventions.
9. Editorial disputes, particularly concerning the addition of captions on drawings not intended to "illustrate," eventually caused divisions among the staff, leading to a "strike" by the artists. Zurier, supra, note 7, 52–57.
10. *The Masses* was consciously modeled after visually sophisticated European satiric journals such as *Le Rire, Simplicissimus,* and *Jugend.*
11. The magazine was distributed through Socialist Party offices in a number of states. All records, including subscription lists, have been lost. Thus it is impossible to know if *The Masses* reached its namesake. Zurier, supra, note 7, 66.

1921 Warren G. Harding, Calvin Coolidge

Artistry and Industry

Art direction bolstered its professional and artistic stature when the Art Directors Club was formed in 1920. An annual exhibition and catalogue of "advertising art" were the club's chief means of publicity. The first exhibition, held in the prestigious galleries of the National Arts Club in New York, displayed paintings and drawings that had been commissioned for advertisements — the ads themselves were not shown, however. This blurring of the distinction between fine art and mass media was reinforced by the catalogue: paintings and drawings appeared as large-format reproductions at the front of the catalogue, while their "application" in actual advertisements appeared in an appendix of small images at the back.

The exclusion of actual advertisements — which represent the art director's use of the artist's work — was not repeated in the second exhibit, a decision considered "valuable" by the exhibition committee, even though a reviewer felt it "detract[ed] a bit from the neat and orderly arrangement."[1] The second exhibition also included photography, a medium pervasive in advertising yet relatively new to the art gallery. Throughout the early catalogues the work is described as not merely equal to fine art but *more* significant, since it is an art for the masses, able to "create a new state of mind in a nation."[2]

The artistic status of advertising art and the professionalization of the art director were part of a much larger expansion of advertising in the 1920s. As manufacturers increased in number and output, market research became an important agency service.[3] J. Walter Thompson, then one of the largest firms in the country, added, in 1919, a statistical and investigation department and two planning departments — one for male and one for female consumers. Such bureaucratic complexity had a twofold appeal: it mirrored the structure of the corporations that such agencies served, and it helped convey the image of advertising as a full-scale science.

Stanley Resor, the president of J. Walter Thompson, hoped to create a "university of advertising" at the firm, instituting a two-year course for incoming employees and hiring John B. Watson, a former Ivy League professor, who was well known for his controversial books on behavioral psychology. Watson believed that three instincts guide human behavior: fear, rage, and love. These result from, respectively, a loss of support, constraints on bodily movement, and stroking of the skin. For Watson, all other emotional responses are conditioned from this original trio; advertising could learn to guide consumers by triggering such sensations. Fear was frequently turned to the advantage of business through advertisements that played upon the insecurities of women as inadequate dates, wives, mothers, or housekeepers. Behaviorism lent to advertising the rhetoric of science, serving to legitimize an increasingly irrational conception of human nature.[4]

1. *The Second Annual of Illustrations for Advertisements in the United States* (New York: Art Directors Club, 1922), 14.
2. Ibid., 13.
3. For the expansion of advertising agency services see Pope, *The Making of Modern Advertising*. The expansion of agency services has continued into the present: the JWT Group, a holding company for J. Walter Thompson, has subsidiaries specializing in recruitment and medical advertising, two public relations firms, and a market research company.
4. For information on Watson's career in advertising, see David Cohen, *J.B. Watson: The Founder of Behaviorism. A Biography* (London: Routledge and Kegan Paul, 1979), 168–194. For the cultural context in which behaviorism came to fruition, see Lucille Birnbaum, "Behaviorism in the 1920s," *American Quarterly* 7, 1 (Spring 1955): 15–30.

Modernistic vs. Modern

Before the 1920s industrial design was a largely anonymous service, with neither artistic nor professional recognition.[1] The profession emerged in the mid-1920s out of the promotional ethic of advertising and was evidenced particularly in packaging. Many first-generation industrial designers — including Walter Dorwin Teague, John Vassos, and Lurelle Guild — began their careers as illustrators for advertising.[2] Others, such as Norman Bel Geddes, Donald Deskey, Russell Wright, and Henry Dreyfuss, started out designing sets for theatrical productions. These people were hired by ad agencies and manufacturers as "consumer engineers" and "product stylists," who could create consumer demand by applying art to industry.

Many of the celebrities of industrial design were also recent immigrants, including the French-born Raymond Loewy. Loewy's illustrational style exemplifies the conflation of monumentality, fashion, and opulence common to the design arts of the 1920s. The success of Loewy and other Europeans reflected the American fascination with the European style variously known as Art Moderne, La Mode 1925, Modernistic, Skyscraper Style, and Jazz Moderne.[3] The profusion of names indicates the plurality of the style; the name *Art Deco*, common today, came from the title

of the 1925 Paris Exposition Internationale des Arts Décoratifs et Industriels Modernes, devoted to the design arts.[4] The essential conservatism of Art Deco has been noted by the historian Rosemarie Haag Bletter, who has characterized the Art Deco architect as "an avant-garde traditionalist." The term aptly describes the way elements of avant-garde art — Futurism, Expressionism, Cubism, and Constructivism — were used to inflect a mass, commercial style with an appealing, uncontroversial, modernity.[5]

In America awareness of the style spread through the publicity surrounding the French exposition; Art Deco soon became the architectural expression of New York's major department stores, corporate headquarters, and automated restaurants.[6] In graphic design and illustration it did not constitute a singular aesthetic but was rather a loose set of ideas and motifs, ranging from reductive geometry, elongated torsos, and a mannered angularity, to the repetition and regularity associated with the machine, as in M.F. Benton's typeface Broadway (1929).

The opulence of Art Deco was curbed by the October 1929 stock market crash. For industrial design the Great Depression would have a positive effect, maturing it into a profession with direct economic and social value. The use of new materials — aluminum, plastic, black Vitrolite glass, Masonite, linoleum — in the industrial forms of sheets, bars, rods, and tubes, encouraged a vocabulary of simple forms, making the decorative quality of Art Deco appear fussy and anachronistic.[7]

This interest in modern materials and technologies led many designers to look to the machine as both a functional and aesthetic model. The European heritage of machine aesthetics, represented by De Stijl, Constructivism, the Bauhaus, and Le Corbusier, was largely rectilinear, elementary, and geometric; the American interpretation of the machine combined these European precedents with the seamless, complex curves and tapering forms of aerodynamic streamlining then being developed for airplanes, boats, and automobiles.[8] Parallel stripes, "speed whiskers," and the airbrushed appearance of Monel metal made streamlining a particularly graphic expression of speed, progress, and modernity.[9]

Walter Dorwin Teague's facade design for a 1932 exhibition, *Design for the Machine*, epitomizes

the curvaceous, streamlined aesthetic of continuous, flush surfaces and spare detail. The customized typeface combines the residual angles and step-motifs of Art Deco with the "ascetic" modern interest in the reductive, elementary forms of the circle, square, and triangle.[10]

Within much literature on modern design and architecture, Art Deco and streamlining are seen as the derivative bastardization of a purer, nondecorative, and "functionalist" Modernism, exemplified by the Bauhaus and by the Purism of the French architect and painter Le Corbusier.[11] While Art Deco and streamlining often provided pleasing, legible public symbols, it was devalued by proponents of the purportedly "nondecorative" Modernism of the Bauhaus and Le Corbusier. This more abstract, severe aesthetic was championed in America when The Museum of Modern Art, New York, presented *Modern Architecture: International Exhibition* in 1932, which set forth a restricted model of "true" Modernism.[12] This influential exhibition was followed in 1938 by the first American survey of work from the Bauhaus.

abcd

Through these exhibitions, and their related publications and publicity, The Museum of Modern Art positioned itself as an arbiter of modern design and, by definition, an opponent of Art Deco and "misapplied" streamlining.[13]

The effort to draw a line between modern and modernistic betrays the interconnections and shared reference points of design and architecture in the 1920s and 1930s. For example, M.F. Benton's Broadway and Teague's facade lettering share with Herbert Bayer's "universal alphabet" an interest in standardized, geometric elements. Bayer's typeface, designed from 1925 to 1928 at the Bauhaus in Dessau, is composed on an armature of lines and circles; like the Benton and Teague faces, geometric forms and the assembly-line logic of interchangeable parts are transferred to typography. All three examples aim to express the modernity of their age, yet the universal alphabet issues from the esoteric, avant-gardist heritage of the Bauhaus, while the American faces are heir to a more self-consciously decorative tradition. The unquestioned separation of these traditions, however, obscures a more complex relationship between mass culture and "progressive" design.

1. For the emergence of the industrial designer and the contributions of that profession, see Arthur J. Pulos, *The American Design Ethic: A History of Industrial Design to 1940* (Cambridge, Mass.: MIT Press, 1983).
2. The conflation of advertising, packaging, and industrial design at this time is evident in the motto of the influential trade journal *Advertising Arts*: "Devoted to the Design of Advertising, the Creation of Printed Literature, and the Styling of Merchandise and Packages."
3. Other names by which the style was known were New York Style, Moderne, Style Chanel, Style Poiret, Vertical Style, Zigzag Moderne, and Modernism.
4. While the American government had been invited to exhibit in Paris, Secretary of Commerce Herbert Hoover declined the invitation and instead sent a committee representing manufacturing and trade groups to observe. In its report the committee stated that Americans were living "artistically largely on warmed-over dishes" and called on them to "initiate a parallel effort of our own upon lines calculated to appeal to the American consumer." For the American response to Hoover's decision not to participate, see Pulos, supra, note 1, 304–305.
5. Rosemarie Haag Bletter, "The Art Deco Style," Cervin Robinson and Rosemarie Haag Bletter, *Skyscraper Style* (New York: Oxford University Press, 1975), 41.
6. The Parisian exposition encouraged an understanding of Art Deco as a French style with roots in Cubism; its stylistic antecedents, however, also include the Vienna Secession and the Glasgow School. Even though Germany and the De Stijl artists, with the exception of Frederick Kiesler, were excluded from the exposition, the avant-garde was also influential. America's interest in French fashion and style preceded the 1925 Paris exposition. In 1913 the American fashion magazines *Vogue* and *Vanity Fair* followed the example of French magazines and published illustrations derivative of the highly stylized drawings of the Parisian couturier Paul Poiret. The exotic and ornamental drawings of the French illustrator Erté became the signature style for *Harper's Bazaar* when he was signed to a ten-year contract. Patricia Frantz Kery, *Art Deco Graphics* (New York: Harry N. Abrams, 1986), 118, 119. The exposition did, however, bring the style to the attention of a much wider public. In 1927 Lewis Mumford noted that "American designers, instead of designing directly for our needs and tastes, are now prepared to copy French Modernism, if it becomes fashionable, just as habitually as they copy antiques." Pulos, supra, note 1, 305.
7. Ibid., 337.
8. The anonymous, industrial architecture of American grain silos was an important source for European modern architecture and the "machine aesthetic." See Reyner Banham, *A Concrete Atlantis: U.S. Industrial Building and European Modern Architecture, 1900–1925* (Cambridge, Mass.: MIT Press, 1986). For information on streamlining, see Donald J. Bush, *The Streamlined Decade* (New York: George Braziller, 1975); and Jeffrey L. Meikle, *Twentieth Century Limited: Industrial Design in America, 1925–1939* (Philadelphia: Temple University Press, 1979).
9. The graphic nature of streamlining was commented upon in an article reviewing the 1930s: "Among the current manifestations of [the] persistent search for a 'modern' ornament is the curious cult of the 'three little lines' … few objects have escaped the plague of this unholy trinity." "Design Decade," *Architectural Forum* 73 (October 1940): 221.
10. Teague refers to the "ascetic manner" of Le Corbusier, Mies van der Rohe, and "a number of others" in his *Design This Day* (New York: Harcourt Brace, 1940), 172.
11. The term *Bauhaus* is not used here to denote a stylistically or philosophically unified body of work or ideals. A number of often conflicting agendas characterized the Bauhaus at different points in its history. Much of the literature that excludes Art Deco and streamlining from the history of modern design also tends to reduce the work and ideas of the Bauhaus to a set of formal characteristics arising from the function, materials, and production of the object. For a reevaluation of the Bauhaus mythology, see Marcel Franciscono, *Walter Gropius and the Creation of the Bauhaus in Weimar: The Ideals and Artistic Theories of Its Founding Years* (Urbana: University of Illinois Press, 1971); and Gillian Naylor, *The Bauhaus Reassessed* (New York: E.P. Dutton, 1985).
12. The exhibition was accompanied by a book, *The International Style: Architecture since 1922*, by Henry Russell Hitchcock and Philip Johnson. The text is credited with establishing the term *international style*.
13. John McAndrew, "Modernistic and Streamlined," *Bulletin of The Museum of Modern Art* 5, 6 (December 1938): unpaginated. Art Deco is still not part of the canon of Modernism maintained by The Museum of Modern Art. Describing the criteria for acquisitions, Arthur Drexler, the late curator of the department of architecture and design, wrote: "the department's definition of quality excludes unsuccessful or ephemeral styles, no matter how numerous their examples may be. Even such popular manifestations as Art Deco and other 'modernistic' furniture which, in the twenties and thirties, imitated the stepped contours of skyscrapers, are not eligible for inclusion." *The Museum of Modern Art, New York: The History and the Collection* (New York: Harry N. Abrams, 1984).

Fashion Plates

The eclectic quality of "modernist" American design in the 1930s may be attributed in part to the fact that European Modernism was filtered to American audiences through the transient media of fashion and interior design magazines.[1] These media deployed the resources of European Modernism as a range of stylistic options, without the weighty dogmas that characterized the various "isms" of the avant-garde. In the 1920s *Vogue* and *Vanity Fair* had brought European illustration and industrial and graphic design to an American audience. This tradition was pursued more actively in the 1930s through the European designers Alexey Brodovitch at *Harper's Bazaar* and Mehemed Fehmy Agha at *Vogue*, *Vanity Fair*, and *House & Garden*.[2]

While Agha preceded Brodovitch and provided a model for his work at *Harper's Bazaar*, the two designers can be said to have worked in a situation of mutual influence, bringing similar backgrounds to similar tasks. Agha came to America from Berlin in 1929 at the invitation of the publisher Condé Nast; and Brodovitch, who had come from Paris to teach in Philadelphia, was invited to New York by *Harper's Bazaar* editor Carmel Snow in 1934. Thus both men were "imported" and then empowered to bring a specifically European quality to American magazine design. Their pluralistic

The field of the cloth of Gold

approach to European art and design is evident in the range of artists they employed: A.M. Cassandre, Man Ray, Cartier-Bresson, Salvador Dali, Lisette Model, Brassaï, Jean Cocteau, and Isamu Noguchi.

Prior to the work of Brodovitch and Agha, magazines such as *Harper's* and *Vogue* used traditional layouts and, like newspapers, relied on framing techniques — circular insets, overlapping corners — which treated photographs and

illustrations as discrete compositional units. Brodovitch and Agha often let images cross the binding and bleed off the page, bringing an unprecedented centrality and force to photography in publication design. By considering the coherence of each spread and the sequential rhythm of the entire magazine, Brodovitch and Agha came to play a primary role in the total look of the magazine, transforming the role of the art director in publication design.[3]

Representing the New Deal: Stylization and Documentation

The Works Progress Administration (WPA), instituted by President Roosevelt in 1935, was designed to employ the millions of workers left jobless by the Great Depression.[1] Although most WPA programs, such as the Rural Electrification and National Youth administrations, utilized unskilled labor, the Federal Art Project (FAP) employed professional writers, painters, actors, and musicians.[2] At the height of the New Deal these artists constituted only two percent of the total number of WPA employees, and the arts projects received less than seven percent of the total budget.[3]

Divisions within the FAP ranged from easel painting and community art centers to film and stained glass. The poster division was one of the most visible and prolific, since it acted as a design/publicity service for many governmental agencies.[4] The posters, produced locally and hung in public buildings, publicized health care issues, cultural events, and WPA programs. The reduced, bold shapes employed in the posters were

1. Fashion and arts magazines were an important factor in introducing European art and design to America. Frank Crowninshield, the editor of Condé Nast's fashionable arts and letters magazine *Vanity Fair*, was a key member of the organizing committee for The Museum of Modern Art, New York. Russell Lynes, *Good Old Modern* (New York: Atheneum, 1973), 11–18.
2. For more information on Brodovitch, see Andy Grundberg, *Masters of American Design* (New York: Documents of American Design, Harry N. Abrams, 1989). For information on Agha's contribution to magazine design, see Sarah Bodine and Michael Dunas, "Dr. M.F. Agha, Art Director;" and M.F. Agha, "Reprise: On Magazines," *Journal of Graphic Design* 3, 3 (March 1985): 3. Brodovitch and Agha are profiled in R. Roger Remington and Barbara J. Hodik, *Nine Pioneers in American Graphic Design* (Cambridge, Mass.: MIT Press, 1989).
3. In addition to his impact on the profession as a practitioner, Brodovitch taught classes and seminars at a number of schools, influencing a generation of art directors and photographers, including: Irving Penn, Richard Avedon, Art Kane, Henry Wolf, Otto Storch, Bob Gage, Sam Antupit, Steve Frankfurt, and Helmut Krone. Allen Hurlburt, "Alexey Brodovitch: The Revolution in Magazine Design," *Print* 23, 1 (January–February 1969): 55.

influenced partly by the artistic vanguard of A.M. Cassandre, Stuart Davis, and Joseph Binder but even more strongly by their method of production. Silkscreen printing, a relatively inexpensive process used for small-scale commercial printing, was almost the exclusive medium of WPA poster artists. The opaque, stencillike quality of silkscreening, seen in a poster by the Detroit designer Merlin, accounts for the remarkable consistency of WPA graphics: transparency, layering, bold expanses of solid color, and hard-edged silhouettes.

The poster division began as a primitive atelier in New York City where artists hand painted individual posters, often reproducing several "copies" from a model. Through the efforts of the artist Anthony Velonis, whose experience producing window displays and wallpaper introduced him to silkscreening, New York's poster division moved into the age of mechanical reproduction, and its output increased to six hundred posters a day.[5]

Anti-New Deal sentiment was, from the very beginning, intense and constant. The FAP was one of the more contentious programs, since the arts were traditionally seen as elitist and urban. Much of the overtly political work produced under the WPA, such as the Federal Theater Project's "Living Newspapers" and the documentary photographs of the Farm Security Administration, garnered the hostility of conservatives, who claimed the project's membership was comprised of left-wing radicals.[6] The words and pictures of poverty and decay reported by writers and photographers compose an image

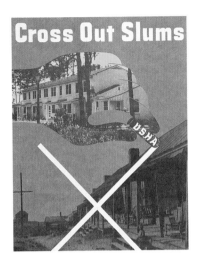

of the era quite different from that conveyed by the bright compositions of the poster division. Neither the textual conventions of "documentary expression," techniques such as quotation, statistical evidence, and direct address, nor the photographic "evidence" that inspired so many of the popular photo-texts in magazines and books, seems to have influenced the poster units.[7]

The absence of photography in the poster projects may have been a result of the organization of labor. In the New York poster unit, which was a model for the rest of the country, employees deemed "unacceptable" as artists were put to work cutting the silkscreen films according to the direction of the designer. Photographic processes, in addition to being more expensive and complex than film cutting, would

1. For an overview of WPA programs, see Francis V. O'Connor, *Federal Art Patronage: 1933 to 1943*, exh. cat. (College Park: University of Maryland Art Gallery, 1966). For firsthand accounts of how the programs functioned, see *The New Deal Art Projects: An Anthology of Memoirs*, Francis V. O'Connor, ed. (Washington, D.C.: Smithsonian Institution Press, 1972).
2. Basil Rauch, *The History of the New Deal, 1933–38* (New York: Capricorn Books, 1944, 1963).
3. William Stott, *Documentary Expression in America* (University of Chicago Press, 1973, 1986).
4. Christopher DeNoon, *Posters of the WPA* (Los Angeles: Wheatley, 1987).
5. Of an estimated thirty-five thousand WPA poster designs, only two thousand have survived. DeNoon's *Posters of the WPA* is the first book published on the poster project. As DeNoon notes, "the works remain largely undocumented in any written history of poster art, and with the exception of an article published in *Print* [magazine] in 1978, virtually no periodical since the FAP's demise has published them." 33.
6. Opposition to the New Deal peaked in 1939 when the United States House of Representatives Committee to Investigate Un-American Activities began questioning the union and political affiliations of those involved in programs such as the FTP. The committee, organized by Representative Martin Dies, manipulated public opinion through unfounded accusations, prefiguring the government's anti-Communist campaign of the late 1940s and early 1950s. The committee's widely reported investigations enabled it to succeed in disbanding the Federal Theater Project.

1937 Franklin Delano Roosevelt

Corporate Design, Corporate Art

have eliminated jobs in a program designed to create jobs.

That photography gave some designers a powerful tool for visualizing the New Deal is made clear in a poster designed by Lester Beall for the United States Housing Authority in 1941.[8] Beall combines the flat colors and schematic shapes characteristic of the poster projects with a documentary style of photography. Probably influenced by the political photomontages of John Heartfield and Hannah Höch, this style carries a sense of urgency and contemporaneity that is absent from the more painterly posters.

In 1934 Walter Paepcke, founder and chairman of the Container Corporation of America, hired the Chicago designer Egbert Jacobson to redesign nearly every surface of his company: factories, offices, trucks, stationery, and advertising.[1] This kind of commercial "packaging," which encases not the product but the company that manufactures it, is known today as "corporate identity" or "corporate image."[2]

CCA's most influential contribution to business culture was its advertising program. At the advice of the agency N.W. Ayer & Son, Paepcke commissioned designs from European modernists, including A.M. Cassandre, Herbert Bayer, and Gyorgy Kepes; the first ad ran in the luxurious, design-conscious business journal *Fortune* in 1937. Some of these early images incorporated photomontage, and would have been considered aesthetically radical, departing from the more established Art Deco and streamlining styles of Modernism.

After World War II CCA advertising shifted away from avant-garde design toward contemporary "fine art." Two 1940s campaigns

featured tentatively cubist, expressionist, or pseudo-primitive illustrations; here typography ceased to be integral to the design and served instead as discrete captions for autonomous "paintings."[3] CCA's most celebrated series is Great Ideas of Western Man, in which artists interpreted famous quotations from the "Western tradition," from Aristotle to John F. Kennedy. A 1959 collage by Herbert Bayer makes no reference to packaging; such ads act as autonomous works of "art" with an oblique advertising function.[4]

CCA thus promoted itself through the act of patronage, representing itself as a benevolent sponsor of artistic creativity. As the artist Hans Haacke has pointed out, corporate patronage

7. Documentary is examined as "a genre as distinct as tragedy, epic, or satire" in Stott's *Documentary Expression in America*. The documentary photo-texts of the Great Depression are critically examined in John Rogers Puckett, *Five Photo-Textual Documentaries from the Great Depression* (Ann Arbor, Mich.: UMI Research Press, 1984).
8. Beall, who emerged as a major designer in the postwar period, earlier had produced a series of strikingly simple and forceful posters for the Rural Electrification Administration that have become icons of sophisticated American design of the 1930s.

1. A comprehensive history of the cultural projects of Walter Paepcke and CCA is James Sloan Allen, *The Romance of Commerce and Culture: Capitalism, Modernism, and the Chicago-Aspen Crusade for Cultural Reform* (University of Chicago Press, 1983). See also Neil Harris, "Designs on Demand: Art Nouveau and the Modern Corporation," *Art, Design, and the Modern Corporation: The Collection of the Container Corporation of America, A Gift to the National Museum of American Art* (Washington, D.C.: Smithsonian Institution, 1985), 8–30.
2. One of the earliest total design programs for a corporation was the German architect Peter Behrens's work for the AEG, an electrical utility, in the 1910s. See Alan Windsor, *Peter Behrens: Architect and Designer* (New York: Whitney Library of Design, 1981).
3. See Container Corporation of America, *Modern Art in Advertising: Designs for Container Corporation of America*, exh. cat. (Chicago: Paul Theobald, 1946). The works in "United Nations" and "United States" were exhibited as fine art at The Art Institute of Chicago in 1946; the show also included graphics by Bayer, Cassandre, Carlu, and others.

1941 Franklin Delano Roosevelt

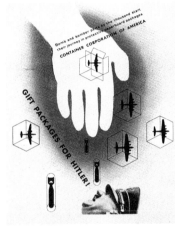

The New Bauhaus: Rationalism and Expressionism

The New Bauhaus was founded in 1937 by The Association of Arts and Industries, a group of citizens who wished to revitalize Chicago manufacturing through design.[1] The school was directed by the Hungarian artist, designer, and theorist László Moholy-Nagy, who had taught at the German Bauhaus.[2] After one year the association withdrew its support, unprepared for the radicalism of the school; only Walter Paepcke, well-known patron-client of the avant-garde, remained loyal.[3] Moholy-Nagy reopened the institution under the name School of Design in 1939, financing it independently; it became the Institute of Design in 1944 and is now part of the Illinois Institute of Technology.

The name *Bauhaus* is commonly associated today with "functionalism," the theory that an object's use, materials, and means of production should dictate its form.[4] A lettering system designed by Hin Bredendieck, a student at the New Bauhaus, was published in the magazine *More Business* in 1938.

All angles are drawn with a T square and a right triangle, and all curves with a compass; thus the letters meet one of functionalism's basic criteria: their method of production helps generate their visual form.[5]

The notion of functionalism is useful for understanding many projects of the New Bauhaus. Functionalism, however, rarely worked as a completely objective, value-free design method, or as a self-contained formula for decision-making. Design strategies such as simplified form, exposed structure, and standardized elements were weighted with philosophical significance and thus were not fully neutral, "scientific" processes of deduction. Furthermore, criteria such as faithfulness to materials and fitness to purpose rarely dictate every aspect of a design but require instead some degree of personal taste and intuition. Thus while functionalism is commonly associated with an excessive dependence on intellect, it was allied at the New Bauhaus with expressionism.[6]

The New Bauhaus student lettering project was inspired by Herbert Bayer's "universal alphabet," designed at the Bauhaus in Dessau from 1925 to 1928.[7] Bayer's reduction to simple geometric forms was part of a broader search for a basic "language" of vision. For example, Wassily Kandinsky's Bauhaus Book *Point and Line to*

of the arts buys respect from a public which might be suspicious of business while admiring "high culture."[5] The CCA collection was eventually donated to the National Museum of American Art at the Smithsonian, an event celebrated with a major exhibition in 1985. The museum catalogue chose to represent all the works as if they were fine art,

even those conceived of as applied design. Thus the early ads, which had actively integrated word and image, are reproduced without typography. Like CCA's later advertising programs, the museum's presentation favored fine art over applied design, finding cultural prestige in autonomous, nonutilitarian objects.[6]

4. Trade articles dealing with CCA's Great Ideas campaign include Walter J. Johnson, "The Case for Management's Advertising," *Public Relations Journal* 19, 10 (October 1963): 10–12; and Andrew J. Lazarus, "Corporate Advertising — A Fad or Fundamental?" *Public Relations Journal* 20, 10 (October 1964): 35–37.
5. Haacke has written on and made works of art about corporate patronage. See Brian Wallis, ed., *Hans Haacke: Unfinished Business* (New York: The New Museum and Cambridge, Mass.: MIT Press, 1987).
6. The book *Art, Design, and the Modern Corporation*, supra, note 3, is the catalogue for this exhibition. Other corporate patrons of the fine arts have included the Johnson Wax Company, which commissioned its corporate headquarters, in Racine, Wisconsin, from Frank Lloyd Wright in the 1930s. The company also sponsored the fine arts. See "Art: USA: Now Thanks to a Wax Company," *Fortune* 66, 3 (September 1962): 133–139.

48

abcdefghi
jklmnopqr
stuvwxyz
a   d d

Plane (1926) tried to identify a "vocabulary" of simple graphic elements underlying all pictorial expression.[8] Bayer's geometricized alphabet offered a simplified medium for the written word — writing, for thinkers such as Bayer and Kandinsky, was a conventional, nonuniversal, culturally limited code, and was thus an enemy of the sensual, immediate "language" of vision.[9] Bayer eliminated capital letters from his alphabet, contending that the uppercase-lowercase distinction does not occur in speech and thus distances writing from direct "natural" communication.

Bayer's alphabet is functionalist insofar as it was created to revise the codes of writing. This act of rationalization was not, however, a verifiably "correct," neutral solution to a utilitarian problem but a critical gesture that discovered — or created — a "problem" that had not existed before. In short, Bayer's font is too radical to be fully explained by a strictly utilitarian definition of functionalism. The student alphabet is more routinely functionalist, but its meaning is nonetheless tempered by the spirit of Bayer's design.

Whereas some Bauhaus exercises yielded rigidly geometric designs, the results of others looked amorphous, organic, or random. For example, an object called a "hand sculpture" was a smooth, irregularly shaped piece of wood designed to be comfortably held; it gave the student a "tactile experience" that could be tapped later in the design of telephones, glassware, or handles.[10] A statement in a 1939 brochure read: "Mastered Technique = Freedom of Creation ... discipline merges with fantasy and genuine results for application begin to appear."[11] Thus Bauhaus design theory projected the objectively identifiable criteria of functionalism over a base of subjective experience.[12]

1. Documents related to the New Bauhaus appear in Hans M. Wingler, *The Bauhaus: Weimar Dessau Berlin Chicago* (Cambridge, Mass.: MIT Press, 1969). See also *50 Jahre New Bauhaus: Bauhaus Nachfolge in Chicago* (Berlin: Bauhaus-Archiv, 1987).
2. A collection of writings by László Moholy-Nagy, with a historical essay by Richard Kostelanetz, ed., is *Moholy-Nagy* (New York: Praeger, 1970).
3. Allen provides an account of the founding of the New Bauhaus in relation to the career of Walter Paepcke in *The Romance of Commerce and Culture*.
4. The term *functionalism* is only an approximation of the German *sachlicheit*, which has also been translated as "sobriety" and "objectivity." Thus "functionalism" does not refer only to utility but also to philosophical notions of the rightness and clarity of form. See Stanford Anderson, "The Fiction of Function," *Assemblage* 2 (February 1987): 19–31.
5. The image is reproduced in *50 Jahre*, supra, note 1, 141.
6. The most famous example of functionalism used in its most literal sense is in Tom Wolfe, *From Our House to Bauhaus* (New York: Farrar, Straus and Giroux, 1981).
7. On Herbert Bayer, see Gwen Finkel Chanzit, *Herbert Bayer and Modernist Design in America, 1926–1976* (Ann Arbor, Mich.: UMI Research Press, 1987).
8. See Wassily Kandinsky, *Point and Line to Plane* (New York: Dover, 1979), English translation, circa 1947; first published as a Bauhaus Book in 1926. For a detailed account of Kandinsky's pedagogy, see Clarence V. Poling, *Kandinsky's Teaching at the Bauhaus: Color Theory and Analytical Drawing* (New York: Rizzoli, 1986).
9. Kandinsky expresses hostility toward "literary" values in his description of the birth of the "point." When the point ceases to be a mark of punctuation and takes on purely visual, abstract qualities, it gains its "voice" (Kandinsky, supra, note 8, 26). Moholy-Nagy makes aggressive statements against verbal language in his book *Painting Photography Film* (Cambridge, Mass.: MIT Press, 1969), originally published as a Bauhaus Book, 1925.
10. Information about the "hand sculpture" project appears in *50 Jahre*, supra, note 1, 116, 117; and in Moholy-Nagy's account of the New Bauhaus, *Vision in Motion* (Chicago: Paul Theobald, 1947).
11. *50 Jahre*, supra, note 1, 114.
12. A 1945 article stresses the liaison of rationality and individuality as the inheritance of the Bauhaus tradition. The phrase that occurs again and again in the essay is "creative and functional." See Edward J. Frey, "Postwar Graphic Arts Education: What Changes Will Come in Teaching Design?" *Print* 3, 4 (Fall 1945): 4–7.

1945 Franklin Delano Roosevelt, Harry S Truman

"Good" Design

Designers who came into prominence in the years following World War II — notably Bradbury Thompson, Paul Rand, Alvin Lustig, and Ladislav Sutnar — were heir to the innovations of Cubism, Dada, Constructivism, the Bauhaus, and Surrealism. They brought the self-expressive sensibilities of the modern artist to advertising and graphic design. Paul Rand's influential book *Thoughts on Design* (1947) is representative of this development, setting forth the role of the designer as a figure who tempers the instinct and intuition of the artist with the professional requirements of advertising: "That which makes for good advertising is one thing, and that which makes for good art is another; but that which makes for good advertising art is an harmonious resolution of both."[1] *Thoughts on Design* is both a polemic against the mediocrity of mass advertising and a statement of Rand's ideas about modern design. It identifies the "abstract, expressive symbol," which results from the designer's mental process, as the key to progressive design; the designer "restate(s) his problem in terms of ideas, pictures, forms, and shapes.

He unifies, simplifies, eliminates superfluities. He symbolizes ... abstracts from his material by association and analogy."[2]

The symbols and techniques employed by Rand and others were often derived from modernist painting and sculpture. Strategies such as collage, montage, childlike drawing, visual puns, biomorphic shapes, and asymmetry came from artists including Klee, Picasso, Braque, Kandinsky, Arp, Miró, Chagall, Ernst, and Heartfield. Such forms were seen as "attention-getting devices" whose obscurity may need to be "balanced with universally recognized forms."[3] Rand's use of abstraction and visual punning can be seen in a 1949 cover for a Museum of Modern Art catalogue. He and other designers divorced themselves from the

unsophisticated tradition of what Rand referred to as the "bromidic advertising [that caters to] bad taste" by infusing their design with the high culture of modernist painting and sculpture.[4]

Modern art and design had established a foothold in America because of the immigration of European artists, designers, and architects in the 1930s; the spread of Modernism was also facilitated by The Museum of Modern Art, New York. When the museum was established, in 1929, its primary focus was painting and sculpture, but after 1932 it included architectural, industrial, and graphic design. In a series of exhibitions called Useful Objects, initiated in 1938, the museum defined its notion of what constituted "good design" in mass-produced consumer items. Although the pretext of these shows was the utility and quality of consumer objects, function, durability, and safety were of secondary importance to appearance: items were generally selected for their formal affinities to modern sculpture and painting. Useful Objects was followed by a series of shows called Good Design, which continued from 1950 to 1955. By advocating modern design in home furnishings, the museum hoped to influence the taste of both furniture manufacturers and the public.[5]

The popular success of the Useful Objects and Good Design series inspired similar exhibitions in museums and department stores throughout the United States. The 1949 Museum of Modern Art exhibition and publication *Modern Art in Your Life* is exemplary of the position museums took in championing the cause of modern art and design. Industrial and graphic design are elevated through their association with painting and sculpture: "when the [book] jacket designer makes up his page with a few rigorous lines against large immaculate areas, when the package designer limits his appeal to square-cut letters and a minimum of balanced rectangles, they ... share Mondrian's delight in a bold and subtle simplicity." At the same time, fine art is democratized because it is shown to influence everyday life: "the artist [gives] form to a vision which the designer then makes his own ... [contradicting] the point of view that the modern artist is isolated from the rest of the world, and his work therefore without meaning to his fellow men."[6] The *Modern Art in Your Life* exhibition displayed the products of the art world alongside the advertisements, book covers, and consumer goods of mass culture. The message of the exhibition

The Expansion of Corporate Identity

is forcefully conveyed in book form through layouts that juxtapose design for mass markets, such as a 1947 book cover by Alvin Lustig, with their high-culture "precedents" — in this case, paintings and sculpture by Miró, Arp, Calder, and Noguchi.

1. Paul Rand, *Thoughts on Design* (New York: Wittenborn, Schultz, 1947), 1.
2. Ibid., 4.
3. Ibid., 54.
4. Ibid., 136.
5. For information on this promotional phase of modern design in America, see Arthur J. Pulos, *The American Design Adventure* (Cambridge, Mass.: MIT Press, 1988); and Lynes, *Good Old Modern*.
6. Robert Goldwater and René d'Harnoncourt, *Modern Art in Your Life*, exh. cat. (New York: Museum of Modern Art, 1949), 5.

The CBS "eye" is the most persistent feature of that corporation's design program. Since 1951 it has appeared on everything from television screens and print advertisements to napkins, matchbooks, wallpaper, and adhesive tape. William Golden, who became art director at CBS in 1949, went so far as to design his own postal meter slugs, with colored inks to match the printing on various packages.[1]

Advertising was the main product advertised by the witty and elegant campaigns of CBS, promoting the television and radio media to potential advertisers and agency account executives. A relatively design-conscious community, this was an appropriate audience on which to lavish innovative ads. Several other early corporate identity programs also used sophisticated design to sell design-related products — the Container Corporation of America began employing modernist graphics in 1934, the West Virginia Pulp and Paper Company published designs by Bradbury Thompson beginning in 1938, and the modernist furniture manufacturer Knoll International first commissioned graphics from the Swiss designer Herbert Matter in the 1940s.[2]

By the end of the 1950s, however, professionally designed identity programs had been adopted by more diverse industries, marking a step in the professionalization of graphic design and the expansion of corporate bureaucracy. The new genre was enthusiastically embraced by trade magazines, which heralded corporate "image" as a lucrative field for ad agencies and public relations departments as well as a legitimate concern of business.

A writer for *Advertising Age* magazine in 1959 coyly offered business as a subject for psychoanalysis: the corporation is "just as subject to neuroses and inner searchings and optimism and depression ... as any single person is."[3] The 1950s was a decade when psychoanalysis was popular, when Americans saw Freudian overtones in films such as *The Seven Year Itch* (1955) with Marilyn Monroe, and the psychoanalyst Erik Erikson coined the term "identity crisis."[4] In the midst of this popular fascination with the invisible histories controlling human will, the corporation emerged as a new personality type, seeking to transcend the "invisible" forces of the market; designers and public relations officers were called on for diagnoses and cures.[5]

Print magazine was particularly energetic in promoting and documenting corporate graphics; in 1953 it exchanged its bookish, scholarly image for a big, glossy format, and the editors announced a new focus on design and business. Especially well documented in *Print* at the end of the 1950s

1. Responding to the rapid growth of television, CBS management divided its television and radio network into separate units in 1951. Golden became CBS television's creative director of advertising and sales promotion, and his assistant Lou Dorfsman took charge of radio. In the years after Golden's death, in 1959, Dorfsman assumed responsibility for the company's complete graphic identity; he was named vice-president, creative director of the CBS Broadcast Group in 1968. This position in upper management indicates the importance of design to the company's then president, Dr. Frank Stanton. Dorfsman remained with CBS until 1988. See William Golden, "My Eye," *Print* 13, 3 (May–June 1957): 24–29; Cipe Pineles Golden et al., eds., *The Visual Craft of William Golden* (New York: George Braziller, 1962); and Dick Hess and Marion Muller, *Dorfsman and CBS* (New York: American Showcase, 1987).
2. On Herbert Matter's work for Knoll, see Eric Larrabee and Massimo Vignelli, *Knoll Design* (New York: Harry N. Abrams, 1981). On Bradbury Thompson, see Bradbury Thompson, *Bradbury Thompson: The Art of Graphic Design* (New Haven, Conn.: Yale University Press, 1988).
3. See Howard Gossage, "Give Your Company a Clear, Consistent Identity, and its Advertising Will be Easier, Better," *Advertising Age* (9 March 1959): 59ff. A textbook for designers is H.F.K. Henrion and Alan Parkin, *Design Coordination and the Corporate Image* (New York: Reinhold, 1967). A recent textbook for public relations professionals is James G. Gray, Jr., *Managing the Corporate Image: The Key to Public Trust* (Westport, Conn.: Quorum Books, 1986).
4. See Erik H. Erikson, *Childhood and Society* (New York: W.W. Norton, 1985).

were identity programs directed by mature designers who had established their careers in the 1930s and 1940s. Paul Rand and the architect Eliot Noyes collaborated on a design program for IBM, initiated in 1956. Rand, Noyes, Herbert Matter, and Charles Eames collaborated on the 1959 identity program for Westinghouse. Matter designed graphics for the New Haven Railroad in 1955, and Lester Beall established a program for International Paper in 1960.[6]

Thus in the same decade that International Style architecture became the official idiom for new office buildings, the rise of "corporate image" signaled the integration of modernist graphic design into corporate culture.

5. Alfred D. Chandler's *The Visible Hand* discusses corporate economics in terms of the demise of Adam Smith's notion of the "invisible hand" of market forces and the rise of the "visible hand" of management, which is able to manipulate capital independently of such simple concepts as "supply," "demand," and "profit."

6. *Print* devoted its May–June 1957 issue to corporate identity. See also "Four Major Corporate Design Programs," *Print* 14, 6 (November–December 1960): 31–50.

Chambers of Commerce

The postwar increase in marriages and the "baby boom" created an expansive housing market and the consequent rush to the suburbs, where the automobile was an indispensable piece of household equipment. The heavy concentration of middle-class consumers encouraged urban retailers to establish branches whose proximity to the suburbs and large parking lots offered an alternative to long commutes into congested cities. The core of many suburbs became the strip of retail stores, eateries, movie theaters, and small businesses whose colored, illuminated, blinking and revolving signs created a dense, graphic corridor of commerce.

While restaurant chains had been pioneered as early as the 1870s, the first to standardize its architectural image was White Castle. In the early 1920s the White Castle System of Eating Houses had established a fiefdom of crenellated, rusticated, and turreted snack shops whose uniformity symbolized consistent quality. The stainless steel shimmer and lavatory whiteness that had become the hallmark of clean and economical lunchroom *interiors* was turned inside out to advertise that White Castle served princely, hygienic hamburgers. By 1929 a movable, fireproof, porcelain-enameled steel

"castle" made of interchangeable parts became the company standard.[1]

McDonald's was among the first and most successful postwar chains to adopt the White Castle model of standardized food and imagery. In 1952 Richard and Maurice McDonald, working with Ray Kroc, began to franchise their successful self-service restaurant, which adapted the self-service concept from retail selling in order to minimize wage labor. By 1953 the yellow parabolic arches, entirely nonstructural and purely symbolic, were established as the company trademark. This zealous expression of technology and modernity merely updated the White Castle strategy: in both cases building and sign are collapsed into a single image.[2]

Franchises that came of age in the 1950s and 1960s incorporated novelty rooflines and futuristic appendages to compete for motorists' attention. The resulting visual chaos of the commercial strip came under attack from environmentalists

1957 Dwight D. Eisenhower

Magazines: Visual Thinking

The rise of television had a twofold impact on the magazine industry: TV's imagery and kinetic variety required a greater level of visual excitement from print graphics, and television also cut into the time many people had formerly spent reading. In a 1955 design annual the impact of television on magazine design was described as marking "a transition from word thinking to visual thinking."[1] The new double-imperative of magazine graphics — greater attention to images and faster delivery of content — created a situation wherein the art director held an increasingly important role in shaping content. Many of the leading art directors of this period — Henry Wolf (*Esquire* and *Harper's Bazaar*), Otto Storch (*McCall's*), Sam Antupit (*Esquire*) — had studied with Alexey Brodovitch, who was influential in magazine art direction and photography from the 1930s to the late 1950s. Others, such as Bradbury Thompson (*Mademoiselle*), Cipe Pineles (*Charm*), Allen Hurlburt (*Look*), Alexander Liberman (*Vogue*), Art Kane (*Seventeen*), Tina Fredricks (*Glamour*), and Will Burtin and Leo Lionni (*Fortune*), also came to prominence in this era.

A distinguishing feature in this phase of magazine design is the growing attention to the relationship between words and images. Typography, photography, and illustration are used provocatively to suggest both the subject and editorial angle. Henry Wolf's magazine covers for *Esquire* are exemplary: clever visual punning expresses urbane, "gentlemanly" sophistication. The fusion of images and words extended to page layouts as well, in staged photographs incorporating text type and in typography composed of three-dimensional objects. In these efforts to collapse the verbal and visual, the magazine attempts to compete with television's seamless flow of imagery overlaid with spoken and typographic messages.[2] Wolf's techniques were pursued in a more aggressive way when *Esquire*, facing economic collapse in 1962, enlisted advertising designer George Lois. The high impact of his covers, informed by the aggressive imagery of advertising and television, can be seen in a 1965 feature on "the masculinization of the American woman."[3]

and community leaders by the late 1960s. In 1969 McDonald's unveiled the first of its environment-conscious, restrained, brown brick buildings, with "tastefully" illuminated ribs on a mansard roof.[3] The industry-wide shift from futuristic bombast to domestic and historical references — the colonial, the Southwest, the Victorian, the Cape Cod — suggest that franchises are now following standards set by the eclecticism of suburban residential architecture and the tastes of municipal zoning boards.

1. For information on the development of fast-food architecture and the growth of roadside commerce, see Chester H. Liebs, *Mainstreet to Miracle Mile;* Philip Langdon, *Orange Roofs, Golden Arches: The Architecture of American Chain Restaurants* (London: Michael Joseph, 1986).
2. Langdon offers a good analysis of the symbolic import of the arches, noting their relationship to "progressive" modern design and their antecedents in Le Corbusier's unrealized plan for the Palace of Soviets in Moscow (1931) and other kinds of "dynamic structural modernism," ibid., 84–109.
3. Fast-food restaurants began combating the effects of over-standardization in the 1970s by miming local building styles and displaying photographs and memorabilia of local history. In the 1980s chains have introduced one-of-a-kind designer units by "signature" architects. See Regina S. Baraban, "Eat and Run," *Metropolis* 7, 8 (April 1988): 52.

1. Wallace F. Hainline, "Editorial Layout," *The 34th Annual of Advertising and Editorial Art and Design* (New York: Watson-Guptill, 1955).
2. By 1966 the experimentation that characterized magazine design in the late 1950s and early 1960s was being referred to as "circus graphics." In 1965 Otto Storch, recalling his dramatic 1958 redesign of *McCall's*, stated that it was "over-designed" and "tricky." The inventive engagement of text and photography that distinguished Storch's work shifted to isolated, full-page photographs. A contemporary review suggested that this conservatism was a response to the complexity of issues such as civil rights, Vietnam, and birth control, which "it might seem an impertinence to dress-up." The implication that design should neutrally deliver "serious" content and that fluff journalism is the art director's domain is unfortunately supported in the publishing. Thomas Barry, "Winds of Change in Magazine Design," *Print* 20, 1 (January–February 1966): 20–26, 75. For a contemporary review of the state of magazine design in the 1980s with remarks by Wolf, Pineles, and Antupit, see "Symposium: Magazine Design, The Rationalist's Dream?" Steven Heller, ed., *Journal of Graphic Design* 3, 3 (1985): 1, 2. Further, see Joseph Giovannini's essay in the present book.
3. Lois's work for *Esquire* is situated in the context of American political graphics in Victor Margolin, "Rebellion, Reform, and Revolution: American Graphic Design for Social Change," *Design Issues* 5, 1 (Fall 1988): 59–70.

The New Advertising and the New Ad Agencies/The Old Advertising and Pop

"The new advertising" is a term that has been applied to the unorthodox strategies that widely transformed the practice and character of advertising in the 1960s.[1] The campaign that has become the icon of the new advertising was created by the firm Doyle Dane Bernbach (DDB) for Volkswagen.[2] A simple layout, a

Lemon.

sober black-and-white photograph, and an unexpected caption are the antithesis of the hard sell. Irreverent humor, disarming wit, and a new self-consciousness about advertising were the hallmarks of the Volkswagen campaign and set the tone for sophisticated advertising in the 1960s. The Volkswagen ads epitomized DDB's ability to frame a fertile campaign strategy — in this case, the modest appearance of the car served to underscore

Detroit's obsession with styling at the expense of engineering and economy.[3]

The creative director of DDB and acknowledged "father" of the new advertising was Bill Bernbach.[4] Aside from his advertisements, Bernbach's most important contribution to the profession was his insistence on the "creative team," composed of a copywriter and an art director. In his own career as a copywriter, Bernbach had found that the traditional bureaucratic separation between writing and art directing led to advertisements whose text and imagery were arbitrarily or awkwardly related.[5]

The new advertising transformed not only the look of ads but also the structure of traditional agencies. Previously, the copywriter and art director had served the will of an executive staff that relied heavily on market research and demographics to form its campaigns. Bernbach and others, sensitive to the mediocrity of mass advertising, dismissed the use of such research in favor of intuition, provocation, and humor. As the new advertising flourished, creative

Recognizing the importance of skilled art direction, a number of corporations enlisted the service of designers to upgrade their company magazines. In the postwar period the rise of "in-house" publications, directed at company employees, stockholders, and patrons, reflected the increasing tendency of privately owned companies to go public. While designers who art directed *The Refresher* (Coca-Cola), *What's New* (Abbott Labs), and *Transition* (Litton Industries) did not enjoy the cachet of working for *Vogue* and *Esquire*, they did find within this field a lucrative area for professional design. By 1962 nine thousand different company magazines constituted a five-million-dollar-per-year business.[4]

An outstanding example is the West Virginia Pulp and Paper Company, which in 1939 enlisted

Bradbury Thompson to design its company magazine. Because *Westvaco Inspirations* was intended to demonstrate printing processes and papers, its primary audience consisted of thirty-five thousand designers, printers, teachers, and students.[5] With complete control of content and design, yet restricted to using existing artwork, Thompson turned the *Westvaco Inspirations* series into a platform for recycling available imagery and experimenting with the properties of printing. In the example reproduced here Thompson placed typographic history within the context of art and architecture. Rather than mimic the typographic conventions of a given era, Thompson viewed the letter forms through a modern lens, drawing attention to their relevance to contemporary design.

4. "Sixteen Pace-Setting Company Magazines," *Print* 16, 1 (January–February 1962): 45.
5. The readership of *Westvaco Inspirations* is characterized in *Bradbury Thompson: The Art of Graphic Design*, an excellent source on his singular contribution to graphic design.

teams gained directorial positions within the agencies. One result was the proliferation of "boutiques," small agencies headed by creative teams that often had broken away from larger firms. Another result was the dismantling of the Anglo-Saxon, upper-middle-class, old-boy network of Madison Avenue. Opportunities for Jewish, Greek, Irish, Italian, and female writers and art directors opened up partly because of the sudden increase in the number and variety of agencies and partly because media imagery of a homogeneous, WASPy America reflected the composition of Madison Avenue more than it did the actual consumer groups, especially those in important urban centers.[6] The extent to which ethnicity influenced the profession was humorously recognized in a 1964 trade ad that portrayed twelve leading Italian-American art directors and asked "Are Italian Art Directors More Talented?" It was followed, a month later, by an ad featuring twelve prominent Jewish art directors de-

manding equal time.[7] Despite the activities of civil rights groups, however, the ad industry rarely employed blacks.

The sophisticated agencies of the 1960s waged a campaign against the glut of trite advertising that characterized the affluent society of postwar America.[8] Confrontation, wit, and understatement replaced predictable celebrity endorsements, comparison strategies, and hyperbole. The skillfully art-directed photograph replaced dated illustration techniques and highly retouched photography.[9] The new advertising tried to revamp an industry whose services were expanding as rapidly as its influence was ebbing. In a trade ad produced by DDB the headline announced "DO THIS OR DIE," and the copy urged truth in advertising and quality in manufacturing: "Unless we change, the tidal wave of consumer indifference will wallop into the mountain of advertising and manufacturing drivel."[10] Indifference was a reaction advertising could not afford.

While Doyle Dane Bernbach represented the sophisticated avant-garde of American advertising, it existed alongside a larger mainstream. In London in the mid-1950s the term *Pop Art* was coined by a collective of artists and designers called the Independent Group; Pop named a class of objects banished from

the realm of good design — stylish Detroit automobiles, Hollywood film posters, and routine Madison Avenue ads were held up as symbols of freedom against the austere Modernism promoted in Britain after World War II.[11]

In 1955 the critic Reyner Banham praised the American Cadillac as a paragon of Pop values — it was impermanent, emotional, sensual, and symbolic. Banham attacked the Volkswagen in 1961 as a product of false modesty, whose lack of superficial design "styling" belied

an absence of technical and aesthetic imagination: the VW's "overwhelming virtue in the eyes of men of liberal conscience was that in a world of automotive flux its appearance remained constant.... In other words, it was a symbol of protest against the standards of Detroit, the mass media and the Pop Arts."[12]

In New York Pop Art emerged in the early 1960s as a response to the heroic Abstract

1. The term has become a convenient way of referring to the sophisticated and often humorous advertising that came of age in the 1960s. It is unclear where the term originated. See Robert Glatzer, *The New Advertising* (New York: Citadel Press, 1970), 10; and Larry Dobrow, *When Advertising Tried Harder* (New York: Friendly Press, 1984), preface.
2. In *When Advertising Tried Harder*, Dobrow writes: "if the sixties were the best of creative times, then the Volkswagen campaign is not merely the best of the sixties, but the best of all time," 81.
3. The Volkswagen campaign was orchestrated by Julian Koenig (writer) and Helmut Krone (art director). Over the years VW ads were worked on by ten different teams of writers and art directors. As creative director, Bernbach (and, later, Bob Gage) assigned writers and art directors to various clients. The other two partners of DDB, Maxwell Dane and Ned Doyle, served as financial manager and account representative, respectively.
4. Bernbach may be considered the father of the new advertising because his work was among the first to depart from established conventions but also because so many important figures in the new advertising, including George Lois, Mary Wells, and Julian Koenig, worked with Bernbach at DDB before opening their own offices.
5. Bernbach began working with an art director when he teamed with Paul Rand on playful advertisements for Ohrbach's department stores in the late 1940s.
6. Dobrow, in *When Advertising Tried Harder*, places great importance on the role of graduates from urban art schools and colleges in transforming the profession: "To compete effectively and successfully in the sixties, advertising agencies were suddenly faced with the need to recruit a new kind of employee with non-traditional attitudes and unconventional notions. How could talent like that be found? Where was it developed? Mainly, in the streets and schools of New York City, with an occasional assist from Chicago and points West," 68.

Black Markets, Black Power

Some American advertisers are color-blind.

Ebony.

Expressionism of the previous decade; Pop tried to find a less personal brand of abstraction in the flat colors, halftone screens, and mechanical repetition of the mass media. Most of the material incorporated by the American Pop artists was not modernist design or sophisticated conceptual advertising, but rather the slick mainstream of fast-food, comic strips, supermarket packaging, journalistic photographs, and commonplace automobiles, as in James Rosenquist's 1963 *Untitled (Broome Street Truck).*[13] While celebrating the common life of the present, Pop Art also offered nostalgia, recalling a golden age of truly "American" media and design.

Two advertisements represent opposite sides of "black America" in the 1960s: an ad designed by Herb Lubalin for *Ebony* magazine (1969) urges manufacturers to recognize that "the Negro is not the white man's burden ... he's earning $30 billion dollars a year; ... he spends a greater percentage of his income on food, home furnishings, and personal care products than white people of comparable income do."[1] The *Ebony* ad, which appeared as a full-page in *The New York Times*, makes a baldly economic bid to the advertising community, appealing to business interests rather than social responsibility. The other ad, designed by Lou Dorfsman in 1968 and photographed by Ron Borowski, also appeared as a full-page in *The New York Times*; it announced a CBS television program, "Black History: Lost, Stolen, or Strayed." The text in the ad underscores the urgency of the issue by stating that "the frustrations of [the black American's] search for identity and recognition underlie much of today's crisis of alienation in American society." The model bears a resemblance to Martin Luther King, Jr., who had been assassinated three months before the ad appeared.

Both images derive their impact from face-painting: the "design" of each ad occurs on the skin of the subject rather than in the composition of the page or photo-

graph. The CBS ad turns an emblem of democracy into a provocatively ambiguous mask suggestive of tribal face-painting; unlike native African traditions, however, this painting is not the result of *self-* adornment. The Lubalin ad picks up on another convention of facial painting by reversing the blackface worn by white vaudeville entertainers as well as by the singer Al Jolson in the 1920s and 1930s. Both ads rehearse the controversial issues of the representation of blacks in mainstream media.[2] The fact that they deal with the subject of race in a theatrical and aggressive manner is indicative of the "dilemma of integrated advertising."[3]

The *Ebony* ad is typical of the strategy employed by black media to encourage national advertisers to solicit the black community through publications such as *Ebony*, *Jet*, *Negro Digest*, and *Tan*. John H. Johnson, the publisher of all four of these periodicals, was a major influ-

7. The first DDB ad on "ethnic" art directors appeared in *Advertising Age* (2 November 1962): 75.
8. The economist John Kenneth Galbraith's influential book *The Affluent Society* (1958) contended that America had attained a level of prosperity enabling it to shift from the production of goods to the development of public services.
9. Photography played a major role in the new advertising, and several important photographers emerged in this period, notably Henry Wolf, Bert Stern and Carl Fischer.
10. The "DO THIS OR DIE" ad is reproduced in Bob Levenson, *Bill Bernbach's Book* (New York: Villard Books, 1987), 167.
11. For a history of the British Pop movement, with reprints of contemporary magazine articles, see Brian Wallis, ed., *This Is Tomorrow Today: The Independent Group and British Pop Art*, exh. cat. (New York: The Clock Tower and the Institute for Art and Urban Resources, 1987); it includes reprints of 1950s articles by Reyner Banham, Richard Hamilton, and others.
12. Reyner Banham, "Design by Choice," first published in *Architectural Review*, July 1961, and reprinted in Penny Sparke, ed., *Design by Choice* (New York: Rizzoli, 1981), 97–107.
13. Lucy Lippard, ed., *Pop Art*, with contributions by Lawrence Alloway, Nancy Marmer, and Nicolas Calas (New York: Praeger, 1966).

ence in creating an awareness of black consumers: "Our cities are growing darker every day. Negroes already represent 28% of the aggregate central city population in 78 key cities. Some 95% of the country's 23,000,000 Negroes live where two-thirds of all retail sales are made. And you can see why businesses operating in central city markets with white-oriented images and marketing techniques are experiencing increasing difficulty in relating to black consumers."[4]

While advertisers were quick to realize the wisdom of creating ads with black models for black publications, the white (and black) readership of magazines such as *Life*, *The Saturday Evening Post*, and *Time* still found few black models in national ad campaigns. A senior vice-president of the National Urban League stated that "no segment in America has done so much to make Negro Americans the invisible men as the advertising industry."[5] Whereas Johnson urged advertisers to reach the black market through black publications, the Congress of Racial Equality (CORE) and other civil rights groups began to call for a fairer representation of blacks in the "mainstream" media, countering the practice of "separate but equal" ad campaigns.[6]

In 1963 CORE and the National Association for the Advancement of Colored People (NAACP) addressed the issue by bringing pressure upon advertisers "to include Negroes in advertising layouts, to use more Negro actors in television programming, and to hire more Negroes into the advertising industry." By informing top national advertisers of their belief in the importance of integrated advertising, CORE acted as both a catalyst and a watchdog. "Selective buying groups" were established in major cities as a leverage against uncooperative advertisers, and CORE's threat of expanding a local boycott to the national level forced Lever Brothers, then the country's sixth-largest advertiser, to direct attention to the black community.[7] Efforts toward integrated advertising reflected the extension of civil rights activity from the primary issues of education and voting into the areas of

1. The stereotyped characterization of blacks as a group that spends more on personal-care products was a consistent feature of *Ebony*'s appeal to advertisers. The research director of Johnson Publishing Company, which publishes *Ebony*, referred to "the Negro's propensity to consume," and stated that "the Negro family ... spends a larger percentage of its disposable income for goods yielding immediate or relatively short-run satisfaction." See "Ads Must Enhance Negro's Prestige, *Ebony*'s Davis Says," *Advertising Age* 29 (6 October 1956): 87. The Lubalin ad, although more aesthetically sophisticated than *Ebony*'s earlier campaigns, maintains a stereotyped characterization of black consumers. W. Leonard Evans, the editor of *Tuesday*, the black-oriented newspaper supplement, astutely claimed that the term *Negro market* is a misnomer, preferring to characterize the market economically rather than racially. See Arnold M. Barban, "The Dilemma of 'Integrated' Advertising," *Journal of Business* 42, 4 (October 1969): 477.
2. Several studies were conducted on the nature and extent of images of blacks in print and television. The American Civil Liberties Union conducted a television content analysis in December of 1965, which found that "Negroes were given only .65 percent of the speaking roles on commercials and 1.39 percent of the non-speaking roles." See "TV Ads, Shows Still Lag in Use of Negro, Other Races: ACLU," *Advertising Age* 37 (11 April 1966): 128. A study by Harold H. Kassarjian looked at twelve "mainstream" magazines for the years 1946, 1956, and 1965 in order to evaluate the nature and frequency of representations of blacks in advertising: "the number of Negro ads comprise less than one third of one percent of the total [ads studied]." See Harold H. Kassarjian, "The Negro and American Advertising, 1946–1965," *Journal of Marketing Research* 6 (February 1969): 32.
3. The term is taken from an article by the same name and is used here to describe a set of concerns voiced on the part of advertisers, marketing consultants, and civil rights groups over fully integrated national ad campaigns and the hesitancy of advertisers to use blacks in "white media" and whites in "black media." See Barban, supra, note 1: 477–496.
4. Johnson was quoted at an Advertising Age Media Workshop; see "Use of Negro Models in Ads Won't Reduce Sales to Whites, Johnson Advises Workshop," *Advertising Age* 40 (9 December 1969): 24. Johnson's appeals to the advertising community urged an awareness of the potential market *without* raising the issue of integrated advertising. At the time Johnson, his mother, and his wife were the sole owners of the Johnson Publishing Company.
5. The statement was made by Ramon S. Scruggs, who was also manager of public relations for AT&T. See "Admen Rapped for Keeping Negro 'The Invisible Man'," *Editor and Publisher* 100, 46 (18 November 1967).
6. Many corporations produced ads with black models for use in black publications, paralleling the separate-but-equal doctrine upheld by the Supreme Court ruling in the 1896 *Plessy v. Ferguson* case. The ruling stated that so long as equal accommodations are made for blacks, separation based on race is sanctioned by the Constitution. *Plessy v. Ferguson* was overturned by the 1954 ruling *Brown v. The Board of Education* (of Topeka, Kansas).
7. The New York chapter of CORE began its campaign by sending letters to the heads of corporations, inviting representatives to attend a meeting with other national advertisers and to submit monthly progress reports. See "CORE Intensifies Drive for Negroes in Ads; Zeroes in on Pepsi-Cola Co.," *Advertising Age* 35 (9 November 1964): 3; and "CORE Pleased with Advertisers' Attitudes in Latest Meeting," *Advertising Age* 35 (30 November 1964): 46.

Poster Protest

affirmative action and antidiscrimination. The Voting Rights Act was signed in 1965 amid the national publicity focused on the Selma-to-Montgomery march. This photograph, taken during the march by Matt Herron, documents the grass-roots activism that brought national media attention to the Voting Rights Act. Many of the four thousand people marching had covered their faces with zinc oxide to protect their skin from the sun during the fifty-four-mile journey. One marcher inscribed the message of the march on his forehead, bringing the resources of page, typography, and illustration into the service of political struggle. Likewise the efforts of civil rights groups for integrated advertising began at a grass-roots level and managed to change the public face of some of America's largest corporations.

Collecting stylish Art Nouveau posters that advertised literary periodicals and cultural events was a fashionable pastime in the 1890s. The poster craze of the late 1960s and early 1970s was just as fashionable, yet it had no pretensions to the genteel world of the salon. This second wave of poster art had its origins in youth and pop culture, specifically in the promotion of San Francisco-area rock groups during the late 1960s and early 1970s.[1] The psychedelic colors and writhing letter forms of these posters, suggestive of drug-induced hallucinations, quickly gained an audience and became commercially available through several poster houses.[2] As their popularity increased, distributors began to offer a wider selection, reflecting the disparate sources and influences of youth culture in the 1960s: themes of peace and protest, underground comics, science fiction, political heroes and despots, nineteenth-century temperance images, and pop stars.[3]

A recurring strategy was to amend the American flag. For the disillusioned of the 1960s, the flag

had become a symbol of militaristic, right-wing America. Protest posters of the 1960s demonstrate how visual punning helped revive an icon whose meanings had become diffuse and contradictory.

As a commercial trade, the poster boom was conducted through mail-order houses, which often advertised according to genres such as "political and ideological," "psychedelic-abstract," "peace and love," and "posters for art exhibitions and reproductions of modern art." They were also sold through retail "poster galleries" that opened in urban centers and near campuses throughout the country in the late 1960s.[4]

While the posters collected at the end of the 1800s originally functioned as advertisements, the bulk of poster production in the 1960s and 1970s did not. Most of these late twentieth-century posters had some public life — on board fences, kiosks, or newsstands — but were primarily intended for domestic display. The political posters available from the retail stores

and distribution houses were purchased and hung to express solidarity with a cause. They were not, like the street posters produced by student groups in the late 1960s, tools of a specific political struggle.

The popular interest in posters and their often didactic role made them a particularly effective medium for the cause of groups lacking access to radio, television, and newspapers. From 1968 to 1970 student demonstrations reached a peak on campuses throughout the country; two of the major issues were the struggle for black recognition and increased student power. At Columbia, as at many other colleges and universities, students called into question the separate relationship between the school and the community it inhabits. The war in Vietnam — particularly as it affected the university through ROTC, on-campus recruiting, and military research — was another major issue in student protests.[5]

One 1969 poster was anonymously produced in response to the violent police action taken when students occupied an administration building at Harvard University. The takeover began after negotiations to initiate a black studies program had proven ineffective.[6] The poster employs the boldly simplified

1973 Richard Nixon, Gerald Ford

forms, terse language, and deliberately crude typography that had become the hallmarks of the posters of the student/worker uprisings in Paris of May 1968.[7] For many activists in the United States the events of May had served as a model, proving that revolutionary action was still possible in a modern industrial state.   Few examples of student-protest posters remain, for their role was related more to the expendability and urgency of newspapers and graffiti than to interior decoration.

1. For information on protest posters, see David Kunzle, *American Posters of Protest, 1966–70*, exh. cat. (New York: New School Art Center, 1971), 15, as well as Kunzle's essay in the present book. For a more general account of political graphics, see Robert Philippe, *Political Graphics: Art as a Weapon* (New York: Abbeville, 1982): 281.
2. Kunzle, *Posters of Protest*, 15.
3. Ibid., 14–16.
4. Ibid., 16.
5. For an assessment of the protest issues as well as the number and distribution of protests, see "Student Protests, 1969" (Chicago: Urban Research Corporation, 1970). For the period 1968–1970, see Ronald Fraser et al., *1968: A Student Generation in Revolt* (New York: Pantheon Books, 1988).
6. The police who had been called to retake the building removed their badges and clubbed students, journalists, and innocent bystanders. Forty-one students and seven policemen were treated for injuries, and 169 students were arrested. Police brutality galvanized student and faculty support for Students for a Democratic Society (SDS), which, along with the Progressive Labor Party, had led the takeover of the administration building. The decision to strike in support of SDS was upheld in a mass meeting of ten thousand students and faculty members (Fraser, 291–292).
7. The posters produced in the Paris uprising were the collective effort of the Atelier Populaire, a group of art students from L'Ecole des Beaux Arts and L'Ecole des Arts Décoratifs, which had seized the schools' printing studios and produced as many five hundred posters a day. The posters were statements of resistance, daily news reports of factory strikes, and notices of police brutality. The posters quickly became desired collectibles, and many were stolen off the streets and sold. See James C. Douglass, "The Graphics of Revolution," *Print* 22, 5 (September–October 1968): 15–20.

Signature Styles, International Styles

By the end of the 1960s a major stylistic trend had emerged in American graphic design, which coincided with a widespread reaction against Modernism or the International Style among architects. A group of graphic designers, including Milton Glaser, Seymour Chwast, and Herb Lubalin, rejected such ideals as functionalism and neutrality in favor of a witty, eclectic style having immediate consumer appeal, which was assembled out of bits and pieces of art history, popular culture, and personal experience.[1]

Milton Glaser, after receiving a professional art school education from The Cooper Union for the Advancement of Science and Art, New York, in the early 1950s, studied etching in Italy with Giorgio Morandi, a conservative artist who had worked with the avant-garde "metaphysical" painters early in the century. Glaser's experience with classical art would inform his lifelong commitment to drawing. As early as 1960 he criticized designers who work with found images and collage, and he delivers similar dicta today: "A designer who must rely on cutouts and rearranging to create effects, who cannot achieve the specific image or idea he wants by drawing, is in trouble."[2]

Glaser founded the Push Pin Studios with Seymour Chwast, Reynold Ruffins, and Edward Sorel in 1954. Although the studio's

early work employed expressionist mannerisms typical of 1950s design, the "Push Pin style" came into its own in the 1960s, yielding images that were personal yet highly controlled, characterized by bright colors, flattening outlines, exaggerated, fattened forms, and funny or bizarre juxtapositions. According to Glaser, designers should work within a "vernacular language," manipulating culturally familiar elements in a new way.[3] In a 1968 poster Glaser inserted the client's product — a portable plastic typewriter designed by Ettore Sottsass — into a landscape borrowed from the fifteenth-century painter Piero di Cosimo. Glaser thus depicted Pop-inspired Italian design with references to Renaissance classicism,

metaphysical surrealism, and American comic book illustration.[4]

Seymour Chwast's cover for *Idea* magazine (1976) is a manifesto of eclecticism, applying a catalogue of separate styles to a single subject.

Like the illustrations of Glaser and Chwast, the typography of Herb

Lubalin is marked by a love of exaggeration and familiarity. Lubalin abandoned modernist standards of "invisible" text and classical proportions in favor of intensifying the distinctive features of an alphabet — thinner thin strokes, rounder "o's," sharper serifs, and inventive ligatures. In Lubalin's own corporate logo, used from 1967 to 1975 (a collaboration between Lubalin and his partner Tom Carnase), the sinuous swashes recall Victorian and Art Nouveau calligraphy, but their heavy, almost uniform weight

makes the mark bold and "contemporary."

The attitude toward style expressed by Lubalin and the Push Pin designers parallels the architectural theory of Robert Venturi and Denise Scott Brown, popularized in their 1972 book *Learning from Las Vegas*, which offered the eclectic commercial vernacular of that city as a popular alternative to the elitism and abstraction of modern architecture.[5] Their book did not suggest that architects should literally copy the landscape of Las Vegas but rather that they should "learn" from it — commenting, interpreting, adapting.

Similarly, the Push Pin artists do not baldly "copy" styles but personalize their historical quotations. Although these designers adopt "vernacular" imagery, they do not emulate the Duchampian collage

aesthetic of the Pop artists, who appropriated commercial forms without altering them stylistically. Pop's direct incorporation of ready-made material is closer to the Modernism of El Lissitzky and John Heartfield, for whom lens, type, scissors, and glue were tools for recording and reorganizing cultural signs rather than for expressing their own personalities.[6] Whereas the aesthetic of the camera has dominated much avant-garde design since the 1920s, the work of Lubalin and the Push Pin designers is dominated by an aesthetic of the hand, returning to a concept of the designer as a unique, individualistic "artist."

While these designers appealed to the changeable tastes of middle-class consumers, other members of the American design profession searched for a style that would have permanent, universal validity, communicating through a supposedly neutral, universal vocabulary of photography, geometry, schematic drawings, systematically applied grids, and spare, sans-serif typefaces.[7]

A set of pictorial symbols completed in 1974 for use in airports, hospitals, office buildings, and other public spaces, was endorsed by the United States Department of Transportation (DOT) and selected by a committee that included Thomas Geismar, Rudolph de Harak, John Lees, and Massimo Vignelli, each of whom had built successful businesses during the 1960s designing signage and identity programs based on rational modernist principles. Seymour Chwast also belonged to the committee — for the rigorously eclectic Chwast, Modernism, like any historical style, has its appropriate uses.[8]

The project aimed to express not the personalities of individual designers but rather committee consensus and neutral scientific methods. The group analyzed past examples and instructed the design firm Cook & Shanosky to create a new set of symbols. The committee based its evaluations on semiotics (the science of signs), a theory outlined in the 1930s by the American philosopher Charles Morris, who believed that an analysis of visual and verbal signs could result in a more reliable and efficient system of communication.[9] The committee's use of semiotics added to the "scientific" authority of its report, and it reflected an interest which had long been part of modernist design theory: to find a stable, universally valid, visual "language."

International picture signs were originated in the 1920s in Vienna by Otto Neurath, whose

system Isotype was used to present social and economic statistics to a general public.[10] The American designer Rudolf Modley worked with Neurath and used the method for educational publications in the United States in the 1930s.[11] A similar social orientation motivated much International Style design in the 1940s and 1950s; some

avant-gardists believed that rational design would reorder society, bringing the benefits of technology to a mass public and creating a unified global culture. By the end of the 1950s, however, many modernists realized that the industrial system that had provided a broad population with new goods depended on the continual obsolescence of those products in order to perpetuate itself.[12] The notion of a stable, universal style thus seemed invalid for advertising most consumer products, but it was embraced in the 1960s as the official visual "language" of corporate, institutional, and governmental communications, in the tradition of design for the public good.

1. Coffee-table books on these designers are: *The Push Pin Styles* (Palo Alto, Calif.: Communication Arts Magazine, 1970); Seymour Chwast, *The Left-Handed Designer* (New York: Harry N. Abrams, 1985); Milton Glaser, *Graphic Design* (Woodstock, N.Y.: Overlook Press, 1973); and Gertrude Snyder and Alan Peckolick, *Herb Lubalin: Art Director, Graphic Designer, and Typographer* (New York: American Showcase, 1985). Other artists who worked with the Push Pin Studios include John Alcorn, Sam Antupit, Paul Davis, Herb Levitt, Reynold Ruffins, and Barry Zaid.
2. Glaser is quoted in Sterling McIlhany, "Milton Glaser," *Graphis* 16, 93 (November–December 1960): 508. See also, Milton Glaser, "Some Toughts on Modernism: Past, Present and Future," *Journal of Graphic Design* 5, 2 (1987): 6.
3. Glaser, *Graphic Design*, 14.
4. Glaser connects his work to comic book art in the article "Comics, Advertising, and Illustration," *Graphis* 28, 160 (1972–1973): 104–117. The article focuses on a device Glaser has often used in which a series of boxes contains a narrative sequence of illustrations. Articles about the historicizing trend in 1960s design include "Art Nouveau: Then and Now," *Print* 18, 6 (November–December 1964), which compares work by Chwast, Glaser, Paul Davis, and others to Koloman Moser and Aubrey Beardsley.
5. Robert Venturi, Denise Scott Brown, and Steven Izenour, *Learning from Las Vegas* (Cambridge, Mass.: MIT Press, 1972).
6. On John Heartfield's graphic work, see Maud Lavin, "Heartfield in Context," *Art in America* 73, 2 (February 1985): 84–93.
7. A tradition of "modern" design, which held up the twin ideals of a "universal," formal vocabulary and personal, abstract expression had been established in the United States in the 1930s and 1940s by Lester Beall, Paul Rand, Herbert Bayer, Gyorgy Kepes, Will Burtin, and others; this tradition, influenced by developments in Europe — particularly Switzerland — was expanded and to some degree codified in the late 1950s. See, for example, R.S. Gessner, "Swiss Designers of the Younger Generation," *Graphis* 13, 69 (January–February 1957): 12–39; and Emil Ruder, "Typography of Order," *Graphis* 15 (September 1959): 404–413.
8. See American Institute of Graphic Arts, *Symbol Signs* (New York: Hastings House, 1981).
9. Morris was a professor at the New Bauhaus in Chicago, and his ideas became relatively well known among rationalist designers after World War II. See Charles Morris, "Foundations of the Theory of Signs," Otto Neurath, ed., *International Encyclopedia of Unified Science* (University of Chicago Press, 1938): 77–138.
10. See Otto Neurath, *Empiricism and Sociology*, Marie Neurath and Robert S. Cohen, eds. (Dordrecht: D. Reidel, 1973); and Otto Neurath, *International Picture Language/Internationale Bildersprache*, Robin Kinross, ed. (Reading, England: Reading University, 1980). For a critical essay on Isotype, see Ellen Lupton, "Reading Isotype," *Design Issues* 3, 2 (Fall 1986): 47–58.
11. Rudolf Modley, *The United States: A Graphic History* (New York: Modern Age Books, 1937). Modley's book *Handbook of Pictorial Symbols* (New York: Dover, 1976) is a collection of pictograms by Modley and others; it includes a brief essay about Neurath's ideas. See also Henry Dreyfuss, *Symbol Source Book: An Authoritative Guide to International Graphic Symbols* (New York: McGraw-Hill, 1972).
12. The reevaluation of functionalism was expressed through professional conferences and trade journals. For example, the theme of the Seventh International Design Conference in Aspen, Colorado (1957), was "Design and Human Values," which dealt with the idea that human "values"—and also the contemporary economy—are not static but rather in constant flux. Members of the conference used the phrase "form *is* function" to mediate the contradictions between consumerism (the culture of pleasure) and the stoic laws of "good design." See George D. Culler, "Design and Human Values," *Art Direction* 9, 7 (October 1957): 50–51.

Newspaper Design

In the 1930s and 1940s many newspapers adopted "modern" headline typography, such as flush-left lines, lowercase letters, and limited type families, resulting in clean, orderly designs that echoed the journalistic ideal of "objectivity," while sensational tabloids continued the use of dramatic type, images, and layout.[1] Several papers changed more dramatically during the 1960s, a period when labor disputes and intense competition with magazines and television devastated many papers — *The New York Herald Tribune* was redesigned by Peter Palazzo with large magazine-style photographs and type, but the paper did not survive the decade.[2]

The notoriously conservative *New York Times* developed an entirely new graphic image by the mid-1970s. Louis Silverstein, an advertising designer who had been head of *The Times*'s promotion department since 1952, brought techniques from progressive advertising, such as large type and photographs and witty juxtapositions of image and text, to the newspaper. With an imaginative use of typography, the emotional power of a headline can exceed its strictly "informative," journalistic function.[3]

The national daily paper *USA Today*, founded in 1982, exemplifies innovative newspaper design of the 1980s. By using full-color photography, bold information graphics, and a telegraphic editorial style, *USA Today* has brought the spirit of network television to the newspaper industry, condensing events into an easy-to-read, ready-to-serve, nationally uniform package.[4]

1. For a detailed history of newspaper design up to 1960, see Hutt, *The Changing Newspaper*. The designer behind Mergenthaler Linotype's program for newspaper reform was John Allen. Many of the examples of "good" newspaper design shown in his 1936 book feature dynamically cropped and juxtaposed photographs, influenced perhaps by the magazines of the 1920s and 1930s; these dramatic pages are omitted from Allen's 1947 book, in favor of more order and stability. Allen also exchanges the traditional term "makeup" for the more prestigious "designing" in the later book. See John E. Allen, *Newspaper Makeup* (New York: Harper and Brothers, 1936); and idem, *Newspaper Designing* (New York: Harper and Brothers, 1947).
2. On the *Herald Tribune*, see Peter Palazzo, "Behind the Trib's New Look," *Print* 17, 5 (September–October 1964): 32–35.
3. For more information on the redesign of *The New York Times*, see Ellen Lupton and Jennifer Tobias, *Louis Silverstein: Design and The New York Times, 1952–1986*, exh. cat. (New York: Herb Lubalin Study Center of Design and Typography, The Cooper Union, 1988).
4. For information on *USA Today* and related trends, see Mario R. Garcia and Don Fry, *Color in American Newspapers* (St. Petersburg, Fla.: Poynter Institute for Media Studies, 1986).

New Wave, Neo-Conservative

For the classic Swiss Modernism of the 1950s and 1960s, grids, sans-serif type, and photography represented such values as clarity, simplicity, objectivity, and neutrality. By the early 1980s members of a younger generation were making the same elements express an apparently contradictory set of values: ambiguity, complexity, subjectivity, and individuality. Proponents of "Postmodernism" or the "new wave" in America include April Greiman, Dan Friedman, and Willi Kunz.[1]

The logo for the retailer Vertigo, designed by April Greiman and Jayme Odgers, is composed of rules, geometric letter forms, and primary shapes — the ingredients of classic Modernism. But here the elements form an inconsistent collection of marks, separated by white space and enclosed by an external framing device. Whereas classic modernist design aims to produce unified, "organic," self-contained wholes, this logo is composed of discontinuous parts. Compare, for example, Lester Beall's 1960 mark for International

INTERNATIONAL (A) PAPER

Paper where the framing element is formally consistent with the interior symbol, having the same heavy line weight and geometric clarity.

Although the work of new wave designers in the 1980s stylistically revises classic Modernism, it maintains one of its central theoretical principles: the belief that abstract composition is the designer's central problem, to be solved through both analytical and intuitive thought processes. Many Bauhaus projects had combined a faith in rationality with a search for innocent, nonverbal, sensual experience; in the 1950s Armin Hofmann and others at the Basle School of Design refined Bauhaus principles into a pedagogical method that gained international influence; revealing his antagonism toward verbal, intellectually based expression, Hofmann wrote in 1965 that the picture, unlike the word, "contains an inherent message ... [it] speaks to us directly ... [it] radiates movements, tone values and forms as forces which evoke an immediate response."[2] The Basle School furthered the Bauhaus idea that the designer speaks through a visual "language" that operates separately from the intellect.

The clientele for new wave design in the early 1980s consisted largely of art- and fashion-oriented businesses — clothing stores, architectural firms, restaurants, museums, and the art schools where the style was taught. As the 1980s progressed, however, the new wave became attractive to corporate clients.[3] For a growing population of "young urban professionals," the new wave offered a fresh, forward-looking companion to fashionable Postmodern architecture, established as an official corporate idiom during the age of Ronald Reagan and George Bush. The new wave offered visual innovation without disturbing the modernist framework that offers the designer dominion over the realms of taste and personal expression but discourages the understanding of design's broader cultural meaning.[4]

1. The influence of the Basle School of Design has traveled in the United States both through the example of its design and through the educational programs it has inspired, including the graduate program at Yale and the program at the University of the Arts, Philadelphia. April Greiman and Willi Kunz studied at the Basle School of Design; Dan Friedman studied at the Hochschule für Gestaltung, Ulm, and the Basle School. An article in which the terms *Postmodern, new wave,* and *Swiss-punk* appear is Jean W. Progner, "Play and Dismay in Post-Modern Graphics," *Industrial Design* 27, 2 (March–April 1980): 42–47.
2. In the late 1950s Swiss design was publicized in America in the multilingual Swiss trade journals *Graphis* and *Gebrauchsgrafik*. See, for example, R.S. Gessner, "Swiss Designers of the Younger Generation," *Graphis* 13, 69 (January–February 1957): 12–39; and Emil Ruder, "Typography of Order," *Graphis* 15 (September 1959): 404–413. Gessner's article indicates that Swiss design in the late 1950s was by no means monolithic; much of the work reproduced resembled the expressionistic, illustrative advertising popular in the United States at the time. Armin Hofmann taught seminars at the graduate program in graphic design at Yale University beginning in 1956; through these courses and the graduate program at the Basle School of Design, which welcomes American students, Hofmann has had a major impact on American designers. See Armin Hofmann, *Graphic Design Manual: Principles and Practice* (New York: Van Nostrand Reinhold, 1965); and idem, "Thoughts on the Study and Making of Visual Signs," *Design Quarterly* 130 (1985).
3. A presentation of new wave corporate graphics is Michael Bierut, "Corporate Design: A Cutting Edge in the Age of Entropy?" *ID* 35, 2 (March–April 1988): 30–33.
4. An educator who has offered an alternative to the visually dominated approach of the Basle School is Hanno Ehses, who has applied the theory of verbal "rhetoric" to visual-verbal expression. See Hanno Ehses and Ellen Lupton, *Design Papers 5: Rhetorical Handbook, An Illustrated Manual for Graphic Designers* (Halifax: Nova Scotia College of Art and Design, 1988).

Desktop Publishing: Off-line and On-line

During the 1980s the microcomputer — a powerful, inexpensive, general-purpose computer scaled to fit on a desktop — became a relatively commonplace office machine.[1] The term *desktop publishing* refers to a broad range of tasks accomplished with the aid of microcomputers and such "peripherals" as scanners and laser printers. Commonly, a computer file is sent to a digital typesetter, which can deliver either traditional galleys, to be pasted up by hand, or camera-ready layouts.[2]

By making type less expensive, microcomputers have encouraged more organizations to publish more documents — with or without the help of professional graphic designers. It is possible that microcomputers will democratize design and lessen the need for professionals. At the same time, the demand could increase for visually sophisticated publications; the professional designer might then function more commonly as a consultant than as a manager of start-to-finish production.[3] By centering many tasks in one compact machine, microcomputers have made it easier for young designers to go into business for themselves. The new technology could also make a space for more grass-roots, low-volume publishing activity.

The New Primitives

There is no "computer graphics" style. Microcomputer typography can closely approximate the look of conventional typesetting, or it can be emphatically crude. For example, the designers Zuzana Licko and Rudy VanderLans have chosen to dramatize the potential harshness of bit-mapped typefaces and images; labeling themselves "the new primitives," they refuse to use the computer as an instrument for replicating traditional typographic norms.[4]

But for writers and designers with a less style-based approach, the significance of the microcomputer lies not in the look of its letter forms but in the flexible, dynamic working process it enables. The computer has softened the boundary between writing and designing a text, giving us the license to repeatedly rewrite and rearrange.

However dynamic the process of desktop publishing may be, the final result is a static "off-line" printed document, such as a museum catalogue. An entirely different genre of computer-aided publishing is the "on-line" text, a document stored and transmitted in an electronic form. Whereas off-line texts are usually produced as a quantity of identical objects, the on-line text is "published" on demand, its contents customized by the reader.[5]

Since the 1970s a major form of electronic text has been the bibliographic database, a service transmitted through telephone lines to libraries and other users from a storage center.[6] Smaller databases can be contained entirely on current desktop machines. Programs such as Apple's Hypercard or Owl's Guide for the PC allow users to build customized databases and interactive documents in a desktop environment.[7]

The design considerations involved in an on-line text are quite different from those of print.[8] A designer working with electronic media might be concerned with shaping the content of the document as well as attending to its aesthetics: What is the appropriate output? How is the body of information organized and accessed? How is the user oriented within the document? Does the interface imitate a familiar environment, such as an office desktop or design studio, or does it try to develop a "vernacular" language for the new culture of the computer?

1. Currently, two basic types of computer are used for desktop publishing: those manufactured by Apple Computer, Inc. and those that are compatible with IBM's microcomputers. Their basic hardware is similar; what makes them "incompatible" is the software "operating systems" that communicate between the machine and software applications.
2. On desktop publishing, see the series of articles in *PC Magazine* 6, 17 (13 October 1987); and 7, 7 (12 April 1988). See also Chuck Byrne, "A Designer's Guide to the Computerized Studio, or, How to Stop Worrying and Start Exploiting the Tools of Desk-Top Publishing," *Print* 42, 3 (May–June): 128–139.
3. Philip Meggs surveyed the opinions of twenty graphic arts professionals as to the impact of computers on graphic design in his article "The Future: New Discoveries, Old Skills," *Journal of Graphic Design* 4, 4 (1986): 1, 2; most of these designers were enthusiastic about computers. In contrast, Dorothy Spencer's article "Much Ado about Desktop," in the same issue of the *Journal*, analyzes electronic publishing as a puffed up, design-poor industry with little to offer either aesthetically or economically.
4. Zuzana Licko and Rudy VanderLans, "The New Primitives," *ID* 35, 2 (March–April 1988): 60.
5. Material on electronic publishing rapidly becomes outdated. Some works that were current during the writing of this essay include Oldrich Standera, *The Electronic Era of Publishing: An Overview of Concepts, Technologies, and Methods* (New York: Elevier Science Publishing, 1987); and Joost Kist, *Electronic Publishing: Looking for a Blueprint* (London and New York: Croom Helm, 1987); and the series of articles in *BYTE* 12, 10 (October 1988). The article that is said to have initiated the "hypertext" idea is Vannevar Bush, "As We May Think," *Atlantic Monthly* 176, 1 (July 1945): 101–108; Bush was a scientist involved in weapons development during World War II and was concerned with peacetime applications of the new information technologies.
6. Some currently available database services include *Academic American Encyclopedia* (Danbury, Conn.: Grolier); in 1987 it contained thirty thousand articles and was accessible to two hundred fifty thousand on-line subscribers. For the history of reference works, or texts designed to be accessed in a "random" or nonlinear manner, see Tom McArthur, *Worlds of Reference: Lexicography, Learning, and Language from the Clay Tablet to the Computer* (Cambridge, England: Cambridge University Press, 1986).
7. For a textbook on Hypercard—which, incidentally, is pleasant to read—see Danny Goodman, *The Complete Hypercard Handbook* (New York: Bantam, 1987). Information on Guide, a hypertext program for computers compatible with the IBM PC, is available from Owl International, Bellevue, Washington.
8. See Stephen T. Kerr, "Instructional Text: The Transition from Page to Screen," *Visible Language* 20, 4 (Autumn 1986): 368–392.

1989 George Bush

History of Design, Design as History

Graphic design has now been established as a relatively unified "profession" for several decades, with tacitly understood aims and limits.[1] Today design training is offered by college-accredited art programs that tend to cultivate individual artistic sensibilities and encourage aesthetic innovation. Graphic design has thus emerged as a humanistic discipline, which, like painting and architecture, aims to transcend pure profit and utility to enrich sensual and intellectual experience. Some designers and critics, however, have recently noted that graphic design lacks the historical self-awareness common to other humanist disciplines, which have long traditions of debate over theory and style.[2]

Some design historians have worked to identify a base of important movements and individuals: a humanist discipline needs a humanist heritage. Philip Meggs produced the first encyclopedic history of graphic design in 1983, forworded with the assertion that "if we understand the past, we will better be able to form a cultural legacy of beautiful form and effective communication."[3] Meggs's narrative begins with cave painting, but it progresses toward the more concrete "cultural legacy" of the modern profession, the achievements of individual designers, and their affiliations with modern art movements.

The emergence of professional

design has been a recurring theme of this time line; in some essays the work of well-known individuals has been contrasted with anonymous, popular, or culturally marginal modes of expression. A history of professional design could be fortified, complemented, or even engulfed by a study of those forms existing beyond or beneath the domain of "graphic design" — the bulk of graphic communication, from interoffice mail to anonymous soapboxes, does not appear in the annuals of professional societies. If design history limits its study to paragons of good taste and aesthetic innovation, then those products and images that could be branded distasteful, subcultural, amateur, or artless become discredited as objects of study.[4]

Scholarship that fits this more inclusive conception of design includes Adrian Forty's 1986 book, *Objects of Desire*, which analyzes the politics and economics of design through case studies on subjects including the sewing machine, the automated office, and the graphics of the London Underground.[5] During the last twenty years *Design Quarterly*, published by the Walker Art Center,

has sponsored criticism on some topics outside of professional or high-culture design, such as information graphics, "consumerist vernacular" architecture, and the signage system of Julia Child's kitchen.[6] Since 1984 the journal *Design Issues* has published essays that address such subjects as drawing techniques, the grid, and watch faces.[7]

For design history to be valuable to contemporary practitioners, it must address the origins and aims of the profession;

this orientation helps make history directly relevant to design practice. But the profession can be studied as a changing institution that has interacted with and defined itself against other modes of expression; design history can then serve as an information source with theoretical, ethical, and political — as well as aesthetic — functions.

1. The American Institute of Graphic Arts (AIGA) published this definition of graphic design in 1987: "the aesthetic ordering of type and image in order to interest, inform, persuade, or sell." Sharon Helmer Poggenpohl et al., "An Outline for Design Education," *Journal of Graphic Design* 5, 3 (1987): 8, 16. Despite the apparent generality of this definition, not *all* acts of "aesthetic ordering" — such as writing a letter or painting a sign for a supermarket window — belong to what is commonly understood as *professional* design.
2. Victor Margolin has surveyed developments in design history, relating it to the various fields into which design-related studies are currently distributed, such as decorative arts, American studies, and popular culture. See Victor Margolin, "A Decade of Design History in the United States, 1977–87," *Journal of Design History* 1, 1 (1988): 51–72. Margolin is a founding editor of the journal *Design Issues*. As the editor of the *Journal of Graphic Design*, a newsletter published by the AIGA, Steven Heller has encouraged designers to write historical and critical essays. Heller has organized an annual conference on design history at the School of Visual Arts, New York, since 1987.
3. For one writer's identification of designers and design styles, see Philip B. Meggs, *A History of Graphic Design* (New York: Van Nostrand Reinhold, 1983).
4. Clive Dilnot has laid out a variety of roles and sources for design scholarship in his essay "The State of Design History, Part II: Problems and Possibilities," *Design Issues* 1, 2 (1984): 5.
5. Adrian Forty, *Objects of Desire: Design and Society from Wedgwood to IBM* (New York: Pantheon Books, 1986).
6. See Richard Saul Wurman, "Making the City Observable," *Design Quarterly* 80 (1971); John Chase, "Unvernacular Vernacular: Contemporary American Consumerist Architecture," *Design Quarterly* 131 (1986); and Bill Stumpf and Nicholas Polites, "Julia Child's Kitchen: A Design Anatomy," *Design Quarterly* 104 (1977).
7. Articles in *Design Issues* include Richard Porch, "The Digital Watch: Tribal Bracelet of Consumer Society," 2, 2 (Fall 1985): 46–49; and Jack H. Williamson, "The Grid: History, Use, and Meaning," 3, 2 (Fall 1986): 15–30.

Matthew Carter

[born 1937]

During the fifteenth century a printing craftsman was often a type designer, and not infrequently a type designer was also an author. As time and technology advanced, these functions became fragmented and specialized; the designer designed, the punch cutter cut, the printer printed, and so on. In this age of digital typesetting Matthew Carter, a former printer's devil and printing historian, has effectively come full circle, bringing together the related, but disparate functions of typography. As the creative director of Bitstream Inc., a computer "type foundry," Carter has not only revived elegant metal faces, now redrawn for digital composition, but he has also developed programs that put design and production capabilities back into the hands of the single user. Under Carter's aegis the computer and laser printer are not wellsprings of outrageous computer-generated tricks but tools for typographic expression. Though Carter might very well be a perfectionist in matters of aesthetics, he also makes an effective case in word and deed for the democratization of printing and graphic design. Through Carter's experiments, written communications will certainly be enhanced by the professional but made friendly and available to the amateur.

In 1978 AT&T asked Mergenthaler Linotype to create a new typeface for its telephone books. Matthew Carter, then a staff designer at the company, developed the face called Bell Centennial that has been used ever since. Its numerals were digitized by hand, bit by bit, to provide increased control. The inked bitmaps opposite appear in their final printed form overleaf.

In 1965 I became a staff designer at Mergenthaler Linotype (having come to the United States from England in 1960), where I worked on new faces and on converting metal faces to phototypesetting. Many of them were problem-solving or opportunity-taking faces, i.e., faces that compensated for the early defects of photocomposition. When the first commercial digital typesetter came out, I did similar compensatory work.

Ultimately, I designed an alphabet commissioned by AT&T for use in the phone book; it was Bell Centennial. Mergenthaler Linotype had made Bell Gothic (designed in 1930 by Mergenthaler's Chauncey Griffith) for AT&T before the war. But, for a variety of reasons, some technical, some aesthetic, AT&T wanted to revisit the whole question of the typeface for phone books.

It was a complicated problem, because everything that Western Electric came up with in the way of measuring the degradation of the typeface in the realistic conditions in which it was produced and printed was contradictory. A typeface can be modified to compensate for under-inking, but then what can be done when it's over-inked? And both conditions occurred. Another problem was that the heavier face, which was used for the name and the number, was on the same width as the address face, which was lighter. One of the very

The Bell Centennial typeface family
consists of four related type weights
designed for use in small sizes —
6 or 7 point, each with its own
function in phone directory entries.
Reading the letter "h" from left to
right: name and number, address,
sub-caption, boldface listing.

The letters "h o d" demonstrate the
differences between the Bell Gothic
face formerly used by AT&T and
Centennial, which is bolder and
wider and has slightly more space
between characters.

The four-part Centennial family is
shown here in 6 point type.

useful bits of guidance I got from the Bell
people was the decision that the addresses
were only there to make the distinction between John Smith who lived on Eighth Street
and John Smith who lived on Ninth Street. This
was a very subsidiary part of the entry. But, for
technical reasons, it couldn't be subsidiary in
Bell Gothic. Because the lighter face was the
same width as the heavier one, no space could
be saved. So the first thing we did was make
the light face narrower, and the name and
number face a little wider. There was a net
space gain, and we were able to save some
lines on the page and some millions of dollars.
Multiply the additional lines by the number of
directories, and the number of forests that go
into that is very considerable.

There are two things that are not
open to debate in type design. One is that we
tend to work with what we've inherited. As
Frederic Goudy has been variously quoted: "The
old boys stole most of our good ideas." The
other is a tension between the functional attrib-
utes of type — what makes an "A" different

from a "B" different from a "C" — that obviously have to be preserved, and the stylistic at-
tributes that make them appear to belong together. Reconciling those two things is the job
of the type designer. We are working with an
alphabet that can't be tampered with very
much. So we design slightly different clothing
to be hung on the same skeleton. And the
clothing, of course, has to be consistent. It's
difficult to work much originality into type design without offending the reader. Typographers are there to help authors communicate,
and if we introduce any disharmony in that, we
are not serving the interests of the author, the
printer, or the reader.

Although type designers draw let-
ters, letters are not the product. The product is
words. But it's not until they become words
that you can tell whether the letters are good or
bad. In addition, there is a certain emotional-
ism connected to typography. It's difficult to
measure readability. Legibility can be measured because successive degradations demonstrate how the letter forms hold up. But readability is difficult to measure. People read and
comprehend best those typefaces with which
they are most familiar. There is a congeniality
factor where type is concerned; it is even
harder to measure than readability.

But fine points aside, I think that
the democratization of printing and publishing
with the personal computer is the most interesting thing to happen to typography since the
invention of movable type. The fascinating
thing today is that people without any background in the discipline can produce typography. The fact that those people are unschooled
means that a certain freshness will surface,
and typographers will need to take on a series
of new challenges.

Most of my life I have avoided
questions at parties such as, "What do you do
for a living?" Because God forbid I should have
to explain what type is. But I was in a restaurant the other day with a friend, and the waiter
came up and said, "Did I hear you talking about
fonts?" I said "Yes." And he said, "Oh, I have
a computer, and I'm really into fonts."

Matthew Carter

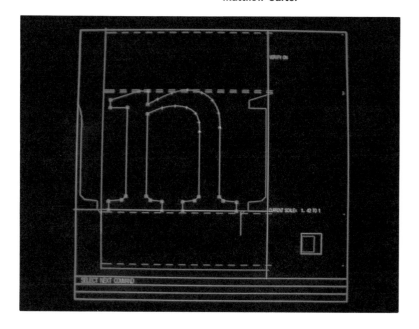
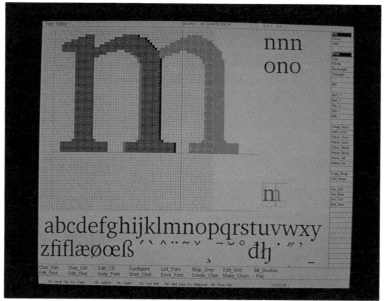

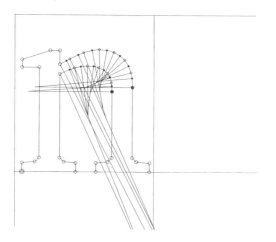
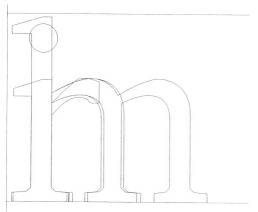
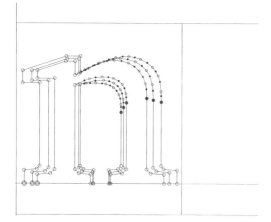

Bitstream Charter is a typeface that was designed by Carter in 1987. In the lowercase "n," digitized on a computer (top, left), the letter form is defined by points stored around the outline. Individual pixels in the bitmaps viewed on an editing display (top, right) can be turned on or off to refine the shapes. The bitmaps have been derived by a computer program from the definitive outlines. Here the "n" and "m" are superimposed to study the consistency of the shapes.

In the outline format all shapes are made up of straight lines and/or arcs of circles. The radii of the arcs have been plotted on the letter "n" (bottom, left). The center image shows lowercase characters with shared elements overlaid. Once the roman and black weights of the Charter family were designed, the intermediate bold weight was interpolated electronically, as demonstrated in the letter "n" (right).

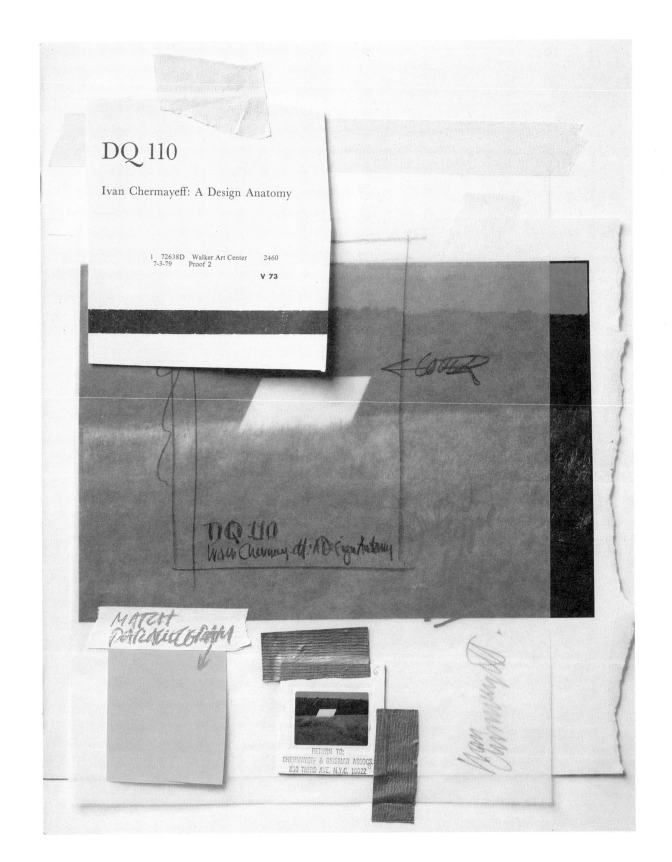

Ivan Chermayeff

[born 1932]

As a principal of Chermayeff & Geismar Associates since 1960 (originally Brownjohn, Chermayeff & Geismar Associates, 1957–1960) Ivan Chermayeff has created hundreds of graphic, environmental, and exhibition designs. Though divorced from the rigid ideology of his forebears, Chermayeff is a second-generation modernist, and he adheres to the doctrine of fitness of purpose, which in his hands is often applied with visual eccentricity. His positive impact on the environment is seen in various corporate identities, book and record covers, and civic and cultural posters for such clients as Mobil, Xerox, and The Museum of Modern Art, New York. The design of large-scale exhibitions has been a remarkable achievement of the firm, from the American pavilion at the 1958 Brussels World's Fair to the Smithsonian Institution's *Nation of Nations* exhibition, created for the United States Bicentennial celebration. Like Paul Rand and Saul Bass, Chermayeff has extended the modernist vocabulary into the 1980s by making graphic design that provides information and visual stimulation.

The analysis of Chermayeff's working environment in *Design Quarterly* 110, by his longtime friend Russell Lynes, reveals the essence of the designer's method. A brilliant collagist, Chermayeff assembles a lively cover with bits of tape, photographs, and colored papers.

Design Quarterly 110 1979
"Ivan Chermayeff: A Design Anatomy"
cover: 11 x 8 1/2 format
Published by Walker Art Center

Good design, at least part of the time, includes the criteria of being direct in relation to the problem at hand — not obscure, trendy, or stylish. A new language, visual or verbal, must be couched in a language that is already understood. When I began there were some brave people around — mostly publishers. In those days — the late 1950s, early 1960s — all of us who were involved in graphic design produced many book jackets and record album covers. Milton Glaser and Seymour Chwast, for example, also started out by doing tons of book jackets, but they were more involved with illustration than I, and although they graduated into other things, they always had a base in illustration. I never had the confidence in drawing that the others had and rarely made illustrations that were purely illustrative responses to assignments.

My work had more to do with typography. It was in the world of products, too, which meant architecture and industrial design — how things are put together. In that sense, exhibitions — communications of a larger sort — have always been a significant part of my work. I trained at the Institute of Design in Chicago, which was much more aligned to painting in all its forms, and much more European (because of Moholy-Nagy, who was its founder), than the American experience.

Mobil Showcase presents

BETWEEN

THE WARS

American Diplomatic History from Versailles to Pearl Harbor
A unique 16-week television series   Host: Eric Sevareid
Wednesday evenings beginning April 5 at 7:30   Channel 5

Mobil

World War I and World War II helmets separated by a black fedora require no additional words of explanation in this poster for a television documentary series.

Between the Wars 1977
46 x 30
Published by Mobil Corporation, New York

A retrospective of the sculpture of Claes Oldenburg was accompanied by this shiny plastic-bound book. In its design Chermayeff captured the essential character of the artist's soft sculpture.

This book about the work of Claes Oldenburg was written by Barbara Rose for The Museum of Modern Art
1970
Heiner Hegemann, design production
8 1/2 x 14 3/8 format
Published by The Museum of Modern Art, New York

The three trademarks shown here by Chermayeff & Geismar Associates are among the hundreds of memorable symbols created by the firm. These marks appear in a variety of formats.

(from top)
WGBH Educational Foundation
Channel 2, Boston

Graphic Arts USA
Traveling exhibition for the
Soviet Union and Eastern Europe
United States Information Agency

Mobil Corporation

I didn't really get that much out of school. It took a lot of years for me to recover from preconceived notions about what design was all about, because I came from a rigorous Bauhaus background of dogmatic insistence on a certain kind of vocabulary and sensibility, which is counterproductive to good communications. That discipline is okay, and there are certain parts of that vocabulary that are terrific. But where the Bauhaus hallmarks — order and cleanliness — become coldness, rigidity, and repetitiveness was not clear at that time.

My attitudes toward design evolved from working with a very broad series of problems. Graphic design, and design generally, is a cooperative activity. Inevitably, that means working on other people's problems. I have been lucky to work with very bright, talented people — Tom Geismar and Robert Brownjohn.

I never wanted to have a style, because it's contrary to the meaning of good communications to have one. It may be good for the business of communications but not for communications itself. So I always rejected the idea that something was supposed to look a certain way. But no matter how hard you try, you carry along a certain amount of baggage.

One of my daughters, who is a painter, congratulated me not long ago on a poster that she had seen from the window of a subway car. In fact, I had not done it. But I knew exactly what she meant, because it was my way of going about things, which is to incorporate the process of thinking about the problem into the work itself. I enjoy having people know what my decisions are along the way. It's rather difficult to explain. I like to incorporate handwriting and the physical process of putting things down ... nails, tacks, tape, stickers, and things that hold other things together on a temporary basis, because they are signals of the act of inclusion. Which is another way of saying that I like to make things come together by collage, assemblage, pulling bits and pieces together — things that may not necessarily belong together in the normal course of events.

My natural tendency is to reveal that relationship as much as is possible, rather than to hide or disguise it.

To pursue that freewheeling course one needs brave clients. And finding such clients who trust you isn't a case of one fine day ... but as your network expands what you're really doing is building, essentially by performance and hard work, a level of trust. After many years of practice you're treated the way one hopes any professional would be. Then you can say to a client, "This is what you should do. This is the poster that you should have. This is the typeface it should use." And they say, "Yes, sir; yes, doctor" — instead of telling you that their wives don't like yellow or some other nonsensical distraction. As time goes by, it is possible to shift the amount of time that one spends solving problems to time defining problems. And the more one can define them, the more interesting it is to work on them.

Quite often, clients don't know what they want. They just know that they have a problem. A designer can thrash it out with them and help define it. That becomes very true when dealing with communicative exhibitions in which the subjects have to be expressed and evolve structure and form in other media. All the decisions along the way need to become part of a grand scheme. That is clearly more than graphic design. But then, graphic design just becomes design in the larger sense.

Graphic Art for the Public Welfare

Neil Harris

Massive changes in printing, mechanical reproduction, and paper-making technologies transformed the graphic arts in late nineteenth-century America. The volume of material now available in the interest of amusement, inspiration, instruction, and advertisement was unprecedented, and the community of American designers increased in number as well as ambition.

Instruction and inspiration, however, were overshadowed by commerce. Support for the new design came from clients such as mail-order houses and manufacturers demanding trade catalogues, restaurants seeking menus, hotels ordering stationery, theater companies and circuses in search of posters, and industrialists soliciting labels, logos, and packaging materials. An almost inexhaustible variety of graphic opportunities existed. But the clients shared fundamentally private objectives. Illustrators, typographers, catalogue-makers, brochure designers, and poster artists normally labored to sell some commodity or service.

Some of the work was of extremely high quality. By the early twentieth century Hart Schaffner and Marx, the Packard and Pierce-Arrow motor car companies, Steinway and Sons pianos, and other major firms would employ artists such as Franklin Booth, Earl Horter, Adrian J. Iorio, Walter Dorwin Teague, and Adolph Treidler to produce imaginative, often dramatic, and highly expressive publicity. The better printing firms, including Bartlett-Orr, the Cheltenham Press, the Stetson Press of Boston, and Munder-Thomsen of Baltimore, retained accomplished artists on their staffs to prepare designs for their varied sets of clients.[1] And, during the 1890s particularly, magazine and book publishers supported audacious and even avant-garde work for their art posters.

But artists' attitudes toward advertising remained ambivalent. Printing journals and advertising associations insisted that the publicity arts reflected

Frank Crerie
Get Rid of Rats 1921
four-page circular
cover: 7 3/4 x 5 3/8 format
Collection the Metropolitan Life
Insurance Company Archives,
New York

high levels of professional skill and merited critical applause. Many commercial artists, however, hoped for more serious careers in the high arts; advertising was simply a way station, not worthy even of their signatures. Despite the fact that they would remain tied to commercial art for the rest of their working lives, these artists anguished over the function they performed.[2] Status in the arts was retained by those engaged in gallery and museum exhibitions, the production of murals for civic and religious structures, and serious illustration.

By 1910 commercial advertising loomed larger as a source of employment than ever before. Constrained by private interests, challenged by photography and mechanical reproduction, and doomed to glamorize consumer appetites, American graphic designers remained in the shadows of their more elegant senior colleagues in painting and sculpture. Even the greatest among them depended on commercial clients. Celebrated American poster artists, such as Will Bradley, Will Carqueville, J.J. Gould, and Edward Penfield worked primarily for book publishers, periodicals, bicycle-makers, piano manufacturers, and department stores. They were nurtured in their short-lived glory years by a few reform-minded editors and book publishers.[3] And while typographers and book designers found enthusiastic support among American followers of William Morris and their range of private presses, this enthusiasm was short-lived as well.[4]

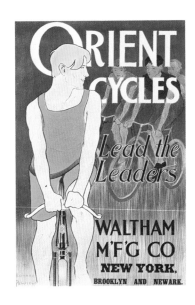

Edward Penfield
Orient Cycles circa 1896
chromolithograph
41 1/2 x 27 1/2
Collection Merrill Berman

1. The volume, variety, and character of the new commercial art can best be seen in periodicals of the day, particularly those concerned with printing and advertising. Journals that featured the work of designers and printing firms, along with samples and reviews of typographical and graphic trends include, for the United States: *American Printer*, *Inland Printer*, *Printing Art*, *Graphic Arts*, and *Graphic Arts and Crafts Yearbook*. See also Victor Margolin, Ira Brichta, and Vivian Brichta, *The Promise and the Product: 200 Years of American Advertising Posters* (New York: Macmillan, 1979); and Frank Presbrey, *The History and Development of Advertising* (New York: Doubleday, Doran: 1929).
2. Edward Hopper was one of those resentful of having to do work as an illustrator and a commercial artist. See Gail Levin, *Edward Hopper as Illustrator* (New York and London: W.W. Norton, 1979). For further contemporary discussions, see *Fame* 7 (May 1898): 180; "From the Inside," *Fame* 10 (October 1901): 479–480; Will B. Wilder, " 'Art' and Advertising," *Fame* 18 (October 1909): 217–218; and "Art Commercialized and Commercial Art," *Fame* 20 (September 1911): 106–107. A somewhat more benign view of the graphic arts community (this one in Chicago) and its commercial commitments can be found in Ralph Fletcher Seymour, *Some Went This Way: A Forty-Year Pilgrimage among Artists, Bookmen and Printers* (Chicago: Ralph Fletcher Seymour, 1945), chap. 2.
3. David W. Kiehl, *American Art Posters of the 1890s*, exh. cat. (Metropolitan Museum of Art, New York, 1988) examines this movement carefully. The essays by Kiehl and Nancy Finlay are particularly relevant here. See also Victor Margolin, *American Poster Renaissance* (New York: Watson-Guptill, 1975).
4. The fullest discussion of graphic design, typography, and the American Arts

The American story was made the more striking by the contrast abroad. European designers also served commercial and industrial markets, publicizing breweries, restaurants, camera firms, magazines, stores, vintners, resort hotels, and other private interests. But they found support from public sources, civic causes, and cultural institutions as well. They designed for trade fairs and international expositions, for museums, art galleries, national theaters, concerts, and for reading programs.[5] Official printing, under royal patronage in earlier centuries, had proud graphic traditions that were not obliterated by the developing private markets.

A new state of affairs came to this country only after certain national crises had forced it upon us. Twentieth-century American governments turned to the graphic arts under the threats of wartime emergency and economic catastrophe. Then, highly varied and original approaches to public aesthetic needs appeared, and traditions of cultural and civic publicity developed. But only then.[6]

It is impossible to deny the fundamentally private character of the graphic arts market in early twentieth-century America. But it would be equally shortsighted to deny the presence of alternative legacies, quietly but rather significantly developing voices of their own, even before World War I and the Great Depression mobilized the graphic arts into public service. Like much advertisement and book design, a large portion of this art was unsigned. But this anonymity was not ubiquitous, and even when the artists remain unknown the designs still speak. They found their reason for being in some novel blends of public and private authority, many formed in the heady period of early twentieth-century reform that has come to be known as the Progressive Era.

and Crafts movement can be found in Susan Otis Thompson, *American Book Design and William Morris* (New York: R.R. Bowker, 1977). See also Nancy Finlay, *Artists of the Book in Boston, 1890–1910*, exh. cat. (Houghton Library, Harvard University, Cambridge, Mass., 1985); and Wendy Kaplan, *"The Art That Is Life": The Arts and Crafts Movement in America, 1875–1920*, exh. cat. (Museum of Fine Arts, Boston, 1987).

5. Surveys of European graphic art and poster design make this point, particularly when they treat the late nineteenth and early twentieth centuries. "As in most countries at the turn of the century, business, which in following a fashion had been able to concern itself with producing images of an artistic quality, fell back into banal mediocrity. From then on only public events and exhibitions permitted artists to express themselves." Alain Weill, *The Poster: A Worldwide Survey and History* (Boston: G.K. Hall, 1985), 91. Dawn Ades has argued that the distinction between poster and art poster "was not necessarily between the function of advertising an aesthetic as opposed to a consumer product, but was rather a reference to the status of the designer." This is certainly true, for both Europe and America, but she goes on to note that the term *art poster* "was most frequently used for those concerned with cultural as opposed to commercial interests. Within this, there were posters with a specific relationship to an art

movement and which therefore acted as a visual manifesto, as aesthetic propaganda." Dawn Ades, "Function and Abstraction in Poster Design," idem, *The 20th-Century Poster: Design of the Avant-Garde*, exh. cat. (Minneapolis: Walker Art Center and New York: Abbeville, 1984), 27. My point is that American graphic artists had fewer calls from political, cultural, and civic clients, and made their artistic statements within a commercial context. For a brief period in the 1890s some commercial clients, particularly magazines and publishers, encouraged self-consciously aesthetic appeals. But such patronage was not sustained.

6. A large literature treats official support for art during World War I and federal art patronage during the Great Depression. For the former, see Stephen Vaughn, *Holding Fast the Inner Lines: Democracy, Nationalism and the Committee on Public Information* (Chapel Hill: University of North Carolina Press, 1980), chap. 8; and Walton Rawls, *Wake Up, America!: World War I and the American Poster* (New York: Abbeville, 1988). For the latter, see Francis V. O'Connor, ed., *Art for the Millions: Essays from the 1930s by Artists and Administrators of the WPA Federal Art Project* (Greenwich, Conn.: New York Graphic Society, 1975); and, most recently, Christopher DeNoon, *Posters of the WPA* (Los Angeles: Wheatley, 1987).

Anticipations of some new directions for American graphic artists came in Chicago's World's Columbian Exposition of 1893. A landmark in the history of American architecture, public art, city planning, mass amusements, and civic consciousness, this exposition also proved to be a significant opportunity for graphic artists and illustrators. Timely advances in color printing, photographic reproduction, and process printing methods helped make the exposition the best-covered peacetime event of the American nineteenth century. The great fair palaces, the Midway, the exotic exhibits, amusements such as the Ferris wheel, and the statuary and fountains were all memorialized in an outpouring of newspaper and magazine articles, pamphlets, brochures, plates, pennants, ashtrays, costume jewelry, shawls — in short, any surface that could take an image.[7] Many of the items, of course, were privately sold souvenirs, and much of the coverage was designed to make profits for publishers and printing companies. Nonetheless, the focus upon an event of such magnitude, on its host city, and on its relationship to certain ideal forms of civic life created something of a watershed in the history of American graphic arts.

The larger exhibition experience of the fair had an analogous impact. Exhibitions of this type were nothing novel in American life. State fairs, industrial expositions, county fairs, and several major international shows — notably Philadelphia's United States Centennial Exposition in 1876 — were common by 1893. But the splendor and scale of the new exhibitionism, the size of the visiting crowds, and the increasing focus, within the palaces, on matters of social policy, public health, culture, and education were all new. Maps, charts, models, posters, mounted photographs, reconstructed interiors, relics, and commodities of all kinds were pressed into service. The World's Columbian Exposition, and the half-dozen or so major expositions that followed it during the next twenty years, provided a forum for developing expertise among exhibit planners, museum specialists, curators, and architects; in essence they were working out a science of national display.[8]

It was not surprising, then, that a new generation of social reformers turned to exhibitions and their graphic support as instruments through which to

7. Although much has been written about the Columbian Exposition, a full history of its graphic presentation has not yet been published. Some varieties can be seen in Stanley Appelbaum, *The Chicago World's Fair of 1893: A Photographic Record* (New York: Dover, 1980), particularly the listing of visual sources, 109–111; Peter B. Hales, *Silver Cities: The Photography of American Urbanization, 1839–1915* (Philadelphia: Temple University Press, 1984), chap. 3; and Howard M. Rossen and John M. Kaduck, *Columbian World's Fair Collectibles: Chicago (1892–1893)* (Des Moines, Ia.: Wallace-Homestead, 1976).
8. For more on this subject, see Robert W. Rydell, *All the World's a Fair: Visions of Empire at American International Expositions, 1876–1916* (Chicago and London: University of Chicago Press, 1984).

Designer unknown
The Youth's Companion – World's Fair Extra Number
4 May 1893
cover: 16 1/4 x 11 3/8 format
Collection The Wolfsonian Foundation, Miami

awaken public interest. By the 1890s scholars, settlement-house leaders, clergymen, social workers, economists, journalists, and sociologists had begun to repudiate older, sentimental notions of poverty, insisting that "indigence is an effective bar to opportunity" and that the "curse of want" was neither necessary to character development nor socially inevitable.[9] Many demanded legislative action. But before effective public action could be taken, the public conscience needed to be aroused.

And here both the new art of photographic reproduction and some traditional methods of graphic representation proved vital. Before the 1890s quite a few American magazines had featured articles dealing with the desperation of urban poverty. Their lurid descriptions prompted some governmental replies. The most dramatic response, however, came not to words but to pictures. In 1890 the Danish-born journalist Jacob Riis published his famous examination of New York slum life, *How the Other Half Lives*. Riis's reports for the *New York Tribune* had helped stimulate the creation of the Tenement House Commission half a dozen years earlier, but he was now armed with the skills of a photographer. Riis's pictures enjoyed their first effectiveness as lantern slides that accompanied lectures, for during the late 1880s it was still impossible to reproduce photographs inexpensively and accurately. By the time he was ready to do his book, however, he was able to use a considerable number of halftones in the text, avoiding, in those pictures at least, the mediation of line drawings. This gave his work an extraordinary immediacy.[10]

The photograph fit the spirit of scientific documentation sought by the new social workers. But it did not work alone. Just as it could not entirely dislodge illustration from advertisement and fiction, so it could not take over the entire cause of reform. Its central status was never in doubt, but the graphic skills required for reform literature's charts, maps, graphs, and drawings constituted an equally essential element. It was the dialogue between photography and other graphic arts that helped give these American texts their power.

Such a combination — along with papier-mâché models — dominated the influential *Tenement House Exhibition* of 1900, mounted by New York's Charity Organization Society, one of Riis's favored institutions. The displays proved to

9. These quotes are taken from Robert W. Bremner, *From the Depths: The Discovery of Poverty in the United States* (New York: New York University Press, 1964), chap. 1. Bremner's book was one of the first to study the subject. In chapters 7, 9, and 11 he reviews some of the aesthetic strategies employed to publicize the existence of want and deprivation in turn-of-the-century America.
10. For more on Riis, see Hales, *Silver Cities*, chap. 4; and Alexander Alland, *Jacob Riis: Photographer and Citizen* (Millerton, N.Y.: Aperture, 1974).
11. Roy Lubove, *The Progressives and the Slums: Tenement House Reform in New York City* (University of Pittsburgh Press, 1962), provides an excellent summary of this movement.

be a means by which to galvanize public demand for housing reform. The data in the exhibitions were reproduced in a two-volume report, *The Tenement House Problem*, published two years later.[11] Other such exhibitions and publications followed, and in 1909 a kind of high point in the genre was reached through publication of the Pittsburgh Survey, which eventually would become a massive six-volume examination of that city's numbing range of health, housing, and social problems.[12]

The Pittsburgh project owed its origin to an investigation of social conditions in Washington, D. C. The resulting article, "Neglected Neighborhoods," was published in a special issue of the Charity Organization Society's journal, *Charities and the Commons*, in March 1906. One Pittsburgher, Alice B. Montgomery, the chief probation officer of the Allegheny Juvenile Court, was excited by the article and wrote to editor Paul Kellogg requesting a similar study in her city. The new Russell Sage Foundation, based in New York City, offered financial support, and a team of investigators moved to Pittsburgh for several months. There, aided by local professionals and civic leaders, they compiled an exhaustive examination of the city's pressing social problems. The results appeared first in *Charities and the Commons* and then in book form.

There had, of course, been earlier examinations of urban life published in Europe and America, notably the enormous study sponsored by Charles Booth, *Life and Labour of the People in London* (1891–1903), B. Seebohm Rowntree's *Poverty: A Study of Town Life* (1901), *Hull-House Maps and Papers* (1895), and *The Tenement House Problem* (1903).[13] All had featured photographs, diagrams, and innovative maps and graphic interpretations. The multicolored maps used in Booth's volumes were exploited by the Hull House investigators as a basis for their own brilliant designs, the resulting color quilt vividly illustrating the ethnic and racial heterogeneity of Chicago neighborhoods.[14] Such documentation had begun to achieve an artistry of its own, although the specific cartographers and colorists frequently remain anonymous.

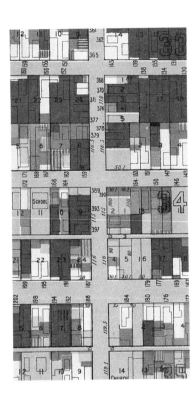

One of a series of *Hull-House Maps and Papers* presenting the nationalities and wages of the residents in a congested district of Chicago.

(detail)
Nationalities Map No.1 1895
Polk Street to Twelfth,
Halsted Street to Jefferson
Published by T.Y. Crowell & Co.,
New York and Boston
Collection Chicago Historical Society

12. The Pittsburgh Survey began its serialized appearance in *Charities and the Commons* 21 (2 January 1909) and continued through a series of special issues. The covers were specially designed; drawings, graphs, maps, charts, and photographs were interspersed. The Survey was continued as a series of books, published from 1909 to 1914. For background on the project, see Clarke A. Chambers, *Paul U. Kellogg and the Survey: Voices for Social Welfare and Social Justice* (Minneapolis: University of Minnesota Press, 1971), chap. 3; and Roy Lubove, *Twentieth-Century Pittsburgh: Government, Business, and Environmental Change* (New York: Wiley, 1969). For more on the Pittsburgh Survey and reform photography, see Hales, *Silver Cities*, chap. 5 and epilogue.
13. These reports and surveys are discussed in Bremner, *From the Depths*, passim. See also "Social Surveys," *Encyclopedia of the Social Sciences* (New York: Macmillan, 1934), 14, 162–165; and Shelby M. Harrison, *The Social Survey: The Idea Defined and Its Development Traced* (New York: Russell Sage Foundation, 1931).

But the Pittsburgh Survey was novel in both scope and intensity. Its capacity to arouse indignation owed much to the dramatic power of Lewis Hine's photographs and to the drawings of the young Joseph Stella. Both photographer and artist, aided by layout designers and typographers, combined their talents to produce a document that was simultaneously a distinctive graphic achievement and a persuasive piece of social research. Impact required both. The combination could also be seen locally at the Pittsburgh Typhoid Fever Commission, where the twenty-one-year-old Douglas McMurtrie, who was to become a typographer for the Cheltenham Press as well as an influence on the design of *The New Yorker*, found his first job; he took charge of the commission's printing.[15] Such documentation drew upon certain established aesthetic conventions but inevitably developed its own aesthetic vocabulary. And, in time, it would influence commercial publications — business magazines, annual reports, advertising formats — that sought to present concentrated doses of statistical and graphic information.

The power of design as a shaper of public opinion was quickly recognized. The Russell Sage Foundation, for one, confronting the impact of the Pittsburgh Survey and the growing popularity of social exhibits, created a special Department of Surveys and Exhibits, headed by Shelby Harrison, and published a Survey and Exhibit Series. Evart Routzahn, the department's associate director, and his wife, Mary, produced a series of texts with titles such as *The ABC of Exhibit Planning*, along with reading lists on publicity methods for social work.[16] Harrison published a surveys bibliography in his *The Social Survey* (1931), paying tribute to Riis, Addams, Booth, DeForest and Veiller, and Rowntree, but also pointing to the special contributions made by the Pittsburgh investigation and to the role of journalistic graphic portrayal. He quoted Paul Kellogg, who called for exploiting "all that the psychologists have to tell us of the advantages which the eye holds over the ear as a means for communication. The survey's method is one of publicity."[17] Kellogg's journal, in its very title and carefully

14. *Hull-House Maps and Papers* (New York and Boston: Crowell, 1895) was the first book produced at the settlement house Jane Addams founded. See the discussion in Allen F. Davis, *American Heroine: The Life and Legend of Jane Addams* (New York: Oxford University Press, 1973), 98–101.

15. See the entry on McMurtrie by James M. Wells, Edward T. James, ed., *Dictionary of American Biography: Supplement Three, 1941–1945* (New York: Scribner's, 1973), 492–493.

16. See, for example, Evart G. Routzahn and Mary Swain Routzahn, *Publicity Methods Reading List: Selected References on Publicity in Social Work and Kindred Fields* (New York: Russell Sage Foundation, 1924). *The ABC of Exhibit Planning* (New York: Russell Sage Foundation, 1918) included analyses of labels, maps, stereopticon showings, and convention exhibits, as well as illustrations of effective and ineffective graphic displays.

1899 14,591,000
ONE MILE

1911 32,837,000
ONE MILE

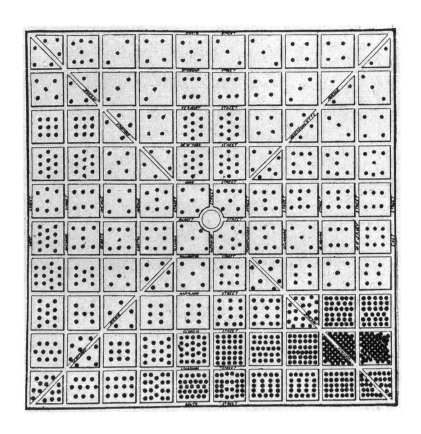

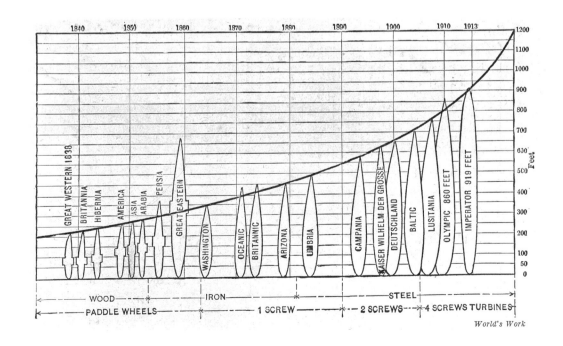

World's Work

82

chosen symbol, as well as the articles it ran, underscored the role of graphic art in stimulating social consciousness.[18]

Between publication of the Pittsburgh Survey and American entry into World War I many other social surveys were commissioned, analyzing housing stock, mortality figures, family relations, crime, recreation patterns, employment opportunities, industrial pollution, and traffic congestion, among other subjects. Most were undistinguished in their graphic strategies, but some merit close analysis. One such is George Kenngott's *The Record of a City* (1912), a social survey of Lowell, Massachusetts, filled with photographs, graphs, and handsome colored maps by Chester Wheeler showing the residence patterns of foreign nationalities.[19] In 1915 specialized (as opposed to community) surveys, began to be undertaken. By 1928 almost three thousand surveys, most of them specialized but including more than one hundred fifty community studies, had been recorded by the Russell Sage Foundation. Many combined extensive research with innovative exhibit methods and sophisticated graphic presentation.

By this time, as well, the first textbooks on graphic techniques had appeared, most notably Willard C. Brinton's *Graphic Methods for Presenting Facts*. The author, a lecturer at business schools throughout the country, geared his presentation to "the business man, the social worker, and the legislator." He pointed out that data collection was but half the task. "The larger and more difficult part of the work is to convince the minds of others that the proposed solution is the best one — that all the recommendations are really necessary.... As the cathedral is to its foundation," Brinton solemnly observed, "so is an effective presentation of facts to the data."[20] In the course of suggesting a grammar of graphic presentation, Brinton could now draw on work done for the Russell Sage Foundation and from material that had appeared in journals such as *Engineering Magazine*, *Good Housekeeping*, and *Scientific American*, from utility company and railroad reports, from statements by municipal departments, and from the *Statistical Atlas of the United States Census* (a 1900 innovation) — sources all of which indicated the spread of graphic sophistication. Graphic representation can "awaken

Three diagrams from
Willard C. Brinton's *Graphic Methods for Presenting Facts* 1914
Published by The Engineering
Magazine Company, New York

(clockwise from left)
Number of Passengers Carried on the
Railroads of the United States in
1899 and in 1911 Compared;
Relative Soot Deposits in
Indianapolis, March, 1912; and The
Growth in the Length of Ocean
Liners, 1840–1913.

17. Harrison, *The Social Survey*, 15. The Kellogg quote came from a 1912 essay, "The Spread of the Survey Idea," *Proceedings of the Academy of Political Science* 2 (July 1912).
18. Chambers, *Paul U. Kellogg and the Survey*, 20–24, 84–85, discusses Kellogg's interest in the journal's format and appearance as well as its content. For example, he commissioned the artist and illustrator Hendrik Willem van Loon to design a new sailing ship trademark for the Survey in 1921, replacing the caravel it had used as a symbol since 1909.
19. George F. Kenngott, *The Record of a City: A Social Survey of Lowell, Massachusetts* (New York: Macmillan, 1912).
20. Willard C. Brinton, *Graphic Methods for Presenting Facts* (New York: Engineering Magazine Co., 1914), v, 1–2.

interest ... vivify dry statistical details, and ... stimulate analytical thought," another writer had announced, more than a decade earlier, analyzing recent advances in mapmaking.[21]

The survey-makers and textbook writers were joined by another large group absorbed by the possibilities of graphics for reform: the health campaigners and insurance interests concerned with dress, diet, and sanitary improvement. During the first decade of this century, for example, the National Tuberculosis Association dramatically expanded its public education programs, distributing circulars, pamphlets, posters, and messages by the tens of millions and sponsoring exhibitions that toured more than a dozen states over a six-year period. With the help of statistical tables, maps, photographs, charts, and models the NTA warned about the dangers of spitting, the problems of dry sweeping, explored ways in which the disease was spread, and urged the need for regular medical examinations.[22] Evart Routzahn of the Russell Sage Foundation helped set up the first traveling show in 1905, and in 1908, at the NTA's Sixth International Congress, held in Washington, D.C., hundreds of exhibitors contributed to a massive publicity display. The *Journal of the Outdoor Life* ran reproductions of anti-tuberculosis posters that were distributed around the country, and streetcar companies made space available for car cards and permitted health messages to be stamped on transfers. Early among health and reform organizations, the NTA realized the value of a logo, adopting the double-barred cross that had been used by such societies in Europe and registering it as a trademark in 1920.[23]

It was at about this time that the NTA, along with the Red Cross, adopted the most successful reform graphic of the era, the Christmas Seal. The idea of selling postal seals to help raise money to fight tuberculosis had originated in Denmark; it was described in a 1907 *Outlook* article by Jacob Riis, who had received a letter from his homeland bearing such a seal. Emily Bissell, a Delaware resident who read the article, immediately put the idea to work in her state and soon persuaded the Red Cross to adopt the method. From one hundred thirty-five thousand dollars raised in 1908, the sales of the seals under the joint supervision of the NTA and the Red Cross reached two million dollars in 1919, at which time the NTA took over the entire operation. With its

This poster (by an unknown designer) advocating the study and prevention of tuberculosis was reproduced in the January 1910 issue of the *Journal of the Outdoor Life*.

Christmas Seals have been the major source of funding in this battle; shown here are the Seals from 1910 and 1939.

21. W. Z. Ripley, "Notes on Map Making and Graphic Representation," *Publications of the American Statistical Association* 6 (1898–1899): 313.
22. Michael Teller, "The American Tuberculosis Crusade, 1889–1917: The Rise of a Modern Health Campaign" (Ph.D. diss., University of Chicago, 1985), vol. 1, 135–159, contains an excellent summary of the programs of publicity and public education. Richard H. Shryock, *National Tuberculosis Association, 1904–1954: A Study of the Voluntary Health Movement in the United States* (New York: National Tuberculosis Association, 1957), also treats the subject in some detail.
23. Shryock, *National Tuberculosis Association*, 133.

annual change of design the Christmas Seal not only raised money for the fight against tuberculosis but also reminded millions about the NTA's objectives and advice.

Insurance companies, too, some of them with enormous numbers of policyholders, began to turn to graphic publicity as a means of protecting health and aiding longevity. As early as 1898 the Metropolitan Life Insurance Company was publishing booklets devoted to personal health.[24] Insurance companies had long been sensitive to the selling power of graphics; Thomas Nast, for example, was employed to draw cartoons for insurance periodicals in the late nineteenth century. Now, with their large printing plants and experience in distributing chromolithographed calendars and booklets containing recipes, essays, poems, and well-known quotations, the insurance companies, led by Metropolitan Life, began to take health education and nursing care seriously. In 1909 the company hired Dr. Lee Frankel, a chemist who was also a self-educated sociologist, to head its new Industrial Department. Frankel had been examining workingmen's insurance for the Russell Sage Foundation. Metropolitan Life promised to make its future policy insurance "not merely as a business proposition, but as a social programme."[25] Persuading the directors that aggressive warfare against disease would ultimately profit the company (as well as benefit the public), Frankel and a young associate, a high school teacher named Louis Dublin, put out an eight-page pamphlet, *A War upon Consumption*, in 1909. Printed in an edition of 3,500,000 and in ten languages, the pamphlet was carried by Metropolitan Life agents into homes across the United States. *The Metropolitan*, the company's periodical, which was distributed free to policyholders, began featuring elaborately illustrated pages offering health advice; one issue even argued for the creation of a federal department of health. In time these pages would be distributed as circulars. Other publications, many of them strikingly designed, followed — booklets with titles such as *Get Rid of Rats*, *A Day in the Life of a Fly* (illustrated by a *New York American* cartoonist, Hal Coffman), *Teeth, Tonsils and Adenoids*, *How to Live Long*, and *The Magic Book of Health*.[26] By the end of 1916 Metropolitan Life had distributed some eighty million health-related circulars to its

24. The first Metropolitan booklet devoted exclusively to health was published, in French and English, by the company's medical supervisor in Canada and was entitled *A Friend in Need*. John Gudmundsen, *The Great Provider: The Dramatic Story of Life Insurance in America* (South Norwalk, Conn.: Industrial Publications Co., 1959), *passim*, provides some information on such life insurance publicity. Dozens of pamphlets and broadsides published before 1920, along with the policyholder magazine, *The Metropolitan*, founded in 1901, reveal the growing sophistication of graphic design at the company.
25. *The Metropolitan* 25 (26 January 1909), unpaginated.
26. A list of the Metropolitan's publications, annotated and in chronological order, along with a history of its welfare work through 1924, can be found in *An Epoch in Life Insurance: A Third of a Century of Achievement*, 2d ed. (New York: Metropolitan Life Insurance Company, 1924), 204–242.

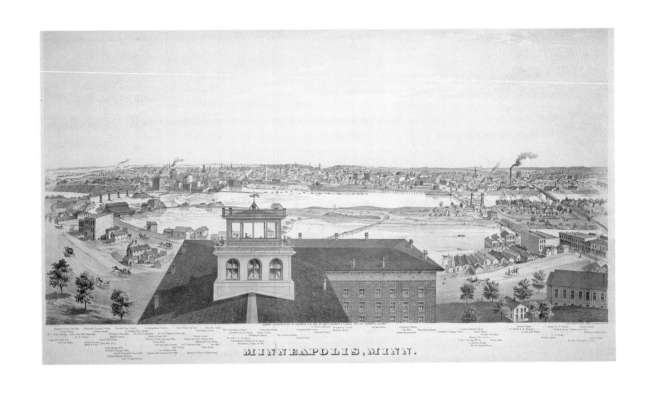

MINNEAPOLIS, MINN.

policyholders. Eight years later, this figure reached almost three hundred fifty million. One booklet alone (on child care) would by 1945 achieve almost thirty-two million copies.[27]

Some of the insurance literature mimicked established graphic techniques for juveniles, using lavish color and cartoonlike drawings. Other pieces employed the heavily allegorical styles exploited by some advertisers and poster-makers. And still other examples were far more austere, principally relying on dramatic lettering. In general, from the turn of the century on, companies like Metropolitan Life moved from highly sentimental vignettes emphasizing children, pets, and holiday scenes to more didactic and explicit illustrations. Compared with commercial advertising, the sophistication of this graphic art was quite limited, although by the 1910s it showed great progress. But the developing social conscience that was part of the Progressive movement was nonetheless providing, for the first time, an outlet for designers to serve a clear public cause and to promote not a product but the distillation of the latest scientific advice.

Still a third new arena allowed for a much higher level of graphic skill, since it tapped into certain established artistic conventions. This was the growing movement to transform the often squalid, haphazardly planned, congested, and inefficient American city into a more elegant, rational, and impressive grouping of buildings, parks, boulevards, transportation nodes, plazas, and public conveniences. From the 1890s through the 1920s hundreds of American communities turned to architects, city planners, and landscape architects for assistance.[28] From these "city beautiful" and "city efficient" campaigns emerged a literature with graphic as well as planning significance, adorned with an even richer mix of plans, charts, illustrations, graphs, and diagrams than the social surveys had featured.

There were various reasons for the graphic richness of the published city plans. One was an extant tradition of architectural rendering, which, aided by the improvements in printing now available, could project enticing visions of the urban future. Trained in architectural schools to prepare elaborately finished drawings of assigned projects — with premiums placed on speed and polish — architects were able to adorn the published plans with elegant illustrations.[29]

Another tradition easing the path for this new literature was the presence of the bird's-eye city view. For more than half a century these detailed,

George H. Ellsbury
Minneapolis, Minn. 1874
chromolithograph
15 x 30
Published by George H. Ellsbury and
Vernon Green, Chicago
Collection Minnesota Historical
Society, St. Paul

Jules Guérin
*Chicago, View Looking West of the
Proposed Civic Center Plaza* 1908
from *Plan of Chicago* 1909
by D.H. Burnham and E.H. Bennett
pencil and watercolor on paper
29 11/16 x 41 1/2
Collection The Art Institute of
Chicago

27. These figures are taken from James, *The Metropolitan Life*, chap. 11.
28. Much has been written on the City Beautiful movement. For a useful survey of the literature, see William H. Wilson, "The Ideology, Aesthetics and Politics of the City Beautiful Movement," Anthony Sutcliffe, ed., *The Rise of Modern Urban Planning, 1800–1914* (New York: St. Martin's, 1980), 186–198.

dramatic, and highly stylized renditions of small towns and large cities alike had been promoted by their publishers and by local boosters. Designed to interest potential investors and immigrants (and to excite local pride), such graphic exuberance fed a tradition of civic self-consciousness, no less intense because it was harnessed to an essentially private production.[30] This genre was supplemented, moreover, by a large number of multi-colored railroad company maps and views, many of which, like the bird's-eye views, were exercises in corporate pride and boosterism.[31]

Finally, there was the overriding objective of the new urban publications: to persuade citizens that the costly improvements being proposed were worth the tax increases that would surely follow. City plans of the Progressive Era were often campaign documents, statements of grandiose intentions requiring a future vision that could be easily grasped and widely admired. The plantings, widened boulevards, new public buildings, and rationalized transportation corridors had to be realized on paper, at least, before enabling legislation could be approved.[32]

The most elaborate plan of this period, as well as the most ambitious and probably the best fulfilled, was Daniel Burnham's *Plan of Chicago* (1909).[33] Superbly printed by the local firm of R.R. Donnelley and Sons and beautifully illustrated

29. *The Brickbuilder* 23 (1914) ran a series of eleven articles, entitled *Monographs on Architectural Renderers*, examining ten American renderers; this remains an excellent source of information on illustrators Alfred M. Githens, Rockwell Kent, Birch Burdette Long, and Floyd Yewell, among others. For a well-illustrated survey of one city's experience with architectural illustration, see Alex Krieger and Lisa J. Green, *Past Futures: Two Centuries of Imagining Boston*, exh. cat. (Harvard University School of Design, Cambridge, Mass., 1985). George E. Thomas, "Pecksniffs and Perspectives: The Changing Role of the Drawing in the Architectural Profession after the Civil War," James F. O'Gorman et al., *Drawing toward Building: Philadelphia Architectural Graphics, 1732–1986* (Philadelphia: University of Pennsylvania Press, 1986), 117–125, establishes the growing importance of drawing to the profession. And Pauline Saliga, "The Types and Styles of Architectural Drawings," John Zukowsky et al., *Chicago Architects Design* (Art Institute of Chicago, 1982), 20–30, analyzes techniques and processes.
30. In a series of books John W. Reps has discussed and reproduced large numbers of these views. For one of his most exhaustive studies, see John W. Reps, *Views and Viewmakers of Urban America* (Columbia, Mo.: University of Missouri Press, 1984).
31. Some of these railroad graphics may be found in Andrew M. Modelski, *Railroad Maps of North America: The First Hundred Years* (New York: Crown, 1987).
32. For more on this, see Paul Boyer, *Urban Masses and Moral Order in America, 1820–1920* (Cambridge, Mass. and London: Harvard University Press, 1978), chaps. 17–18; and Thomas S. Hines, *Burnham of Chicago: Architect and Planner* (New York: Oxford University Press, 1974), chaps. 7–9, 14.
33. Daniel H. Burnham and Edward H. Bennett, *Plan of Chicago* (Commercial Club of Chicago, 1909). This volume was reprinted in 1970 by the Da Capo Press as vol. 29 of the series *Architecture and Decorative Art*, ed. Adolf K. Placzek.

by Jules Guérin and Fernand Janin, the publication set a standard few others could hope to equal. Its production was subsidized by the Commercial Club of Chicago; such generosity was not usually available.[34]

Nonetheless, the book's approach, inspiration, and impact did have parallels elsewhere, progeny as well as ancestry, and showed the willingness of city reformers to make use of the new weapons that graphic designers had brought them. Like a number of other far less expensive productions, the *Plan of Chicago* mixed its media. Photographs of existing conditions, and of impressive accomplishments in other (mainly European) cities, were complemented by clearly drawn, multicolored maps exploring the logic of new street and transportation plans, by reproductions of scenes from the city's past (to indicate just how far recent growth had progressed), by renderings, drawings, and perspectives of what the city's new public buildings and lakefront might look like from both the air and the ground, and by diagrams, tables, and charts — all intended to promote the practicality, and aesthetic advantages, of the recommendations. Reviewing the *Plan* in Liverpool's *Town Planning Review* in 1910, Patrick Abercrombie pointed out that it had "the great merit of transforming a dull and inchoate city plan into a magnificent centralised conception," the "vivid and atmospheric impressions" produced by Guérin's renderings of the lakefront, the new boulevards and plazas, and the Chicago River helping to make the recommendations "as attractive and engaging as possible."[35] A later critic argued that the *Plan* gained so much attention because Daniel Burnham, the architect in charge, saw it as "a picture book. It is like an exhibition of pictures with captions or a series of slides with commentary, but put into permanent printed form."[36]

The skillful architectural rendering and drawing that made these city plans so appealing was a relatively recent achievement. Before 1880, noted *The Brickbuilder* magazine in 1916, American architectural draftsmanship had languished. Most magazine perspectives were made with triangle and T square and were "marvels of

34. In graphic terms the only rival to the *Plan of Chicago* before 1920 was probably Edward H. Bennett and Andrew Wright Crawford, *Plan of Minneapolis* (Minneapolis: Civic Commission, 1917), a handsomely printed volume done for the Minneapolis Civic Commission. It also featured the art of Jules Guérin and was designed in the spirit and on the scale of the *Plan of Chicago*.
35. Patrick Abercrombie, "Chicago," *Town Planning Review* 1 (April 1910), 56. This was one in a series of reviews focusing upon recently published American town plans, including those for Washington, D.C., Milwaukee, Boston, and Philadelphia.
36. Robert Bruegmann, "Burnham, Guérin, and the City as Image," John Zukowsky et al., *The Plan of Chicago: 1909– 1979*, exh. cat. (Art Institute of Chicago, 1979), 16. Bruegmann reviews the role of exhibitions and publicity in developing public interest in city plans.

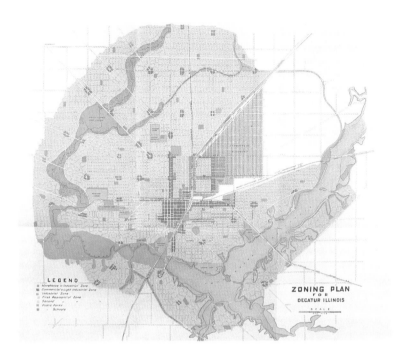

ZONING PLAN
FOR
DECATUR ILLINOIS

LEGEND

ELEMENTARY NEEDS

How principal business streets are given a disordered appearance and made to look narrower by multitudes of projecting signs

Views east and west from the corner of Court and State Streets

uninteresting distortion of effect."[37] Gradually, artists such as Hughson Hawley, Birch Burdette Long, and Floyd Yewell, as well as celebrated architects such as Cass Gilbert, Alfred M. Githens, and John Russell Pope accustomed clients and architectural firms alike to handsome and highly individualistic renderings. "The time to educate the client is before he builds," wrote Samuel Swift in an article on Jules Guérin, who illustrated several of the major plans. In Swift's words, Guérin had the special ability to eliminate "from the layman's view of a design, the non-essential elements, and to make clear to him the oft-quoted distinction between truths and facts."[38] In the 1920s architectural journals, increasingly able to exploit color, featured the elegant graphics produced by these draftsmen — usually on behalf of a specific architectural firm.[39]

The flood of city plans that appeared at roughly the same time made excellent use of this new proficiency, establishing a dialogue between the photographic record of what had been with a graphic promise of what might be — cities that were beautiful, healthy, and efficient — centers of local pride, tourist patronage, and business investment. The city plans, like the social surveys and the health campaigns, mingled scientific fact and careful research with dramatic, sentimental, and idealistic social hopes.

Along with Chicago, other large cities, including Boston, Philadelphia, Cleveland, Detroit, Minneapolis, St. Louis, Denver, and San Francisco, considered monumental improvements and landscape changes. But smaller municipalities — Albany, New York; Hartford, Connecticut; Providence, Rhode Island; Springfield, Illinois; Fort Wayne, Indiana; Madison, Wisconsin; Palm Beach, Florida; and Pasadena, California, among others — went to planners and architects such as Bion J. Arnold, Edward H. Bennett, Arnold W. Brunner, Daniel Burnham, and Charles Mulford Robinson for help in taking control of their physical destinies. Their plans have been considered as exercises in spatial management, but the literature the plans produced has yet to be considered as a genre.[40] Here graphic artists, book designers, architectural draftsmen, and cartographers could combine forces to create a new kind of document in the interests of a civic cause: graphics for the public good.

Zoning Plan for Decatur Illinois 1920
from *The Decatur Plan*, by Myron Howard West
Published by the Association of Commerce, Decatur, Illinois

Illustration from *Better Binghamton* 1911
by Charles Mulford Robinson
Published by the Mercantile-Press Club, Binghamton, New York

37. *The Brickbuilder* 25 (October 1916): 274. The comment came in an obituary tribute for D.A. Gregg, an architect and renderer.
38. Samuel Swift, "The Pictorial Representation of Architecture: The Work of Jules Guérin," *The Brickbuilder* 18 (September 1909): 177. For more on Guérin, a crucial figure in this movement, see Mark A. Hewitt, *Jules Guérin: Master Delineator*, exh. cat. (Farish Gallery, Rice University, Houston, 1983). Guérin worked for a number of architects besides Burnham and Bennett, including Cass Gilbert and John Russell Pope.
39. Most notably *Pencil Points*. Many of this journal's color illustrations are reproduced in Arthur L. Guptill, *Color in Sketching and Rendering* (New York: Reinhold, 1935).

Howard Chandler Christy
Fight or Buy Bonds 1917
34 x 22 (approx.)
Collection Minnesota Historical
Society, St. Paul

More careful study of this literature would expose its graphic varieties, some of them associated with particular planning firms. Different styles in the approach to persuasion developed, with greater or lesser reliance on maps, commissioned drawings, photographs, and diagrams. But by the late 1920s traditional beauxarts renderings coexisted with fascinating new color abstractions, as exemplified by the land use studies of the great Regional Plan of New York. Some of the artists working in this genre, like their commercial colleagues, remain anonymous. But they were contributing to a powerful instrument of public enlightenment.

The printing magazines, which in the 1890s and first years of this century had run elaborate monthly reviews of commercial design and typography, reproducing specimens of almost every kind of paper ephemera — from menus and brochure covers to remittance forms and ticket stubs — paid remarkably little attention to the civic arena.[41] This genre was limited and comparatively unimportant; moreover, in some areas, such as public health, it was less sophisticated than standard commercial work. And tight budgets meant few economic rewards. But a new public market was being created, and graphic designers were increasingly consulted in creation of the new signage, the seals, symbols, and posters, the lettering, and the street furniture that well-appointed communities were demanding. By 1917 this market was still in its infancy, though it was quickly beginning to grow.[42]

It would be permanently transformed, that year, by the wartime emergency. Faced with the task of mobilizing the public to buy war bonds, accept

40. My characterizations are based on examination of dozens of city and town plans. A few striking examples of the genre include (in chronological order): Arnold W. Brunner and John M. Carrere, *Preliminary Report for a City Plan for Grand Rapids* (Grand Rapids, Mich., circa 1909); *Partial Report on "City Plan"* (Baltimore: Municipal Art Society, 1910); Arnold W. Brunner et al., *A City Plan for Rochester* (Rochester, N.Y.: Civic Improvement Committee, 1911); Charles Mulford Robinson, *Better Binghamton* (Binghamton, N.Y.: Mercantile-Press Club, 1911); John Nolen, *Greater Erie* (Erie, Pa.: City Planning Commission, 1913); and Myron Howard West, *The Decatur Plan* (Decatur, Ill.: Association of Commerce, 1920).

41. Occasionally, the printing journals would give a civic cause or cultural event the same attention and critical review they expended on commercial materials. Thus *Printing Art* 18 (July 1909): 285–286, reviewed a competition for a program cover sponsored by the Beethoven Society Symphony Orchestra in Baltimore. Or it might examine an announcement form created by Boston's Museum of Fine Arts in order to raise money for a new building, noting that it was much better than "the usual document of this class, which generally looks like some legal notice." *Printing Art* 11 (July 1908): 204. But such instances were rare.

42. Among other things, one might point to the commissioning of posters by The Art Institute of Chicago and the Chicago Opera Association, described in *The Poster* 8 (November 1917): 42–44. Ralph Fletcher Seymour designed the program cover for the Chicago Grand Opera company in 1913, title pages for the Pageant of Illinois in 1909, and bookplates for The Art Institute.

conscription, save food and fuel, and generally support the war effort, government propagandists turned to American artists for help.[43] Illustrators, painters, and poster-makers were more than eager to participate, forming voluntary committees and generally exhibiting the same patriotic fervor that captured other professions at the time. The posters produced during a relatively brief period remain among the best-known pieces of graphic design in our history, a testament to the skills that had developed among commercial designers and illustrators during the previous twenty years.

World War I coincided with the first municipal and institutional efforts to harness design to cultural and civic causes. Cities such as Milwaukee, Newark, and Springfield, Massachusetts, sponsored their own poster contests. So did the State of Illinois, to celebrate its centennial in 1917, and the National American Woman's Suffrage Association.[44] Large railroad companies, such as the Santa Fe, had a tradition of promoting the areas served by their lines, and they had developed distinctive methods of mapping out their routes and terminal facilities.[45]

By this time, too, the huge new public utilities companies, privately owned but publicly regulated and ultimately answerable to the electorate, had begun to appreciate the values of corporate personality that graphic artists could create for them. Electrical companies in particular, such as New York Edison, worked attentively to assure their customers that they held their interests at heart.[46] Fred Cooper did the honors for New York Edison, with his affable Knickerbocker figure reassuring New Yorkers of his company's good intentions. In Chicago the electric-traction interests of Samuel Insull turned to Willard Elms, Oscar Rabe Hanson, Ervine Metzl, and other artists to combine chamber of commerce imagery with the striking graphic approaches that had been so well developed in private industry.[47]

43. The most complete survey is Walton Rawls, *Wake Up, America!*, supra, note 10.

44. For the suffrage campaign, see Paula Hays Harper, "Votes for Women?: A Graphic Episode in the Battle of the Sexes," Henry A. Millon and Linda Nochlin, eds., *Art and Architecture in the Service of Politics* (Cambridge, Mass.: MIT Press, 1978), 150–161. *The Newark Posters Catalogue* (Newark, N. J.: Committee of 100, 1915) describes the contest for a poster celebrating the city's two hundred fiftieth anniversary.

45. The Santa Fe program is depicted in several issues of *The Poster*; see particularly, *The Poster* 8 (March 1917): 44, 46.

46. Henry Lewis Johnson, "Keeping the Public Informed about Electricity," *Graphic Arts* 6 (January 1914): 49–56, described Fred Cooper's work for New York Edison. The firm's advertising manager, who was supportive of Cooper, was Cyril Nast, son of the cartoonist Thomas Nast.

47. *The Poster* 15 (May 1924) discussed the Chicago campaign. See also Dana M. Hubbard, "How Chicago Elevated Is Advertising Chicago to Chicagoans," *Printers' Ink Monthly* 5 (November 1922): 53. Churches were also active patrons of poster and other advertising in the 1920s, as was the Red Cross.

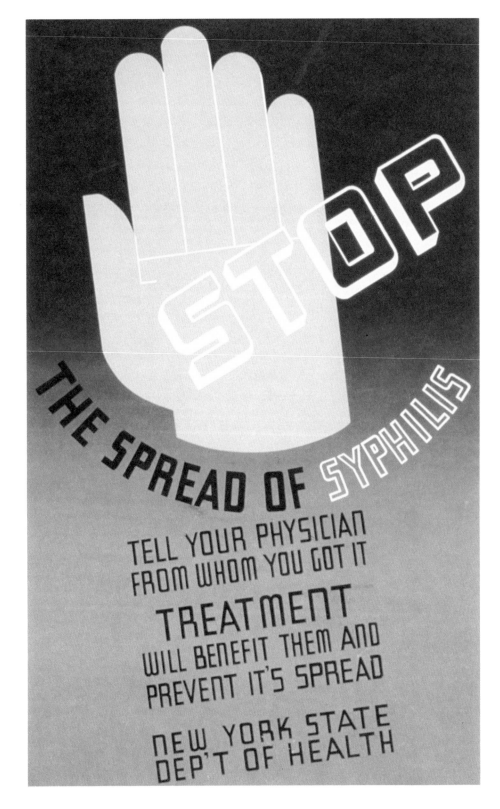

During the 1910s and 1920s also, American libraries, museums, zoos, art galleries, and other cultural institutions began concerning themselves more seriously with their graphic identities, partly stimulated by the need to raise private funds to support their programs. With guidebooks, gift shops, posters, annual reports, and exhibition catalogues assuming new importance, several of these organizations turned to printing enthusiasts such as Henry Watson Kent for help. A few even found permanent positions for them.[48] Creation of new courses in design and printing at major universities, the establishment of new professional groups such as the Society of Typographic Arts (an offshoot of the slightly older American Institute of Graphic Arts), and annual exhibitions of advertising art provided further occasions to review the public function of design.

Such growth in these years, while significant, was also limited. The involvement of the graphic arts with civic and cultural causes would increase far more substantially in the 1930s, when for a variety of reasons federal involvement in the arts, recreation, health, and environmental planning became pervasive. Posters, brochures, instruction manuals, exhibits, photographs, films, and books flowed from federal agencies. State governments and municipal agencies also turned to artists for interpretative support, along with cultural institutions and philanthropic societies seeking public aid. By the time of World War II officials could draw on a well-developed, flourishing partnership between the graphic arts and public causes — a situation quite different from the wartime experience a generation earlier.

Nonetheless, those first somewhat hesitant and occasionally crude steps taken during the Progressive Era remain absorbing. They constitute the beginnings of what has since become a broad and impressive program of public education and information, the world of museum posters, exhibition catalogues, public health leaflets, civic guidebooks, survey maps, charitable campaigns, consumer reports, traffic and road signs, university bulletins, governmental agency handouts, and voter and literacy aids, among others, on a very long list. In all these, graphic artists have played a major role, enhancing and expanding the work of the arts, the humanities, and the sciences. As we look back on such accomplishments it is appropriate to recall their early practitioners, unheralded in their day and largely forgotten in ours. They remain part of the surprisingly rich graphic heritage that is ours to claim.

Neil Harris is a professor of history at the University of Chicago. He has written extensively on the history of American culture. A collection of his essays entitled Cultural Excursions *will be published by the University of Chicago Press in 1990.*

Ben Kaplan
Stop the Spread of Syphilis circa 1935
silkscreen
22 x 14
Collection Library of Congress,
Washington, D.C.

48. Henry Watson Kent, *What I Am Pleased to Call My Education* (New York: Grolier Club, 1949), chap. 10, reviews his work for the Metropolitan Museum of Art. The Museum Press was praised by major figures in American graphic and typographic design, such as Bruce Rogers, Carl Rollins, and Daniel Berkeley Updike.

DAS BAUHAUS IN DESSAU.

leitung: walter gropius.

[German text, largely illegible]

42

The Bauhaus in Dessau
Direction: Walter Gropius
Advertisement published in Dessau newspapers,
1925

The Bauhaus in Dessau
direction: walter gropius

purpose:
the training of artistically talented people to become creative designers in the fields of the crafts, industry, and architecture
I. design instruction:
basic instruction
craft instruction (goal: journeyman's certificate)
architectural instruction
II. practical research:
production of prototypes for the crafts and industry
building and furnishings
workshops:
cabinetmaking, wall-painting, metal, weaving, printing (typography, commercial art, and art prints)
start of the winter semester: october 14, 1925. admission to the basic course (compulsory for everyone) from age 17 onward—experienced craftsmen, technicians, mechanics, and architects will also be admitted—apply now
basic instruction (1 year) per semester: 30 marks. admission fee: 10 marks. workshop training: free of charge.

under the same direction:
school of arts and crafts and trade school, dessau
I. school for the building trades: prussian curriculum
in the winter: architecture classes V and III
II. school for mechanical engineering: four progressive half-year classes; good grades confer the right of admission to the last semester at the engineering school in zwickau (fall admission for classes III and I)
(easter admission for classes IV and II)
III. trade school: teaching workshops for those employed in the trades
evening classes: drafting, mathematics, etc.; preparatory courses for factory foremen with final examination
day classes for the trades (yearly courses, beginning in april)
beginning of the winter semester: october 14, 1925 enrollment and payment of tuition
september 21 to 30, 1925
late enrollment: 10% penalty

106

das bauhaus in dessau

lehrplan

[text, illegible]

42

Bauhaus Dessau
The City of Dessau
From "Bauhaus Dessau," booklet of the Dessau Bauhaus (1927)
At this time Dessau had 70,000 inhabitants—about one fifth of the entire population of the state of Anhalt. The tremendous growth of industry had changed its residential character, making Dessau appear a modern and cosmopolitan city by comparison with Weimar, and this despite its significant and quite noticeable tradition.

Dessau lies between the Elbe and the Mulde rivers in a large area of parks, the most important of which is the Wörlitzer Park. Duke Friedrich Franz, called "Papa Franz" by his people, who created the Wörlitzer Park, was the founder of the cultural tradition in his Duchy of Anhalt. just as Karl August had been for Weimar. His friend and adviser Erdmannsdorff had influence as an outstanding master-builder. Among those who once lived here were Johann Lavater, Friedrich von Matthisson, a friend of Schiller's (Beethoven set his "Adelaide" into music); von Knobelsdorf (architect of Sans Souci), who directed the alterations of the castle; and the philanthropists Basedow, Campe, and Salzmann, who made Dessau the point of departure for educational endeavors during the Age of Enlightenment. At that time, the Chalcographic Society was founded, important art collections were started, Johann Friedrich August Tischbein was court painter. Goethe reports at length about repeated visits to Dessau where, together with Karl August, he received important inspirations for the Weimar Park.
Under the successors of "Papa Franz," Dessau acquired a good reputation as a center for the performing arts which it has kept to the present day. The significant names in this area are Rust, Friedrich Schneider, and Wilhelm Müller.
The preceding generation provided Dessau with large industrial companies. The Berlin-Anhalt Engineering company built several large plants. Dessau became known through the German Continental Gas company, the Askania Works, the Polysius Machine Factory, the Dessau Sugar Refinery, the various Junkers works, especially the internationally known Junkers aircraft factory, a railroad-car factory and a number of medium- and small-sized industries. The other important industries in the vicinity of Dessau, Agfa works at Wolfen, the nitrogen-fixation plant at Piesteritz, metallurgical works at Rodleben, the Riedel company at Rosslau, the power plant at Golpa-Zschornewitz, offer a chance to get acquainted with the different branches of industry by inspection visits at their plants. Dessau is two hours by train from Berlin. Almost equidistant are the cities of Halle, Magdeburg, and Leipzig. The Harz mountains can be reached in three or four hours. The site at the rivers Elbe and Mulde, between vast areas of green, promotes outdoor sports.
[Original without capital letters]

The Bauhaus in Dessau
Curriculum (1925)
Broadside, published in November 1925
In addition to the general curriculum and the program of the principles of Bauhaus production, the Dessau Bauhaus—during the last months of 1925 and the beginning of 1926—issued separate plans for the work of the workshops. The typographical design was done by Herbert Bayer, who also did the other Bauhaus printing during that period.

Curriculum
Purpose:
1. a thorough craft, technical, and formal training for artistically talented individuals with the aim of collaboration in building
2. practical research into problems of house construction and furnishing. Development of standard prototypes for industry and the crafts.
Areas of instruction:
1. Practical instruction. in
a. wood (cabinetmaking workshop)
b. metal (silver and copper work)
c. color (wall-painting workshop)
d. fabrics (weaving and dyeing workshop)
e. printing—books and art prints
Supplementary areas of instruction:
study of materials and tools
rudiments of bookkeeping, cost estimating,
and contract law
2. Form instruction (practical and theoretical)
a. perception
science of materials
study of nature
b. representation
study of geometric projection
study of construction
technical draftsmanship and building of
107

Symbol in Space Before Form in Space: Las Vegas as a Communication System

The sign for the Motel Monticello, a silhouette of an enormous Chippendale highboy, is visible on the highway before the motel itself. This architecture of styles and signs is antispatial; it is an architecture of communication over space; communication dominates space as an element in the architecture and in the landscape. But it is a new kind of landscape. The paradoxical aspect of this giant roadside is evoked subtle and complex meanings to be savored in the double shapes of a traditional landscape. The commercial persuasion of roadside eclecticism provokes bold impact in the vast and complex setting of a new landscape of big spaces, high speeds, and complex programs. Styles and signs make connections among many elements, far apart and seen fast. The message is basically commercial; the content is basically new.

A driver 30 years ago could maintain a sense of orientation in space. At the simple crossroad a little sign with an arrow confirmed what he already knew. He knew where he was. Today, the crossroad is a cloverleaf. To turn left he must turn right, a contradiction poignantly evoked in the print by Allan D'Arcangelo. But the driver has no time to ponder paradoxical subtleties within a dangerous, sinuous maze. He relies on signs to guide him—gas, food, motel to the right at the next exit.

The dominance of signs over space at a pedestrian scale occurs in big airports. Circulation in a big railroad station required little more than a simple axial system from door to train, by ticket window, stairs, waiting room, and platform—all virtually without signs. Architects object to signs in buildings: "If the plan is clear, you can see where to go." But complex programs and settings require complex combinations of media beyond the pure architecture of the structure, form, and light at the service of space. They suggest an architecture of bold communication rather than one of subtle expression.

2. The sign. Allan D'Arcangelo.

WELCOME TO FABULOUS LAS VEGAS, FREE ASPIRIN – ASK US ANYTHING, VACANCY, GAS

All cities communicate messages — functional, symbolic, and persuasive — to people as they move about. Las Vegas signs let you at the California border and before you land at the airport. On the Strip three message systems exist: the heraldic (the signs) dominant; the physiognomic, the messages given by the faces of the buildings (the continuous balconies and regularly spaced picture windows of the Dunes say "HOTEL"); and the suburban bungalows converted to chapels by the addition of a steeple; and the locational (service stations are found on corner lots, the casino is in front of the hotel, and the ceremonial valet parking is in front of the casino). All three message systems are closely interrelated on the Strip. Sometimes they are combined, as when the facade of a casino becomes one big sign or the shape of the building reflects its name, and the sign, in turn, reflects the shape. The sign for the building or the building the sign? These relationships, and combinations between signs and buildings, between architecture and symbolism, between form and meaning, between driver and the roadside are deeply relevant to architecture today and have been discussed at length by several writers. But they have not been studied in detail or as an overall system. The students of urban perception and imageability have ignored them, and there is some evidence that the Strip would confound their theories. How is it that in spite of "noise" from competing signs we do in fact find what we want on the Strip? Also, we have no good graphic tools for depicting the Strip as message giver. How can the visual importance of the Stardust sign be mapped at 1 inch to 100 feet?

3. Map of Las Vegas Strip showing heraldic symbolism.

4

[born 1925]

Muriel Cooper

In 1982 the Massachusetts Institute of Technology was awarded the second AIGA Design Leadership Award. The three groups at the university so honored were Design Services, the design department at The MIT Press, and the Visible Language Workshop; each of these was initiated by Muriel Cooper. In the 1950s MIT was first among universities in its commitment to a coherent design expression in all of its print material. The early works of the Office of Publications (now Design Services) were characterized by the use of graphic design to express and clarify scientific and technological information.

In the early 1970s MIT Press became known for the design of its books on architecture, design, and popular culture. The ascetic yet provocative formats designed by Muriel Cooper were perfect for the presentation of such texts. Her magnum opus for *The Bauhaus* (1969) by Hans M. Wingler, an in-depth account of this legendary academy, used a grid that built upon the school's teachings of the relationships of form to function and technology. It is not surprising that she would be drawn to the computer as a tool not only to extend traditional graphic design capabilities but also to investigate new graphic communications in an electronic environment.

MIT's Visible Language Workshop, of which Cooper is director, began as a laboratory for making experimental graphics using traditional reproduction technologies in unconventional ways and soon became the site of an extended love-hate relationship with the computer.

The work at The MIT Press covered all aspects of publishing, including some outstanding books among the five hundred-odd volumes of that period. The genres were both individual and systematic and ranged from unique art and architecture books, photography, and history of science to complex technical and scientific works. The bulk of the work was standard and repetitious and required a set of systematic but variable design solutions for limited budgets. Developing systems that would accommodate a wide range of variable elements was very much like designing processes.

The people and works of the Bauhaus were my conceptual and spiritual ancestors, so I felt a particular bond with the material. While the structure of the book evolved from the Swiss grid system, it was devised to be rich enough to encompass the complex panorama of the archival textual and visual material. Because the color plates had to be salvaged from other publications for economy's sake, they determined size constraints. All of the material was archival and could not be cropped. My approach to design always emphasized process over product, and what better place to express this than in a tome on the Bauhaus, the seminal exploration of art and design in an industrial revolution. All of my books explored implicit motion. *The Bauhaus* was designed both statically and filmically with

The Bauhaus 1969
by Hans M. Wingler
pp. 106–107: 14 1/4 x 10 1/4 format
Published by The MIT Press,
Cambridge, Massachusetts

Learning from Las Vegas 1972
by Robert Venturi, Denise Scott
Brown, and Steven Izenour
pp. 4–5: 14 1/4 x 10 7/8 format
Published by The MIT Press,
Cambridge, Massachusetts

a mental model of slow motion animation of the page elements.

Later I made a film of the Bauhaus book that sped up the reading process by shooting three frames for each double page, a view of the information that revealed the conceptual structure of the book as would a stop-motion movie of the construction of a building over time, or of a seed growing into a blossoming flower. This book has a life of its own that I believe is due to an unusually symbiotic relationship of form and content. I was very fortunate to have been at the right place at the right time.

Learning from Las Vegas [1972], by Robert Venturi, Denise Scott Brown, and Steven Izenour, was an exercise in using design to resonate content with subject. The visual materials were not only graphically rich, but as content-laden as the text, so the interdependent rhythms of those relationships were important. I wanted to arrange visual and verbal materials spatially in a nonlinear way to enhance the reader's comprehension. Creating virtual time and space in two dimensions has always intrigued me.

Many of the books contained mathematics. Mathematical notation is a self-contained symbolic language. Its conventions are well established and devised to clarify

Four images and three text segments are used to explore ways simultaneously to represent multitiered information using changes of size, placement, color, and translucency. Each frame changes as the "reader" browses in real time, with text and image cues dependent on the linkages that have been designed for browsing. The tools for this series were developed at the Visible Language Workshop by Suguru Ishizaki; the series was designed by Muriel Cooper.

Design Quarterly 142 1989
"Computers and Design"
cover detail: 11 x 8 1/2 format
Published by The MIT Press for
Walker Art Center

information hierarchically with little concern for overall visual coherence when mixed with text formats. Normally, centering is the rule. I found the problem of redefining conventions based on function that would maintain coherence and yet allow integration with the text format to be a significant challenge. Devising a means of displaying these conventions in a flush-left design was a subtle but by no means a small accomplishment.

The Donald McCullin book *Is anyone taking any notice?* [1973] is a collection of appalling and at the same time beautiful photographs of the effects of war in many parts of the world. It touched me deeply, and I coupled the images with excerpts from Aleksandr Solzhenitsyn's Nobel Prize acceptance speech, trying to counterpoint the words and images in a message of hope rather than despair. I remain very proud of this work. It was an interesting example of a designer's view integrated with that of a photographer and writer. I was also concerned with making the photographic book more of a spatial and psychological experience than the typical "framed photograph" metaphor.

But the inequitable constraints placed on verbal and visual information by the double page; the early closure demanded by the mass-production cycle; and the crush of deadlines that prevented research into new solutions for communication problems all contributed to my growing frustration with the print medium. It was clear that the computer would soon have a profound impact on these limitations.

Consequently, MIT Press formed a small research and development group to work on experimental books and to explore new media — in particular the computer.

I was convinced that the line between reproduction tools and design would blur when information became electronic and that the lines between designer and artist, author and designer, professional and amateur would also dissolve. We had one of the first color copiers in New England — 3M color on color — which we used both for experimentation and for color presentations. Nicholas Negroponte, director of MIT's Media Lab, put a couple of computers in our department at the Press and a couple of undergraduate hackers were assigned to us to develop early versions of word processing with some minimal graphics. We were actually inventing a primitive form of desktop publishing.

At the same time I met Ron MacNeil, who had been in Minor White's Creative Photography Laboratory and had bootstrapped an experimental print shop using a neglected darkroom and an offset press. We complemented each other's resources and created a course called "Messages and Means." It was design and communication for print that integrated the reproduction tools as a part of the thinking process and reduced the gap between process and product. The principles of this class led to the formation of the Visible Language Workshop.

Computers had already influenced me enormously, and while I was dazzled by their potential, I was frustrated by their opacity and their limitations. The Visible Language Workshop became the experimental bridge between the computer and four hundred years of printing. While the first phase of the VLW was experimental print, integrating the computer into the array of design and reproduction tools, it became clear that the computer would soon emulate and integrate all of those traditional tools. Looking back at the history of the VLW, it seems like a microcosm: the phases that we went through are currently the phases that the design professions are now going through in relation to computers. We expect that our current concerns will be those of the design community in the next three to five years.

Today we are integrating traditional design methodology with the computer, a chameleonlike tool, and seeking ways to represent both articulated and intuitive design knowledge. Artificial-intelligence tools seem a promising approach to help us represent design knowledge to the computer so that it can become not only an aid but an assistant to the designer and the user. Unlike print or any of the traditional communication media, the computer is interactive and nonlinear, capable of real-time display of multimedia and of interconnecting information with dynamic pathways. This new world demands a new kind of designer who will provide opportunities, pathways, and processes for a more independent user, a designer who will create rich structures for users who will be able to acquire, browse, and gather information on their own terms.

Another thing that is around the bend is the elimination of the distinction between graphics for print and graphics for animation or television. All tools are soon going to be together, which will change specialized design professionals into something called design generalists. The design of the Bauhaus book, for example, would no longer be limited to text and photographs but would include film, video or animation, and three-dimensional or holographic visualizations of the sculpture, architecture, or performances of that moment of history. Hypertext and hypermedia principles would extend the editing and authorship of such an archival database so that a reader interested particularly in the political and social influences of the Bauhaus would be able directly to pursue multimedia bibliographic information in depth, rather than referencing footnotes and other sources.

Without new design principles and concepts we will be faced with a multimedia Tower of Babel. The computer is a totally different medium from any that we have ever known. Today it resembles old tools and, as with any new medium, that's the way it is being absorbed into the culture. I agree with people who say it is a process maker. It is so fast that it seems to resemble the way we think: one need only observe children interacting with talking computers as if they were intimates. The most advanced computer research is trying to understand the way we think and see and mapping those things into the computer. Some people believe that the computer eventually will think for itself. If so, it is crucial that designers and others with humane intentions be involved in the way it develops.

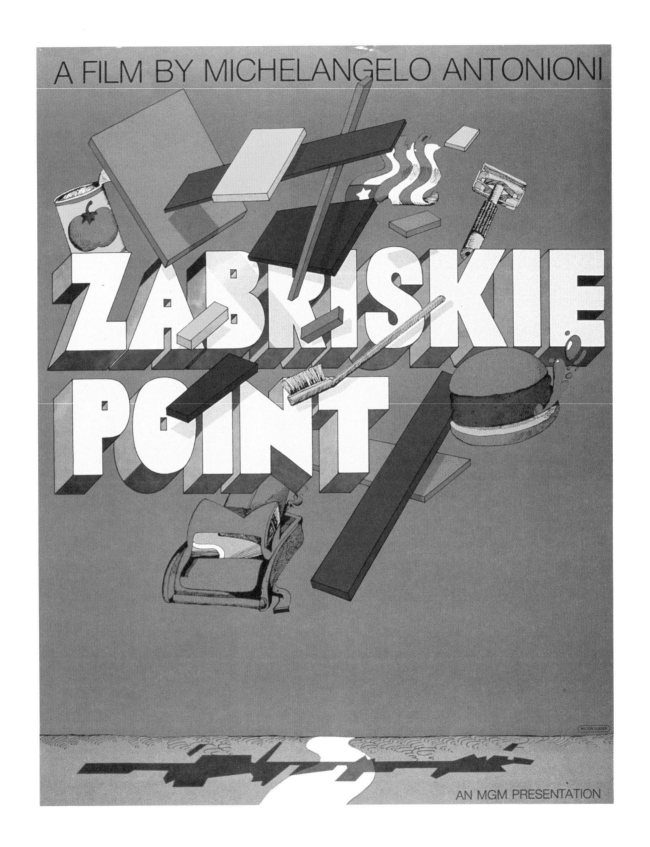

Milton Glaser

[born 1929]

Responding to what he felt was a cold, mechanistic approach to design taken by many modernists, Milton Glaser reintroduced narrative drawing and historical references in his design and illustration. As cofounder in 1954 of Push Pin Studios (with Seymour Chwast, Reynold Ruffins, and Edward Sorel), Glaser offered the field an eclectic alternative to systematized design. And the Push Pin style, characterized by a reprise of Victorian, Art Nouveau, and Art Deco forms, evolved into a distinctive revivalist fashion that spanned the mid-1960s to the mid-1970s. The style added color and humor to posters and record and book covers, among other consumer products. In keeping with his eclectic nature, Glaser left Push Pin in the 1970s to pursue interior, furniture, product, and architectural design, as well as a wider range of print projects.

When Push Pin Studios was starting out in the mid-1950s conformity was the norm. But I have always railed against ideological purity, or any other kind. At Push Pin we found corruption was more interesting than purity. My greatest dread was that I might become a mediocre painter. I realized that my life was in this profession, and I had to figure out a way to dig in.

I learned to draw properly in Italy. I always had a pretty good reputation as a draftsman, but I never felt confident about it until after I spent two years at the academy drawing from casts. It gave me the confidence that I needed and a basis for understanding a formal vocabulary. After the war Italy was almost a third-world country, but everybody was doing everything as the opportunity arose. Even today, Italian students train as architects and then become industrial or graphic designers. There's a nice blurring of distinctions. I found the idea of being well rounded very attractive. When I came back, Seymour Chwast, Ed Sorel, and Reynold Ruffins had already started Push Pin Studios, and my newly acquired European sensibility was added to the mix.

When you have a current, every once in a while you have individuals or groups that break out of the current with an alternative sense of purpose or vision. The current was

In this poster Milton Glaser's skills as a draftsman provide a preview of this film's concluding sequence, in which a large American house is blown up, and its material contents are scattered into space over a desolate landscape.

Zabriskie Point 1972
28 x 21 1/2
Collection the designer

101

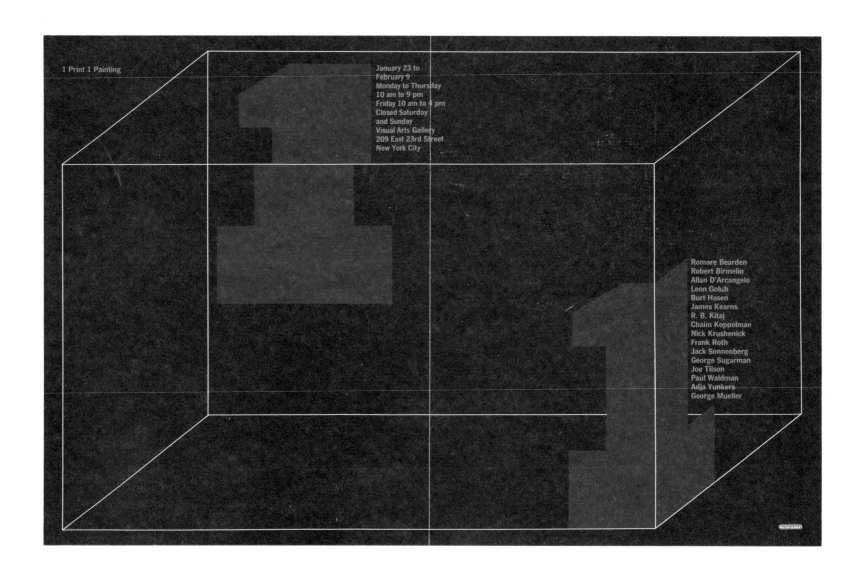

1 Print 1 Painting

January 23 to
February 9
Monday to Thursday
10 am to 9 pm
Friday 10 am to 4 pm
Closed Saturday
and Sunday
Visual Arts Gallery
209 East 23rd Street
New York City

Romare Bearden
Robert Birmelin
Allan D'Arcangelo
Leon Golub
Burt Hasen
James Kearns
R. B. Kitaj
Chaim Koppelman
Nick Krushenick
Frank Roth
Jack Sonnenberg
George Sugarman
Joe Tilson
Paul Waldman
Adja Yunkers
George Mueller

The Case Against F. Lee Bailey, by Barry Farrell
I Left My Heartburn in San Francisco, by Gael Greene
The School Principal Who Said No, by Ken Auletta

75 CENTS   MAY 3, 1976

NEW YORK

Why Everybody's Talking About

GOSSIP By Alexander Cockburn

In this atypical poster image, Glaser relies exclusively on type, and its manipulation at the hands of an isometric cube, to portray his subject.

1 Print 1 Painting 1968
11 x 17
Published by Visual Arts Gallery, New York

Magazine design went through radical changes in the late 1960s and early 1970s. In an effort to bring back readers lost to television and to develop new ones, Glaser applied his narrative acumen and the Push Pin penchant for revivalist design to *New York* magazine. Originally a Sunday supplement of *The New York Herald Tribune*, *New York* appeared as a smaller-scale weekly magazine after the demise of the *Tribune*.

**Milton Glaser and
Walter Bernard**, Art Directors
New York 3 May 1976
cover: 11 x 8 1/2 format
© News America Publishing, Inc., New York

Modernism, and the idea of purity of form, of the unadorned, and of honesty applied to graphics, architecture, and to some extent, painting. There was a kind of moralistic obsession with reducing elements to their simplest, most primary expression. There was nothing wrong with that ideology; it manifested itself very strongly in Swiss and German design, and it came here at the same time that Modernism began to emerge in the United States. It was a very powerful force on the theoretical side of design, in the schools, and in intellectual publications.

But on the street commercial artists were hacking away, trying to make ends meet without any formalistic vocabulary. It is ironic, of course, that those banal, nonintellectual expressions later became the basis for Pop Art and now are reemerging in the work of people such as Tibor Kalman and Steven Doyle, with the investigation of banal, vernacular forms. But at that time we were also interested in banal, discarded forms that violated the idea of purity. It was a conscious, yet an intuitive, rebellion. On the intuitive level we at Push Pin felt that there was another way to approach things, and we had other preferences. It seemed silly to have a single source of ideas. We liked Victorian typography. Seymour Chwast was particularly interested in romantic

typography, and he also liked woodcuts and American primitives. We didn't believe in eating vegetarian food all the time. Sometimes you want a greasy burger.

One other thing was essential to our approach: the idea of narration. Nobody seemed interested in telling stories; a concern with formalism and purity leads to abstraction. So the work that emerged elsewhere was non-narrative, non-storytelling abstraction designed to be perceived on the highest platonic level. Our interest in storytelling was the element that set our work apart. Also, we recognized the danger of losing drawing as an essential element in design. We all felt that we had to draw to control the idiom. When I was teaching in the 1960s it was almost impossible to convince an art student that there was any validity in the drawn image. As a result, a whole generation of people grew up unable to represent their ideas through drawing. (That may be the reason that collage became so universal as a technique.)

In the late 1960s the Push Pin style came to represent an attitude toward design. It isn't an attitude, incidentally, that I am entirely comfortable with now. But Push Pin was definitely on a roll in those days. However, if you look at the actual jobs that won awards, they are really dinky little things. There are a lot of Push Pin publications: book jackets, magazine illustrations, record sleeves, but no big corporate programs, no annual reports. You can take intellectual risks on book jackets.

At a certain point we were accepted, and once that happened everything became less interesting. All my life I've wanted to be accepted but not by accommodating myself to the world. The question is: Where does one go once the work has been seen, perceived, accepted, and finally discarded? We are doomed by our own history — and storytelling is still central to what I do.

Changing Technology Changes Design

Estelle Jussim

Here we are in the most profligate age of media, when printed paper inundates our mailboxes, films repeat themselves endlessly on cable television, once-humorous television series run forever on commercial channels, and computers spew forth not only lava flows of data but also surprise us with futuristic color animations. All this would have astounded the first graphic designers, those ingenious few of our ancestors in dimmest prehistory who began to draw symbols for animals they hunted and later invented shapes for the sounds we make when we speak. Pictographs, hieroglyphics, characters, and phonetic alphabets were our first graphic designs. With them, and with the development of representational pictorial communication, the human race has recorded its history and maintained its archive of discoveries and ideas. In a very real sense, the history of human communication is simultaneously the history of graphic design, whether we think of the Roman letter forms chiseled on triumphal arches or the convolutions of the *Book of Kells* (circa 800 A.D.). When we examine the history of graphic design we find not only human records but human art, beautifully exemplified by the medieval book.

The hand-produced medieval manuscripts gave us a magnificent treasury of combined pictures and calligraphic letter forms, many of them revived in the nineteenth century, when the idea of complete "creative control" over the design of books became increasingly important. Johannes Gutenberg's mid-fifteenth-century invention of movable metal type succeeded in mechanizing the bold calligraphy of late Gothic letter forms. From Gutenberg came the impetus toward typographic innovations based on the technology of punch, matrix, and poured lead, formally composed in even lines and closely woven columns. Through the next four centuries, with the successive typographic designs of Claude Garamond (d. 1561), William Caslon (1692–1766), and John Baskerville (1706–1775) — all the way to the so-called modern type fonts of Giambattista Bodoni (1740–1813) — the ideology of the even line and the solid column of text did not

R/Greenberg Associates, Inc.
Still from the title sequence for
Superman
© 1978 Film Export A.G.

falter. Ottmar Mergenthaler's invention in 1886 of the Linotype, the first successful automatic typesetting machine, seemed only to emphasize the left-right, left-right marching of even columns of type. Amply suited to newspaper composition, the Linotype was much more an aid to printers than an encouragement to new creation on the part of the graphic designer. An anti-mechanistic, aesthetic revolution in typographic imagination did occur from the 1880s to the early 1900s with the Arts and Crafts movement, inspired by William Morris's Kelmscott Press and T.J. Cobden-Sanderson and Emery Walker's Doves Press. Meanwhile, graphic designers of posters and advertisements in large-circulation popular magazines continued to use ornate wooden display faces and execrable woodcuts to attract attention. The contrast between the standard magazine ad of the 1890s and the high art and purism of William Morris's followers was a typical example of the schism between socioeconomic classes that was unconsciously maintained by the popular media. No one could deny, however, that the availability of cheap reading material, no matter how poorly designed, was anything but a substantial benefit to literacy among the so-called masses.

The first decades of this century saw a technologically based rebellion against the supposed inexorable linearity of book and journal design — the lockstep of tightly set texts within even margins — the linearity that would so vex Marshall McLuhan in the 1960s. He preferred the "words in liberty" of the early twentieth-century Futurists, who exploded typographic uniformity with the aid of offset lithography. Placing cutout letters of different sizes and fonts in sprays of words, and reproducing them with the camera and the offset press, the designers of Futurist and Dada publications immeasurably expanded the artistic freedom of graphic designers. Without the specific reproductive technology of offset lithography, ultimately the product of photographic technologies, it is possible that no avant-garde design would have emerged.

While technological determinism cannot completely explain the interconnections between graphic process and graphic design without considering the all-important context of social and economic demand, certain inventions, like that of photography, ultimately transform not only art and information but also the societies in which they appear. Just as Gutenberg's typographic inventions spread the written word throughout the Western world, so did the application of photographic technologies to printing make possible the mass distribution of images. The transformations of still photography into the motion picture, television, and digitized images via the computer have made us the most visually oriented society in human history.

Curiously, the invention of still photography was encouraged by the Bavarian Aloys Senefelder's discovery of lithography in 1796. Nicéphore Niépce, a practicing French lithographer familiar with the chemistry of producing planographic plates, wanted nothing less than to automate the copying of engravings. His first impressive success, in 1822, was the reproduction of a line print of which he intended to sell copies. Ten years later, the English scientist William Henry Fox Talbot, frustrated by his inability to draw a landscape even with the aid of an artist's prism, wanted nothing less than to automate the recording of nature. Niépce led to Daguerre, Talbot to paper negatives and paper prints and all subsequent developments in photographic technologies. Prophetic of future mercantile advertising, Talbot's *The Pencil of Nature* (1844–1846), the first book illustrated with mounted paper prints, resembled a commercial catalogue rather than an art enterprise, for in it he displayed everything he believed the "sun drawing" process could reproduce: copies of text pages, copies of engravings, pictures of sculptures, of glassware, of shelves of books — in other words, anything that light could illuminate and chemicals could record. By itself, early negative-positive paper photography did not alter design. Mounted photographic-print illustrations, while different in content and appearance from etchings, engravings, or any other intaglio process, were nevertheless simply additions that had, somehow, to be incorporated into a bound book. Any process that could not be printed simultaneously with relief-metal or wood type demanded special (and expensive) treatment by publishers, at least until lithography made it possible to combine words and images on planographic surfaces.

Lithography was in wide use by the third decade of the nineteenth century. Combined with various photo-technologies, it had a tremendous impact on book design. Unfortunately, the autographic qualities of lithography led to a reckless abandoning of traditional layouts, especially in text design and letter forms. In the 1880s and 1890s these often raucous liberties carried over to designs incorporating the newly invented screened halftone process photoengravings used for the reproduction of photographs. For publishers — the employers of designers — screened halftone plates meant freedom from the relatively expensive wood engravings that had dominated newspaper as well as book illustration. Photo-technologies vied one with the other for commercial success in often cutthroat competition. At the height of their powers of reproduction, wood-engravers found themselves technologically unemployed; they were perforce slower and therefore more expensive than photo-engravers. There was so much technological innovation in graphic reproduction that by the beginning of the twentieth century a full-fledged media war can be said to have been staged, fought, and won by both lithography and photography. Thanks to various transfer techniques, by which a freshly inked page of type could be imprinted on a lithographic stone and then simultaneously printed with an artist's drawing, the problem of combining text and picture for ease and economy of printing in one press was permanently solved.

The development of lithographic color techniques was rapid. By the 1840s chromolithography was in high gear. Essentially a hand process requiring exact registration of multiple plates, it found its apotheosis in books of the English designer

and writer Owen Jones and, later, in the posters of designers such as Jules Chéret, Toulouse-Lautrec, Will Bradley, and Theophile-Alexandre Steinlen. But by 1900 the glorious chromolithographic posters that had adorned kiosks and walls throughout the major cities of Europe and America had been vanquished by offset lithography. The children's books, valentines, merchants' cards, and omnibus-carriage cards — many of them handsomely designed by the artists who worked for chromolithographic firms such as Louis Prang — were challenged by the new three- and four-color halftone process printed by offset. If graphic designers were to defend themselves against technological unemployment, they had to acquire new skills. What they had to do first was to understand the new technologies and the new presses, as well as the new process inks used for four-color reproduction. It was not until the 1940s, however, that the ingenious Bradbury Thompson separated the idea of four-color process inks from that of screened process halftones and created bold double spreads for *Westvaco Inspirations*, the West Virginia Pulp and Paper Company's journal displaying its printing papers. In that influential publication Thompson printed black-and-white illustrations separately in each of the four-color process inks, moving the repeated images around the page to invoke the idea of motion. He had an exceptional knowledge of the history of typography, and was sympathetic to the Bauhaus emphasis on sans-serif typefaces such as Futura. The Bauhaus master Herbert Bayer also believed that capital letters should be abolished, and Thompson, his acolyte, agreed that there were, in reality, *two* alphabets: uppercase (or capital letters) and lowercase. Nevertheless, Thompson's designs for what he called Alphabet 26, while of considerable influence and artistic interest, failed to revolutionize typography.

During World War I photographic images were reproduced by rotogravure, an ungracious medium that coupled text and picture in an intaglio screened process suitable for the huge newspaper presses that had been developing along with paper manufacturing. And while this mass-media expansion of the reproduction and distribution of words and images transmitted floods of information and pseudo-information to a greedy public, graphic design languished. The advertising pages of magazines such as *Collier's*, for example, were gaudy, often so dominated by photography that the editorial matter increasingly relied upon drawings and paintings for the sake of contrast.

While still photography, interpreted or reproduced by screened halftone processes, continued to dominate book and magazine publication, billboards, and posters, another medium was achieving an unexpected maturity and artistic potential: the cinema. The Lumière brothers, Auguste and Louis, had perfected the silent motion picture as early as 1895, but it was not until D.W. Griffith directed *Birth of a Nation* (1915) and *Intolerance* (1916), with their epic panoramas, rhythmic counterpoints, structural

Using the stylistic flourishes of Art Nouveau, Will Bradley's posters for *The Chap-Book* — an avant-garde literary and art magazine of the 1890s — typify America's late-Victorian graphic style.

Will Bradley
The Blue Lady December 1894
chromolithograph
18 7/8 x 13 1/4
and
The Twins May 1894
chromolithograph
19 1/2 x 13 1/2
Collection Norwest Corporation,
Minneapolis

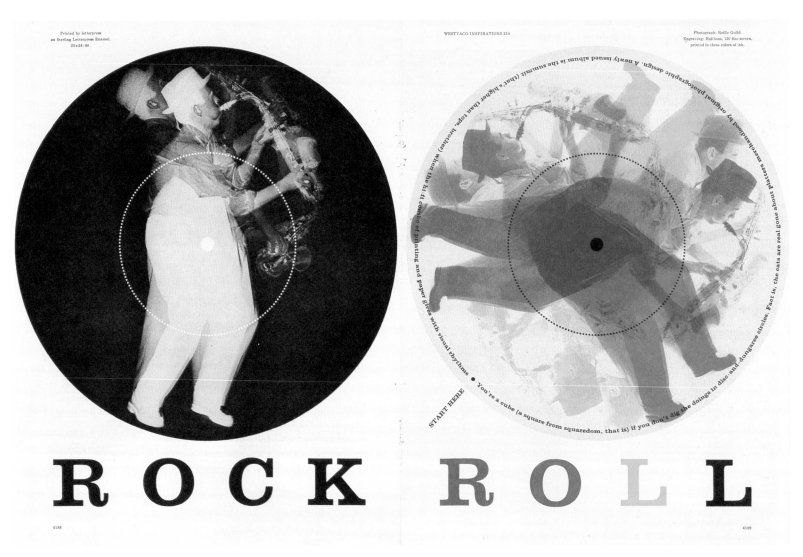

Printed by letterpress
on Sterling Letterpress Enamel.
25x38-80.

Photograph: Rolfe Guild.
Engraving: Halftone, 120 line screen,
printed in three colors of ink.

START HERE • You're a cube (a square from squaredom, that is) if you don't dig the doings in disc-and-dungaree circles. Fact is, the cats are real gone about platters meandering by original photographic design. A newly issued album is the summit (that's higher than tops, brother) when the hi-combo of printing and paper gives with visual rhythms

R O C K R O L L

4188

4189

Instead of the standard four-color separation process, in *Rock Roll* Bradbury Thompson uses one halftone plate printed first in black and opposite in three process inks. In this piece, and in a number of others of this period, Thompson uses the transparency of the colored inks to create a layering of images; here that overlapping implies the motion of a spinning record.

Bradbury Thompson
Westvaco Inspirations 210 1958
letterpress
12 x 9 format
Published by Westvaco Corporation, New York

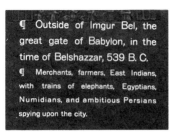

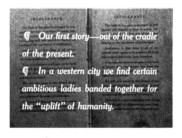

Title cards for D.W. Griffith's masterpiece *Intolerance* (1916) preceded the four sections of the film: 1) "The Babylonian Story;" 2) "The Judean Story;" 3) "The Medieval French Story;" 4) "The Modern Story." The title messages were superimposed on background images appropriate to each theme.

innovations, and narrative complexities, that cinema was recognized as having significant artistic potential.

With the motion picture came the need for the designer of what were called "title cards," those two-dimensional placards bearing typographic or hand-lettered dialogue, advertising messages and warnings, announcements and general information. Characteristically, Griffith went several steps beyond such relatively simple design requirements. For *Intolerance*, for example, he wanted different designs to precede each of the four sections of the film as these interwove with one another. So, for the narrative concerning ancient Babylon, the screen displayed text superimposed on Babylon's sculptural friezes; for the segment about the French Huguenot massacre of 1572, nothing would suffice but a background of fleur-de-lis overlaid with pompous Griffithian morals. While fascinating in myriad details, *Intolerance* was a visual hodge-podge, a graphic designer's nightmare created by the need to offer some visual clue as to which of the four stories was about to be continued.

In terms of visual effectiveness, the coming of sound was at first a technological catastrophe. Talking pictures were so feeble at first that actors literally had to cluster themselves within reach of the microphones. But the novelty of sound made such movies popular. As a result the visual sweep of silent films came to an abrupt, if temporary, end. It was not until sound technologies were vastly improved that other delights, such as the extravagantly designed musicals of the 1930s, could develop. Color film also offered new opportunities for dramatic design. In *Gone With the Wind* (1939), many scenes ended with a black silhouette of Scarlett O'Hara framed against a distant view of a faked Tara, bathed in the tangerine glow of a painted Southern sunset. In the 1950s the norm for B-movie main titles was the superimposition of letter forms over live action. Later, along with other increasingly sophisticated uses of color and hand-lettering, a cartoon Inspector Clouseau could pursue his pink cartoon prey through the zany intricacies of the credits in the Pink Panther comedies. Created by Hollywood animator Friz Freleng for the first film, *The Pink Panther* (1964), and designed for later productions such as *The Return of the Pink Panther* (1975) by the Richard Williams Studio in London, these credits constituted entire comic sequences in and of themselves.

For many well-established graphic designers, adapting to motion picture demands was something of a trial. Of his first encounter with designing movie credits, Saul Bass wrote: "A graphic and industrial designer heretofore, I now found myself confronted with a flickering, moving, elusive series of images that somehow had to add up to communication."[1] His striking credits for *The Man with the Golden Arm* (1955) and *Anatomy of a Murder* (1959) demonstrated the ingenuity of a brilliant graphic designer conquering the difficulties of a new medium. Bass introduced a modernist approach to sequences of images, all coordinated with music, with the rhythm of the

HONOR BLACKMAN
AS PUSSY GALORE

DIRECTOR OF PHOTOGRAPHY
TED MOORE B.S.C.

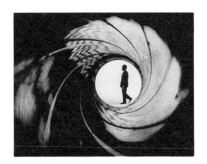

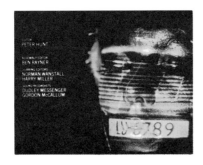

EDITOR
PETER HUNT

ASSEMBLY EDITOR
BEN RAYNER

DUBBING EDITORS
NORMAN WANSTALL
HARRY MILLER

SOUND RECORDISTS
DUDLEY MESSENGER
GORDON McCALLUM

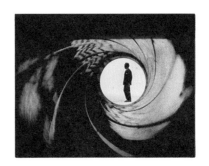

ASSISTANT DIRECTOR
FRANK ERNST

CAMERA OPERATOR
JOHN WINBOLT

CONTINUITY GIRL
CONSTANCE WILLIS

MAKE UP
PAUL RABIGER
BASIL NEWALL

ACTION SEQUENCES BY
BOB SIMMONS

opening scenes of each motion picture, and, usually, with billboard advertising as well. He encapsulated individual lines of type or lettering in bold cutout forms. For *Anatomy of a Murder* white type dropped out of silhouetted and abstract anatomical parts, all of which sprang to the screen in rhythm with Duke Ellington's jazz.

Bass was certainly a pioneer, yet it was the gaudy and titillating opening credits for the James Bond films of the 1960s that completed the shift from two-dimensional designs to three-dimensional illusionism. The most spectacular — and certainly the most talked about — credit designs for the Bond flicks were those for *Goldfinger* (1964), created by Robert Brownjohn. They featured a seminude woman glistening with gold paint who seemed transparent. The trick, later divulged to the press, was to project scenes and faces from the film itself directly onto her body. This startling image was preceded by the standard opening for the Bond adventures: the audience looks through the barrel of a revolver as if it were an enormous tunnel. The implied gun is aimed at Bond, who walks casually into sight. In an instant he whips around, his own gun blasting, as red "blood" courses down the screen, and the imaginary assailant sways and falls. This brief introduction served as a trademark for the invulnerability of the protagonist.

When the aspect ratio of movies — the relationship of image width to height — changed from 35mm to 70mm, and in ultrawide-screen formats such as Cinemascope, designers had new problems to solve. *The Boston Strangler* (1968), for example, exploited the new widths by using multiple split-screen effects, from the credits through to the end of the film. *The Robe* (1953), *The Ten Commandments* (1956), and other religious extravaganzas, may have been ultrawide and ultra-colorful, but their credit designs lurched backward toward the kitschy effects of D.W. Griffith. Technological splendor did not always bring graphic progress.

The ultrawide films were partly a response to the insidious encroachments of television, a medium the motion picture industry did its best to vilify, mock, and ignore. None of these stratagems worked. From the early 1950s on, television dominated America's attention. For graphic designers, the small screen, the weakness of image resolution, and the peculiar new technological vocabulary of the medium seemed irritatingly retrograde. *I Love Lucy* (1951–1957), with its vapid valentine heart filling the screen, or *I Dream of Jeannie* (1965–1970), introduced by linear cartoon figures, were hardly what Saul Bass might have wished for in new design. Designers discovered to their dismay that, while television posed as a visual medium, its early characteristics were largely auditory, more suited to the comic shenanigans of Jackie Gleason than to stirring vistas or epic battle scenes. The networks soon discovered that, in addition to live

Seen here in the title sequence for Albert Broccoli's *Goldfinger*, the view of 007 through the barrel of a revolver became, starting with *From Russia with Love* (1963), the standard opening for James Bond films.

Robert Brownjohn
Partial title sequence for *Goldfinger*
Goldfinger © 1964 Danjaq S.A.
All rights reserved
Gun Logo Symbol © Danjaq S.A.
and United Artists Company, 1962

1. Saul Bass, "Movement, Film, Communication," in Gyorgy Kepes, ed., *Sign, Image, Symbol* (New York: George Braziller, 1966), 200.

113

newsworthy events, what played best on the tube was film, and Hollywood swiftly accommodated itself to the making of television movies of often dubious artistic value. As the medium matured, graphic designers who had a gift for visual sequences marked by sharp timing, a striking rhythm of graphics coordinated with music, and an appreciation for the drama of human movements and gestures as backgrounds for, or in combination with, graphics, were increasingly successful. However, what they had learned from designing for the photographic medium of film was a vocabulary of effects only partly appropriate for the electronic medium of television.

Design for motion took a giant step forward with Stanley Kubrick's film *2001* (1968), particularly in the climactic "Jupiter and beyond the Infinite" sequence, a fantastic voyage hurtling the viewer through an eye-boggling display of color pyrotechnics. Slit-scan filming, with its exceedingly complex technology, would be responsible for the later propagation of many of television's most intriguing credits effects, especially animations such as the titles for weekly movie slots. R/Greenberg Associates would later use slit-scan exposure techniques for the main titles of the film *The Untouchables* (1987). With such dynamic titles, which stress diagonal movements into space and out again toward the spectator, graphic designers had obviously departed from the traditions of the flat page, with its organization of typography and images inside a rectangle. This was "Goodbye, Gutenberg!" with a vengeance. But even moving, three-dimensional designs based on the achievements of Kubrick's film technology were only portents of what was to come with computer graphic design and computer-aided animation.

A mountainous landscape created by fractal geometry (a way of depicting nongeometric forms mathematically): numbers and numbers alone programmed into a specialized image-generating computer. Metallic dinosaurs roam a bleak horizon. Transparent sparrows fly through a glassy sky filled with shimmering globes. The eye effortlessly skims across skeins of wired connections into a futuristic living room. Obviously, the computer artist-technicians sitting at their consoles with an array of keyboards and computer menus have at their disposal an astonishing range of effects. In *Young Sherlock Holmes* (1985), for example, a knight in armor, part of a stained glass window in a church, suddenly begins to move. Then the knight jumps from the window, wielding an enormous sword, and moves in three dimensions toward a terrified priest, a real-life actor. Walt Disney Studios's *Who Framed Roger Rabbit* (1988), of course, represents the more humorous side of this live actor-computer combination.

The graphic designers themselves may not necessarily manipulate the wonders of the computer keyboard, although they must know what to expect from it. Their talents are needed to create the storyboard, a hand-drawn visual sequence organizing image and words into the patterns of the story that guide the camera or the computer technician in frame-by-frame detail. Graphic designers visualize each step in

With the advent of computer animation, graphics such as these for the film *Superman* became an option explored very early by R/Greenberg Associates. Because of its amusing "streamlined" movement and variety, this sequence of extremely extensive credits holds the viewer's attention.

R/Greenberg Associates, Inc.
Partial title sequence for *Superman*
© 1978 Film Export A.G.

the story, promotion, or advertisement, and provide specific instructions as to color and directions of movement. Many computer animations have the visual complexity of an M.C. Escher drawing, coupled not only with intense colorations but also with variations in motion through three-dimensional space. And the computer continues to increase its spectacular ability to rotate imagined objects, turn them inside out, expand them, deflate them, color them, transform them into other objects or animals, fling them toward infinity, and return them magically transformed into total environments.

A peculiarity of graphic design in any medium is that the end product is not visible until the design elements have been reproduced. The mechanical for a magazine illustration may consist of a basic outline on pasteup board on which several overlays have been mounted, each supplying a few words to be printed, say, in red, the next in blue; photostats show where photographs are to be inserted. Finally, a tissue overlay presents as close an idea of the finished work as is possible. To turn this mélange into print requires skillful coordination by camera personnel, platemaker, and printer. Finally, when the plates are completed, inked, and run through presses that may be sixty feet long with multiple rollers and colors, pieces of paper appear printed with the advertisement or editorial display. The realization of the graphic design occurs only through replication technologies requiring enormous capital investments.

Perhaps nothing better demonstrates the economic requirements of advanced graphic design for motion pictures than the productions of R/Greenberg Associates. With spectacular mid-Manhattan facilities, this firm combines specialized visual talents with state-of-the-art technologies that are immensely more complex and capital intensive than the average production house can afford. With these technologies it has created ingenious advertisements — for AT&T, Kodak, and IBM, among others — as well as eye-catching motion picture titles, credits, and advertising trailers for films such as *Superman* (1978), *Alien* (1979), *All That Jazz* (1979), *Ragtime* (1981), *Tootsie* (1982), *Gandhi* (1982), *The World According to Garp* (1982), *Back to the Future* (1985), and *Dirty Dancing* (1987). To produce the special effects in these titles and trailers, R/Greenberg commands the following technologies, as described in its promotional brochure: the Oxberry CompuQuad, "the only fully computerized optical printing facility reserved exclusively for in-house work;" the Elicon Camera Control System, combining "the flexibility of live-action animation;" the digital-imaging system includes the Evans & Sutherland Multi-Picture System, and Ikonas Raster Graphics System with "real time capabilities and over 16 million colors simultaneously" available.[2] There has been some criticism that the capital investments required for such instrumentations have

2. R/Greenberg Associates, *Moving Pictures. By Design,* brochure (New York: R/Greenberg Associates, 1987), unpaginated.

led to an elitist aristocracy of designers, a kind of monopoly, with little of this munificence of design capability available to the average graphic designer.

No technological innovation is better than the imagination using it, and it may be that the extraordinary technological advantages described above can invite graphic complexity beyond what is needed for a particular production. The dazzling opening credits for *Dirty Dancing* are a good example. In subdued grainy grays, writhing dancers, interrupted by an intervalometer (a device that regulates the opening of the camera shutter) or similar animation technique, dominate the screen and are wonderfully sexy. Superimposed on the dancers are the vivid pink letters of the title. The avant-garde energy displayed here, however, is abruptly dissipated by the film, which quickly proves itself to be realistic, undirty, and even rather gentle. At the end, the opening sequence is repeated with the title. No matter how much we can admire what was achieved for *Dirty Dancing*'s titles, it is obvious that they have a very different feeling and rhythm than the film, and a totally different look. R/Greenberg's brilliantly appropriate designs for the ominous *Alien* and the fantastic *Superman*, on the other hand, did much to set the mood for those movies. A legitimate question therefore can be raised as to the visual and emotional relationship that credits should have to the films they introduce.

Tibor Kalman, founder of M&Co., another adventurous graphic design house, categorically asserts that "if done properly, titles can contribute to the point of view the director wants to achieve. . . . You have to understand how to create the mood the director wants and, at the same time, do your job, which is putting the names in front of the film."[3] His title sequences for Jonathan Demme's *Something Wild* (1986) and *Swimming to Cambodia* (1987), David Byrne's *True Stories* (1986), and especially the end titles for John Sayles's *Matewan* (1987) have all excited critical attention. He makes claim to be a "practiced imperfectionist," since he has observed that "designers are taught [that] elegance is beautiful. I don't find it refreshing any more, partially because everyone's gotten to be so good. . . . Everything is now nice. It puts me to sleep." This may explain why M&Co.'s end credits for Catlin Adams's *Sticky Fingers* (1988), instead of marching along in vertical perfection, roll up the screen like sluggish snakes. Such graphic innovations may seem "kicky," but they hardly do justice to the movie crews for whom credits are all-important and must be legible. For a Talking Heads video, "(Nothing But) Flowers" (1988), Kalman, truly an enfant terrible of the graphic design industry, superimposed lyrics over the face of the group's lead singer, David Byrne. Kicky or not, this kind of design relies upon advanced technological skills and instrumentation of an expensive, complex variety. The work of both the R/Greenberg and M&Co. groups

For the titles of Jonathan Demme's film *Something Wild*, M&Co.'s Tibor Kalman and Alexander Isley created a multicolored idiosyncratic typography that is seen over views of Manhattan.

M&Co.
Partial title sequence for *Something Wild*
© 1986 Orion Pictures Corporation, Los Angeles

3. Quoted in John Leroy Calhoun, "Where Credit Is Due: The Heads and Tails of Title Design," *Theatre Crafts* 21, 7 (August–September 1987): 79.

comprises evidence of the increasing demand for electronically based dazzlements to overwhelm the viewer.

In a real sense, graphic design is a type of conceptual art. The *idea* for a design in any medium is *unique*; its realization is through technologically produced artifacts that are multiples, distributed to large audiences. This multiplicity of reproduction has generated the primary objection to accepting graphic design as a "fine" art. Acutely aware of this kind of condemnation, Paul Rand, one of America's most influential designers, has argued vehemently that "the designer's work, like any good artist's, is unique. He produces one design, one advertisement, one poster, even though his work gives birth to countless reproductions — no different from the *one painting* that is reproduced in numerous art books and catalogs."[4] Even accepting this statement, it is still possible for critics to assert that it is the essentially commercial function of graphic design that denies it the status of "art." Graphic design, they insist, is primarily devoted to advertising, to selling commodities by sometimes unethical psychological persuasions. Furthermore, anything that requires so many technological manipulations must be considered a craft rather than an art. If the human hand is not observed to have been operating in the creation of an image, they conclude, it cannot be accepted as fine art.

Marcel Duchamp offered a way out of this dilemma by suggesting that art is anything that is regarded in an art context. While this suggestion resembles the fallacy of tautology, what it simply implies is that it is possible to judge any object from the point of view of aesthetics. Typographic forms, for example, can provide aesthetic satisfaction both in themselves and in the appropriateness of their fonts for a particular design. The configurations of images and words can achieve clarity and beauty in the hands of designers who exploit a reproductive technology with creativity. Indeed, William Blake, that inventor of techniques to integrate words and images, that poet-painter of vibrant pages, that seer of prophetic visions, perhaps unexpectedly believed that mechanical excellence is the only vehicle of genius. It is inherent in graphic design that the technologies of its reproduction and multiplication influence aesthetic ideology; and it is only by accepting the limitations and opportunities of those technologies that genius can emerge.

Estelle Jussim is the author of Visual Communication and the Graphic Arts *(1974);* Slave to Beauty *(1981);* Stopping Time *(1988); and* The Eternal Moment *(1989), a complete collection of her essays. She is a professor on the graduate faculty at Simmons College, Boston.*

4. Quoted in John Kouwenhoven, *Half a Truth Is Better Than None* (University of Chicago Press, 1982), xiii.

Richard and Robert Greenberg

[born 1947 and 1948]

Even the Futurists would not have imagined the advent of motion graphics when their first manifesto was published in 1908. Nor could those Bauhaus masters such as Moholy-Nagy, who appreciated the potentials of film, ever have dreamed that such graphic tricks as image enhancement, matting, or flying and streaking letter forms would be possible on film. And neither could Saul Bass have anticipated the remarkable computer aids that would have made his stark film animations so simple to produce. In 1977, when Richard and Robert Greenberg, started R/Greenberg Associates in New York to make graphic design techniques come alive on film, they realized the need for advanced technology to achieve the unprecedented effects they were after. For each project the Greenbergs invent tools to realize their visions. The firm is described by its founders as a mini-Bauhaus, an intimate mixture of craft and creativity with science and technology. Though the work is diverse — including television commercials, film titles, industrial films, and videos — the overriding sensibility derives from classic modern design principles. In a field where visual clichés abound, the Greenbergs successfully transcend convention.

By panning a motion-control camera over the wiggling body of a baby lying on a white background and combining those images with shots of a cloud-filled sky, R/Greenberg Associates created an amazing and touching film opening.

Partial title sequence for *The World According to Garp*
© 1982 Warner Bros. Inc., Burbank, California

Richard: When I was a student at the University of Illinois one of my teachers showed me books on Swiss and German graphic design; the one that most influenced me was Emil Ruder's *Typographie* [1967], because in it I discovered a very systematic approach that was also quite beautiful.

My film work began one summer between my fourth and fifth years at the university. I had the idea that since letter forms have implied motion, it would be interesting to make movement of those forms. So I bought a Bolex movie camera and cut some letter forms apart and filmed them as I moved them around. I realized that typography could have an emotional and filmic quality. In a film title such as the one we made for *Alien* [1979], we apply that graphic thinking. The title is a kind of sequential Swiss poster. Combined with the proper music, pure type has an emotional impact and can make one feel joy, fear, or heartache.

There is a direct parallel between graphic design with a two-dimensional image and graphic design with a three-dimensional illusion. The primary difference is that film unfolds over time, while a poster must give the information in one take. So a film designer has to know how to keep building suspense without giving away the story.

Robert: Another aspect of time is the issue of speed. At twenty-four frames per

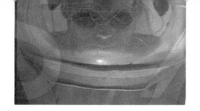

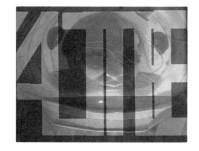

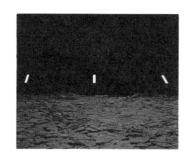

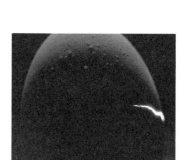

Executive Producer **Daniel Melnick**

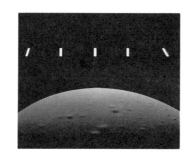

ALIEN

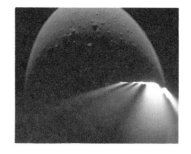

LTEREDSTATE

Produced by **Howard Gottfried**

120

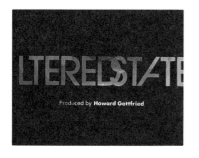

second one has to think in terms of how the image will read on the big screen, which is different from seeing a still image through a projector. There are a lot of different rules in film design as opposed to print, but there are also a lot of rules to be broken.

In film, an idea must be pared down to its essentials. What *Altered States* [1980] showed, for example, was just a big, grotesque, sans-serif face that looked like one of the chapter headings in Emil Ruder's book. The impact came from what was done with it emotionally and from what was not shown.

Our early work was done with very simple tools. Now the content and quality of our work is greatly affected by new, complex technologies. Computers came into play first not as a creative tool but as a way of being able to control information and memory and as a means to do something in hours that would otherwise take days. We moved from graphic design and animation to optical printing — which meant that we could merge graphics with graphics on one piece of negative — to optical printing with live action, eventually moving into motion control, which is a robotic device that controls the live-action camera. We just recently opened up digital video post-production, merging three fields that connect to design applications and integration possibilities; computer-assisted filmmaking with cameras.

Richard: But technology is simply the means to an end. We don't have people who are exclusively technicians. We train visual artists in technology, and they are directly involved in our work. We also spend much of our time trying to discover or invent the best way to solve a problem but do not want the technology showing in the final piece. If the viewer is aware of the technology, the image doesn't work. When the viewer is not aware of the hidden technology, the image is warmer, more luminous. For example, the close-ups of the flying baby in the titles for *The World According to Garp* [1982] would have been impossible before the computer. (It would have been against the law actually to throw a baby!)

Our design philosophy was constant from the beginning. What we do at our best is allow the viewer access to the movie. For example, when we made the titles for a film called *Blow Out* [1981], which is about a sound editor who hears some gunshots while editing a recording, we had decided on an idea that was simply decorative typography, but it just didn't work for me. Ultimately, the image I wanted was a close-up of the gauge line on a sound meter, an entirely different concept, one that was more revealing of the story the film would tell. The first was conventional design, the second contributed to the telling of the story.

Robert: Sometimes our ideas are ahead of our technical capabilities. We sold our *Superman* [1978] titles by presenting frames that showed streaking light, which gave the impression of speed coming from the letters. Once we sold the idea, there was a lot of scurrying around to figure out how to do it. It was a week to ten days of panic! There were no rules. That's why I don't believe in film schools, and/or editors who say you're crossing over the line, because once you do it wrong, and it works, then the rule doesn't matter any more. Whenever possible we try to get the designers to become more technically astute and the engineers and the technicians to become more sensitive to design.

The important thing is interaction between people in various disciplines. We have eighty-some-odd people on the staff, and many free-lance people we bring in for specific jobs. Each area that we're in could be a separate company, so to integrate it and have a common design philosophy is very difficult. But the concept of having everything under one roof is very important to us. Without it one can lose the creative thrust that holds the entity together.

In the titles for *Altered States*, live-action shots of the actor William Hurt are seen through abstract shapes that only very slowly emerge to become the letters of the film's title. The opening for *Alien* is similarly mysterious; white blocks gradually become letter forms as the audience watches an oval egg crack open to emit an eerie, otherworldly light.

Partial title sequence for *Altered States*
© 1980 Warner Bros. Inc., Burbank, California

Partial title sequence for *Alien*
© 1979 Twentieth Century Fox Film Corporation, Beverly Hills, California

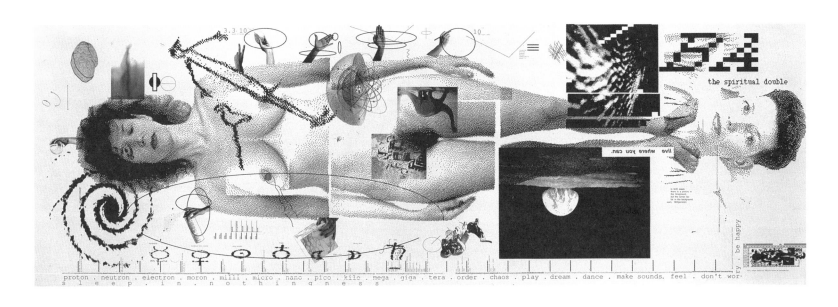

the spiritual double

live where you can.

rry . be happy

proton . neutron . electron . moron . milli . micro . nano . pico . kilo . mega . giga . tera . order . chaos . play . dream . dance . make sounds . feel . don't wor

sleep . in . nothingness

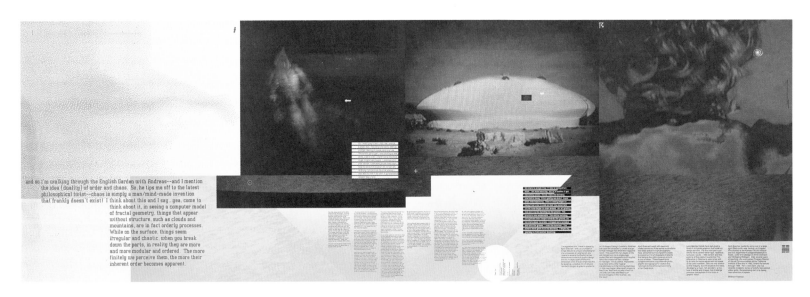

and so I'm walking through the English Garden with Andreas--and I mention the idea (duality) of order and chaos. So, he tips me off to the latest philosophical twist--chaos is simply a man/mind-made invention that frankly doesn't exist! I think about this and I say...yea, come to think about it, in seeing a computer model of fractal geometry, things that appear without structure, such as clouds and mountains, are in fact orderly processes. While on the surface, things seem irregular and chaotic, when you break down the parts, in reality they are more and more modular and ordered. The more finitely we perceive them, the more their inherent order becomes apparent.

April Greiman

[born 1948]

The doyenne of computer-generated design and a courageous visual experimenter, April Greiman is an inspiration for a generation of designers whose tools are advancing at hurricane speed. During a period of continual change in all the arts, Greiman is expanding the boundaries of graphic presentation and, hence, its perception. Both forward and backward thinking are perfectly acceptable today, meaning that the rules by which design was once practiced are completely blurred. The computer has upset the equilibrium by making possible myriad effects that were never before available to the studio designer. The question of how best to integrate this new technology into the creative process has been difficult, yet Greiman deftly attempts reconciliation by pushing the limits of legibility and accessibility. Using the classic syntax of graphic design, which she learned at the Basle School of Design, Greiman allows herself — and many of her clients allow her — great freedom to create.

In this issue of *Design Quarterly*, April Greiman has used the computer to create a large-format montage that denies the magazine format. The usual thirty-two pages of this magazine are reorganized into a single-page, foldout poster filled with ideograms and thoughts about the creation of humankind — a large-format topic!

Design Quarterly 133 1986
"Does It Make Sense?"
25 1/2 x 75 3/4
Published by The MIT Press for
Walker Art Center

After working in New York for a few years in the early 1970s I became a bit frustrated with the lack of ideas and the wall-to-wall printing typical of much of the design industry. Sometimes you could smell a job in your mailbox — "Ah, a new brochure." I began to feel that many things that I was seeing were all form and no content. That propelled me toward a more open environment, and I moved to Los Angeles in 1976.

When I first went to the West Coast I had so little work and such low rent that I started to paint and make color Xeroxes and collage — personal things — for quite a few years. I was very influenced spiritually and culturally by L.A., by the art scene and also the entertainment business.

In the early 1980s I became director of visual communications at the California Institute of the Arts, and because it was a great interdisciplinary environment I started working in the area of video and computer graphics. I was questioning what the quality and texture of the image on the page could be. Many people were afraid of the computer, but I found it to be somehow very soft and inspiring emotionally. Then I began to have connections with high-tech computer companies such as Pearlsoft, which was one of the first personal computer software companies, Windfarms, a

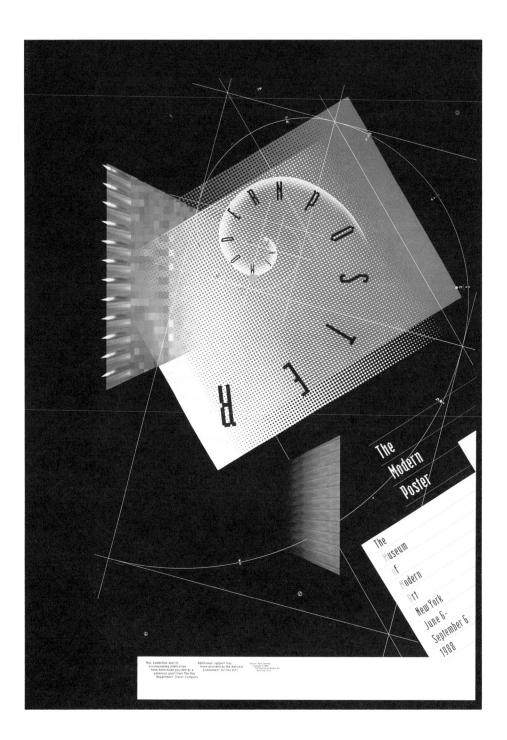

The (di-zīn') mark was created by Greiman in the mid-1980s for a furniture, lighting, and accessory shop in Los Angeles.

In 1981 Greiman developed an identity scheme for the Los Angeles restaurant China Club that included a logotype and various ephemera, such as matchbooks and menus.

For a 1988 exhibition at The Museum of Modern Art in which an overview of the twentieth-century poster was presented, Greiman used a variety of new technologies to create the poster image.

The Modern Poster
39 x 25
© 1988 The Museum of Modern
Art, New York

large-scale wind energy development corporation in San Francisco, and Interac, which was an early interactive video corporation.

I was trying to make a three-dimensional statement in two dimensions, to incorporate time and space. Even now, I still apply most high-end paint boxes with video imagery in traditional ways to all kinds of problems. For example, I may use the Macintosh computer to develop a logo, but ultimately it is typeset. The client is unaware that the workhorse in that process was a computer. Computer technology is a wonderfully profound tool for collapsing all kinds of seemingly disparate kinds of disciplines (including traditional ones) into one language, one digital language. It's a hybridizing process, a means of bringing together a diversity of technologies and imagery. On the one hand it's very good for linear thinking, but it also has a way of suggesting new and unexpected ideas.

In the last few years I've been applying new technology and expression in the area of poster-making. A 1988 poster for The Museum of Modern Art is a good example; it's based on the idea that television is the new poster. I used a television screen as an icon and generated the central image, which was a gradation, by using Image Studio, a good

Macintosh retouching program. Then I laser-scanned that into the graphic paint box at super-fine resolution. I videotaped some landscapes, went back to an editing bay, and made video-feedback shots; then I froze the videotape and shot off the monitor. That image was then scanned back into the video paint box to be distorted into a perspective shape, and finally downloaded into the graphic paint box.

The genius of the graphic paint box is that it's designed to communicate with print technology. So while I'm working on a giant monitor, a small monitor breaks down the image into four-process colors. On the small monitor I can select an area and change its color. I can go out not only to film but to videotape or to printing plates.

One result of this hybridizing investigation is a project with the architect Barton Myers: nine tile building roofs for a theater in Cerritos, at the very far reaches of L.A. I spent most of the budget cutting and pasting with colored paper to make a special illusion happen within the pattern. But I also worked with landscape images on the graphic paint box. Some wonderful things are going to happen on those roofs. I want to take some of the forms and break them down so that they disappear into the atmosphere, or change shape, depending on the light and what's happening in the sky.

There are other people working in their own new ways, of course. The whole electronic revolution is so much more powerful than any of us can even begin to comprehend. I like looking at the work of very young designers and wishing I had done it! Furthermore, I'd like to see people sharing resources. Every designer does not need to have a laser printer, sixteen computers, and a stat camera — it's such a waste. More designers should share space, share resources. Sort of an upscale communism.

Design in the Service of Commerce

Maud Lavin

General Electric has not striated its trademark. The corporate design logic that has given Prudential's symbol the look of universal cost-code bars and has abstracted other company logos out of recognition is less evident with GE. Indeed, despite its recent, global-scale corporate identity program — researched and designed by Landor Associates from 1986 to 1988, with implementation beginning in 1988 — General Electric has essentially retained its original logo. Citing the universal recognizability of the corporation's trademark monogram, Landor recommended altering only a few curlicues. What the designers changed instead was the trademark's "visual environment," that is, the graphics surrounding it. This focus is characteristic of the evolution of corporate identity programs; following the lead of IBM (and other precursors, such as Olivetti and the Container Corporation of America), it is now the norm for multinationals to seek to control their environment visually in order to communicate omniscience and stability.[1] But while this has come to be standard practice, GE's new identity program has expertly refined a particular psychological aspect of the design challenge: it links the corporation's claim of all-knowingness to the celebration of the corporation as an individual.

In general, the 1980s has been a period during which advertising and design have increasingly promoted corporations (and products as their stand-ins) as sanctified individuals. Such promotion entails more than simply giving a company a personality: it involves ascribing to the company a hyper-individualism, a supremacy as an individual above society. Some dictionary definitions of individualism already conflate personal conduct with economic theory; the word has come to denote "the leading of one's life in one's own way without regard for others," and laissez-faire economics, "the

Landor Associates
Tractor-trailer graphics for
GE lighting using the "Dynamic
Monogram" 1986–1988
Creative Director: Tom Suiter
Project Director: Don Bartels
Designers: Karl Martens, Rebecca
Oliver, Randall Dowd,
Virginia Zimmerman

---

1. Adrian Forty, *Objects of Desire: Design and Society from Wedgwood to IBM* (New York: Pantheon Books, 1986).

127

doctrine that individual freedom in economic enterprise should not be restricted by governmental or social regulation."[2] With the increased implementation of corporate identity programs, advertising and design in the service of commerce have become more explicit and skilled in practicing this conflation. As we live in a society already worshipful of individualism, it is important to ask how this picture of the corporation as an idealized individual is conveyed and how it has evolved, how it has affected the design profession, and how certain designers have tried to work outside its framework to address social issues.

In advertising, a range of visual strategies has been used to personify the corporation. We can see the expert application of one such strategy by looking more closely at the Landor/GE logo. What is innovative about it is that GE has employed design not only to mark the company as an individual but also to identify that individual as the father. Lacanian psychoanalytic theory leads us to recognize that any time authority and regulation are transmitted through the use of a proper name, what is invoked is the name of the father; in this sense most corporate names and logos can be classified as paternalistic. In the case of GE, however, it is important to notice how the entire visual environment has been mobilized to enhance this kind of paternalism.

The visual sign of this paternalism, in GE/Landor language, is called the "dynamic monogram." Accompanying the familiar round and self-enclosed logo is a projection of that same logo, enlarged so greatly that either one-quarter or three-quarters of the sign — depending on which version the given vendor wishes to use — is visible; the rest bleeds off the edges. The dynamic monogram, which appears in light tones, cannot be contained by borders; it looks like a shadow thrown by a giant GE logo looming outside the frame. The design is consistently used on packaging, trucks, ads, signage, and stationery, creating oversized graphic fragments that implicitly place the viewer in the position of a child. In both its size and ubiquity this projection of the logo connotes the role of the archetypal father, promising safety and protection through the authority of his name. The symbolism of Landor's dynamic monogram of course fits neatly into the concurrent BBDO (Batten, Barton, Durstine and Osborn Worldwide, Inc.) ad campaign, particularly the slogan characterizing GE as procreator: "We bring good things to living. We bring good things to life."

If the goal of an identity program is to communicate corporate individualism and paternalism simultaneously, then the Landor design is an especially felicitous one for the promotion of GE's consumer goods, home appliances, medical technology, and aerospace industries. Domesticity and technology are spheres in which paternalism is generally deemed acceptable.

2. See, for example, *Webster's New World Dictionary of the American Language* (Cleveland: World Publishing Company, 1966), 743.

In tracing the development of the kind of corporate identity that the GE logo represents it is necessary to begin by asking a large and complex question: How have graphic design and advertising treated issues related to the individualism that is an integral part of American culture? In answering this question we should not necessarily assume that advertising is received exactly in the spirit it is pitched. Indeed, the sociologist Michael Schudson has argued that the opposite is true, that advertising fails to persuade the American public. Instead, he claims, advertisers merely follow and encourage existing buying trends.[3] However, the main focus of the present essay is on ideology rather than on sales figures, on the significance of the methods and messages designers use to connect corporate interests with those of society and with those of the individual.

In order to clarify such complex subjects as individualism and ideology in this context, a few historical markers are needed. Additionally, it is necessary to recognize that advertising is not able simply to celebrate individualism. For its primary task, the promotion of products on a mass scale, is not always congruent with the promotion of individualism. In fact, tension between the individual and a mass of people has been inherent in much of twentieth-century advertising. Ads are pitched to individual consumers with the implication that the product will make each buyer better and special. At the same time, ads must reach as many people as possible and exhort them to act in an identical way (i.e., to buy the product). Still, acting the same is different from acting in concert, and advertising has long been and can still be criticized for promoting individualistic behavior as opposed to cooperative action. Given that general criticism, issues of individualism can be seen as central to three periods in American advertising during this century: 1) the 1930s, during which the grim effects of the 1929 stock market crash took hold, ending what had been a period of unparalleled economic growth and consumer purchasing power; 2) the 1950s, characterized by the buying sprees of postwar prosperity, conformism in the interest of business and country, and labor unrest; and 3) the 1980s, a period of conservative, pro-business government during which the identities and images of United States-based multinational corporations have been solidified as never before in the face of serious threats to American economic hegemony.

In his book *Captains of Consciousness*, the sociologist and historian Stuart Ewen finds that advertising functioned as early as the 1920s to aid "the business community ... setting up itself, or its personified corporate self, as a model for emulation.... The authority of industry was being drawn as a sustaining *father* figure while the traditional arenas of social intercourse and the possibility of collective action were

Chiat/Day, Inc., Los Angeles
Apple Computer introductory
commercial for the Macintosh 1984
Film Director: Ridley Scott
Creative Director: Lee Clow
Art Director: Brent Thomas
Copywriter: Steve Hayden

3. Michael Schudson, *Advertising: The Uneasy Persuasion* (New York: Basic Books, 1984).

pictured as decrepit, threatening and basically incapable of providing any level of security."[4] Similarly, the cultural critic Raymond Williams accuses advertising of promoting a hyper-individualism and a turn away from communal action.[5] Yet the historian Roland Marchand, in his survey of American advertising from 1920 to 1940, finds that advertising during that period addressed anxieties produced by modernization and shows that the preaching of consumerism functioned not only to sell products but also to "re-personalize" American life and finesse the complexities of national scale. Implicit in Marchand's approach is the premise that advertising underscores the contradictions between the experiences of an individual and the mass focus inherent in modernization.[6]

Indeed, in surveying print ads of the 1920s and early 1930s a dual appeal to the individual and to the community can often be found. In some instances the idea of community is directly tied to the corporation — the corporation as a substitute for other forms of community. But in others community is celebrated as a valuable social organization in and of itself. Two ads that appeared in *Fortune* magazine during 1930 illustrate these trends. In the first one, for United Hotels, the organization of the hotel chain is likened to that of large-scale steel and automobile companies. Graphics and copy combine to summon up the image of the chain as the community of the future. The drawing shows blocks of city buildings towering upward, illuminated by beams of light, with modern block type breaking in from below. The headline, which must have held appeal in light of the recent stock market crash, reads: "UNITED FORTUNES." The ad copy promises both "centralized control and supervision" and inspired service by individuals, which, it claims, cannot be standardized.[7] In such ways advertising during the Great Depression alluded to frictions among the individual, the community, and the corporation. Yet what is troubling about the United ad is its suggestion that the whole range of issues surrounding the identity of an individual in a community can be resolved within a framework that relates the individual exclusively to the corporation.

The second *Fortune* ad, for the H.K. McCann advertising company, also seeks to make the notion of community fall within a corporate definition. The ad stands out for us today because of its misguided tribute to Italian fascism, which is part of its larger call for collective behavior. Underneath a drawing of a bundle of rods, the headline "Fascisti All!" is followed by: "The bundle of rods which is on the United States ten cent piece; the red strapped fasces that lay over the left shoulder of the Roman

Designer unknown
Advertisement for United Hotels
Company of America
Fortune February 1930
p. 15: 13 x 10 1/4
© Time, Inc., New York

4. Stuart Ewen, *Captains of Consciousness: Advertising and the Roots of Consumer Culture* (New York: McGraw-Hill, 1976), 102.
5. Raymond Williams, "The Magic System," idem, *Problems in Materialism and Culture* (London: Verso, 1980), 170–195.
6. Roland Marchand, *Advertising the American Dream: Making Way for Modernity, 1920–1940* (Berkeley: University of California Press, 1985).
7. *Fortune* 1, 1 (February 1930): 15.

"...and I'll live like a princess in a house that runs like magic..."

Lictor; the name of the Italian Fascisti — all these signs and names say strength is in union. You can break a stick — but not a bundle of sticks. This is the kind of strength acquired by an advertising agency of many offices of many experienced men and women, of many accounts widely diversified."[8]

The appeal to community, however garbled in some Depression-era ads, is grossly simplified in ads from the World War II years and the 1950s. In these community *is* the corporation and/or a militaristic patriotism, and individual experience is defined as allegiance to company and country. It is widely recognized that postwar economic prosperity, besides initiating a surge in buying, created a desire to build a new world rooted in the private family dwelling and increased consumerism.[9] A full-page ad in the May 1944 issue of *House & Garden* anticipates the coming of this climate. At the top of the page is an image of a woman lying in a bubble bath who wears a crown and is surrounded by angels. Below we see the same woman, hanging up clothes with the help of her husband outside their single-family house. The head, "...and I'll live like a princess in a house that runs like magic," is followed by copy reading, "I have a wonderful post-war dream ... I'm always fresh as a daisy, pretty as a picture ... and housekeeping — in my new all-Gas home of the future — seems like play!"[10]

In ads of the 1950s identification between the consumer and the product (and therefore the corporation) is stressed. Design of that decade contributed to this emphasis by allowing only a highly simplified, condensed, seemingly essential reading of the message. It was in this same period that the necessity of an equally hard-hitting, unambiguous corporate image was recognized. As *Print* magazine reported in 1959: "The merchant is realizing that unless the prospective customer can consciously or unconsciously see a 'fit' between her own self-image and the image of the store, she will not patronize it, no matter what price offerings are made. It is perfectly logical, therefore, for the manufacturer to inquire whether a similar attraction or repulsion may be taking place between the consuming public and his company's personality which would have bearing on the sale of his products."[11]

Designer unknown
Advertisement for the H.K. McCann Company
Fortune April 1930
p. 4: 13 x 10 1/4
© Time, Inc., New York

Designer unknown
Advertisement for the American Gas Association
House & Garden May 1944
p. 18: 11 x 8 1/2
© The Condé Nast Publications, Inc., New York

8. *Fortune* 1, 3 (April 1930): 4.
9. See Dolores Hayden, *Redesigning the American Dream: The Future of Housing, Work, and Family Life* (New York: W.W. Norton, 1984); and Roland Marchand, "Visions of Classlessness, Quests for Dominion: American Popular Culture, 1945–1960," in *Reshaping America: Society and Institutions, 1945–1960*, Robert H. Brenner and Gary M. Reichard, eds. (Columbus: Ohio State University Press, 1982), 163–192.
10. *House & Garden* 85 (May 1944): 18.
11. Pierre Martineau, "Sharper Focus for the Corporate Image," *Print* 13, 3 (May–June 1959): 22. The designers Lou Dorfsman and Herb Lubalin served as guest editors of this issue, which was devoted to the corporate image.

WHO
ME?

Yes, *you* in the Handmacher. The most beautiful suit of the season. Look how softly it curves to the figure. How charming in every detail. Ample evidence of the genius of styling and mastery of tailoring that is uniquely Handmacher's. Tailored in Striette woolen. The bib effect is its own perfect linen blouse revealed. Misses and Junior Sizes. $89⁹⁵

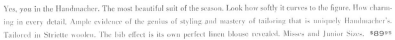

TAILORED BY

handmacher ® "YOU CAN FEEL THE GOOD FIT"

Postwar ad design, in contrast to the storyboard and cartoonlike ads of the 1930s, is stark, with large, legible images. This tendency is evident in an ad for Handmacher's women's suits that appeared in a 1954 issue of *Vogue* magazine; the photo fills five-sixths of the page. A woman in a suit stands with three men in business suits. She points to herself, and the type next to her reads: "Who Me?" The copy answers: "Yes, *you* in the Handmacher. The most beautiful suit of the season." Her identity and ability to be distinguished from men ("Look how softly it curves to the figure") are attributable wholly to the product.[12]

The 1980s have brought a diversification of advertising approaches and an interest in event advertising and micro-marketing. Nevertheless, to generalize, it is easy to see a continuation of the advertising trend to subsume individual experience within the parameters defined by corporation/brand name/product. In the characteristic ad of the 1980s the consumer exists through the product, and the product is author of a lifestyle; that is, the product takes the place of the person within American myths of individualism. (Which is not to say that prospective buyers are necessarily brainwashed by this message, for consumers during this decade have voiced vigorous skepticism about advertising while at the same time acknowledging their delight in its high production values.) If one ad could be said to be exemplary of the 1980s "you-*are*-the-product" (as compared with the 1950s "you-are-*identified*-with-the-product") trend, it is the first TV Michelob beer commercial in "The Night Belongs to Michelob" series, which aired in 1986. The entire sixty-second spot is a sequence of dark liquid and night-light shots, all of which dissolve to approximate a look of gleaming fluidity. This is not a narrative but a montage of the coolness, wetness, comradery, and sexuality available in the proffered night. The beer personifies the night, and the ad suggests that the viewer can attain this nocturnal experience not just by consuming Michelob but by becoming Michelob.

Where does design fit into this framework of advertising, individualism, and the corporation? What is its function, and does it have any power to change an ad's message, to reflect the interaction between the individual and society or between the individual and the community? Does design, within the limits of corporate advertising, have the power to raise questions about the notion of the corporation as an individual? The skeptical answer to these questions is no. Design in the service of commerce is subordinate, after all, to the desires of its clients as well as to the canons of the design profession, which typically emphasize "simplicity," "honesty," "legibility," and "abbreviation." Some postwar designers have reacted to these restrictions by employing wit and humor and by pursuing formal innovation; The Pushpin Group and Dan Friedman, both based in New York City, immediately come to mind. But it must be

12. *Vogue* 123 (1 February 1954): 32.

Designer unknown
Advertisement for Handmacher
Vogue 1 February 1954
p. 32: 10 x 8
© The Condé Nast Publications, Inc., New York

DDB Needham Worldwide Inc.
"Night Moves/Collins"
Sixty-second television commercial for Michelob, 1986
Film Director: Joe Pytka
Creative Directors: Susan Gillette, Nancy Jordan
Art Director: Bruce Ritter
Copywriters: Jeff Holinski, Peter McHugh
Agency Producer: Hank Sabian

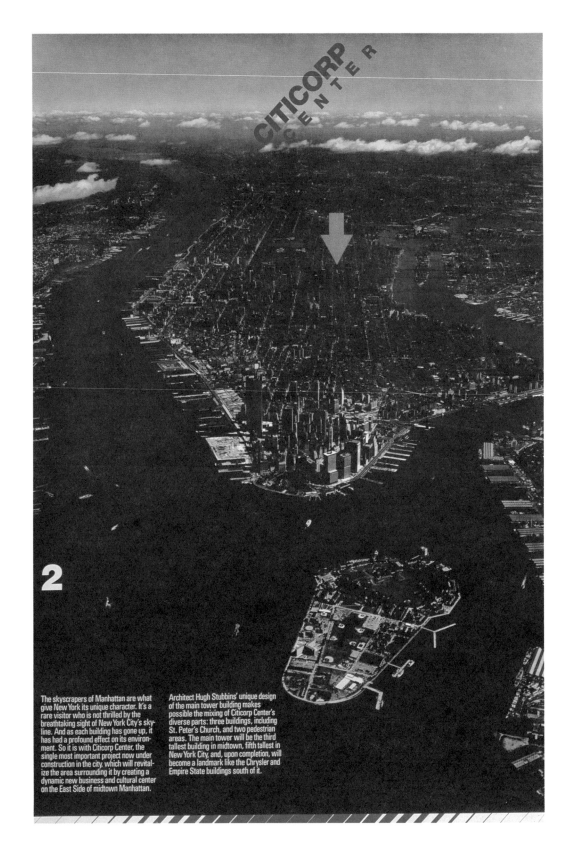

2

The skyscrapers of Manhattan are what give New York its unique character. It's a rare visitor who is not thrilled by the breathtaking sight of New York City's skyline. And as each building has gone up, it has had a profound effect on its environment. So it is with Citicorp Center, the single most important project now under construction in the city, which will revitalize the area surrounding it by creating a dynamic new business and cultural center on the East Side of midtown Manhattan.

Architect Hugh Stubbins' unique design of the main tower building makes possible the mixing of Citicorp Center's diverse parts: three buildings, including St. Peter's Church, and two pedestrian areas. The main tower will be the third tallest building in midtown, fifth tallest in New York City, and, upon completion, will become a landmark like the Chrysler and Empire State buildings south of it.

134

asked whether formal innovations are really able to effect substantial change in the message communicated.

The argument can be made that, in graphic design, formal innovation is not so important as the selection and juxtaposition of signifying fragments. For design is montage, a recycling of common symbols in new combinations and visual environments. It is precisely because design recirculates easily understood and shared imagery — and is widely distributed — that it is so powerful. Given this immense ability to communicate, graphic designers need to focus less on formal concerns and more on the context and content of the message. While designers are by definition dependent on clients, they can choose clients, as well as colleagues, in such a way as to increase their involvement in the shaping of messages.

What does this selectivity mean in specific cases? Consider a comparison of Paul Rand's work with that done by William Golden during the 1950s. The two men shared attitudes toward design and even much visual vocabulary, although Rand more clearly embraced certain visual standards established by avant-garde art. Despite these parallels, some of Golden's designs for CBS and Rand's for IBM evince quite distinct philosophical differences.

In his writings Rand talks of simplicity, repetition, striation, letters, and brevity, and he designs accordingly; his logos for ABC (1962) and IBM (1956) are cases in point. Perhaps Rand's noncorporate work is formally more challenging, as is evidenced by the covers he did during the late 1930s and early 1940s for the antifascist cultural magazine *Direction*. However, in his corporate identity programs, visual puns are as far as he goes in the direction of complexity. (Recall his rebus for a 1981 IBM poster, in which the *I* is represented by the image of an eye and the *B* by a bee.) Rand believes the designer should pursue simplicity in order to divine some abstract "truth." His argument seems to be that essentialism of form is equivalent to the essence of truth, a common modernist maxim but one that does not bear close scrutiny. If we think in particular about how design represents a multinational corporation such as IBM, Rand's client for decades, it is clear that striated letters do little to reflect the "truth" of this enormous technological, economic, and cultural complex. In his book *Paul Rand: A Designer's Art* he endorses the statement made by Irwin Miller of the Cummins Engine Company that "Good design at heart is simply honesty."[13] Variations on this ingenuous claim pass for received wisdom in many design courses and among many working designers; it is a claim that keeps the focus of the profession on visual minutiae and away from the responsibilities that come with its tremendous power to communicate.

Dan Friedman
Poster for Citicorp Center real estate
project 1975
48 x 32
Collection the designer

13. *Paul Rand: A Designer's Art* (New Haven, Conn.: Yale University Press, 1985). The statement was made in a talk given by Miller, then chairman of Cummins's executive committee, on 14 June 1984, after his company had received a design award from the American Institute of Graphic Arts.

There seems to be a shared belief system operating in the cases of effectively implemented corporate identity programs. By and large, the design profession has since the 1950s accepted IBM's proposition that "IBM's 'Corporate Image' can be summed up: good design itself is the image."[14] In the course of praising Rand's fresh and clean IBM logo in 1959, Joe Carty, then the organization's head of advertising and corporate promotions, said, "All we're trying to do is to communicate IBM as a company that is serving in an orderly, efficient and honest manner."[15]

But such deceptively bland credos are of course not the entire basis for this belief system. As the designer Wally Olins points out in his 1978 book *The Corporate Personality*, corporate identity programs were primarily developed after World War II, emerging with the establishment of the huge multinationals and reflecting their desires to monopolize markets globally and to communicate continuity and stability in a variety of cultures. Olins observes that these desires have produced identity programs that seek to make the clients appear "homogeneous," "strong," "cool," "distant," "controlled," "smooth," "unwrinkled," "all-knowing," "ubiquitous," "all-seeing," "ordered," "superhuman," "expensive," "modern," and in charge of nature.[16] "If companies share the idea of corporate omniscience," he contends, "it is inevitable that they will tend to look similar," going on to complain that "corporate design is for the most part as stiff, sullen, aggressive and self-glorifying as it was 10 or even 20 years ago."[17]

Given the restrictions of this belief system, and the willingness of most designers to accept them, it is illuminating to look at the career of William Golden. He worked for CBS radio and television in the 1940s and 1950s and was the television network's creative director of advertising and sales promotion from 1951 until his untimely death in 1959. Golden is well known for designing the CBS trademark, which symbolizes both the viewer's eye and the camera's lens. Outside his corporate work he produced designs for political causes, such as posters for the Presidential candidate Adlai Stevenson. But even at CBS, Golden, with collaborators such as the leftist artist Ben Shahn, was able to make certain liberal social statements. Take for example two newspaper advertisements designed by Golden with artwork by Shahn for Fred Friendly and Edward R. Murrow's "See It Now" documentary series (1951–1958). Both featured simple blocks of boldface type and pen-and-ink drawings. Golden laid the drawings out to take up more than half the page, increasing their impact further by not framing them. For a 1958 show on the effects of nuclear fallout Shahn drew two bald people anxiously looking skyward. A similarly humanistic approach is evident in the ad for a 1957 "See It

William Golden
Drawing by Ben Shahn
Program advertisement for the
CBS program "See It Now," 1958
various formats

William Golden
Drawing by Ben Shahn
Program advertisement for the
CBS program "See It Now," 1957
various formats

14. "IBM's 'New Look,'" *Print* 13, 3 (May–June 1959): 25.
15. Quoted in ibid.: 25.
16. Wally Olins, *The Corporate Personality: An Inquiry into the Nature of Corporate Identity* (London: Design Council, 1978).
17. Ibid., 77.

Now," entitled "The Puerto Ricans — Americans on the Move," for which Shahn drew a family of immigrants standing together, looking apprehensive, their belongings gathered around them. It is important to bear in mind that this kind of work was possible only because of the liberal self-image CBS News had during the early days of television. And, if Golden's departures from the post-World War II design norm were unusual then, they look freakish now, thirty years later, when the corporate design climate is altogether more rigid.

In his writings Golden shares Paul Rand's adulation of order, simplicity, and legibility. Yet unlike Rand he does not conflate these formal issues with the communication of a mythic essential truth. Moreover, Golden is skeptical about the function of design in the service of commerce: "For Business wants him [the designer] to help create an attitude about the facts, not to communicate them. And only about some of the facts. For facts in certain juxtapositions can offend some portion of the market. So he finds himself working with half-truths, and feels that he is not using all his talents. He finds that he is part of a giant merchandising apparatus in which the media of mass communication have reached a miraculous degree of technical perfection and are being operated at full speed to say as little as necessary in the most impressive way."[18]

Adding Golden's comments to the bulk of the foregoing material, we can see that even when a given corporation allows a graphic designer to comment on broad social issues, the designer, quite naturally, will not be able to communicate insights about the operation of the corporation or its relationship to the economy and society. Instead, by focusing exclusively on the corporation, design in this context contributes to a celebration of the organization as a supreme individual in society. And yet, while graphic design as a field is dependent upon funding and clients, it need not be entirely reliant on corporations.

Given that corporate design is virtually closed to the more critical varieties of social commentary, it is necessary for graphic designers who wish to address social issues in their work — and to have that work widely disseminated — to choose between two alternatives: liberal *pro bono* work, generally done for public-service groups and well-funded socially oriented organizations; and more politically radical work, addressing systemic issues, which typically relies for funding on a variety of marginal sources. The latter designs treat subjects ranging from sexism and racism to international trade and the environment. Besides dealing with social questions, both types of work can also raise questions about how graphic design produces meaning

18. Cipe Pineles Golden, Kurt Weihs, and Robert Strunsky, eds., *The Visual Craft of William Golden* (New York: George Braziller, 1962), 61. For a different yet related comparison of Rand and Golden, see Lorraine Wild, "Art and Design: Lovers or Just Good Friends," AIGA *Journal of Graphic Design* 5, 2 (1987): 2–3.

formally, for example, counteracting the prevalent essentialism-above-all ethos through such techniques as layering and montage.[19]

Free or low-paid *pro bono* work is done by small and large design firms alike seeking both to do public service and to receive recognition. Most of these firms feel they cannot afford to alienate anyone and so stick to safe subjects. Landor Associates, for instance, is aggressive in pursuing blue-chip *pro bono* projects, lending a helping hand to such needy clients as the America's Cup, the Nobel Foundation, and Prince Philip. These designs most frequently take the form of logos and letterheads. On the other hand, there are many designs done for less glamorous projects, such as the numerous peace posters Art Chantry has created in Seattle and the hand-painted literacy billboards Sheila Levrant de Bretteville, Ave Pildas, and the Brookl7n Design Workshop produced in Los Angeles in 1988.[20] And yet *pro bono* work, by its very nature, is often circumscribed. The liberal client organizations in question are characteristically more interested in patching up society — focusing on such single-issue problems as drunk driving and drug abuse — than in working to effect broader, long-term societal change.

Nevertheless, graphic design, with its inherent ability to communicate broadly through a recycling and reordering of our common visual vocabulary, is ideally suited to address larger problems and societal change. While there are relatively few opportunities for designers to do this — in part because funding for such projects is, as suggested, erratic and difficult to solicit — a number of designers have independently managed to produce effective activist work, conceived of according to the urgency of issues rather than the demands of clients. Facilitating this work is the fact that design technology is becoming increasingly accessible and personalized; small groups and even individuals can now approach large issues via a cottage industry route.

The work of two designers (also commonly identified as artists) who engage in such activism can be used to illustrate the point.[21] Barbara Kruger, who was employed for eleven years as a graphic designer at Condé Nast Publications (full time as an editorial designer for *Mademoiselle* from 1967 to 1971 and then part time as a general-assignment designer and picture editor until 1978) was by 1982 taking the

19. In this context it is important to stress again that formal innovation in and of itself is not enough: the challenge to the profession is to learn to assert itself more in terms of the messages it produces, the contexts in which it produces them, and the audience and reasons for which it produces them.
20. Sheila Levrant de Bretteville in letters to the author and to Linda Krenzin, 29 August 1988 and 23 March 1989, respectively.
21. It bespeaks our restricted concept of graphic design that a designer who begins producing politically independent work with support from noncorporate sources is reclassified as an artist.

cottage industry approach as her privately produced graphics began to sell. Her livelihood today comes mainly from the art market, but she has produced a great number of explicitly political posters, billboards, and works in related media with funding from a variety of public and cultural organizations. In 1986 and 1987, for example, she created a series of some eighty billboards addressing militarism and myths of masculinity that appeared in Australia, New Zealand, the United States, Great Britain, and Israel.[22] Working in her signature style, which incorporates emphatic white-and-black photomontages, often framed in red, with text, Kruger coupled the title of a popular Tina Turner song, "We Don't Need Another Hero," with a stereotypical image from a 1940s print ad of a girl admiring a boy making a muscle. In Philmont, New York, the hometown of onetime White House aide Oliver North, the billboard went up in the summer of 1987 during the House-Senate Iran-contra hearings, from which the indicted lieutenant colonel was emerging as the man of the hour.

The work of Leslie Sharpe comprises a second example of design activism. Sharpe, who works as a graphic and product designer at Think Big, a chain of upscale gift and novelty stores in New York City, has since 1986 been producing a series of design projects dealing with women employed in the garment industry in this country and abroad. Concentrating on problems involving illegal immigrants, home workers, and women workers in the Third World, as well as on the stereotypes that women's fashions help perpetuate, these projects question the way capitalism works — placing a particular emphasis on corporate inequities. In *Industrial Homework* (1989), a series of six street posters, for example, she juxtaposes images of home workers with an image of a model that becomes increasingly distorted as the series unfolds. The posters are accompanied by text that provides facts about the Bush Administration's policy on legislation concerning home workers.

Sharpe's garment worker projects take different forms and are aimed at various audiences; these range from the constituency of the International Ladies Garment Workers Union (ILGWU) to pedestrians to readers of the California Institute of the Arts journal *Revenge*. Work such as hers challenges the representation of the corporation as a supreme, infallible individual and disrupts the corporation = individual equation by focusing instead on the individuals who, as employees and consumers, are affected by a company's activities.

The ever-increasing tendency of corporations, beginning in the 1920s, to use graphic design to promote their products and enhance their images, and the postwar belief that even small businesses should look "modern" or "designed," have,

The designer Sheila Levrant de Bretteville is chair of the department of communication design and illustration at Otis Art Institute of Parsons School of Design in Los Angeles, where she started the Brookl7n Design Workshop to provide an opportunity for students to produce *pro bono* work for nonprofit clients who do not have design budgets. There were seven students in the original group, and their teacher was born in Brooklyn — thus the logotype.

Brookl7n Design Workshop
Can You Read? 1988
Art Director: Shelia Levrant de Bretteville
Faculty Advisor: Ave Pildas
Student Designer: Diana Cain
painted billboard
14 x 18 feet
Billboard donated by Patrick Media, Los Angeles

22. The project was funded in Great Britain by England's Channel 4 and the Art Angel Trust and in Israel and this country by various art museums. In Ireland and Israel, Kruger's billboards served to comment upon the fatalistic attitudes young men imbibe growing up in those heavily militaristic societies.

while providing much-needed livelihood for the design profession, combined to work against it in other ways. Indeed, the growing popularity of design within the business community has led the profession to see itself as chiefly client-oriented. The accepted function of the designer has become one of providing a service rather than generating ideas to be communicated; this self-definition discourages explicitly political expression. However, there are possibilities open to those who would imaginatively pursue activist design projects that are alternative or supplementary to work for businesses and large organizations. Beyond this, the challenge to the profession as a whole is to redefine the societal role of the designer in a way that more broadly engages the mass-communicative powers of graphic design.

Maud Lavin has written frequently on photography and design. Her essays have appeared in the periodicals Art in America *and* New German Critique *and in the anthologies* Global Television *(1989) and* The Divided Heritage: Themes and Problems in German Modernism *(1989).*

Barbara Kruger
Untitled (We Don't Need Another Hero) 1986–1987
painted billboard (installed in London)
various dimensions:
10 x 20–14 x 40 ft.
Collection the artist

Leslie Sharpe's series of posters was designed on a Macintosh computer using PageMaker, SUPERPAINT, and Thunderscan software, thus bringing the artist into the realm of design via technology.

Leslie Sharpe
Industrial Homework: Into the 21st Century, Back to the Dark Ages 1989
laser prints
8 1/2 x 11 each
Collection the artist

NOVEMBER

SOUP   BOUDIN & WARM TARTS

GUSTY WINDS

HIGHS UPPER 40S TO MID 50S

LOWS UPPER 30S TO MID 40S

FLORENT

OPEN 24 HOURS 989 5779

WATCH FOR HEAVY RAINS

WEAR YOUR GALOSHES

MNCO

144

Tibor Kalman

[born 1949]

M&Co. is the cryptic name of a New York graphic design firm whose distinctive "studio" persona is not based on a recurring typographic or pictorial style but on the sense of wit and irony of its principal, Tibor Kalman. Though Kalman says that M&Co.'s is a collaborative process, his particular vision and taste for the visual language of vernacular graphic forms helps determine the characteristically unpredictable direction in which M&Co. has moved since its inception in 1979. M&Co. is not a design firm whose members adhere to certain strict rules or ideologies, for within the constructs of a specific assignment Kalman, who had no formal design training and happened into the field doing ad hoc window displays for a Barnes and Noble bookstore, pushes the perceptions of both client and customer about what design should be. Rather than standardize its solutions or conform to the dominant trends, M&Co. customizes "campaigns" for clients as diverse as real estate developers, restauranteurs, and arts magazines. Personalization in this case means subjectivization — building upon cultural phenomena — and imbuing each problem with the unexpected. Formal design tenets concerning balance and harmony are of secondary importance to strong concepts. In Kalman's view elegant typography will not improve a bad idea. In addition to two dimensions, M&Co. has ventured into product and motion design. M&Co. is well known for its collaborations with the composer-performer David Byrne and other representatives of current culture, but Kalman's primary contribution to contemporary practice is a keen ability to use design not as an end in itself but as a tool to break from convention.

I was born in Budapest to a father who is a man of science and a mother with an artistic nature. M&Co. was born out of my love for these two disciplines. Passionate exactitude. Mad reason. I went into my room at the age of twelve with a huge stack of books and didn't emerge until I was eighteen. I could have been an inventor seeking unexpected solutions to absurd problems. But instead, chance found me at the age of nineteen working in a bookstore when a window dresser called in sick. My future was framed.

I studied journalism in college, intending to expose the world's ills. It was the late 1960s, and radicalism was pervasive. I learned valuable lessons: that bell bottoms are truly unattractive; that you can successfully challenge the status quo; and that you are free to use your imagination to change the real world. And within the inevitable self-seriousness of this process, I discovered that humor can be a critical medium. Everywhere, especially where it least belongs.

M&Co. is now ten years old. And in that time we have developed not a style but a method. We are not content (except when the rent bills hover overhead) to be mere corporate stylists. That seems to me to be the path of least resistance. It brings in the most money but is a terrible waste of the opportunity

M&Co.'s work for Restaurant Florent in New York could only be a product of a close collaboration between client and designer. The M&Co. group often eats (one does not dine) at Florent, and they have taken clues from the simple charms of its environment and applied them, with a dollop of wit, to the old "downtown" look of these 1987 newspaper ads.

Shorts, et al., 6 1/2 x 10
Steak, 6 1/2 x 10
Menu Board I, 14 x 11

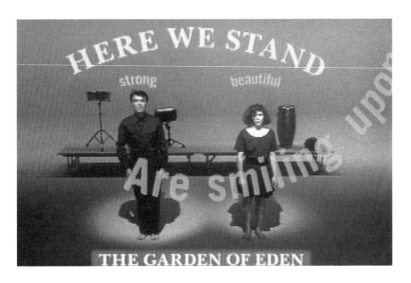

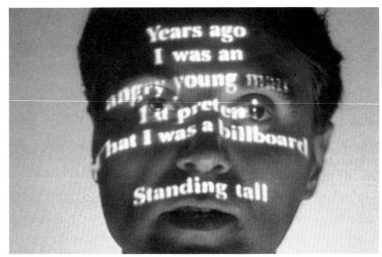

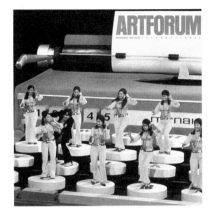

that designers have to create meaningful, passionate communication.

What we strive to do, whether the client likes it or not, is to examine a problem and contribute both content and a form to its solution. We try to create work based on the communication of ideas that engage our client's audience. However, we are in the throes of an era that I find especially troublesome. Designers seem no longer to work for entrepreneurs but rather for "marketing departments." As a result, the work is designed not so much to serve the needs of the audience or even the client but to serve the needs of the marketing department. The audience wants to be involved, to be moved, to be touched by the work of designers. The marketing department wants the work to be safe. Thus there is little room for quirkiness or passion or point of view. Too many people are in the way trying to make too much money. Appealing only to their perception of the safest course, the "least common denominator," finally creates a sterile, limp, homogenized visual landscape.

At M&Co. we spend most of our energy fighting this fight. We have no account executives. We avoid working for marketing types. The few clients who understand the essence of our laboratory mentality are precious to us. They want to think, and they want us to think. They want to redefine the questions. We want to discover and rediscover by drawing on literature, history, art, and from the clarity of the fast-disappearing American vernacular landscape.

M&Co. has always been a collaborative. A changing group of talented designers has always changed its course, its style, its content. A large part of the credit for the work and the thinking belongs to those designers. Of course, if they disagree with me I fire them.

My wife, Maira, is an artist and an important collaborator. She always makes me approach a problem backward and upside down. I also listen to my children, who provide a constant inspirational whirlwind of difficult questions and free association.

M&Co. was commissioned by *Artforum* to design a series of issues of the magazine from September through December 1987. They worked closely with the editor, Ingrid Sischy, who wanted the typography and images to develop around the content of each article, moving away from the traditional makeup of the publication.

Artforum November 1987
cover: 10 1/2 sq. format
Still from *Bombay Talkie*, 1970
A film of James Ivory and Ismail Merchant
© Artforum International Magazine, Inc., New York

Artforum December 1987
pp. 100–101: 10 1/2 sq. format
"The World in a Bottle"
© Artforum International Magazine, Inc., New York

David Byrne of Talking Heads band fame was one of M&Co.'s earliest clients. For him they have designed record albums, tape boxes, posters, film titles, and in 1988 a remarkable music video, "(Nothing But) Flowers," by Index Video. In it, letters and words fall like flower petals around the musicians, and sentences wrap around the players' faces creating a "closed-caption" video that uses typography as description but most of all for the pure pleasure it provides.

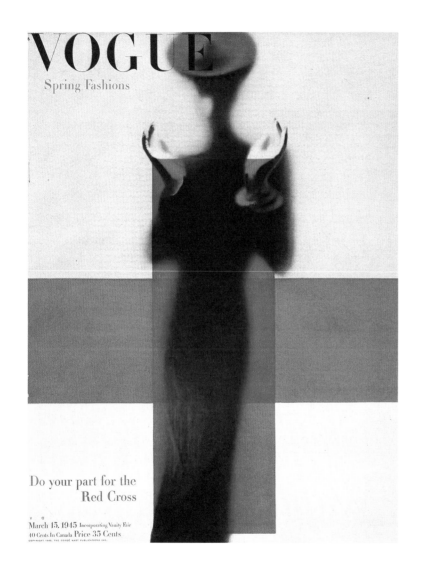

VOGUE

Spring Fashions

Do your part for the
Red Cross

V O
March 15, 1945 Incorporating Vanity Fair
40 Cents In Canada Price 35 Cents
COPYRIGHT 1945, THE CONDÉ NAST PUBLICATIONS INC.

ANC

VOGUE

1950

MID-CENTURY
FASHIONS
FACES
IDEAS

TRAVEL
HANDBOOK

Incorporating Vanity Fair
★ ○ January 1950
Price 50 Cents in U.S. and Canada
$1.00 All Other Countries
COPYRIGHT 1949, THE CONDÉ NAST PUBLICATIONS INC.

Alexander Liberman

[born 1912]

One of the great strengths of Alexander Liberman's long reign as editorial director at Condé Nast has been his sensitivity to what makes an arresting magazine cover image. These two pages of *Vogue* examples (opposite and overleaf) from 1945 through 1951 look as fresh today, if not as startling, as they did then.

Vogue 15 March 1945
cover: 12 3/4 x 9 3/4 format
Erwin Blumenfeld photograph
© 1945 (renewed 1973) The Condé
Nast Publications, Inc., New York

Vogue January 1950
cover: 12 3/4 x 9 3/4 format
Erwin Blumenfeld photograph
© 1950 (renewed 1978) The Condé
Nast Publications, Inc., New York

Alexander Liberman, the current editorial director of Condé Nast Publications, Inc., grew up in Paris before World War II, when European graphic design was at its zenith. He briefly worked for the master posterist A.M. Cassandre and while still quite young became the chief layout man and later art director of *VU*, France's influential picture weekly. Like so many designers and artists, he fled the specter of war and landed on the steps of Condé Nast in New York, which hired him as an assistant to Mehemed Fehmy Agha at *Vogue*. In 1942 he became its art director. Liberman guided the visual personality of *Vogue* through its most elegant era in the 1950s and elevated its editorial and pictorial content from a magazine of just fashion to one with journalistic intent. In the 1960s he was given almost total command of all Condé Nast publications, including *Vogue, Mademoiselle, House & Garden*, and more recently, *Vanity Fair, Traveler*, and *Self*. Liberman insists his magazines are not designed to serve style but rather to report it.

I started at *VU* as a layout man. Very soon I was running the art department and was named art director about 1933. *VU* was an illustrated magazine, so every morning the photographers and all the agents would present pictures, and in the afternoon we had to think about what to do with them. I designed layouts and special projects, assigned photographers, created covers. All the covers signed "Alexandre" are mine. I did a lot of work with André Kertész, Robert Capa, and Brassaï. They were not "great photographers" then, they were good friends who did good work. There was no cult of photography at that time. It was interesting and enriching, but there wasn't the fetishism that exists today.

Vogel, the creator of *VU*, had escaped to America in 1940, and Condé Nast, his old friend and associate in many ventures, invited him to work with him. He couldn't speak English, so he said to Condé, "I need Liberman." When I was able to get to America I was given a job in the Condé Nast art department, and for a little while I did layouts for *Vogue* at $50 a week. The only thing I brought to America was a gold medal I had received for an exhibition design in the Paris World's Fair of 1937.

One day, Dr. M.F. Agha, the art director, called me into his office and said, "I'm terribly sorry, but you're not good enough for

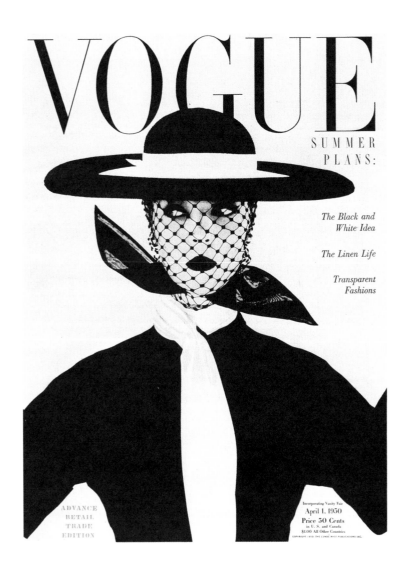

Vogue." So I was fired. That was Friday. On Monday Condé Nast asked to see me, not knowing I had been fired. I brought my gold medal, and we talked; it was very interesting because Condé at that time was reacting against the prevailing cliché presentation of fashion: quaint titles at the bottom of pages, obscure typography, and strange handwritten titles. Nast was full of admiration for *Life* magazine, which had recently started. Condé wanted *Vogue* to be modern and to apply the principles of a newsmagazine, so when he learned from Vogel that I had been involved with a newsmagazine he was very excited, and I think the gold medal cinched it because he said, "Well, a man like you must be on *Vogue.*" He asked Agha to come in and said "I want Liberman on *Vogue.*" Since Condé was an absolute monarch, Agha never told him he had fired me. I was put on the seventh desk in the art department. Cipe Pineles had the first desk.

At *Vogue* there was a special place and time to choose 8-by-10 Koda-chromes for covers. These were very pompous occasions: Condé, Agha, Mrs. Chase, the edi-tor, and sometimes the photographer, all in their hats and "royal robes." (In those days the principal *Vogue* pages were created in Paris. Thirty-two pages would arrive from Paris all laid out. Fashion was dominated by Paris, and so the center of fashion information was there.)

In 1942 I was appointed art direc-tor of *Vogue*. As I had always resented the fussy, feminine, condescending approach to women by women's magazines, I thought it was important to shake up this rather somnolent society. If we had to show hats, I tried to mix hats with contemporary life. So, for example, I might reproduce a Mondrian painting on the same page. A little later, the only way I could get Jackson Pollock into the magazine was to get Cecil Beaton to photograph a model in front of some Pollock paintings.

I greatly admired the portrait pho-tography of Atget, Nadar, and August Sander and began to dislike the artificiality of most fashion photography. Fortunately, Irving Penn came into my life. He worked as an assistant with me in the art department on design and layout until one day I said, "Why don't you go and take the picture?"

Clarity and strength of communica-tion are what interest me. I've always opposed graphic design for its own sake and believe that design is a servant to the communication of information. I was never sensitized to type, and didn't feel that a sixteenth of a millimeter spacing mattered; rather, I felt this or that looked pretty good and communicated the mes-sage. I always wanted to drop the fancy types, and in 1947 we changed the logo of *Vogue* to Franklin Gothic, which until then had been used only in newspapers. I thought it had strength and looked modern. All the captions and the titles were set in Franklin Gothic, which was then revolutionary in women's publications.

At that time *Vogue* had Lee Miller as the magazine's war correspondent; as a photographer she had followed the armies throughout Europe. And to *Vogue*'s eternal credit we were the first to publish her pictures of the Buchenwald gas chambers after libera-tion. Nobody realizes that *Vogue* published them. But for me this was practically a justifi-cation for being on *Vogue*. Moreover, a new approach to women's clothes was brought about through the activity of American women working in factories for the war effort. The arti-ficiality of fashion began to disappear, and it's only after the war, when Christian Dior intro-duced the "New Look" in the 1950s, that the old attitudes returned with a vengeance. But it was never the same. The lessons of Lee Miller's war photography and of Cecil Beaton's photographs of bombed London caused a change in fashion photography. News photog-raphy in general and the emergence of daring paparazzi forced a rethinking at *Vogue*. Although the job of the magazine is fashion, I've always felt that *Vogue* was one of the strong pioneers for democratization, for women's rights, and for breaking down false cultural values.

My concept of layout has always been concerned with flow. I usually lay out se-quences the way a film is cut, trying to commu-nicate moods through a sequence of images. I hate white space because white space is an old album tradition. I need to be immersed in the subject matter.

The most marked change in *Vogue* from the 1960s to the 1980s is in its graphic strength — much bolder type is in-tended for faster communication. White space does not exist, but a certain power, a daring has emerged that wasn't there even when I first used Franklin Gothic. In retrospect it seems dainty. Reversed type and other strong typographic devices are used to accentuate motion, catch the eye, communicate the message.

Vogue 1 April 1950
cover: 12 3/4 x 9 3/4 format
Irving Penn photograph
© 1950 (renewed 1978) The Condé
Nast Publications, Inc., New York

Vogue 1 October 1951
cover: 12 3/4 x 9 3/4 format
Richard Rutledge photograph
© 1951 (renewed 1979) The Condé
Nast Publications, Inc., New York

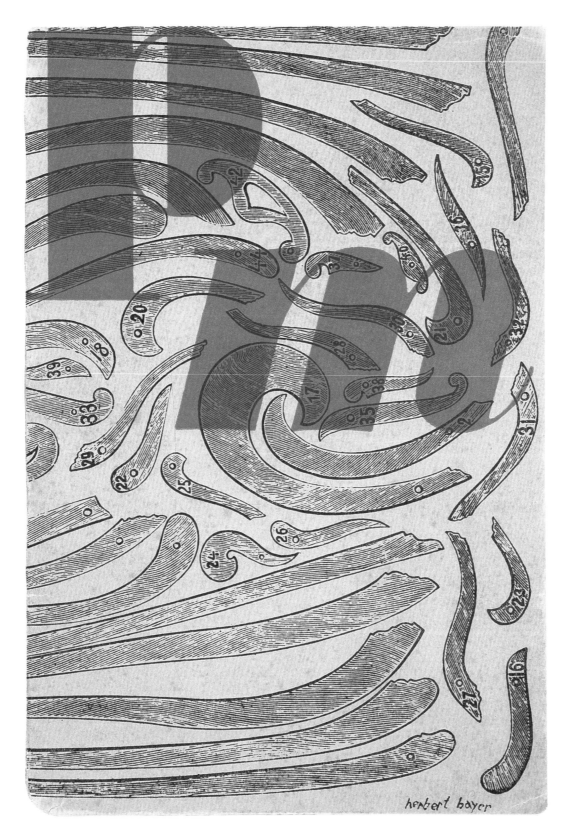

herbert bayer

Europeans in America

Lorraine Wild

A small, worn copy of *PM* ("An Intimate Journal for Production Managers, Art Directors and their Associates") offers a telling glimpse into the state of the graphic arts in America at the start of World War II.[1] The journal was published by Dr. Robert Leslie, a modern-design enthusiast and the owner of The Composing Room, a large New York City typeshop. Along with book reviews and trade news, *PM* showcased various designers and illustrators by giving them pages on which to present their work. The cover of this issue was designed by the Bauhaus veteran Herbert Bayer, newly arrived from Germany. Bayer also contributed and designed the issue's featured piece, which consisted of translations of three articles he wrote in Berlin in the early 1930s on advertising design, on exhibition design, and on his search for a "universal" alphabet. In thirty-two illustrated pages Bayer displayed every aspect of his graphic work, from typography and poster design to painting and photographic experiments. Proselytizing suavely to his new American audience, he conflated art and design, presenting irresistable arguments for the devising of beautiful new forms as the only rational response to modern conditions.

Another article in this issue focused on work by the Art Squad, a student club at Abraham Lincoln High School in Brooklyn directed by Leon Friend, the chairman of the school's art department. The Art Squad produced work in all media, including graphic design. Theirs was an awkward yet energetic interpretation of the modern style that reflected the influence of sources ranging from Bayer to streamlined product design. In the article Friend described his efforts to expose students to working artists and visiting critics, including émigré designers such as Austria's Joseph Binder and Germany's Lucian Bernhard.[2]

Herbert Bayer
PM 6, 2
December 1939–January 1940
cover: 7 7/8 x 5 3/4 format
© 1940 PM Publishing Company,
New York

1. *PM* 6, 2 (December 1939–January 1940).
2. Some Art Squad graduates, such as Alex Steinweiss and Gene Federico (both of whose work appears in the *PM* article), went on to become influential graphic designers working in New York City after the war.

What is striking about the Bayer and Art Squad articles is that, taken together, they vividly represent that moment when Modernism, as a conceptual premise and a visual style, began to take hold in American graphic design. They also point up the pluralistic nature of that movement: although the philosophical basis of Bayer's undiluted European utopianism was never absorbed or adopted by Americans, many of its formal characteristics were. Therefore, where Bayer's Modernism was theoretical and functional, its American counterpart was pragmatic and visual.

So close and unquestioned are the links between present-day graphic design and its modernist antecedents that if you were to ask today's typical well-read American designer about role models, you might expect the names El Lissitzky, László Moholy-Nagy, and those of other European figures from the early twentieth century to be mentioned. That is because the contemporary definition of graphic design as a conceptual activity was largely shaped by the artists and designers of the European avant-garde, who, in the years just before and after World War I, challenged traditional notions of cultural and artistic production and developed theories about form-making and the transmission of meaning that became the basis for modern design. But when Modernism was finally integrated into common design practice in America, both its aesthetic and conceptual bases were significantly altered. As the course of this evolution is not readily apparent, it is necessary to show how graphic Modernism in Europe grew before turning to the main subject of this essay, which is the transference of the visual aesthetic — as opposed to the ideological framework — of Modernism to American graphic design.

During the nineteenth century the rude forces of modernity — invention, technology, industrialization, and urbanization — gave the activity of design the basic form that we recognize today. Before that time design was indivisible from the process of making — the shape of a chair was determined by the woodworker who carved it, the look of a page decided by the printer who locked up the type on the press. Industrialization separated conceptual and visual planning from the process of manufacture; that separation marks the birth of the modern designer. This change was quickly followed by the beginnings of a critique of design from John Ruskin, and especially from William Morris, that demanded spiritual, moral, and conceptual honesty in objects produced in this new, and often alienating, industrialized work environment.[3] Goods made in light of that critique may appear quaint to us now, but they are weighted by the still recognizable conviction that the design of even the simplest things should reflect some truth about the maker, the making, and the reality of the times.

3. Gillian Naylor, "Morris as a Pioneer of Modern Design," Institute of Contemporary Arts, *William Morris Today*, exh. cat. (London, 1984), 84.

As Estelle Jussim shows in her essay in this book, the modernization of printing technology (and concurrent spread of literacy) during the nineteenth century did not initially change the visual form of printed matter. Long-standing typographic customs hung on, particularly in book design. Competition for the new commercial audience did foster a variety of aggressive graphic strategies, ranging from posters bearing slogans in huge, loudly ornamented letter forms to advertisements delivering massive amounts of information and "advice" in tiny, compacted type. Nonetheless, until early in this century, printed matter produced on both sides of the Atlantic typically featured a traditional pictorial realism and a concrete relationship between words and pictures.

Cubism, Futurism, and Dada (and, in a utopian sense, the De Stijl and Constructivist movements) sought to break down the traditional formal and conceptual boundaries of art and to bring form-making into a more direct relationship with modern life. Cubists experimented with the creation of visual equivalents for ambiguity and relativity — essentially modern experiences explored in science, literature, and philosophy. The Futurists and Dadaists went further. Reacting to the violence and perceived hypocrisy of society during and after World War I, they mounted an enraged attack on bourgeois culture in which angry manifestos, outrageous performances, alarming noises, and indecipherable books and broadsides were deployed. The irony of their nihilism was that it opened new avenues of expression, made it feasible for artistic ideas to be realized in nontraditonal forms. Hence the stuff of popular culture became a metaphor for the brutal modern urban experience. As the poet Guillaume Apollinaire declared in 1912, "Catalogues, posters, advertisements.... Believe me, they contain the poetry of our epoch." [4]

Artist-designers who were inspired by these movements began turning words into a new visual medium, fracturing them into sounds, liberating individual characters, driving them off the page with an explosive energy that served as a visual metaphor for the volatility of the times. This "heroic" period of modern typography[5] began with the Italian Futurist F.T. Marinetti's call in 1913 for "parole in liberta" (words in liberty) and continued through the mid-1920s. The preconception that the typographic composition ought to be an unobtrusive support for verbal content was now superseded by the idea that type could itself act upon an audience. Most important, the designer was now seen as responsible for the visual concept of a piece, as the author of strategies that had an elastic relationship to the literal meanings conveyed by the text.

Typography was not the only means by which graphic Modernism

F.T. Marinetti
Zang Tumb Tumb 1912
cover: dimensions unavailable
Courtesy Musei Civici di Rovereto,
Galleria Museo Depero, Italy

4. Quoted in Herbert Spencer, *Pioneers of Modern Typography* (London: Lund Humphries, 1969), 13.
5. Ibid.

expressed itself. The medium of photography was seen as mechanical, infinitely manipulable, and convenient — qualities appropriate to the Machine Age. In addition to its more "objective" uses, photographic imagery could be arranged into montages and could be reduced into the abstracted symbols and basic geometric forms, particularly the circle and the square, that were favored by the De Stijl and Constructivist movements. Both groups were interested in a Platonic idealization of reality, assumed to be universally represented by such forms. Primary colors and geometric shapes also could be transformed into symbols that would communicate to a modern audience impatient with traditonal, complex verbal and visual messages. The De Stijl and Constructivist artists were inventing a new visual identity for their times that would harmonize with (what they perceived as) its functional and spiritual demands.

Other European modernists were occupied with making a functional assessment of society in order to find scientifically rational and practical ways to reform it.[6] This goal informed the Bauhaus, where efforts to unite art and industrial technology found a synthesis with avant-garde experimentation and utopian ideals. The intentions of this institution, which was established in Weimar in 1919, were succinctly described by its founder, Walter Gropius, in 1926: "The Bauhaus workshops were essentially laboratories in which prototypes of products suitable for mass production and typical of our time are carefully developed and constantly improved."[7] "Products suitable for mass production" included printed matter, and both Moholy-Nagy and Bayer worked to delineate new standards for graphic design that responded both to emerging printing technologies and to new aesthetic ideals.

In treatises such as *Offset, Book and Commercial Art* (1926) Moholy-Nagy advocated the use of greatly contrasting typefaces within a text to denote the hierarchy of information, an approach that assumes the availability of machine typesetting (his proposed technique is rather complicated for hand-setting) and of an editor willing to let the designer visually edit the text. The resulting designs would be simplified, commercially feasible manifestations of Marinetti's words in liberty. Moholy-Nagy saw the book of the future as a brightly colored tome with photographs arranged in cinematic sequences and set in typefaces "designed in an objective, scientific manner."[8]

While Moholy-Nagy and others were theorizing, a number of European designers were working to realize avant-garde tenets in concrete form. The German Jan Tschichold wrote *Die Neue Typographie* (1928), which explained the new

6. Kenneth Frampton, *Modern Architecture: A Critical History* (New York: Oxford University Press, 1980), 130–131.
7. John Heskett, *Industrial Design* (New York: Oxford University Press), 101.
8. László Moholy-Nagy, "Modern Typography: Aims, Practice, Criticism," Hans M. Wingler, *The Bauhaus: Weimar, Dessau, Berlin, Chicago* (Cambridge, Mass.: MIT Press, 1969), 80–81.

ideals to typesetter-tradesmen in practical terms. Also in Germany, commercial designers such as Karl Shulpig and O.M. Hadank devised imaginative trademarks that abstracted popular imagery to create instant identification.

The public taste for Modernism was further cultivated by a variety of French architects, furniture and interior designers, and graphic designers who evolved an exuberant style of decoration that used abstract, Cubist-inspired forms in a romantic and traditionally ornamental manner. This style, today referred to as Art Deco or Moderne, evinced a belief in the benevolence of the machine and industrial production and progress, yet its agenda could not be called theoretical. Moderne typefaces, for example, were designed with exaggerated geometry solely for stylistic purposes; type was used in ways that neither enhanced nor interfered with content. The boundaries between Moderne and Modernism were hardly clear, a fact demonstrated by the work of the internationally influential French poster designer A.M. Cassandre, whose compositions freely employed cartoonlike Moderne elements *and* reductive abstraction as well as photomontage and the simplified typography of Modernism.

Thus European modernist designers of every stripe were propelled by the avant-garde's rejection of artistic convention, by its drive to find apposite new ways to respond to the spirit of the times, and by its enthusiasm for the products and symbols of modernity.

To the European artist, New York City, and by extension, the United States, seemed a place free of the tyranny of tradition and dedicated to the fullest expression of Modernism. This image derived in part from reports by avant-garde artists and writers who had visited America, such as Marcel Duchamp, Francis Picabia, and Vladimir Mayakovsky, and from movies and newsreels that tended to show off what technology was bringing to industry and architecture. Magazines had a part in this as well. Walter Allner, a onetime Bauhausler who came over in the early 1950s to work on the design of *Fortune*, has said that when that magazine first appeared on European newsstands, in the early 1930s, it was considered to be the epitome of Modernism precisely because — its conservative layout notwithstanding — it visually glorified American industry.[9] The European designer imagined that in America the modern artist was as highly valued as modern technology. Accompanying this vivid projection was the fact that the same turbulent social and economic forces that drove European artists toward radical experimentation in the years after World War I were now making it impossible for many of them to continue working in their homelands. As a result, during the 1930s the United States became the adopted home for many of Europe's most innovative designers, as an abbreviated list indicates: Alexey Brodovitch from Russia

9. Unpublished talk by Walter Allner, University of Bridgeport, Bridgeport, Connecticut, April 1987.

(1930); Joseph Binder from Austria (1930); Herbert Matter from Switzerland (1936); Gyorgy Kepes and László Moholy-Nagy from Hungary (1937); Will Burtin and Herbert Bayer from Germany (1938); Leo Lionni from Italy (1939); and Ladislav Sutnar from Czechoslovakia (1939). World War II brought over other designers as temporary visitors, such as A.M. Cassandre and Jean Carlu, both from France.

Though Modernism had affected American graphic design before the 1930s wave of European immigration, there was little connection between the appearance of modern tendencies in the design of print (or in product or interior design, for that matter) and any native avant-garde activity on American soil.

Invited to build a pavilion at the 1925 Paris Exposition Internationale des Arts Décoratifs, the United States declined, admitting that, due to its conservative cultural climate, this country did not design or produce "modernistic" objects.[10] American mass-market manufacturers and their advertisers had not yet really focused on the visual style of their objects or advertisements as part of their bid for the consumer's dollar. The most dramatic break with this pattern was the decision by General Motors in 1925 to challenge the primacy of Henry Ford's generic Model T with automobiles whose style would change annually.[11] This lesson in merchandising was soon seized upon by other manufacturers then facing the problem of supply outstripping demand.

"Styling" became the premise on which new-product design was based; for the most part, it was a simple matter of redesigning the casing, eliminating historicizing decoration, or of concealing the mechanism of a product to give it a smooth, organized, simple look. A new approach in advertising emerged at the same time, one that would compel advertising's audience to see the consumption of novel goods as a mark of social status. By the late 1920s the use of exaggerated Art Deco geometric form in print ads had become quite common — employed partly to get the audience's attention and partly to appeal to the elite (and those with elitist aspirations), who appreciated the idea of modern art. Between the popularity of the Art Deco style in illustration and the growing use of photography, American advertising moved from the presentation of largely verbal pitches to an emphasis on visual persuasiveness. There was now a great commercial fascination with the formal qualities of European avant-garde art and with how abstraction and symbolism could be used to express the new.[12]

10. Karen Davies, *At Home in Manhattan: Modern Decorative Arts, 1925 to the Depression*, exh. cat. (New Haven, Conn.: Yale University Art Gallery), 11.
11. Stephen Bayley, *Harley Earl and the Dream Machine* (New York: Alfred A. Knopf, 1983), 32.
12. Roland Marchand, *Advertising and the American Dream: Making Way for Modernity, 1920–1940* (Berkeley: University of California Press, 1985), 117–163.

European avant-garde art was typically explained to Americans in terms of its aesthetics; the complex ideology that propelled most of it was omitted. But a few European journals covering advertising, graphic design, and typography were distributed domestically and did help acquaint Americans with design done in accord with the "new principles," which differed substantially from the "modernistic" style already popular here. One of these magazines, *Gebrauchsgraphik: The Monthly Magazine for the Promotion of Art in Advertising*, was published in Berlin beginning in the 1920s, with English translations. It surveyed projects such as travel posters, pharmaceutical packaging, and exhibition designs. Its editor, Dr. H.K. Frenzel, presented only graphic design; there was no coverage of the other arts or crafts. Yet *Gebrauchsgraphik* was not an advertising-industry trade journal. Catering to an audience specifically interested in the aesthetic development of print, it became the prototype for graphic design magazines that appeared after World War II, such as *Graphis* and *Communication Arts*, which exhibit commercial work in a gallerylike manner — highlighting its formal quality as an applied art and giving it a dignity it generally does not enjoy. Besides featuring commercial examples, *Gebrauchsgraphik* focused on experimental German designers, both in and outside the Bauhaus, and reported on the work of other designers in Europe, such as that by the American expatriate E. McKnight Kauffer, who lived in England until 1940. The respectability of commercial art was enhanced by its presentation in *Gebrauchsgraphik*, and American designers duly noted the benefits of connecting graphic design to art.

Commercial Art and Industry, published in London, was another journal covering modern graphic design that was available in the United States during the 1920s and 1930s. It was more a "publicity" journal than *Gebrauchsgraphik* and was not so selectively edited. However, it did report on important work on the Continent and in England, particularly big public projects such as the design programs for the British Rail Association, the Shell Oil Company, and the London Underground, all of which were carried out in keeping with formal modernist principles. The French journals *Publicité* and *Arts et Métiers Graphiques* treated commercial and experimental design, favoring poster designers such as Jean Carlu, who, like Cassandre, worked in a heavily illustrative style that married Art Deco with techniques such as photomontage. The imagery in their work often glamorized modern icons such as automobiles, phonographs, neon lights, and machinery. The innovativeness depicted in these journals was almost completely formal; the cheerful progressivism of the work would easily translate into a pragmatic approach to domestic design problems.

The most interesting American periodical then covering Modernism was *Advertising Arts*, a supplement to the advertising trade journal *Advertising Buying and Selling*. Published in New York from 1930 to 1935, it was more unruly and

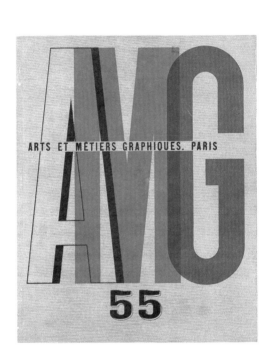

Designer unknown
Arts et Métiers Graphiques 55
1 November 1936
cover: 12 1/8 x 9 5/8 format
© *Arts et Métiers Graphiques*, Paris

eclectic than any of the European magazines yet vividly caught the images and ideas that were firing the imaginations of commercial artists, art directors, and advertisers.

Some articles did attempt to make direct connections between European Modernism and commercial design practice. For example, Clarence P. Hornung, a New York packaging and trademark designer, contributed an article to the July 1930 issue entitled "Architecture as a Source in Modern Design," illustrated with sketches by the German expressionist architect Eric Mendelsohn. Hornung wrote that both the modern architect and the modern graphic designer were concerned with "the conquest of space," and he drew formal parallels between plans and elevations and the schematic design of page layouts.

Among the more intriguing articles in *Advertising Arts* were those by Mehemed Fehmy Agha, the art director of *Vogue* (and, later, *Vanity Fair* and *House & Garden*), who had been an art director in Paris and Berlin before moving to New York City in 1929 at the invitation of Condé Nast. Agha took it upon himself to translate the most experimental European developments into terms the American designer and art director could understand. In his October 1930 article "What Makes a Magazine 'Modern'?" he illustrated the recent history of typography with reproductions of pages from a Bauhaus publication and a Weiner Werkstatte catalogue, while poking fun at the complexity of modernist typographic ideals.[13] Often adopting a world-weary tone in his articles, Agha would reject the ideals of the modern movement and deride the way in which theory attached itself to avant-garde forms. But he illustrated these diatribes with such interesting material — one 1931 article had examples of typography by Richard Neutra, El Lissitzky, Le Corbusier, and Kurt Schwitters — that the sheer novelty of the work would attract attention, no matter what he had to say about it or how far he removed it from its original revolutionary context.

A number of books published around 1930 helped disseminate information about European modernist graphic design. The anthology *Circle: The International Survey of Constructivist Art* (1931) contained the first English translation of Jan Tschichold's *Die Neue Typographie*. *Mise en Page* (1931), by A. Tolmer, published in Paris but translated into English, was an eccentric compilation of the entire range of new graphic techniques and styles. After exhorting the contemporary designer to "work in the spirit of the age" the author proceeded to overlay the modern compositions with classical geometry and Gothic expression, using montage, collage, pochoir, and cello-

13. Mehemed Fehmy Agha, "What Makes a Magazine 'Modern'?" *Advertising Arts* (October 1930): 16. "These vagabond theories," Agha jibed, "originated by Spaniards in France and exported to Germany via Russia, arrived back in France via Holland and Switzerland, only to settle down in Dessau and be taught to Japanese students by Hungarian professors."

phane pages — the idea being that modern design embodies timeless truth while expressing the contemporary spirit.

It would be wrong to assume that American designers were totally dependent on news from abroad to define modern design or to make the crucial connection between form and ideology. Some, like Paul Rand, who visited Europe in the late 1920s, had firsthand knowledge of the new work. Many were interested in art, and, if they had any training at all, had received it in drawing or painting — since there were then no formal design curricula; these designers thus quite naturally turned to the noncommercial media for inspiration.

Publications such as those described above did not only reach designers. They also helped to influence potential clients of design and to create a receptive atmosphere for the new work. And while the Great Depression caused some patrons to become cautious, it led others to take risks. The design and advertising program of the Container Corporation of America, to take one pioneering instance, was created during the 1930s by its founder-chairman, Walter Paepcke, in order both to build a positive image for the company — which, since it did not manufacture consumer goods, had little public identity — and to help combat the anti-big business sentiment prevalent during the Depression. Through a carefully orchestrated campaign that used designers chosen from the pages of *Gebrauchsgraphik*,[14] their advertising helped forge a benign, progressive image by equating the patronage of advanced art and design with enlightened business management.

Despite the publicity that modern design was receiving in the United States in the 1920s and early 1930s, only a small portion of print design was actually being conceived according to the new principles. A review of the Art Directors Club annuals and other contemporary publications that reproduced posters, brochures, and the like shows that it was some years before recognizably modern (as opposed to stylistically modernist) work began appearing. It took time for examples to be widely seen, for clients to be generally convinced, and for arguments justifying the new style to percolate.

When truly modern graphic design did start surfacing, by the mid-to-late 1930s, its strongest expressions were to be found in the work of the European émigrés who had arrived in America during that decade. Fortuitously, many of them found clients who patronized their work precisely because it represented a new approach to visual communication. These designers' experiences were not uniformly positive. While Will Burtin expressed his pleasure in discovering "people less biased by narrow

14. James Sloan Allen, *The Romance of Commerce and Culture: Capitalism, Modernism, and the Chicago-Aspen Crusade for Cultural Reform* (University of Chicago Press, 1983), 30.

IF YOU don't like full skirts, turn your eyes to the left.

ALIX is making these graceful dinner dresses with square necks and

TIGHT DRAPERY pulled over the form and held firmly with

A TWIST of the material. They are not always dead black but often

CHALK WHITE, which looks much newer for little dinners.

LONG SLEEVES replace the done-to-death jacket and

WHITE SANDALS emphasize the whiteness of the white.

SOME have no apparent fulness but cling to the body like

WET CLOTH, flat in front with the new tight drapery behind.

CHANEL also provides for those who hate bouffant skirts by her

STRAIGHT STRAPLESS black dresses with naked tops like

SARGENT'S portrait of Madame X, the line of the decolletage

CUT HEART-SHAPED and the skirts flowing out toward the hem.

MOLYNEUX does slinky black dresses with little

POINTED TRAINS and a series of princesse dresses that are

PLAIN OR PRINTED, and very easy to wear.

MAINBOCHER gives you a new silhouette, with a simple

MOLDED TOP and a slim skirt with a gathered flounce like a

LAMPSHADE put on just below the crucial point of the derrière.

SCHIAPARELLI also makes long-sleeved dinner dresses, but

JACKETS STILL APPEAR in the Schiaparelli collection, and these are

WOOLEN JACKETS embroidered in gold and beads or else

SATIN JACKETS with large embroidered silk motifs. They are worn over

SIMPLE MOLDED DRESSES with brassiere tops. Fresher for spring are

SCHIAPARELLI'S printed evening dresses with their variously

SHAPED HOODS that slip down like capes over the shoulders.

FUR BOLEROS are shown over all these molded

DINNER DRESSES and the smartest are black fox or

SILVER FOX mounted on black crepe de Chine

SKINTIGHT to the figure, stopping short.

The dress at the left is by Alix at Bergdorf Goodman.

TO MAKE YOU THINK that hips are thin as air.

ALIX
HOYNINGEN-HUENE

61

162

interpretations of tradition *or* modernist rhetoric,"[15] Herbert Matter often spoke of his disillusionment with American clients and their visual naïveté.[16] Whatever their individual reactions, the work of the émigrés as a group had a great impact on American design, and they in turn were affected by their new environment. The designs they created in the United States universally reflect a decreasing dependence on modernist doctrine and a willingness to make open, pragmatic interpretations of that style.

In 1934 Alexey Brodovitch, who had been designing theatrical sets and department store ads and displays in Paris in the late 1920s, was recruited by *Harper's Bazaar* editor Carmel Snow to become the magazine's art director; he would hold the job until 1958. Snow and the magazine's publishers, who wanted the luxury goods featured in it to retain their allure despite the Depression, gave him license to make radical design changes. His Parisian work had been strongly geometric and semiabstract, reflecting the influence of Fernand Léger, Man Ray, A.M. Cassandre, and Le Corbusier. Brodovitch brought a predilection for architectural structure and space to *Harper's Bazaar*. He had Cassandre and Bayer create startling, posteresque cover illustrations. On the inside he combined an inventive but restrained typographic approach with a daring use of photography. He hired photographers such as Richard Avedon, Louise Dahl-Wolfe, Hoyningen-Huene, and Man Ray, and gave them free rein; they delivered images that broke away from the photographs of stiffly posed models typical of the time.

Brodovitch had an exquisite eye for cropping, and he composed the pictures without a grid but with full regard for the drama of the layout at hand. Using negative space as powerfully as pictorial space, he designed spreads as discrete entities and sequenced them in a way that gave to each issue a feeling of movement and variety. His palette of typefaces was simple: Bodoni (the quintessential modern serif face), typewriter (a nod to the machine), a genteel script (a note of Dada), and Le Corbusier's stencil typeface. Type was generally set in regular columns using justified type, but the compositions also contained surprises such as type set in shapes that related to forms in the photographs. Overall, his design (along with the editorial content) worked to connect the novelty of fashion to innovation in art, photography, literature, and theater. Brodovitch's *Harper's Bazaar* looks contemporary even today.

Will Burtin was another émigré whose work affected the appearance of popular American magazines. A graphic designer from Cologne, he produced commercial work based on Bauhaus ideals. He applied a simple, functionalist aesthetic to projects he did for *Architectural Record* and the U.S. Army Air Corps from 1938 to 1945, as well as to *Fortune* magazine, where he served as art director from 1945 to 1949.

Alexey Brodovitch, Art Director
Harper's Bazaar 15 March 1938
pp. 60–61: 12 3/4 x 9 3/4 format
Hoyningen-Huene photograph
Courtesy *Harper's Bazaar*
© 1938 The Hearst Corporation

15. Will Burtin, "Integration: The New Discipline in Design," *Graphis* 27 (1949): 230–233.
16. Unpublished commentary by Herbert Matter, Yale University, October 1980.

SCOPE

Vol. IV, Number 3, Fall 1954
Copyright 1954, The Upjohn
Company, Kalamazoo, Michigan

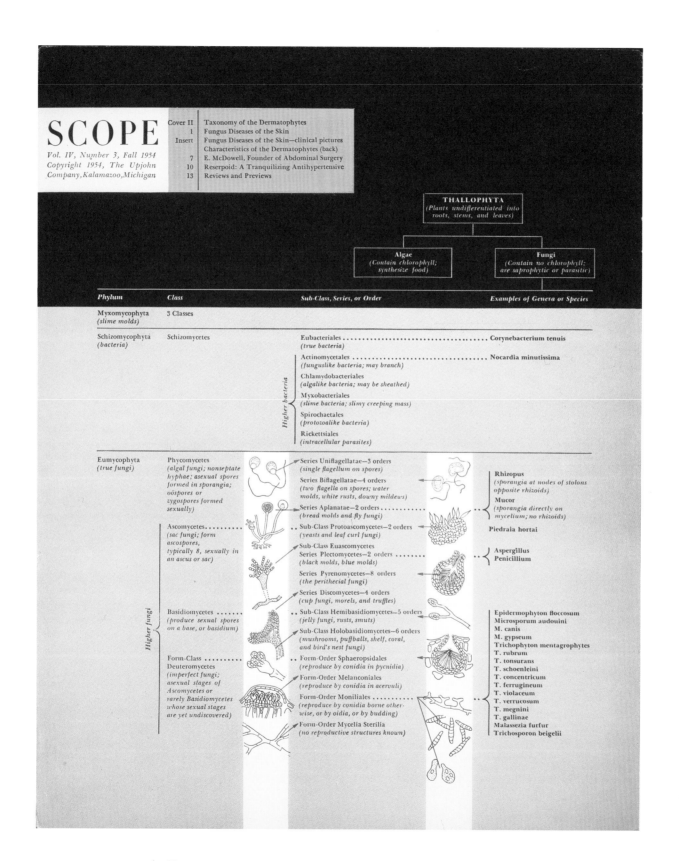

THALLOPHYTA
(Plants undifferentiated into roots, stems, and leaves)

Algae
(Contain chlorophyll; synthesize food)

Fungi
(Contain no chlorophyll; are saprophytic or parasitic)

Phylum	Class	Sub-Class, Series, or Order	Examples of Genera or Species
Myxomycophyta *(slime molds)*	3 Classes		
Schizomycophyta *(bacteria)*	Schizomycetes	Eubacteriales .... *(true bacteria)*	**Corynebacterium tenuis**
		Actinomycetales .... *(funguslike bacteria; may branch)*	**Nocardia minutissima**
		Chlamydobacteriales *(algalike bacteria; may be sheathed)*	
		Myxobacteriales *(slime bacteria; slimy creeping mass)*	
		Spirochaetales *(protozoalike bacteria)*	
		Rickettsiales *(intracellular parasites)*	

Higher bacteria

Phylum	Class	Sub-Class, Series, or Order	Examples of Genera or Species
Eumycophyta *(true fungi)*	Phycomycetes *(algal fungi; nonseptate hyphae; asexual spores formed in sporangia; oöspores or zygospores formed sexually)*	Series Uniflagellatae—3 orders *(single flagellum on spores)*	
		Series Biflagellatae—4 orders *(two flagella on spores; water molds, white rusts, downy mildews)*	**Rhizopus** *(sporangia at nodes of stolons opposite rhizoids)*
		Series Aplanatae—2 orders *(bread molds and fly fungi)*	**Mucor** *(sporangia directly on mycelium; no rhizoids)*
	Ascomycetes *(sac fungi; form ascospores, typically 8, sexually in an ascus or sac)*	Sub-Class Protoascomycetes—2 orders *(yeasts and leaf curl fungi)*	**Piedraia hortai**
		Sub-Class Euascomycetes Series Plectomycetes—2 orders *(black molds, blue molds)*	**Aspergillus** **Penicillium**
		Series Pyrenomycetes—8 orders *(the perithecial fungi)*	
		Series Discomycetes—4 orders *(cup fungi, morels, and truffles)*	
	Basidiomycetes *(produce sexual spores on a base, or basidium)*	Sub-Class Hemibasidiomycetes—5 orders *(jelly fungi, rusts, smuts)*	**Epidermophyton floccosum** **Microsporum audouini**
		Sub-Class Holobasidiomycetes—6 orders *(mushrooms, puffballs, shelf, coral, and bird's nest fungi)*	**M. canis** **M. gypseum** **Trichophyton mentagrophytes**
	Form-Class Deuteromycetes *(imperfect fungi; asexual stages of Ascomycetes or rarely Basidiomycetes whose sexual stages are yet undiscovered)*	Form-Order Sphaeropsidales *(reproduce by conidia in pycnidia)*	**T. rubrum** **T. tonsurans** **T. schoenleini** **T. concentricum**
		Form-Order Melanconiales *(reproduce by conidia in acervuli)*	**T. ferrugineum** **T. violaceum**
		Form-Order Moniliales *(reproduce by conidia borne otherwise, or by oidia, or by budding)*	**T. verrucosum** **T. megnini** **T. gallinae** **Malassezia furfur** **Trichosporon beigelii**
		Form-Order Mycelia Sterilia *(no reproductive structures known)*	

Higher fungi

Published by Henry Luce, *Fortune* was an intensely pictorial survey of the power of American industry that was directed at industrialists and businessmen. During Burtin's tenure the magazine took on an innovative modern look that matched its audience's aspirations. Like Brodovitch, Burtin used excellent photographers, and he employed imaginative designers and illustrators to tackle the vast numbers of charts, maps, and other features dealing with quantified data that were integral to *Fortune*. He also utilized symbols and imagery derived from surrealist and abstract painting to help convey complex scientific, technological, and economic information. This tactic, which he successfully used, too, in his work for *Scope*, the Upjohn pharmaceutical company's periodical for physicians, assumed a fairly sophisticated degree of visual awareness on the part of the reader.

As a consultant to Walter Paepcke's Container Corporation of America, Herbert Bayer demonstrated the usefulness of modern design to the development of a positive corporate image. His work for the organization ranged from internal communications and print ads to special publications such as the *World Geo-Graphic Atlas* (1953). Bayer presented himself to the Container Corporation as an artist first and foremost. This gave him several quite valuable advantages. It first of all led the business executives he dealt with to respect his expertise unquestioningly, whereas a simple designer, presumably steered more by methodological concerns than by aesthetic ones, likely would have found his work subject to much scrutiny. The second advantage of his role was that it freed Bayer to forge links in his work (however thin) between philosophy and form. "Could not certain laws of perception," he wondered in an article entitled "Contributions toward Rules of Advertising Design," "become an ABC of design, based on the psychological nature of the eye?"[17] But Bayer never isolated these "laws," and indeed his advertising design for the corporation chiefly sprang from personal exegesis, intuition, and motifs in his own paintings. In the *World Geo-Graphic Atlas*, on the other hand, he developed an elegantly straightforward cartographic style, which was supplemented by geographical, political, and ecological information conveyed by pictures, symbols, diagrams, and simple modern typography. The forms he chose to work with fulfill the modernist ideal of presenting information "objectively" and were appropriate to the goal of delineating then current global reality.

The Container Corporation's patronage of "good design" helped bring the aesthetic of Modernism into common visual language. But the easy utilization of the formal parlance of avant-garde art by this and, subsequently, by many other corporations had the ironic dual effect of obscuring corporate agendas *and* the socially

Will Burtin, Art Director
Scope 4, 3 Fall 1954
cover and two spreads,
not paginated: 11 x 8 3/4 format
© The Upjohn Company,
Kalamazoo, Michigan

17. Herbert Bayer, "Contributions toward Rules of Advertising Design," PM 6, 2 (December 1939–January 1940): 6–7.

critical notions that were the underpinnings of the modern movement. Over the years a number of designers became uncomfortable with the commercial appropriation of abstract art. In a speech given at the 1959 International Design Conference in Aspen, Colorado, William Golden, CBS television's creative director for advertising and sales promotion, complained that references to painting in advertising constituted "a wonderful panacea.... Business can accept it because it is successful, and oddly enough 'safe' since it says absolutely nothing."[18]

The work of the Czech designer Ladislav Sutnar offers a distinct counterpoint to Bayer's aestheticized Modernism. Beginning in 1941 he spent years reworking *Sweet's Files*, a set of annually updated catalogues of industrial and architectural products whose original design could not expand to fit the growing number of these products. Relying on the standards set by Jan Tschichold and the Bauhaus, Sutnar used simplified modern typography to establish a clear hierarchy of information. Typographic grids, contrasting weights of sans-serif type, and carefully designed systems of rules, heads, subheads, and standards were devised to ease the reader's way through the bales of material. Sutnar's *Sweet's Files* demonstrated the usefulness of modernist functionalism in graphic design to a wide audience of architects, engineers, and builders.

Herbert Matter's reputation in the United States is mostly based on his photographic work. But not long after his arrival, in 1936, he began producing a body of graphic work that furthered the general interest in modern design. In the early 1930s he had been employed by Cassandre in Paris and had designed a series of striking posters for the Swiss National Tourist Office. Consequently, his work in America reflected a predilection for strong posteresque imagery, usually generated and manipulated photographically. Matter was not too concerned with images derived from technology or art; instead, his basic visual vocabulary was derived from the photographic images and the typographic elements of his subject matter. This is demonstrated in a series of covers he created from 1944 to 1946 for the Los Angeles magazine *Arts & Architecture*. The covers were two-color and had little or no text; the images on them were often the result of darkroom experiments with simple objects or were rebuslike messages for the reader to decipher. Matter's covers were graceful and inventive, created without obvious references to the imagery of the European artists who were his early mentors.

Many of the émigrés became educators, and their version of Modernism had an impact on the creation and growth of design curricula in this country. As already noted, such programs had not existed to guide would-be designers. By the late 1930s, however, a few experimental programs emerged to inculcate modern design

Ladislav Sutnar
Sweet's Files trademark 1942
various formats
© McGraw-Hill Information
Systems, New York

Herbert Bayer
Ralph Waldo Emerson 1952
Container Corporation of America
Great Ideas advertisement
14 x 11
Courtesy Denver Art Museum,
Herbert Bayer Collection and
Archive

Herbert Matter
Arts & Architecture September 1946
cover: 12 3/4 x 10 format
Collection The Herbert Matter
Archive, Yale University

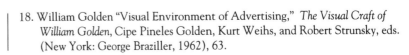

18. William Golden "Visual Environment of Advertising," *The Visual Craft of William Golden*, Cipe Pineles Golden, Kurt Weihs, and Robert Strunsky, eds. (New York: George Braziller, 1962), 63.

theory and pedagogy. The most radical of these were created by ex-Bauhauslers: László Moholy-Nagy reincarnated the German school as the New Bauhaus in Chicago in 1937 with the help of Gyorgy Kepes, a designer and filmmaker from Budapest. Kepes (who in the 1940s would go on to teach at MIT) shared Moholy-Nagy's idea that the designer could be the link between science, technology, and culture and that design education should prepare the student to be a cultural generalist whose specialty would be the ability to create designs that would solve the visual problems at hand, designs that would not serve as ends in themselves. This approach was also pursued from 1933 to 1956 at the progressive Black Mountain College in Asheville, North Carolina, by Bauhauslers Josef Albers and Xanti Schwawinsky, and later by Albers at Yale, where, in the early 1950s, he established one of the nation's first formal graphic design programs. Brodovitch taught a class at the New School for Social Research in New York City, which became one of the most important laboratories for the nurturing of young designers.

Despite the rise of schools rooted in modernist theory, it is clear, looking back at the dissemination of Modernism in design in the United States just before and after World War II, that the look of modern graphic design became much more familiar than the ideas that had helped generate it. The European modernists and their American counterparts found clients who were willing to put the theories into practice for commercial use; there was neither time nor necessity for the manifestos or ideology that had characterized the movement in Europe. Even clients such as the Container Corporation of America, which patronized modern design in part because of the progressive cultural values it held, were doing so primarily because of the forward-looking image they could achieve by associating themselves with contemporary art. The revolutionary ideology behind the avant-garde work of Marinetti and El Lissitzky was ignored; designers in America retained only its formal aspects, which evolved into the visual language of contemporary American institutions and corporations. After World War II the continuing development of Modernism in graphic design was concurrent with the rise of Abstract Expressionism as an indigenous art movement, and much of the enthusiasm for modern design was conflated with that for Modernism in painting. For instance, in 1950 the art historian Thomas Hess wrote an article entitled "Eleven Painters Influencing Graphic Arts,"[19] in which he noted that the best art of the time had two common characteristics: "emphasis on the beauty of order and of the materials them-selves, and absorption in the drama of the individual creator whose intimate expression commands an equally intimate response from the spectator." This spotlight on the "individual creator" is quite contrary to the founding ideals of modern design, with its

Gyorgy Kepes
Advertisement for the School of
Design, Chicago circa 1940
Courtesy University of Illinois at
Chicago
The University Library
Department of Special Collections

19. Thomas B. Hess, "Eleven Painters Influencing Graphic Arts," *Ninth Graphic Arts Production Yearbook* (New York: Colton Press, 1950), 10–21.

bias toward objectivity and functionalism. But Hess was in fact describing a different kind of functionalism, one based on an exchange between the author-artist-designer and the audience that depends less on an accurately conveyed concept than on intuition. To be fair, the shift in interest from objective communication to subjective expression cannot be linked to painting alone; jazz, too, was then in a particularly fascinating stage of development, and it also offered a model of the artist as a solitary improvisor.

The intimate connection of form to concept, and the relationship of those forms to ideas in the culture demonstrated in the work of the European émigré designers, redefined graphic design in America. The vitality of the work created by the European designers and by the best of their American counterparts during the 1930s and 1940s is still admired and often referred to as "timeless." But in fact it is precisely because these designers responded to the ideas of their own time, without formal preconceptions, that their work looks so free and genuine. There is no doubt that some of the current admiration for the graphic design of this period is fueled by a Postmodern nostalgia for the forms themselves. Yet today's designers would do well to look beyond those forms — to the principles behind them — for a revitalization of contemporary graphic design.

Lorraine Wild teaches graphic design and design history at the California Institute of the Arts, Valencia, and is director of the school's visual communication program. Her writing has appeared in ID *magazine and the* AIGA Journal of Graphic Design, *among other periodicals. She also maintains a graphic design practice in Los Angeles.*

Fortune

November 1954

In this issue: The New Age of Mergers   Is Dispersal Good Defense?
Brazil's Big Bid for Dollars   The Web of Word-of-Mouth
Capital Goods: The Crucial Customers   And twenty other timely articles—see page 1

Leo Lionni

[born 1910]

With a doctorate in economics and a passion for art, Leo Lionni cut his teeth as a commercial designer in Italy in the 1930s. Under the wing of F.T. Marinetti, the leader of Italian Futurism, Lionni energetically painted abstract canvases. Later, as an art director and designer for Motta, one of Italy's leading food purveyors, he applied photomontage to advertising for products. One step ahead of the fascists he emigrated to the United States in 1939 and found a job with N.W. Ayer & Co. in Philadelphia, the advertising agency that handled the account of the culturally progressive Container Corporation of America. The company allowed him to employ his modernist principles in their print advertising.

Despite Lionni's significant output during and after the war, his major contribution to American graphic design came with his appointment in 1949 as art director of *Fortune* magazine, which since 1929 had been a wellspring of design innovation. Lionni remade the magazine not by simply changing its typeface or column margins but by giving it another distinctive editorial personality marked by the work of journalist-illustrators and photographers. After leaving the magazine in 1961, he turned to sculpture and painting and to writing and illustrating children's books.

As art director of *Fortune* for twelve years, Lionni had a powerful impact on the magazine's content as well as its imagery.

Fortune November 1954
cover: 13 x 10 1/4 format
Walter Allner illustration
© Time, Inc., New York

Will Burtin had brought a Bauhaus sensibility to *Fortune,* and I felt comfortable with that kind of language. But when I started as art director I moved against it, softening the whole thing up. The Bauhaus idea was that sans serif was better than serif type. Sans-serif type requires a certain kind of layout; serif type is more plastic. It's not necessary to make squares and rectangles with serif type, so I put my functional ideas in other details.

I believe that the great difficulty in a magazine like *Fortune* is making the division between advertising and editorial layout as clear as possible. From a moral point of view, advertising should be declared as advertising. To work with this idea and at the same time make everybody happy is not easy, because the advertisers want to be confused with the editorial. Yet I didn't want design to dominate the magazine. I wanted sections with audacious copy and photographs and was interested in manipulating the spaces in the magazine to enable the use of creative pictures. After several pages of small portraits, farm scenes, or industrial scenes, inserting a full-page chromatic image of a person's face provides a change of pace.

Design during the "monumental era" of *Fortune* was very elegant and spare; during Burtin's reign its emphasis was on information graphics. My interest was in variety

171

Bentley-Farina: a large car by the designer of the Cisitalia.

Simca: a Farina-designed popular French car of great elegance.

It is sometimes said that European automobile designers achieve so high a standard because they are preoccupied with relatively simple problems. The expensive and frivolous sports car is supposed to be easier to design than the inexpensive family-sized car. But sobriety no less than frivolity is entitled to the best, and principles of good design which happen to be applied to sports cars can, of course, be applied just as effectively to larger automobiles, whether they are for sports or family use, patiently tapped out by hand or rolled off the assembly line by the thousands.

Many European cars illustrate this. Pinin Farina's Bentley is a family-sized car matching his Cisitalia for subtlety and verve. The Simca is also based on the Cisitalia. It is a less costly sports car designed for large scale production. The Triumph, a popular British car, is a similar adjustment to technical processes, adapting the razor-edge lines of the custom built Bentley to faster, simpler fabrication. The Jaguar Mark VII is a large, five passenger car designed specifically to compete on the American market. It has many features comparable to American designs, and a remarkably well finished interior.

One of the most interesting European cars is the Volkswagen. This small, rear-engined automobile carries four passengers and is noted for its balance and maneuverability. At first sight the Volkswagen presents a somewhat disquieting contour, but the logic of its form encloses the centered passenger compartment and the front and rear hoods under a metal lid like a walnut shell, with a structural corrugation running along the center of both hoods. Fenders and other details have been treated with equal directness, chromium decoration is judiciously applied, and the reasonableness of the whole design is expressed with considerable style.

The technological skill that goes into the creation of an automobile should be accompanied by a more earnest attention to principles of design than most of the public and most professional designers have given them. An automobile is not a shoe front or a new dress, however much it may be influenced by fashion, and the automobiles in this exhibition represent some of the most serious thought given in our time to the esthetics of automobile design.—A.D.

Triumph: the "razor-edge" style in a popular British car.

Volkswagen: Ferdinand Porsche; rear-engined German family car; both ends cased like a walnut shell.

8 *automobiles*

1 **Mercedes**   Lent by D. Cameron Peck

2 **Cisitalia**   Lent by John Wheelock Freeman

3 **Bentley**   Lent by Briggs S. Cunningham

4 **Talbot**   Lent by Carroll Bagley

5 **Jeep**   Lent by Willys-Overland Motors, Inc.

6 **Cord**   Lent by Charles F. Hewitt

7 **MG**   Lent by Sports and Utility Motors, Mamaroneck

8 **Lincoln Continental**   Lent by Bimel Kehm

Jeep **5**   1951 (model first produced in 1941). Manufactured by Willys-Overland Motors, Inc., Toledo, Ohio. Overall length 10 feet 4 inches.

The admirable Jeep seems to have the combined appeal of an intelligent dog and a perfect gadget. It is an appeal so vast that this wonderful tool for transportation has won approval for much more than its practicality, though the engineers who perfected it worked without the concern for style with which other automobiles are designed.

The Jeep looks like a tray, or perhaps a sturdy sardine can, on wheels. Part of the top appears to have been cut open and folded up, to serve as a windshield. From it a canvas canopy can be stretched over some metal struts to the back of the car, thus affording temporary shelter from rain. Large wheels dominate the design, and insist rather than suggest that the Jeep's primary purpose is transportation.

One of the most striking illustrations of its direct design is the front fender. It is composed of two rectangular platforms placed at the best angle for preventing mud splash. The two sections are connected by an overlap, left plainly visible, and the lower section is joined to a small step. The side walls are low enough for passengers to step in, thus eliminating mechanically troublesome doors. Even refinements of contour grow out of practical considerations: the fenders have rounded corners to avoid cutting passengers as they get in.

With its wheels removed and the windshield folded flat the Jeep fits into a shipping case. Unerated and on the road it can maneuver its way through spaces blocked to larger vehicles. It can be stood on end and pushed through narrow passages; it has on occasion been dismantled and carried, piece by piece, over unmanageable terrain, and with suitable equipment it can be driven underwater. Bolts visible on the wheels and the body facilitate either the removal of parts or periodic tightening.

Those who have used the Jeep will recall certain limitations of comfort. Yet there are few automobiles which give their drivers so exhilarating a sense of speed and control. The Jeep substitutes for a deliberate esthetic program the formative principles of construction; its design is unified by the economy, (disdaining the merely decorative) with which each part is fitted for its purpose. It is one of the few genuine expressions of machine art.

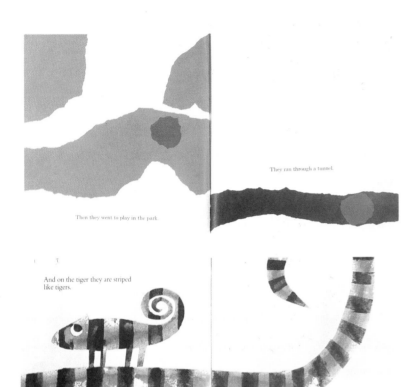

and cinematography. I wanted to make orderliness invisible. I'm an anti-grid man. The best grid is the eye. When you rely on the eye rather than on a grid you're totally free.

I never designed *Fortune* for design's sake but rather to make the magazine look civilized, relaxed, with moments of visual intensity achieved through pacing. After a strong visual impact I wanted restful pages and then another kind of pacing for the story after that. I wanted to attract attention without conventional means and to present the reader with easy choices.

Every art director has to make a compromise between what his client wants and what he himself wants. I can only operate within a certain, let's call it, ideology. I cannot change that. It's a matter of self-expression. I want to be there, not only in name but in spirit.

little blue and little yellow 1959
Written and designed by Leo Lionni
8 x 7 1/2 format
Published by Ivan Obolensky, Inc.,
New York

A color of his own 1975
Written and designed by Leo Lionni
7 1/2 square format
Published by Pantheon Books,
a division of Random House, Inc.,
New York

8 Automobiles 1951
by Arthur Drexler
unpaginated: 10 x 13 format
© 1951 The Museum of Modern
Art, New York

Fortune February 1960
cover: 13 x 10 1/4 format
Leo Lionni design
© Time, Inc., New York

Cipe Pineles

[born 1910]

In 1933 Cipe Pineles, a Viennese-born art student, began working for Mehemed Fehmy Agha, the art director of *Vanity Fair* and *Vogue*. She was infused with his progressive principles of editorial design: generous amounts of white space, unconventionally wide margins, sans-serif type, and photography cropped and framed to heighten the graphic drama of the printed page. Pineles became art director of *Glamour*, and though she was working specifically for a fashion magazine (and would continue to do so until leaving her last magazine job, at *Mademoiselle,* in the late 1950s), she practiced design journalism, not decoration. During the war Pineles worked in Paris with her husband, the designer William Golden, on the army's *Overseas Woman,* a magazine for Red Cross and G.I. women. After the war she took on the art directorship of *Seventeen* magazine, where her most significant achievement was the innovative employ of painters as editorial illustrators, among them Jacob Lawrence, Robert Gwathmey, Philip Evergood, and her longtime friend Ben Shahn. After Golden's premature death she married another design pioneer, Will Burtin, whom she joined as a business partner.

Usually an art director is hired because a change is needed or wanted. In my experience, the first thing a publisher does when a magazine is in trouble, no matter what is wrong, is alter the look, as if change is a panacea for whatever ails it. But design is not a matter of cleaning house, changing the typefaces or column widths just for the sake of doing so. Design is dealing with content.

An exciting magazine comes with tackling issues that are usually reserved for the printed word and using this material in greater visual depth. So the art director on a magazine is responsible for interpreting, in visual terms, the contents of a publication, from the appointment of photographers and artists to deciding whether to use many typefaces or just one. But most important is the ability to harness all that, working with the editor to create momentum so that the reader will keep turning the pages.

Magazine design should never play second fiddle to advertising. If the editorial content is very interesting and has a reason for being, it attracts advertising. A fashion magazine should report on what the industry has to offer. We are journalists in our special field.

Seventeen July 1949
cover: 13 1/4 x 10 1/2 format
Francesco Scavullo photograph
© 1949 Triangle Communications,
Inc., New York

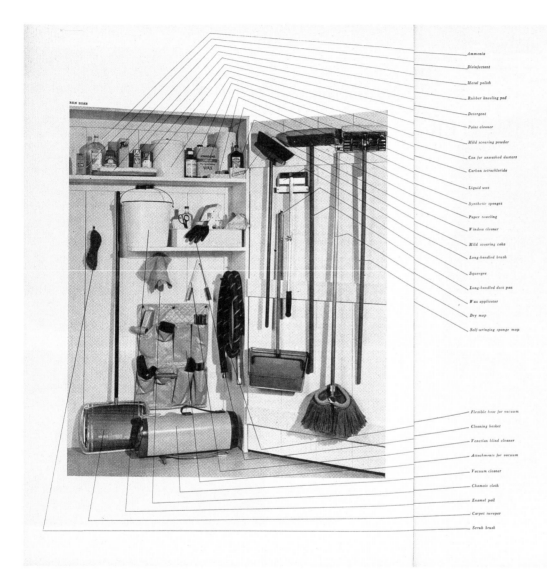

BEN ROSE

Ammonia

Disinfectant

Metal polish

Rubber kneeling pad

Detergent

Paint cleaner

Mild scouring powder

Can for unwashed dusters

Carbon tetrachloride

Liquid wax

Synthetic sponges

Paper toweling

Window cleaner

Mild scouring cake

Long-handled brush

Squeegee

Long-handled dust pan

Wax applicator

Dry mop

Self-wringing sponge mop

Flexible hose for vacuum

Cleaning basket

Venetian blind cleaner

Attachments for vacuum

Vacuum cleaner

Chamois cloth

Enamel pail

Carpet sweeper

Scrub brush

Please don't take a quick glance at our cleaning closet and say in despair that you haven't a tenth of that space in which to store your equipment! We know that few householders have, but we spread out our idea of the basic needs so that you could see it all. Try to devise a compact arrangement in the space you have, even if it must be in several places. We want particularly to help you pick essentials from all the aids and gadgets available.

Let us say firmly at the outset that there are almost no absolutes about the materials and equipment you use for cleaning or about the methods. In instances where we feel strongly, we will tell you which we think are best and why. Of course, you may find other materials, tools and methods which are more suitable to your particular ways of working in your own home.

THE VACUUM CLEANER The most important piece of cleaning equipment is a vacuum cleaner. It can do many tasks which would otherwise require a tool apiece. The big point is to buy all the attachments and *use them well*. You should read and understand all of the instructions and suggestions that come with every vacuum cleaner. And also read and follow directions for keeping the cleaner in order. The tank-type cleaner we show you on the opposite page, for instance, comes with all attachments except the small soft brush which is invaluable for dusting anything and everything in the house. But the brush can be bought for a slight extra charge and is well worth it. Also, these attachments come stored in a sort of box, made like a little satchel. When storage space is very limited, it is practical to hang as much of the cleaning equipment as you possibly can. We bought a shoe bag which we think holds the attachments beautifully.

Of course, some of us can't afford to buy vacuum cleaners. If you can't, you will need, in addition to everything else shown on the opposite page: a horsehair floor brush, a radiator brush, a Venetian blind brush and a whisk broom for upholstery. The cleaner plus attachments can take care of all the jobs these brushes do.

THE CLEANING BASKET Perhaps the next most important adjunct to your cleaning with ease and expedition is a cleaning basket, to carry with you as you work. The one we've shown is metal, but a woven basket of comparable (Continued on page 112)

BY CHARLOTTE ADAMS

109

Blessings
to give and
to receive

Seventeen December 1949
"Blessings to Give and to Receive"
pp. 60–61: 13 1/4 x 10 1/2
© 1949 Triangle Communications,
Inc., New York

Charm October 1951
"Here's What You Need to Clean
Your Home"
pp. 108–109: 11 1/4 x 8 1/2 format
Courtesy *Glamour* © 1951 (renewed
1979) The Condé Nast Publications,
Inc., New York

I never started out with a preconceived idea. Once I took on a magazine, the
ideas for change came with the development of
the magazine. Before I went to *Glamour* as
art director, I was the assistant art director at
Vogue, working for M.F. Agha, where I learned
everything! We used to make many versions of
the same feature. If we did twenty pages on
beauty with twenty different photographers, we
made scores of different layouts in order to extract every bit of drama or humor we could from
the material. Agha drove us to that because he
was never happy with just one solution.

From *Glamour* I went to
Seventeen, where I used many illustrators,
choosing those whose work was appropriate to
the editorial content. The reason an art director makes any decision is to develop a personality for a magazine. Once I made a decision
about whom to use, whether an illustrator or a
photographer, I simply discussed the viewpoint
of the story with them, then gave them free
rein. Out of this would evolve the solution, not
because we forced the artist to do it but because the problem was solved without
constraint.

I asked painters like Robert
Gwathmey and Ben Shahn to contribute illustrations because I wanted to open the magazine
to artists whose work the reader might not
ordinarily see. I also wanted to engage artists
who were not confined by the clichés of illustration. At *Seventeen*, under the pretext that
young people aren't prejudiced about such
things, and that they are interested in anything
in print, I used such artists to broaden the
visual experience of the reader.

From the Poster of Protest to the Poster of Liberation

David Kunzle

The poster, almost by definition, is designated for public spaces, for the street. The streets of the United States, indeed the very breathing spaces around them, have been appropriated and polluted — legally, of course, through purchase — by corporations that assault, deceive, fuddle, and cajole us with posters and megaposter-billboards built on steel scaffolds. (These scaffolds often have access ladders that unintentionally make graffiti possible; indeed, graffiti-making has become the specialty of a handful of "billboard correction artists," who offer us their gestures of liberation.) The idea of appropriating prime time and space remains a poster-maker's dawning fantasy.

Those who have tried to buy space for oppositional posters, as in the New York subway system at various times over the last several decades, have often been frustrated.[1] If we are fortunate enough to work in a place congenial to our feelings (that is, with people who share them), we can put posters in our offices, classrooms, union halls, and factories. But the streets, like the electronic media, are still largely closed. Exceptionally, an artist such as Robbie Conal will post his hostility to the deceptions and iniquities of our leaders on public walls and temporary board fences. Since 1986 he has put up as many as fifteen thousand of his posters in ten cities, despite harassment by civic officials.[2]

The political graphics considered in this essay are invitations to break the shell of media-ted apathy. If we cannot normally post posters in the street, we can at least carry them in and through the street, as we can carry two other poster-related media, bumper stickers and T-shirts, with relative impunity. At a political demonstration,

All of the posters reproduced in this essay are from the collection of David Kunzle. Due to the spontaneous manner in which some of this material was created, certain attributions and dates are unknown.

Designer unknown
Cut Military Spending, Meet Human Needs circa 1980
19 x 14 1/2
Published by Commonworks

1. A few artists, however, have made some headway in this area. For information on their work, see pp. 138–143 of Maud Lavin's essay in this book.
2. The author in a conversation with Conal, November 1988. For an article about Conal's work, see Stacy Title, "Facing the Nation: Guerrilla Artist Robbie Conal Paints the Town Red," *Mother Jones* 14, 2 (February–March 1989): 56.

posters are rightly placed, for they are a form of action — silent, visual, and psychological: weapons in our nonviolent war against violence, doubly potent when allied (as in the multimedia work of Shock Battalion in Los Angeles) with guerrilla theater.

The new wave of what might optimistically be called "posters of liberation" started around 1980, after the revolutions in Nicaragua and Iran and in response to the new Reagan Presidency. An interim of relative quiescence followed the end in 1975 of the Vietnam War, which, in its peak years (1966–1972), generated a vast outpouring of "posters of protest."[3] The production of political posters in the 1980s is probably comparable, numerically, to those, but its nature, quality, aims, and means are rather different. The primary targets of the anti-Vietnam War poster — the draft, the bombing of Vietnam and Cambodia, and domestic repression — were already shifting in the early 1970s to the broader issues of racism at home, women's and gay liberation, labor, the environment, and United States support for Third World dictators. These issues were also taken up in a concurrent nationwide wave of public mural art and were touched upon in many forms of gallery, or "high" modernist, art.[4] And, during the lamentably abbreviated Presidential invocation for worldwide human rights in the late 1970s, it even seemed for a moment that some of these issues would enter the mainstream.

The major foreign situations catalyzing opposition to Ronald Reagan early in his administration were the revolution and contra terror in Nicaragua and the revolutionary activity and United States support of death squads in El Salvador. Solidarity groups sprang up across the country and produced posters as part of their multifarious agitational efforts. Central America (chiefly El Salvador and Nicaragua but also Guatemala) continues, for good and the worst reasons, to spearhead the anti-imperialist poster contingent, which also embraces or embraced Chile and Grenada (the latter, alas, all but forgotten), the Middle East (with accelerating recognition of Palestinian rights, taboo until a few years ago) and southern Africa (Namibia, South African apartheid). In this context Vietnam survives chiefly — but resonantly — in the slogan "No Vietnam War in Central America." The defense of black civil rights in South Africa in some ways parallels the support given the black power movements of the late 1960s.

The domestic front is dominated by threats to the physical environment and to human survival posed by nuclear arms and energy. These threats have given rise to a genre one might call apocalypse posters, intended to be thrilling and awful at the same time, like Albrecht Dürer's *Apocalypse* woodcuts of 1498. In the past popular voices were raised to demand better living conditions; today we beg to be allowed simply to live. The grassroots issues surrounding women's rights, gay rights, and AIDS

3. David Kunzle, *Posters of Protest: The Posters of Political Satire in the U.S., 1966–1970*, exh. cat. (University of California, Santa Barbara, 1971).
4. See Lucy Lippard, *Get the Message?: A Decade of Art for Social Change* (New York: E. P. Dutton, 1984).

are currently among the chief ones generating posters and broadening their social base. Finally, clustered around the big subjects of war, peace, and human rights are an assortment of "lesser" ones, such as handgun control, capital punishment, on-the-job safety, and undocumented workers.

It is hazardous to try to summarize or to compare and contrast the style and quality, the look and feel of the political poster of the 1960s with that of the 1980s, as both share characteristics of individuality, eclecticism, and experimentation — not to mention sheer numerical profusion. These are of course familiar characteristics of any artistic vanguard, but to them must be added a quality such vanguards generally lack: an accessible language. The poster, now acting as a political rather than an artistic vanguard, aspires to reach a broad audience, the more and the less educated, the professional intellectual and the factory worker alike; for the issues addressed, as well as the forms chosen, are broadly based.

The discernible differences of form, which translate into differences of feeling and intention, flow from a new kind of seriousness, a political maturation perhaps. The Vietnam War policies of the United States were greeted by posters that bespoke a heady mixture of scorn, cynicism, and gallows humor, eroticized counter-aggression, and polemics submerged in surreal effects. The Reagan-era poster of liberation, on the other hand, might be said to capture a middle ground: it is more sober than witty and carries none of the cynicism of, say, commercial illustrator Tomi Ungerer's brilliant and often morally and politically ambiguous poster-cartoons of the 1960s. Moreover, the poster today is less apt to parody other media, such as advertising and Pop Art, and is more stringently political, rather than cultural, in its critique.

The poster of protest arose out of a growing sense that the Vietnam War was tearing America apart, just at the time when the civil rights movement promised a measure of integration. The poster of liberation, of the present era, is a poster of integration and of recognition that there is more than a particular war in a particular place to divide us; global issues demand a global view. *A New World of Understanding* is proposed, reversing the view that places the rich northern countries on top, above, and the poor southern countries underneath, below.

A bridge between the two eras is to be found in posters satirizing Presidents: Lyndon B. Johnson and Richard Nixon in the earlier decade, Ronald Reagan in the 1980s. Both LBJ and Reagan are seen as fabricating movie images of themselves and their actions: LBJ the grandiose producer of the great, bloody, Vietnam movie spectacular and Reagan the genial TV game-show host, dispensing huge money prizes to the lucky (i.e., rich) and signing cigarette cartons for his friends and fellow addicts; the jelly beans (pep pills?) are presumably for the masses as well as for himself. His grand-opera audience, attired in Founding Father costume, sits raptly before a screening of the kitsch

David Singer
Master of Ceremonies 1984
27 x 22
Published by Celestial Arts

Nordahl
Vietnam — An Eastern Theatre Production circa 1967
28 3/8 x 22 13/16
Published by Gross National Product

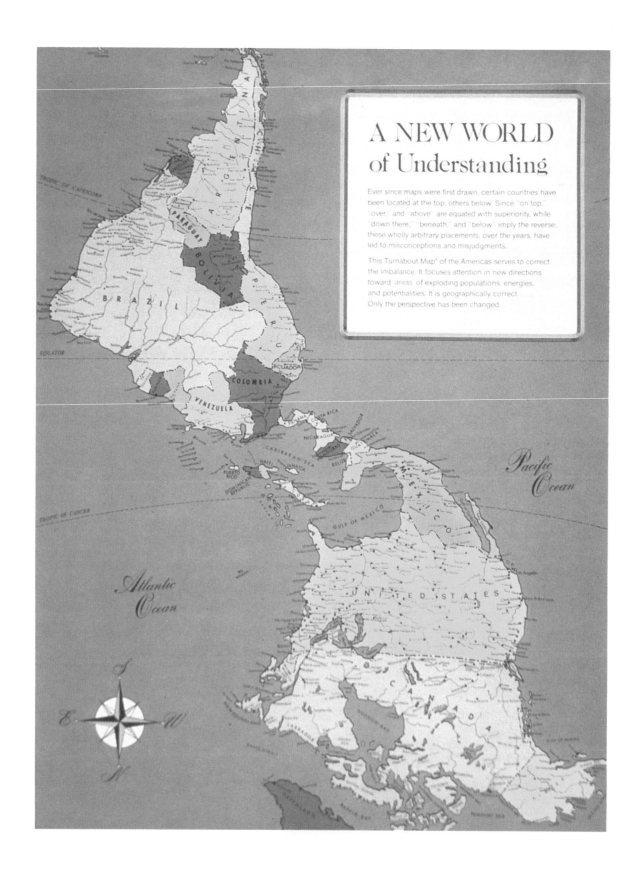

A NEW WORLD
of Understanding

Ever since maps were first drawn, certain countries have been located at the top, others below. Since "on top," "over," and "above" are equated with superiority, while "down there," "beneath," and "below" imply the reverse, these wholly arbitrary placements, over the years, have led to misconceptions and misjudgments.

This Turnabout Map° of the Americas serves to correct the imbalance. It focuses attention in new directions toward areas of exploding populations, energies, and potentialities. It is geographically correct. Only the perspective has been changed.

icons of American prosperity, arrogance, and militarism. In a society taught to see reality as a game and to use media products as a drug, under a President unable to separate political facts from media fictions, it is apposite that he who once peddled a "mild" nicotine drug should now peddle mild-sounding political pap. Scientific reality, however, requires that the statutory health warning be added.

It is inevitable that media constructs such as American Presidents be exposed by the deconstructing of media tricks. High-tech surface realism, which non-commercial posters, aimed at head and heart, normally eschew, is used in the political poster with the force of irony. The *Life*-style magnificence of the nuclear mushroom cloud is instantly deflated by the absurd, plaintive motto — "One nuclear bomb can ruin your whole day" — which has become positively banal through myriad appearances on T-shirts and bumper stickers. Ironically, the mushroom cloud has become a giant personality of our age; a series of "personality posters," advertised in various progressive magazines, lists portraits of Martin Luther King, Jr., Mohandas Gandhi, Albert Einstein, John Lennon, Mushroom Cloud, Karl Marx, and Che Guevara.

Saving the earth is a recurrent poster theme that has led to many poignant images. In one poster we are invited to salvage our precious, imperiled planet through a rescue metaphor, which, though seriously intended, comes off as faintly comic and inadequate. Better the natural metaphor seen in one square of the patchwork quilt-design poster in which a woman is shown carrying and protecting the world in her belly. As for the hard-to-conceive prospect of nuclear annihilation, some West German poster-makers have imagined the unimaginable better than their American counterparts, perhaps because Germans have experienced massive wartime destruction of their homeland and Americans have not. These grim posters indict both the Nazis and the American government, with its policy of planting short-range nuclear missiles in German soil. The unimaginable size of the arsenals accumulated toward a nuclear war is best conveyed in a simple diagram-poster entitled *World Nuclear Firepower 1984*.

Another favorite genre of political poster comprises adaptations of masterpiece paintings. The reclining young woman in Andrew Wyeth's *Christina's World* (1948) turns to gaze along a landscape crowned by an erupting nuclear power station. Normally seen as a broad symbol of existential alienation, she here becomes the prophetess of a future nuclear contamination. The horses in John Constable's *Hay Wain* (1819–1821) ferry American missiles across England's River Stour. A British national icon of domestic tranquility is thus utilized to indict the United States's nuclear terrorization of Europe. Another American icon, Grant Wood's *American Gothic* (1930), has been parodied, with the heads of the farmer and his wife replaced by post-nuclear holocaust skulls. This painting has also been used to address issues such as noise pollution, agricultural policy, and male supremacy.[5] The critique implicit in masterpiece parody is

Jesse Levine
A New World of Understanding 1982
23 x 17 1/2
Published by Laguna Sales

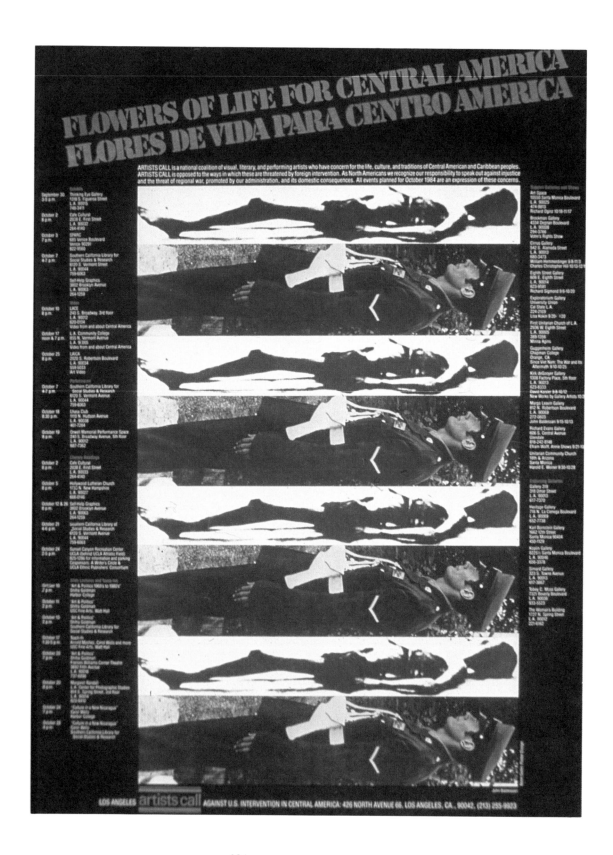

Designer unknown
Amerika Is Devouring Its Children
1970
22 x 15
Published by the College of
Environmental Design, University of
California, Berkeley, to protest the
United States's invasion of
Cambodia

John Baldessari and Norm Gollin
Flowers of Life for Central America
1984
24 1/2 x 18
Published by Los Angeles Artists
Call against Intervention in Central
America

Mark Vallen
Business, as U.$.ual 1984
silkscreen
27 3/4 x 14 3/4
Published by Shock Battalion,
Los Angeles

also of art history as political sanitization, that is, the way art history can work to bleach the politics out of works that in their time were controversial. A few artists are immune to this process. Neither Goya nor Picasso (*Guernica*, 1937), for example, needs parody in order to be updated; their political works may be borrowed and excerpted without violating the spirit in which they were made. Goya's *Saturn Devouring His Children* (1820–1823), for instance, was dramatically adapted in an anti-Vietnam War poster to express the anguished sense of a pacifistic younger generation that it was being devoured by warmongering elders. More recently, the spirit of Goya was called upon in a Matt Mahurin poster showing the nuclear-age Everyman tethered to his missile like a beast condemned to vivisection and devouring itself.

A central theme of the Vietnam War poster was military cruelty, most graphically emblematized in images of napalmed children. The obsession, shared by fine and poster artists alike, with the liquid fire of napalm, which caused such dramatic and "picturesque" disfiguration of civilians, has not passed as such into the age of the Central American wars; however, the continued (if less systematic) use of this and other grisly weapons of United States origin, such as white phosphorus, and the mutilations by Nicaraguan contras and El Salvadoran death squads, remind us that our government continues to condone the worst abuses. Photographs of contra and death-squad atrocities have not, as far as one can tell, been much posterized; pity and guilt are evoked in less sensational ways. The macabre *Business, as U.$.ual* seems less typical than the image of a child gazing in terror out of the darkness; or the minimalist photograph, reminiscent of Hiroshima, of a charred wall with its faint shadow of a crying hand. A poster advertising a program of events organized by the Los Angeles Artists Call against U.S. Intervention in Central America, and entitled *Flowers of Life for Central America*, alternates repeated figures of a smiling military man standing at attention with the corpse (either murdered or starved to death) of his victim. Laid horizontally atop one another, the figures combine to suggest a kind of fossil stratification of a millennial history of repression and killing.

Certain time-honored symbols do not, perhaps cannot, change. The military is typically caricatured as a humanoid monster, as a masked and helmeted dehumanized machine, or as a dinosaur. Characteristically, poster artists do not keep abreast of new weaponry. Thus in the 1980s, for example, we still find bayonets, a hand raised to halt them, in certain posters.

The Central American poster differs in tone from its Vietnam-era predecessor in several essential ways: it evinces a readiness to see not only a victim but a victor; to see not only death and suffering but also a hopeful, even beautiful, revolutionary future; and to see people as struggling for, as well as against. The American peace

5. Wanda M. Corn, *Grant Wood* (New Haven, Conn.: Yale University Press, 1984), 129–142.

"The Assassination of Archbishop Oscar Arnulfo Romero of El Salvador" by J Michael Walker, 1983-84; color pencil drawing, 30"x84" (76x213cm)

Drawn in Solidarity With the People of
Central America and Dedicated to All
Those Who Struggle for Justice in the World

Dibujo Hecho en Solidaridad con el Pueblo
Centroamericano y Dedicado a Toda la Gente
del Mundo que Lucha a Favor de la Justicia

U.S. GOVERNMENT DOESN'T KNOW BEANS

about getting along with our neighbor, Nicaragua. Terrorizing coffee workers and sabotaging storage
facilities are a few tactics used by the U.S. government to intimidate the Nicaraguan community and
destroy its key export crop. In response, hundreds of U.S. citizens have volunteered to help with the coffee
harvest. Support the growing community of North Americans who actively oppose U.S. intervention in
Nicaragua. Contact the Nicaraguan Information Center at (415) 549-1387.

Poster produced and distributed by Noe Valley Community Store, 1599 Sanchez, S.F., CA

©1984 D. Meikle

186

movement during the Vietnam War was split between those who simply demanded withdrawal and those who went beyond that demand to applaud the North and South Vietnamese revolutionaries. Poster-makers typically followed the former, a larger and safer bloc of opinion; it was easier to stand for cutting the losses of defeat than to try justifying victory for "the other side." Thus the Vietnamese were seldom depicted with gun in hand, defending a worthy cause. The idea of armed struggle was not yet generally acceptable to the liberal left, whose ideology was more or less pacifistic.

Attitudes toward the idea of socialist revolutions in the Third World, to be achieved "by any means necessary," have changed fundamentally during the last twenty years. The Cuban revolution, made and defended by guns, has long since been solidified, and Cuba has demonstrated the will to resist attempts at overthrow, such as the aborted April 1961 Bay of Pigs invasion. The Cuban revolution, and the visually splendid Cuban poster, are widely admired. Neither El Salvador nor Nicaragua can draw so readily upon artistic symbols of their historic pasts as can Cuba (or Mexico, of course), so that the spirit of those peoples must be conveyed in contemporary representations. The very features of ordinary present-day Salvadorans and Nicaraguans, much in evidence in the posters, evoke the past: workers and peasants in their natural surroundings, expressive of strength, beauty, innocence, and cultural integrity.

In the solidarity posters the Nicaraguans are not only victims of contra terrorism; they are also workers in the field, in literacy and health, propagators of liberation theology, pickers of coffee beans. Posters appeal for voluntary work brigades of North Americans to help with the coffee harvest ravaged by the contras; brown and pink hands simultaneously reach for the beans.

By contrast, acts of solidarity with North Vietnam (not to mention with the National Liberation Front in the south) were individualistic and rare. To give moral, much less economic, "aid and comfort to the enemy" was seen as treasonable by the government and the press and also shocked those for whom ending the war meant only withdrawing the troops. A Vietnam-era poster shows a pathetic Vietnamese child, juxtaposed with the words "Know your enemy." Such ironic use of terminology would make less sense today because relatively few people in the United States see the Salvadoran or Nicaraguan people as enemies. There are obvious reasons why Central America has more human reality for us than Vietnam did: military factors, not to speak of linguistic, logistical, and geographical ones, impeded visits to that country.

On the other hand, many United States citizens have been able to participate at various levels in the Central American struggles. There have been North American martyrs, such as Ben Linder, killed in 1987 by Nicaraguan contras, and the five religious workers murdered in 1980 by El Salvadoran death squads. They join the native Salvadoran martyr Archbishop Oscar Romero, whose assassination in 1979 is the subject

J. Michael Walker
The Assassination of Archbishop Oscar Arnulfo Romero of El Salvador
1983–1984
10 x 33
Publisher unknown

Douglas Minkler
U.S. Government Doesn't Know Beans about Nicaragua 1984
silkscreen
25 1/2 x 18
Published by Noe Valley Community Store, San Francisco

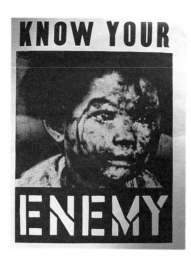

KNOW YOUR ENEMY

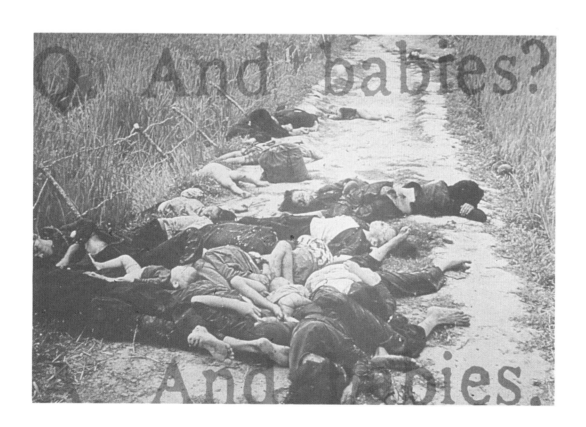

Q. And babies?
A. And babies.

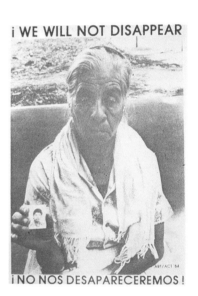

¡ WE WILL NOT DISAPPEAR

¡NO NOS DESAPARECEREMOS!

of a poster design wrought in the monumental style of Renaissance religious paintings, with added modernist electrification.

Many of the thousands of North Americans who have visited Nicaragua since its revolution in 1979 have worked there for long periods. Short- and long-term visitors alike have brought back an understanding of the country's culture and economy, an appreciation for the spirit and life of its people. This has, moreover, been a two-way process: some representatives of the Salvadoran and Nicaraguan revolutions have been able, despite official obstacles, to enter this country and speak openly, in English and Spanish. Posters, too, travel back and forth, are copied, and function the way art often has in the past, as a form of diplomatic gift. Beginning in 1981 exhibitions of posters from Nicaragua have been held in this country, whereas during the Vietnam era we largely saw American posters about Vietnam. Artistic testimony from the country where a war is being waged carries a prima-facie authenticity.

The Vietnam-related poster tended to deemphasize the individuals victimized by the war, while the Central American poster typically stresses the personalizing of the conflict in question. This difference can be seen by contrasting two well-known, and characteristic, posters from each era. The My Lai poster (*Q. And Babies? A. And Babies*), its terribleness derived from the very anonymity of the corpses shown in it, is typical of a physically (though not emotionally) distanced relationship to the Vietnam War. On the other hand, the Central American poster *We Will Not Disappear* (whose defiant, accusatory title is also printed in Spanish) is doubly personalized: it contains the portrait of a particular mother holding the photograph of a particular grandson.

It is not so much the romance of revolution, à la Che, that fires the anti-imperialist cause in the 1980s as the idea of defense of human rights and the struggle for a better life. So while the revolutionary gun has gained a certain visual legitimacy, it is typically laid over with symbols of peace, "flowers of life." "El Salvador" is the butterfly settling over the stacked guns of the FMLN (Farabundo Martí National Liberation Front). The Salvadoran revolutionary is recognizable as a fighter only by his mask; he is bedecked with the flowers of congratulation and celebration, and his bare arm, while raised in the traditional salute of resistance and defiance, is at the same time raised in recognition of us as friends and allies. Guns are not glorified but stand as a last-resort defense, to be superseded as quickly as possible by the tools of peaceful reconstruction.

The Vietnam era acquainted us with the horror of maimed children; one thinks of the famous photograph of Kim Phuc fleeing, screaming, from the bombs. The Central American era, too, has given us the wounded child but shows the child being tended — testimony to the health care available in zones liberated by the guerrillas. The health worker embodies the principle of people's medicine, and he might be a native or an internationalist, such as the American Vietnam War veteran Charles

Designer unknown
Know Your Enemy 1970
29 x 23
Published by the College of
Environmental Design, University of
California, Berkeley, to protest the
United States's invasion of
Cambodia

Designer unknown
R.L. Haeberle, photographer
Q. And Babies? A. And Babies 1970
25 x 38
Published by Art Workers Coalition

Designer unknown
Marcelo Montecino, photographer
*We Will Not Disappear! ¡No Nos
Desaparaceremos!* 1984
26 1/2 x 19
Published by ART/ACT

Clements, who worked as a physician with the guerrillas in the Salvadoran war zones. The *clinica popular* might be equipped with materials sent by a United States solidarity organization such as that which sponsored the poster.

The role reversal depicted here is also significant: man nurses, woman (still with baby) defends. The concept of woman-at-arms, visualized during the Vietnam War on behalf of Vietnam by Cuban rather than American artists, has now become legitimized, particularly through the Nicaraguan revolution, in which many women fought on the front lines. The Salvadoran woman stands, in this poster, as the necessary defender of future life — nature defending itself.

The political poster of the 1980s has not been diluted in a broad youth marketplace, as it was during the 1960s when it was part of the "counterculture" media mix of protest, love, peace, sex, drugs, psychedelia, and pop music. That poster had its faddish aspects and was sold along with Marx and dope paraphernalia, Che and body oils, in the "hippie capitalist" shops that existed in every major city. Today's political poster is ensconced in a handful of left-oriented bookstores and is used to help raise funds at rallies and demonstrations. If it has been "institutionalized" at all, it is through certain poster-distribution and -production wholesale-retail agencies, two of which are large and nationally known: Northland Poster Collective and Syracuse Cultural Workers. Both of these agencies have their roots in politically activist, rather than artistic, milieux; and both rank political integrity above commercial appeal.

Boasting large, well-produced catalogues, the two agencies have achieved national circulation for posters that would otherwise barely reach beyond the often small solidarity groups producing them. Northland Poster Collective was started by artist-activist Ricardo Levins Morales in Minneapolis in 1979. With a semiannual mailing of sixty thousand copies of its catalogue, which offers some one hundred thirty different posters, the collective currently sells between fifteen and twenty thousand posters a year; these address issues revolving around the labor movement, social justice, and peace.

Syracuse Cultural Workers, founded in Syracuse, New York, in 1982 by activist Dik Cool, emphasizes labor, Central America, and Africa. It displays more than one hundred sixty different posters in its current catalogue and sells about twenty-five thousand posters and one hundred thousand cards and postcards annually. It also offers an exhibition service featuring one hundred fifty selected posters and sells a *Peace Calendar*. In addition, it has supplied the movie industry with posters to be used as background "decoration:" *Broadcast News* (1987), a mild comic exposé of TV manipulation of the news, thus honored this medium of truth at its margin.

A third agency, Liberation Graphics, is a maverick one-man show started by Dan Walsh in Alexandria, Virginia, in 1983. It has distributed some one

BOSTON COMMITTEE FOR MEDICAL AID TO EL SALVADOR

David Fichter
In Solidarity with the People of El Salvador 1982
22 x 16
Published by Red Sun Press for the Boston Committee for Medical Aid to El Salvador

hundred thousand posters, mostly on a wholesale basis, since its founding and has between three and four hundred titles currently available. Walsh's specialty has been to work with official, semiofficial, and solidarity organizations abroad in conceiving and marketing posters. His dealings with the Palestinians, which involve about fifteen different agencies internationally, are timely, given the gradual shift of once massively hostile opinion in this country. He has defied the United States trade embargo by bringing in Cuban posters, has smuggled anti-apartheid posters out of South Africa, and has negotiated with the Soviet Union to distribute domestically some of that country's numerous peace posters.

If the political poster of the 1980s is a product of the repression and frustrations of the Reagan years, then one could say that its prospects under George Bush remain "good." With no relief in sight, opposition movements tend to internalize the permanence, almost the naturalness, in our system of a government that provokes, permits, and absorbs peaceful protest.

An example of governmental and corporate co-opting of American political protest is a 1976 poster exhibition organized by the Smithsonian Institution's National Collection of Fine Arts in Washington, D. C. Entitled *Images of an Era: The American Poster, 1945–75* and opening a few months after the United States withdrew from Vietnam, the exhibition contained works chosen to represent the best poster design in all commercial and noncommercial categories. The accompanying catalogue remarked upon the preponderance of socially and culturally oriented works from the period 1967–1972 (and about one-third of the total from this period are actually antiwar), as opposed to those with a commercial message.[6] The exhibition was part of the American Bicentennial celebration and was funded by Mobil Corporation, which also sponsored thirteen of the posters. Designed by well-known American artists (some known as antiwar protesters), the thirteen posters were united by the theme "America: the Third Century."[7] This group constitutes the grand finale to the catalogue, offering a number of patriotic pleasantries designed to flatter corporate ideology. The "Third Century" series is immediately preceded by a poster by Phil Ochs, which depicts a smiling Vietnamese woman — on whose outstretched arms doves are perched — and which declares "The War Is Over!" This poster was intended to help close off an era, but the ugly causes of the Vietnam War remain largely unacknowledged and return to haunt us in Central America.

David Kunzle is a professor of art history at the University of California, Los Angeles. His publications on the subject at hand include Posters of Protest: The Posters of Political Satire in the U.S., 1966–1970 *(1971).*

6. John Garrigan et al., *Images of an Era: The American Poster, 1945–75*, exh. cat. (Washington, D. C.: National Collection of Fine Arts, Smithsonian Institution, 1975).

7. Ibid., 245.

Paul Rand

[born 1914]

During the early 1930s, when Paul Rand was a young designer, most American advertising and magazine layout was performed either by printers who followed established conventions or by commercial artists schooled in accepted graphic styles. The then dominant American "streamlined" forms were often nothing more than superficial coverings that allowed the old to appear new. Rand, however, influenced by European Modernism, embraced a functional, systematic, yet extraordinarily expressive approach to graphic design in both his editorial and advertising work. Though Rand's approach for a book jacket is substantially different from that for a package design or a corporate identity, each solution is underscored by a sensibility that is grounded in wit, simplicity, and of course, appropriateness. In addition to his contributions to the design of books and magazines (he was art director of *Esquire* and *Apparel Arts* when he was only twenty-three years old), Rand has devised benchmark corporate identities for IBM, Westinghouse, United Parcel Service, and NeXT.

In Paul Rand's innumerable book cover designs typography and image are imaginatively deployed to represent the books' contents on their covers.

The DADA Painters and Poets 1951
edited by Robert Motherwell
letterpress
cover: 10 3/16 x 7 5/8 format
Published by Wittenborn Schultz,
Inc., New York

The Anatomy of Revolution 1965
by Crane Brinton
cover: 7 1/4 x 4 5/16 format
Published by Vintage Books,
New York

One summer I discovered an issue of *Gebrauchsgrafik*, the German advertising-art publication, in a little bookshop near the old Brooklyn Paramount theater. And in 1929 I saw my first copy of *Commercial Art*, a British publication that covered the most up-to-date trends in design. I also discovered the Bauhaus in an issue of that magazine. Those things were never mentioned at art school, so my education came essentially from magazines and books.

The term *graphic design* was virtually unheard of in the 1920s. Even though in 1922 W.A. Dwiggins referred to it, it was not a generally accepted term. How could one know about Jan Tschichold in Pratt Institute, or in Brooklyn, or in Brownsville, or in East New York? One knew about "pool sharks" and ice-pick murders but not about Tschichold or the "new typography." Moholy-Nagy's first American book, *The New Vision* [1932], was, in a way, a papal bull for me. I thought that design had to be the way he described it — ordered and systematized. System is a natural need for order. Whether one likes it or not, one lives by a system. You have breakfast every morning, you go to work, you go to sleep. That's system.

If I was influenced by anything, it was architecture — Le Corbusier in particular. If you don't build a thing right, it's going to

From 1938 to 1945 Rand designed a series of covers for the bimonthly cultural magazine *Direction*. His use of photomontage, full-bleed, and historical reference distinguish these designs and reflect the work of the European avant-garde, an influence that Rand readily acknowledges.

Direction
covers: 10 1/2 x 8 format
Editors: W.L. River, Thomas Cochran, and M. Tjader Harris
Published in Darien, Connecticut

Trademark for United Parcel Service 1961
various formats

Design Quarterly 123 1984
"A Paul Rand Miscellany"
pp. 18–19: 11 x 8 1/2 format
Published by The MIT Press for Walker Art Center

cave in. And in a certain sense, you can apply this philosophy to graphic design. Fortunately, nobody's going to die if you do the wrong thing. But that's also one of its difficulties. There's no easy check on bad work. But with architecture, there is — at least structurally.

European painting was also very important for me. When I was doing a cover for *Direction*, I was really trying to emulate the painters. I was trying to do the kind of work Van Doesburg, Léger, and Picasso were doing — to work in their spirit. But there are no rules, no magic bullet, just work. Even in advertising design my models were always painting and architecture: Picasso, Klee, Le Corbusier, and Léger. The model was not the advertising agency. There was always the implication that you do things willy-nilly simply to achieve a certain look. Nonsense. Everything one does must make sense, must be practical, because the problems are practical ones. In this regard design differs from painting. But the formal problems are identical. One still must cope with issues of color, proportion, scale, and myriad relationships.

Even painters have to please non-professionals. Likes and dislikes are often arbitrary. Henry James remarked in the essay "The Art of Fiction" that "Nothing, of course, will ever take the place of the good old fashion of 'liking' a work of art or not liking it: the most improved criticism will not abolish that primitive, that ultimate test." If the guy who owns the business doesn't like what I do, no amount of explanation is going to help. I have to satisfy myself in relation to the problem and to the client. If he wants something done, I try to do it, and if it's right — fine. But if I think it's wrong, I won't do it. If it's ruined, start over! This has always been true for me. The quality of the work always precedes everything else. And the quality, of course, is *my* standard. By quality I mean, if it corresponds to some belief, some painter, or some person whom I respect, then fine. If not, forget it.

Humor is another goal I have always steered toward in my work. People who don't have a sense of humor are a drag. Interesting people are humorous, one way or another. Shakespeare, Mencken, Shaw ... each had a wonderful sense of humor. And humor is important in every arena — especially in business.

In the 1950s I began to do corporate design work. While designing a logo is somewhat analogous to any kind of design problem, it's special. The problems are different from those in advertising. You have to break everything down into the smallest possible denominator. You're not selling a product, so you don't have to persuade anybody except the client. This kind of work wasn't completely new to me. I had done similar things at the advertising agency for firms like Kaiser, Dubonnet, and El Producto.

I was asked to design a logo for IBM because Thomas Watson, Jr., observed, that Olivetti did wonderful things, and he wondered why IBM design couldn't be more distinguished. As IBM was a very conservative organization, especially when Thomas Watson, Sr., was alive, I reasoned that what I produced had to be pretty close to what already existed. The first logo I designed for them was merely a transition — something that was similar to what existed — a slab serif. The stripes didn't occur to me at the time. I believe that if they had, the logo would now be gathering cobwebs. Indeed, questions came up later. Someone quipped that the stripes reminded him of a prison uniform. Fortunately, it wasn't anybody who had too much say. I added stripes because I felt that the letters in themselves were not sufficiently interesting. There was a problem in the sequence of letters, going from narrow to wide. It was just da-daa-daaa, instead of da-da-*da*-da-da-*da*. You were left dangling. I thought of a legal document as a possible solution, a cluster of thin parallel lines used as a background pattern to discourage plagiarism of signatures. Based on this idea, why not make the three letters out of stripes, or into a series of lines? That satisfies both content and

form. Since each letter is different, the parallel lines, which are the same, are the harmonious elements that link the letters together.

I have always believed that if I could understand my own work, anybody could. I use myself as a measure, but I also use other people — not experts or professionals. My daughter, for example, was seven when I showed her a sketch for the United Parcel Service logo. I asked her what it looked like, and she said, "That's a present, Daddy." You couldn't have rehearsed it any better.

When I showed a recent logo design to the plumber, who was working under the sink, I asked him, "What does this say?" And he read it right off. And I knew that it was right because readability was one of the problems I was dealing with. I then showed it to my wife, and she read it without difficulty; then to my accountant, and he read it. I decided that if these three people could read it, it must be right.

Intuition plays a very significant part in design, as it does in life. It's the initial phase of any creative work. It's the factor that makes it possible to be alive. Animals live by instinct, and we do, too. The difference is that they don't reason. We do, and that can be a problem. You get an idea, which comes intuitively. You then look at it and decide whether it's right or wrong. The important thing is not the intuition but the decision — whether it's right or wrong — whether or not to pursue it. Most of the time people simply latch on to trends or to freakish solutions they believe are creative but which have nothing to do with real problems — with right or wrong.

A good solution, in addition to being right, should have the potential for longevity. Yet I don't think one can design for permanence. One designs for function, for usefulness, rightness, beauty. Permanence is up to God.

"All the News That's Fit to Print"

National Edition

Midwest: Chicago, cloudy. High 56. Minneapolis, showers. High 46. Des Moines, showers. High 56. St. Louis, some sun. High 68. Indianapolis, thunderstorms. Weather map is on page 9.

An Elephant in the Bed

By C. L. Sulzberger

BRASILIA, Brazil—Brazil is the world's fifth largest country, contains about 105 million people and borders every South American land except Ecuador and Chile. It is envied by some neighbors, respected by most and feared by all. "Like their attitude toward the United States," says one of the ruling group of generals. "The smaller nations feel as if they were in bed with an elephant."

The capital city, Brasilia, was born fifteen years ago from the combined dreams of Juscelino Kubitschek, President of what was then a democracy, and Oscar Niemeyer, a famous architect whose ideology is Marxist. It was designed as an extraordinarily regimented town without street names but numbered or alphabetical designa-

FOREIGN AFFAIRS

tions, all schools in one area, churches in another, newspapers in yet another and even embassies segregated.

Free-spirited, gregarious Brazilians, forced to move here if they wish to hold their Government jobs, still complain bitterly about the artificially rigid life they are compelled to lead as a result of dwellings assigned according to work, needlessly long boulevards, the impossibility of walking, the absence of public transport. Many families are split, fathers working here, wives and children remaining in Rio—where, incidentally, Brasilia's twin fathers, Kubitschek and Niemeyer, continue to live in comfort.

Brasilia may represent a brave new world that is yet to come but it is a city without a soul. Even its pretentious cathedral leaks like a sieve. Although it was conceived under a freer system, eleven of its fifteen years have been spent under a military government. It is an excellent symbol for an authoritarian regime.

But Brasilia may also be regarded as the token of a democracy that was failing when the armed forces took over in 1964. Inefficiency, guerrilla conflicts, city terrorism and an inept leadership, riddled with corruption, were ruling this enormous country when, like so many developing lands around the earth, it moved to authoritarianism.

The United States, which prior to World War II considered nondemocratic regimes heretical, fails to realize that democracy generally presupposes a literate society with a broad middle class and high living standards as well as a basic political consensus. None of these conditions exist in Brazil, although it is getting there.

The economic growth rate has been phenomenal, comparable to postwar Japan and West Germany, although Brazil really didn't get going until around 1967. All kinds of jiggery-pokery have successfully violated the usual rules. There were back-breaking inflation, enormous deficits, spendthrift waste.

At last these were succeeded by disciplined monetary reforms and ordered planning. Brasilia itself typifies the way this country zigzagged ahead, started off by Mr. Kubitschek in order to move chunks of population into an underdeveloped hinterland.

Although immense gaps exist between rich and poor and it will take decades to level out social disadvantages, South America's giant is in fact moving forward. Its huge nuclear power program, which depends on West Germany as a supplier, is intended to overcome what is already a serious energy shortage. (It may also be designed to balance the threat that Argentina, with India's aid, is probably trying to produce an atomic warhead.)

One potential problem that might yet perplex Brazil is race. Well over one-third of the population has negroid blood. There are numerous people of Indian or Asian ancestry. The Portuguese heritage has always been remarkably tolerant but, at higher levels of Brazilian society, there is evident racial snobbishness.

That is not, however, a popular failing. The all-time hit of Rio carnival songs says: "Your hair gives you away, mulatto girl, because you are colored. But since your color isn't catching, mulatto girl, let's make love."

Politically, Brazil has been in an icebox since 1964 but the freeze is starting to melt. Thirteen parties were abolished ten years ago and re-formed into the pro-Government National Renovation Alliance (ARENA) and the opposition Brazilian Democratic Movement (M.D.B.). Communism is outlawed but the M.D.B. is gaining strength.

Although civil rights were suspended in 1968, they are now slowly working their way back, supported by many elements of the nation from the Catholic hierarchy to some generals. Well-known politicians—notably ex-President Janio Quadros—are clamoring for normal political life.

Where this will all lead is predictable. Some day South America's elephant will have both stability and freedom. But when, is another question. This continent tends to develop spasmodically, with long naps separating sprints.

Punishing the Offenders

By Edward M. Kennedy

WASHINGTON — Violent crime is spreading like a national plague. Since 1968, the national crime rate has risen 57 percent; this year it is up an additional 13 percent. Grim statistics cry out for government action, yet little that government does seems to work. Why can't we make our streets and neighborhoods safe?

The answer is not easy. The problem of crime is elusive and complex. The major first step in fighting crime is to recognize that there is no easy panacea, no magic formula for reducing the crime rate.

For years, perhaps generations, those in government formulating policies to deal with crime have failed to acknowledge the complexities of the problem. Slogans like "law and order" or the more subtle "domestic tranquillity" are poor substitutes for effective action.

Indeed, the tough talkers whose programs have failed to deal effectively with crime over the last eight years have unwittingly encouraged and nurtured the growing sense of hopelessness and cynicism that characterizes contemporary public attitudes toward government and crime control.

But it is futile to counter the law-and-order fallacy with the opposite fallacy that crime cannot be controlled unless we demolish city slums and eliminate poverty and discrimination.

These, of course, are important social goals that must be pursued by conscientious citizens in public and private life. Our heritage requires no less.

But we can no longer afford the luxury of confusing social progress with progress in the war on crime. We face the crime menace now. Perhaps the social policies we initiate in the 1970's will reduce the crime rate in the 1980's. But that is too long to wait. We fool ourselves if we say, "No crime reform until society is reformed."

There are steps we can take now to deal with crime. It is time to fight a more practical, less ideological war on crime. What we need are sound, constructive proposals directed at improving law enforcement and the administration of justice.

We begin by concentrating on the Achilles heel of our criminal justice system: the courts. Their plight is a national disgrace.

Almost everywhere, beset with expanding dockets and shrinking budgets, courts are dispensing stopwatch justice on overloaded assembly lines. The Superior Court of Massachusetts, for example, is struggling with a criminal caseload that has expanded by almost 500 percent over the last few years.

The result in too many cases is that "crime does pay." All too often prosecutors and courts ease the pressures and reduce the bottlenecks by bargains that allow violent offenders to "cop a plea" and return to circulation.

Criminals successfully play the odds time and time again. For many, crime becomes a low-risk, high-profit profession; the hours are short, no professional qualifications are required, taxes are nonexistent, and the risks are minimal.

"Revolving door" justice convinces the criminal that his chances of actually being caught, tried, convicted and jailed are too slim to be taken seriously. In short, our existing criminal justice system is no deterrent at all to violent crime in our society.

What can be done? We can start by promoting *certainty* of punishment and imprisonment for the violent offender. We can require courts to impose a mandatory minimum sentence of two years, without the possibility of probation or parole, in such street crimes as in murder, rape, aggravated assault and burglary; robbery when the victim suffers serious bodily injury; using a handgun or other dangerous weapon in committing a crime; trafficking in heroin; and violent crimes committed by repeat offenders.

The sentencing judge could waive the mandatory sentence on grounds such as age or mental incapacity but only after making a special finding in writing.

A mandatory minimum sentence is not based on a vindicative desire to punish. It arises out of the belief that certainty of punishment is the most effective deterrent to criminal conduct. Such certainty requires that the mandatory sentence receive fair and impartial application. When so applied, it can also eliminate the tarnished view of justice as a commodity subject to bargaining and compromise in the legal marketplace.

But to call for mandatory sentences without providing the courts and prosecutors with the financial resources and technical assistance necessary to meet the challenge of increased caseloads would be self-defeating.

Manhattan District Attorney Robert Morgenthau has said that he lacks the funds needed even to prosecute current cases.

Both the Congress and state legislatures must stop treating the courts as the unwanted stepchild of the criminal justice system. The Congress must require, for example, that a major portion of the funds appropriated for the Law Enforcement Assistance Administration be directed toward improving the administration of justice at the local level.

The need for new initiatives and approaches in the war on crime is compelling. The despairing public attitude about crime can be reversed, but drastic, realistic action is necessary. Mandatory minimum sentences coupled with a crash program of financial assistance to the courts are the two most important steps we can take in the right direction.

Edward M. Kennedy, Democrat, is senior Senator from Massachusetts.

A Critic's View Of the Warren Commission Report

By Jerry Policoff

Twelve years after the assassination of President John F. Kennedy in Dallas, the Warren Commission report, which concluded that the killing was the work of one man, Lee Harvey Oswald, is once again hotly debated.

Recent disclosures show that both the Federal Bureau of Investigation and the Central Intelligence Agency systematically withheld relevant evidence from the commission, and declassified executive session transcripts tell of the untenable circumstances under which the commission operated. Before it had even begun deliberations, one commissioner remarked that "we might as well pack up and go home" in view of the lone-assassin findings being forced upon the commission by the F.B.I., which it relied upon as its principal investigative arm.

Several commission staff members have suggested that the F.B.I., C.I.A. and other agencies be investigated to discover why material was withheld from the commission, but they have maintained that no new investigation of the assassination itself is necessary since none of the fresh disclosures have diminished the commission's essential findings.

This position carries with it the assumption that the original evidence supports the findings set forth in the report—an invalid assumption in view of the facts.

To believe the report, we must also believe that an extraordinary number of improbabilities occurred against the wildest odds. What follows is but a small sample:

- The vast majority of eye and ear witnesses had to have been mistaken about the source of shots from the right front, including several Secret Service agents and the Chief of Police, Jesse Curry, who initially ordered his men to concentrate on that area.
- There must be some nonconspiratorial explanation for the President's head having been rocketed violently backward to the left—a reaction that would seem more consistent with a shot from the right front than from behind.
- All the doctors at Parkland Hospital who examined the President's throat wound before obliterating it with a tracheotomy incision had to have been mistaken when they unanimously described it as an apparent entrance wound.
- Oswald was lucky. A poor shot, he successfully accomplished what none of the commission's expert marksmen were able to accomplish under more favorable controlled circumstances.
- Three employees of the Texas Book Depository, where Oswald worked, must have been mistaken when they said they thought they saw him on the first floor during the 45 minutes preceding the assassination while bystanders on the street were observing a person or persons on the sixth floor.
- A fourth witness was mistaken when he told the F.B.I. on the day of the assassination, Nov. 22, 1963, that he had last seen Oswald on the first floor, but was correct six months later when he told the commission that he had last seen Oswald on the sixth floor after everyone else had gone to lunch.

There also had to have been no connection between a statement by a Dallas police lieutenant that this witness "would probably change his testimony for money," and the apparent alteration in his story.

- Oswald, who said he was on the first floor at the time of the shooting, made a lucky guess in identifying two other employes he said he had observed there and who had in fact been there.
- A policeman who encountered Oswald on the second floor immediately after the shooting did not arrive there as rapidly as he believed since Oswald could not have descended from the sixth floor that quickly.
- The President's shirt and jacket rode up nearly six inches without doubling over in order to produce holes six inches below the collar, since the official autopsy report placed the wound at the base of the neck. Four Secret Service agents, two F.B.I. agents and the President's personal physician were all mistaken when they also located the wound in a position approximating the holes in the clothing. (The higher location was essential to the commission's theory that the throat wound was an exit wound for the bullet that entered the back.)
- Since it has been established that Oswald's rifle was incapable of firing two shots in the minimum time between the wounding of Mr. Kennedy and Gov. John Connally, one bullet must have caused seven different wounds in both men, smashing Governor Connally's fifth rib and right wrist along the way, hitting his left thigh with enough force to leave a fragment permanently embedded in the bone, and then merely falling out of the wound, to be found intact and unscratched by a hospital orderly.

Even test bullets fired through tubes of cotton suffered more damage than this super bullet. The commission's staunchest defenders acknowledge the extreme unlikelihood of the single-bullet theory. They generally argue that it is possible because it happened.

Defenders of the Warren Commission report say that the critics have yet to produce a theory that makes more sense than the one put forward by the commission. On the contrary, the evidence weaves a fabric pointing unavoidably toward conspiracy. The commission with its preconceived notions simply chose to interpret it otherwise, and suppressed that which it could not so interpret.

Jerry Policoff, a New York advertising salesman, has been a student of the Kennedy assassination since 1966.

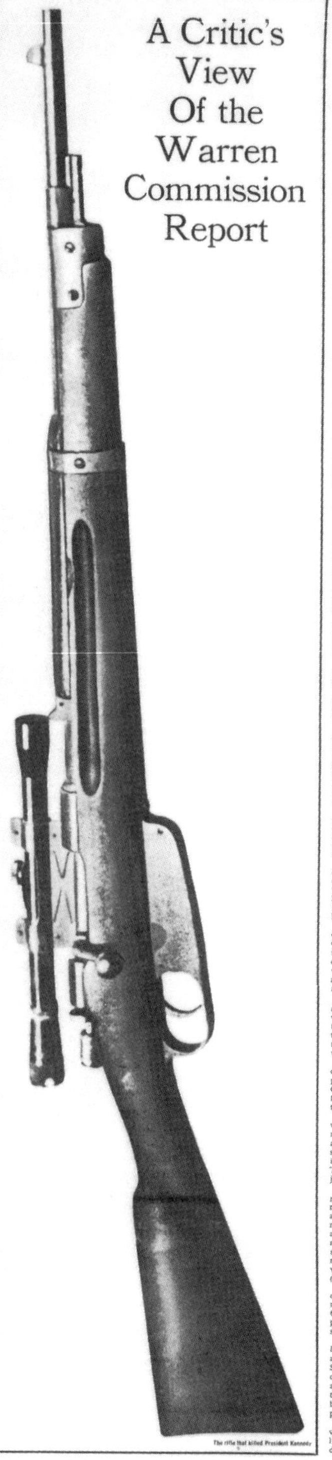

The rifle that killed President Kennedy

Great American Ailments

By Russell Baker

We have all heard that America is a sick society, but nobody has been very specific about what precisely ails us. To fill this gap in the medical sciences, I have completed six hours of research by sitting in front of a television set, as a result of which I can now offer the following Complete Encyclopedia of Leading American Ailments.

* * *

Nagging backache: A mysterious affliction suffered by at least fifteen of every hundred Americans; possibly associated with tired kidneys, or moving the piano.

Rough, chapped lips: A winter ailment which takes half the fun out of kissing. Not to be confused with cracked, ugly hands, which result from washing dishes in inadequately advertised detergents.

Cracked, ugly hands: A scourge peculiar to women. (*See* "Rough, chapped lips" above.)

Razor nicks: All males who use safety razors sold before 1975 suffer at least three per shave.

Mediciney breath: This common ailment invariably attacks persons who, upon being told their breath is offensive, rush off to gargle their own mouthwash. Can be cured only by using a second mouthwash recommended by the person who diagnosed the case in the first place.

Everyday aches and pains: A malaise whose origin still defies medical science, but believed by many to result from getting up in the morning, or being mugged.

Sleepless nights: Characterized by

OBSERVER

intense tossing and turning after retirement. Probably caused by large accumulations of cracker crumbs or problem dandruff (*see* "Problem dandruff" below) in the bedsheets. Medication: Three pages of "Remembrance of Things Past" by Marcel Proust, or three ounces of gin, or pill prescribed by television.

Unneutralized stomach acid: A nasty business in the digestive tract resulting from taking a pill which neutralizes only half as much stomach acid as it ought to.

Tummy bulge: A female abdominal deformity resulting from insufficient girdle elastic in panty hose.

The wet look: A ghastly head ailment in which the patient's hair becomes tightly plastered to his skull. Peculiar to males.

Headache: Another nasty head condition in which nerves that look like steel wires tighten around the sides of the skull, forcing the infamous headache pain to strike, thus producing severe wrinkling around the eyes, tart language to beloved family members and an appalling loss of cosmetic makeup on the facial planes.

Cold miseries: A terrifying mechanical assault on the upper torso in which a fire rages inside the throat, a shower runs at full volume inside the skull and a rope, inserted into the chest cavity, attempts to strangle the lungs.

Problem dandruff: A new and more dreadful form of the male's ancient curse, discovered just last year at the world-famous Dandruff Clinic in Zurich. Unless patient submits to radical shampooing, no rug in his house can be saved.

Unsightly dandruff: Sometimes called the Italian disease because Columbus is thought to have brought it with him from Genoa, unsightly dandruff, if not treated rapidly, invariably leads to loss of job promotion and severe social embarrassment, such as losing the girl.

Offensive foot odor: A hideous pedal ailment secretly suffered by males, who live under unbearable psychic torment because of fear they may be taken to Japanese restaurants where their terrible secret will become known when they are asked to remove shoes.

Cellulite: An affliction in which fatty deposits resembling subcutaneous Jello pockets accumulate on female hips. Can be cured only by buying a book from Ann Miller, the famous doctor of tap dancing.

Iron deficiency: Are you aware that women require twice as much iron as men? Very few of them are getting it, and for this reason they suffer from sluggishness, midafternoon fatigue and inability to put up with small children. Treatment: a large bowl of shredded jail bars at breakfast every morning.

Wetness: Glandular affliction common among Americans who run five miles to the supermarket on August afternoons. Fortunately, home diagnosis is easy: You have only to ask a pair of your talking overalls if you need treatment. If overalls say yes, spray yourself with chemicals. Wetness is not to be confused with "the wet look" or "offensive foot odor." (*See* above.)

Acid indigestion brought on by overindulgence: This dreaded medical mouthful is believed to afflict up to 60 percent of the entire American population on any given day and results from being alive.

Sluggishness brought on by irregularity: More commonly known as the ailment that dares not speak its name, S.B.O.B.I., as scientists call it, most commonly strikes retired men who are about to undertake ladder jobs around the house. It is always accompanied by a more youthful adult who knows precisely what to prescribe.

(Another edition of this encyclopedia will deal with other American ailments, like dull-old-nonvibrating-showerhead depression, which is just emerging.)

Louis Silverstein

[born 1919]

Since the early 1960s (until 1989 under the watchful eye of Louis Silverstein) *The New York Times* has gradually been redesigned. As both the audience and substance of this and all American daily papers are in a constant state of flux, flexible yet concise design is a paramount need. One of Silverstein's most significant moves was the inclusion of more and larger photographs in a newspaper that in the past had used fewer than most. In this 1975 example from the Op-Ed page, the image of the rifle that many presume killed President Kennedy creates a powerful lead-in to the accompanying critical assessment of the Warren Commission Report.

Though some twentieth-century American newspapers were more logical and legible in their design than others, design was not given real importance until the mid-1960s when the Sunday sections of *The New York Herald Tribune* were given new formats by Peter Palazzo. A few years later Louis Silverstein, who was then promotion art director of *The New York Times*, was asked by the publisher of *The Times* to address the need for a more legible text face for the daily newspaper. Silverstein began a chain reaction of change that culminated in the total redesign of the "Old Gray Lady." As assistant managing editor, responsible for visual aspects of the paper, Silverstein was a newsman as well as an aesthetician, and his design of *Times* sections was always based on sound "news judgments." He was most concerned not with how things looked but with how the reader's understanding of the vital information could be enhanced by the addition of new features or the repackaging of old ones. In a field where the word is paramount and designers are suspect, Silverstein's crowning achievement is not only that he brought *The New York Times* (and because of its example, other American newspapers) out of the nineteenth century but that he successfully commingled the art and news departments.

It's fair to say that while the reputation of *The New York Times* remained undiminished, there was a period in the late 1960s when the company simply wasn't making a lot of money. Hence there was great soul-searching at the paper. People went off to executive retreats — spent weekends thinking about the future. There were strikes and union negotiations going on all the time. Several steps were taken. First was the self-examination process that relates to the paper as a product; the others were changes in the structure of the corporation.

At that time newspapers were going through a technological change, from hot metal to cold type. In fact, all the guidelines of a four-hundred-year-old craft disappeared. We had chaos as far as quality was concerned. New guidelines had to be established. What was true in New York was true all over the country. Markets changed, readership changed, people were going out of the city to the suburbs. *The Times* did a lot of surveys in order to establish who we had to reach to continue growing. We realized we were competing with smaller newspapers that were taking full advantage of the same technology that we were having difficulty with.

By the early 1970s magazines like *Life* and *Look* died. Television was growing. The world was becoming visual. Even T-shirts

"All the News That's Fit to Print"

The New York Times

LATE CITY EDITION

Weather: Chance of drizzle today and tonight. Partly cloudy tomorrow. Temperature range: today 51-63; yesterday 59-68. Details, page D24.

VOL.CXXXI . No. 45,094

Copyright © 1981 The New York Times

NEW YORK, WEDNESDAY, OCTOBER 7, 1981

30 cents beyond 50-mile zone from New York City. Higher in air delivery cities.

25 CENTS

SADAT ASSASSINATED AT ARMY PARADE AS MEN AMID RANKS FIRE INTO STANDS; VICE PRESIDENT AFFIRMS 'ALL TREATIES'

Israel Stunned and Anxious; Few Arab Nations Mourning

Jubilation in Beirut

By JOHN KIFNER
Special to The New York Times

BEIRUT, Lebanon, Oct. 6 — There was no mourning in most of the Arab world today for President Anwar el-Sadat of Egypt, whose separate peace with Israel had led to his isolation.

Public jubilation was reported in Syria, Iraq and Libya, and the streets of mostly Moslem, leftist-dominated West Beirut echoed with gunfire in celebration of the assassination. Most public statements attributed Mr. Sadat's death to discontent with the Egyptian-Israeli peace accord.

However, the Sudan, Egypt's closest friend in the Arab world, condemned the assassination and said it stood with the Egyptian Government against all forms of conspiracy and aggression.

Hope for Arab Unity Expressed

There was little public comment in Saudi Arabia. At the United Nations, Gaafar M. Allagany, the acting head of the Saudi mission, expressed sorrow "that this had to happen at a crucial stage." Noting Saudi opposition to Mr. Sadat's policies, he said, "We hope that our sister country will rejoin the Arab states."

An aide to Yasir Arafat, the leader of the Palestine Liberation Organization, said here on hearing of the shooting of Mr. Sadat, "We shake the hand that fired the bullets."

The aide, Saleh Khalef, better known by the code name Abu Iyad, said that "all attempts at dialogue" with Mr. Sadat had failed and that "it was inevi-

Continued on Page A9, Column 1

Cairo Regime's Plans Now Question Marks

The following article is by William E. Farrell, who has reported on Anwar el-Sadat's diplomacy from Jerusalem as well as Cairo.

Special to The New York Times

CAIRO, Oct. 6 — Anwar el-Sadat's rule in Egypt was that of one man who skillfully engineered, in his 11 years in power, the means of controlling every important facet of Egyptian life.

Although he was dismissed by many as a somewhat feckless interim leader when he became President after the death of Gamal Abdel Nasser, Mr. Sadat gradually showed that he had staying power, political skill and an ability that transformed him into a world statesman when he paid his historic visit to Jerusalem in the search for peace.

Now, with his sudden, violent death, many questions about the future of Egypt and its role in the world are beginning to be raised in this saddened capital and in many other countries.

Over the years, Mr. Sadat controlled his political party, the National Democratic Party; he supervised the Egyptian press, which lauded him; he was commander of the military, a key factor in his rule, and he had a facility for calling the pulse of Egypt's masses — about 43 million people. Some 67 percent of them are illiterate, but he was able to reach them by television and radio. He often did, in long speeches that had a pedagogical tone.

Some Egyptians opposed Mr. Sadat.

Though the official 'opening' sealed mortuary chamber that the tomb have been fixed for Sunday was absolutely impossible to predict until then the actual work of living in the entrance. This was involving some hours of work that mean it had to be done with greatest care, so as to keep as many of the seals as possible also to avoid injury to any objects on the other side might be caused by the falling material dislodged.

All this could not be done any day while the official guests kept waiting in the singular pleasant atmosphere of the tomb.

Continued on Page A8, Column 5

AT LEAST 8 KILLED

Speaker of Parliament Is Interim President — Election in 60 Days

By WILLIAM E. FARRELL
Special to The New York Times

CAIRO, Oct. 6 — President Anwar el-Sadat of Egypt was shot and killed today by a group of men in military uniforms who hurled hand grenades and fired rifles at him as he watched a military parade commemorating the 1973 war against Israel.

Vice President Hosni Mubarak, announcing Mr. Sadat's death, said

Mubarak speech excerpted, page A8.

Egypt's treaties and international commitments would be respected. He said the Speaker of Parliament, Sufi Abu Taleb, would serve as interim President pending an election in 60 days.

The assassins' bullets ended the life of a man who earned a reputation for making bold decisions in foreign affairs, a reputation based in large part on his decision in 1977 to journey to the capital of Egypt's foe, Israel, to make peace.

Sadat Forged His Own Regime

Regarded as an interim ruler when he came to power in 1970 on the death of Gamal Abdel Nasser, Mr. Sadat forged his own regime and ran Egypt single-handedly. He was bent on moving his impoverished country into the late 20th century, a drive that led him to abandon an alliance with the Soviet Union and embrace the West.

That rule ended abruptly and violently today. As jet fighters roared overhead, the killers sprayed the reviewing

Of humble origin, Anwar el-Sadat became a statesman known for daring actions. Obituary, pages A8 and A9.

stand with bullets while thousands of horrified people — officials, diplomats and journalists, including this correspondent — locked on.

Killers' Identity Not Disclosed

Information gathered from a number of sources indicated that eight persons had been killed and 27 wounded in the attack. Later reports, all unconfirmed, put the toll at 11 dead and 38 wounded.

The authorities did not disclose the identity of the assassins. They were being interrogated, and there were no clear indications whether the attack was to have been part of a coup attempt.

[In Washington, American officials said an army major, a lieutenant and four enlisted men had been involved in the attack. The mayor and two of the soldiers were killed and the others captured, the officials said.]

The assassination followed a recent crackdown by Mr. Sadat against religious extremists and other political op-

Continued on Page A8, Column 1

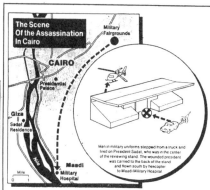

Who Murdered President Sadat?

In the confusion swirling around the assassination of Egypt's President, Anwar el-Sadat, little information was made public in Cairo about the killers. Egyptian authorities were known to have several uniformed men in custody last night, but the Egyptians gave no details about the number or identity of the attackers or the reasons for the attack.

"Islamic fundamentalists" within the Egyptian Army was the characterization offered by Secretary of State Alexander M. Haig Jr. to a group of senators late yesterday afternoon. He also mentioned discontent among some Egyptian officials with the peace treaty that Mr. Sadat signed with Israel.

Reagan Administration officials said their information was that six uniformed men had taken part in the shooting, that three were killed and that the others were captured. They said that at least one was linked to the Takfir Wahigra Society, a radical right-wing Islamic group whose name translates as Repentance and Atonement. Its past actions include the slaying of the Egyptian Minister of Religious Affairs in 1977.

In Beirut, a handful of organizations stepped forward to claim responsibility for the killing, with representatives calling news agencies with their statements. But Reagan Administration officials said they doubted that any of them had been involved in the killing. Details are on page A12.

The Scene Of the Assassination In Cairo

Men in military uniforms stepped from a truck and fired on President Sadat, who was in the center of the reviewing stand. The wounded president was carried to the back of the stand and flown south by helicopter to Maadi Military Hospital.

The New York Times (Oct. 7, 1981)

New York Times.

NEW YORK, SATURDAY, FEBRUARY 17, 1923.

TWO CENTS

THE WEATHER
Fair and cold today and Sunday; moderate winds.

Idaho Assembly Bars Japanese From Leasing Any Lands There

SENATE APPROVES BRITISH DEBT BILL; FINAL VOTE, 70-13

46 Republicans, 24 Democrats Favor It—Borah Among the Four Republicans Opposed.

BITTER DEBATE TO FINISH

Many Assail "British Victory," but Glass Wins Applause by Recalling Allies' Sacrifices.

ONLY ONE AMENDMENT

Settlements With Other Allies Must Have Congress Approval—Bill Now Goes to Conference.

TUT-ANKH-AMEN'S INNER TOMB IS OPENED, REVEALING UNDREAMED OF SPLENDORS STILL UNTOUCHED AFTER 3,400 YEARS

KING IN NEST OF SHRINES

Series of Ornate Coffers Enclose Pharaoh's Sarcophagus.

WHOLE FILLS LARGE ROOM

Mortuary Chamber Opens on Another Room, Crowded With Great Treasure.

EXPLORERS ARE DAZZLED

Wealth of Objects of Historic and Artistic Interest Exceed All Their Wildest Visions.

KING TUT-ANKH-AMEN, wearing the crown and royal vestments, as he appeared to his contemporaries. From a multi-colored decoration on the walls of the tomb of Huy, his Viceroy, discovered some years ago near the tomb of the King.

Courtesy Metropolitan Museum of Art.

ENGINEER AMBUSHED AND SLAIN AT DOOR

Earl Remington of Los Angeles, Who Made Planes in War, Is Found Dead in Driveway.

WIFE ASLEEP IN THE HOUSE

Victim, Shot as He Stepped From Automobile, Met Death He Had Feared.

GOV. REILY RESIGNS PORTO RICO OFFICE

Tells President Ill Health Forbids Him to Resume Executive Duties.

"HAD BEEN LONG UNDER FIRE"

Offended by His Inaugural Address, Unionists Made Many Charges Against Him.

GOETHALS DEMANDS COAL FOR UP-STATE

"We Want Action, Not Conferences," He Says in Message to Federal Fuel Distributor.

SE'ZURE IS THREATENED

Insists Shipments to Canada Be Diverted—People Will Get Coal, He Asserts.

and blue jeans had visual images. And newspapers, which are basically very conservative, were generally waking up to the need to be more visual. Of all the major media, newspapers were the last to recognize the need for professional design. Newspapers were word-oriented and there was confusion about the designer getting in the way of "news judgment." Moreover, there was a built-in antipathy toward designers as somehow coming from the world of advertising. Benjamin Franklin, who was both editor and publisher, designed his own paper, and that tradition persisted. If a paper is lucky, one of the editors is interested in the way things look.

At that time we had a classical, tasteful, dignified page. But we had to change — the world had changed. There was a lot of good designing going on in other print areas, and to stick to the old image was archaic. *The Times* was in dreadful need of professional help, as were most other papers.

The two front pages dealing with Egypt — the opening of Tut-Ankh-Amen's tomb in 1923, and the assassination of Anwar Sadat in 1981 — illustrate how subtle the changes to the paper's format have been. The six-column edition of 1981 replaced the eight columns of 1923, and both text and headline type sizes were increased to adjust to the wider column. The story count on page one dropped from an average of twelve to seven or eight, although the total number of stories in the paper remained the same; as a result, the "Other News" or "Inside" box was added. The logo was "cleaned up" by dropping the period after the word *Times* and revising the side boxes. Silverstein maintains that they did "nothing drastic," but the small changes add up to a cleaner, easier to read, more engaging newspaper.

The New York Times
17 February 1923 (detail)
and 7 October 1981
front pages: 22 x 13 3/4 format

It was a complex process. I maintained that redesign involves three things: a good format that retains its character but is always flexible; the right people — not only art directors but editors and backup staff; and, finally, newsroom and production procedures that can accommodate your new ambitions.

I experienced a gamut of reaction from the editors, from redneck hostility to a simple lack of understanding, which later, with understanding, became, in some cases, support and enthusiasm. *The Times* never announced that it was redesigning itself. We simply took it a step at a time. While this process was going on, I began to be consulted on the design and typography of various parts of the Sunday paper. The issues were legibility and aesthetics. The real beginning was the creation of our suburban sections. But to explain this I have to make an aside.

The Times had two fiefdoms. The news department traditionally is concerned with hard news, and they didn't want design. Creative work was something done in the features — the Sunday departments. The significant thing about the suburban sections of *The Times* was that they came from the news department. I designed them as newspaper-magazines. The idea of a newspaper-magazine was a new one then; now it's become common. We wanted to create sections for Long Island, Connecticut, New Jersey, and Westchester, because we had pragmatic marketing considerations and couldn't afford to create a new newspaper for the suburbs, but we wanted to tell suburban readers that we had something special for them. I thought we should think of ourselves not as newspaper publishers, but as publishers. We can print anything we want on newsprint and in any way we want.

In most newspapers the advertising is put in first, and the news is made to fit around it. The big breakthrough at *The Times* — and that's another reason I think of the suburban sections as the place where our revolution started — was that the news and the advertising departments were cooperating. There's nothing like having anxiety about your

very survival to make you work better! As the catalyst I was working with both the news and with advertising for the common good. That's why this was a watershed. It showed that we could work cooperatively together and intertwine content with design.

The idea for the Sunday suburban sections started with a photograph: when you unfold the paper, the whole top half is a photograph. The second move was the use of a diagonal banner, which is typical of a magazine approach. That diagonal in a newspaper, even today, is arresting. Then the little things: I centered *The New York Times* logo so that it was conservative, just the way it had always been, but placed the diagonal to cut across the logo. Then I did an adventurous thing for a newspaper. I said, "Suppose you have a not-so-terrific story on the inside pages, but it has a terrific picture. Why can't we take the picture from the inside and put it on the front page and run your story without it?" It doesn't sound like much now, but that was a breakthrough!

That was not a news judgment — it was a journalism judgment. When you think of journalism you think first of giving information. You think of truthfulness. You think of the importance of content. You think of communicating clearly and rapidly and relevantly. All kinds of judgments are involved when you're thinking journalistically. And none of those things is inherently present, say, in advertising. Because when you think of advertising, the words that come into your mind are "marketing" or "selling" or "disposing of goods." Our designers can be talented, but unless they also become talented journalists, they fall flat on their faces in newspapers.

Good journalistic design involves the use of explanatory techniques — charts, maps, elements that delve below the surface. I like to think I can explain things in a way that other media can't, if only because they don't have the space, or all those writers, or all that diverse expertise at hand. It isn't a question of enhancement through design. Whether an editor realizes it or not, design is part of what he does every time he prints the paper.

IT'S WHERE THE GIRLS ARE BARE-ING...THE GUYS ARE DAR-ING AND THE SURFS RARE-ING TO GO-GO-GO

In recent years, swimsuit design, like architecture, has

taking the plunge

elastic fantastic

exhibited a kind of free-form eclecticism and historicism.

going to pieces

CONTINUED ON PAGE 62

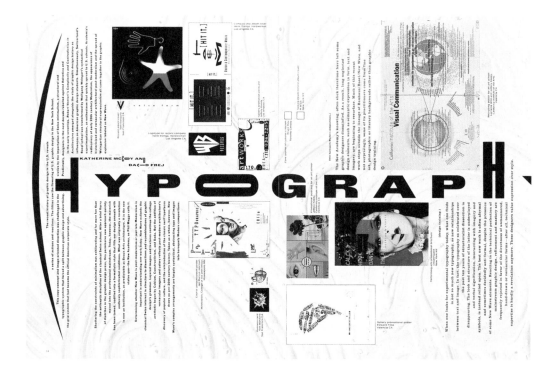

KATHERINE McCOY AND DAVID FREJ

HYPOGRAPHY

California Institute of the Arts
Visual Communication

A Zero Degree of Graphics

Joseph Giovannini

Instead of reading the page, we often graze it: in a dentist's office, at home, on an airplane, we flip through most magazines and many books, back to front, front to back, out from the middle, page hopping among ads, pictures, texts, pre-texts, and sidebars, teased from item to item by pull-quotes and enlarged, decorative capital letters. We emerge with many impressions, some facts, and pieces of stories and personalities. But we have been entertained more than edified.

There is, in a book or magazine, an ecology of words, pictures, graphic devices, sequence, space, and spacing — a delicate balance that makes a publication readable. But readability is often no longer the assumption. Many publications provide instead a kind of perceptual environment, usually a diverting one, in which readers become viewers experiencing the visual tensions of pages designed more for style than for content. Each page, like a poster, stands on its own. The magazine, in particular, is a hand-held gallery.

Victor Hugo believed that the invention of the printing press, at the end of the Middle Ages, killed the building as a text — that the wall of a cathedral, for example, no longer had to illustrate the Bible if people could read its stories in book form. In the philosopher George Steiner's view, the advent and development of photography killed the word on the printed page — the photograph took away its descriptive role, and the presence of a photograph on a page overwhelmed the fragile presence of the word.

In our time, graphics, "liberated" by new photographic and computer technologies and pressed by competition from television, the VCR, and other nonprint media to entertain, is threatening both the text and the photograph with aggressively designed pages that freely mix and cut words, photographs, and graphic devices, creating a page of design rather than a page of text. The reader, typically, no

Helene Silverman, Art Director
Metropolis November 1988
pp. 56–57: 15 x 11 format
Text and photographs taken from
the book *Making Waves: Swimsuits
and the Undressing of America*
Chronicle Books, 1989
© Bellerophon Publications, Inc.,
New York

ID March–April 1988
pp. 34–35: 11 x 8 1/2 format
David Frej spread design
© Design Publications, Inc.,
New York

longer settles in but skims the page; thoughts — rather than being developed — remain impressions. The style and aesthetics of a page are surreptitiously usurping the meaning traditionally posited in words and images. And graphic design is the chief instrument used in the theft. "Reading a magazine just for its design is as valid as reading one for its content," says Helene Silverman, art director of *Metropolis*, an influential New York design and architecture magazine.[1]

Once a service art, graphic design has, during the last decade, rapidly emerged as a strong, often independent force on the printed page, invading it like a virus. In many magazines, most newspapers, and increasingly in books, the texts, photographs, and illustrations are being arranged by designers to capture the attention of the reader and, in higher-quality publications, to achieve what Leonard Koren, the editor and art director of *Wet* magazine, calls "media sensuality." Pages become seductive paintings; the more graphically elaborate books are like pictures in an exhibition. Graphic design has emerged as an independent art, but too often sacrificed to this independence is the legibility of the other arts that design supposedly presents: writing, illustration, and photography.

Designers have learned lessons about fast images and bold juxtapositions from advertisements. Television has influenced print designers by conditioning audiences for the "fast read," for entertainment, and for the presentation of perceptual events in rapid succession. Music videos have made audiences tolerant of nonlinear, disjointed visual formats and have fostered expectations of amusement. The word processor has also affected reading habits and expectations: the quality of writing seems to matter less than the facts, the simple information, and the ability to manipulate the screen. The very words *word processing* signal a shift of emphasis in the acts of writing and reading.

Unless readers — overstimulated by print and screen graphics — are for some reason committed to a particular text, it is likely that they will become bored. "Critics have persuasively argued that extraordinary doses of visual stimuli are needed to engage a viewer brought up on television," writes Steven Heller. "Though the major concern of typographic design in any period is to create an inviting environment for communications, an elegant setting alone is apparently no longer sufficient."[2]

Inspired by television, film, and computer graphics, designers have also reacted against the elegant setting itself, against what has been called "the sterility of the Modern Movement." "Shattering the constraints of minimalism was exhilarating and far more fun than the antiseptic discipline of the classical Swiss school," writes the designer Katherine McCoy, characterizing developments that took place during

1. Helene Silverman, "Design o' the Times," *ID* 35, 2 (March–April 1988): 51.
2. Steven Heller, "The Shock Is Gone," *ID* 35, 2 (March–April 1988): 62.

the 1970s. "After a brief flurry of diatribes in the graphic design press, this permissive new approach quickly moved into the professional mainstream."[3]

Challenged, even inspired, by other media, and liberated from Modernism by eclecticism, an increasing number of periodicals are asserting themselves visually. *Time* magazine, for example — an innovator in graphics among weeklies — has had a history of using new, graphically competitive devices. A long feature on Mikhail Gorbachev and Ronald Reagan, which appeared in the 13 June 1988 issue, for instance, was designed to attain an almost cinematic level of visual stimulation. The screen, whether large or small, has upped the visual ante, putting the printed word on the offensive.

The cumulative effect of liberated graphics on writing, especially in magazines, is that, on the most visually aggressive pages, thoughts are not carried beyond their place in a composition because pages no longer encourage and cultivate a long attention span. The reader's eye falls on a picture, then on a block of text, then on an ad and a caption, as at a buffet. In many magazines it is difficult to distinguish between editorial copy and advertisements; in some, ads themselves are a substantial part of the editorial information.

Overall, ads establish the visual context that editorial design must match in order to survive, and the logic for the design of advertisements affects that for articles. "This is why the most powerful print advertising being done today takes consumers into a world beyond logic and facts, where words can't describe what can be seen or felt," writes Cheryl Heller, chairman and creative director of Heller Breene, a Boston advertising and design firm. "This is not to say that advertising is abandoning words, or that it should. Or that pretty pictures are enough to sell products. But simply that pictures are ideas, too. And when they are good ideas, used in partnership with words, they are attention-getting, memorable and powerfully persuasive."[4] Beyond the world of logic, facts, and words, according to this argument, lies the more potent realm of feeling — the realm of graphic design, with its ability to pair image and word. The resulting periodicals are overwhelmingly visual and visually overwhelming.

The page on which graphics support and enhance rather than compete with the word and image is the exception, not the rule, in many publications, even though much is known about what makes texts and photographs easily legible. Supportive graphics help texts do what words and illustrations do best, allowing them to carry imaginations to other worlds. Hyperactive graphics, on the other hand, hold the reader to the world of a page that has itself become a primary artifact. "Reading today is for many primarily a visual experience," comments Steven Heller.[5]

3. Katherine McCoy, "Typography," *ID* 35, 2 (March–April 1988): 34.
4. Cheryl Heller and Mark Myers, "The Picture as Headline," *ID* 35, 2 (March–April 1988): 49.
5. Supra, note 2.

The effect of graphic design in many publications, then — even when it is handsome design — is the fragmentation or subordination of the text. The result affects no less than how we think: the broken page delivers impressions and even sensations, but it does not lead a reader into the depth that carefully elaborated ideas, crafted writing, and layered passages can create in quiet sequence. There is a strong tendency now to construct each page as a freestanding unit. Several "city" magazines — *New West* and *Los Angeles*, for example — popularize high-energy pages featuring kickers, heads, subheads, sideboxes, and initialing devices. Some publishers are utilizing these and other techniques to produce books that have the look and feel of magazines. Workman, for example, markets softcover books whose pages reflect the graphic strategies of such magazines.

The capitulation of text to layout can also be seen in books about the visual arts, in which texts are often treated as visual blocks that are subservient to pictures. In the most graphically "painted" books each page is a design that may or may not have words, and texts are relegated to introductions that play a minor supporting role. Books about graphic design itself are notorious for having little or no text — they are simply compendia of full-page designs.

In 1987 the jurors at the annual American Institute of Graphic Arts book design awards acknowledged the trend, finding it difficult to establish criteria within the new design climate. A passage from the preface to the 1985–1986 awards book reflects their difficulty: "New technologies and marketing practices are changing the way books are produced and perceived, making it more difficult to determine excellence. The venerable tenets applied to book design and manufacturing are all but ignored in an era of slickly produced coffee table books and mass and trade paperbacks. How does one judge the classically elegant against the souped up visual book? Can the same rules that govern other graphic design forms be applied to the book?"[6]

Some predict that this visual strain of book — for "less literate" people — will enjoy greater popularity in the future. Already in Japan, a sizable part of the book market has been captured by a hybrid that the Japanese call the "mook," a book with softcover magazine binding, headlining devices, and magazine-quality printing and paper.

The battle, finally, is primarily between verbal culture and visual culture, between those who have been called the "word people," and the "image people," between — several decades ago — *Partisan Review* intellectuals and the design department at The Museum of Modern Art in New York. Today those battle lines might be

Meadows & Wiser
All About Old Buildings 1985
cover: 12 x 9 format
edited by Diane Maddex
Published by The Preservation Press,
Washington, D.C.

6. *Graphic Design USA:7: The Annual of the American Institute of Graphic Arts* (New York: Watson-Guptill, 1986), 89.

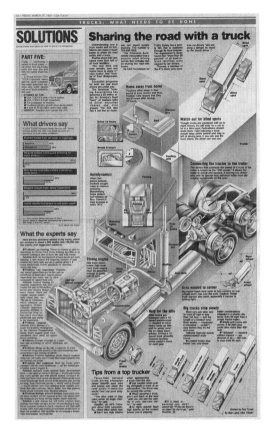

said to be drawn between the editors of *The New York Review of Books* and the graphic and set designers of MTV.

The basic issue is how a person learns by reading; the way a person grasps the thoughts on a given page depends greatly on how those thoughts are presented and developed. It may be alright for *USA Today* to become a print equivalent of television, with color pages and news briefs that do not continue onto a second page. But it is disturbing when the "Arts and Leisure" section of *The New York Times* changes its format, as it did in 1987, to one that visually tends to equate ads, pictures, texts, and captions. Even *The New Yorker*, long a bastion of cool, inconspicuous graphics — one that established the stillness necessary for verbal subtleties — has been threatened in the past several years by twelve-page, four-color inserts, by ads that jump the gutter, and by ads that actually bleat out tunes.

The new presentation upsets the balance: the visual weight of the text becomes lighter than that of the non-text; and only "vocal" writers such as Tom Wolfe or "hot" texts such as those in *Spy* magazine seem audible above the graphic volume. *House & Garden*, once *The New Yorker* of shelter magazines, became the *Vogue* of that genre when it went to a new format in 1988. In this format tightly cropped pictures bled into one another, into texts, and into ads, so that only patterns emerged. Amid this hyperactivity, it was difficult to separate the articles from the ads, to read the words printed over the pictures, and to find the images of buildings and interiors, which had been cropped to enhance the design of the page rather than the architectural design. The elements were all self-canceling; only the look and buzz of the page survived. Most other Condé Nast publications are also marked by overactive graphics. But even *New York Woman* — which is not overactive but clearly presented, with full pictures and long, uninterrupted blocks of text — is not a "reading" magazine; the strength of its graphics pulls the reader's eye from the word and the image to the looks of the page.

Paul Rand, a father of modern American graphic design, suggests that the tendency to consider pure form and visual relationships on a page as independent of content resulted from the abstractions of post–World War II art. The page became distinct from content, "forcing attention on the design of the total surface," he has written.[7]

Whether appearing in a book or on a poster, words in some way became a formal compositional element, particularly in the years following the war; blocks of words acquired a look. Rand has even said that, in his own experience, when

USA Today
27 March 1987
p. 6A: 22 3/4 x 13 1/2 format
© Gannett Company, Inc.,
Arlington, Virginia

7. For a historical review of the pre–World War II typographic innovations that led to the development Rand describes, see Herbert Spencer, *Pioneers of Modern Typography*, rev. ed. (Cambridge, Mass.: MIT Press, 1983). See also the essays by Estelle Jussim and Lorraine Wild in the present book.

he could not evolve a concept for an ad from the given copy he sometimes simply invented copy that worked with his concept for the ad.[8] In the hands of some designers, such as Alexey Brodovitch, pages were composed to be freestanding, each designed so that turning the pages unlocked a sequence of graphic surprises.

The history of the appearance of a page working to support its content is a long one. When the B of the word *Beatus*, for example, was elaborately illuminated at the beginning of a chapter in a medieval manuscript, the intention was to capture visually the spirit that the word revealed — there is a sense of wonder in the illumination; the letter is a portal into the word and the text. In the Haggadah, in which illustrations are not supposed to appear, the typography is often elaborate, yet it is always suggestive of textual meanings and hierarchies — there is a close fit of type to word. In characteristic nineteenth-century books and magazines the text is continuous, gently interrupted by an engraving, perhaps, but never broken.

After World War II, however, with the change from hot to cold type and the development of new photo-printing systems, designers gradually took greater advantage of their technological liberties with more adventurous designs. The availability of the Photostat, for example, allowed a designer like Brodovitch to play every which way with every which size. By the 1960s, especially in magazines, the traditional orthogonal pages with several columns and a picture or two, all registered, was upset. For many designers the construction of a page — even if it remained orthogonal, as in *Time* magazine — now started with the picture rather than with the text. The revolutionary pages and posters by the Russian Constructivists in the 1920s — with their obliquely angled, multicolored, nonhierarchical elements — became everyday, page-by-page commercial reality in magazines. Especially in the 1960s, with the rise in influence of Swiss design, letters within a word themselves became subject to typographic manipulations. Letters were appreciated for their visual character; words erupted from within, with typographic shifts between letters. April Greiman, a leading contemporary "new wave" graphic designer based in Los Angeles, says she tries to paint a word with letters.[9]

Graphic design now challenged the linearity and continuity of text, and, with it, the narrative itself. In 1982 the New York graphic designer Massimo Vignelli reworked *Architectural Record* magazine so that no text would be longer than a single page; and soon other periodicals joined the trend. The results are publications that can be read in almost any direction with the same comprehension — the articles

B.W. Honeycutt, Art Director
Spy October 1988
p. 69: 11 x 8 1/2 format
© Spy Publishing Partners,
New York

8. Rand made this comment in a question-and-answer session with Steven Heller that was part of a symposium, *Modernism and Eclecticism: A History of American Graphic Design II*, held at the School of Visual Arts, New York, 8 October 1988.
9. Greiman in a conversation with the author, Spring 1987.

are short and, like the pages on which they appear, freestanding. The buildup of meaning within the publication does not depend on linear sequence.

If writing is receding on the page, the best contemporary graphic designers are themselves emerging as a new type of writer. Greiman, for example, layers verbal and visual images in what she calls "information texture," so that words and pictures are complementary. Like a concrete poem, all the elements — background, figure, words, punctuation — form a complete text; the elements depend on one another for their meaning. Other graphic designers, especially those applying tenets of Deconstruction, believe everyday experience is made up of different, dissociated experiences and beliefs. They construct pages with multiple texts and juxtaposed narratives in which meaning is comprehended in nonlinear ways. Different orders of information are presented simultaneously; parallel blocks with related and unrelated texts additively sculpt the page, as though the text were a Cubist painting with simultaneous views. Fragmentary pages allow readers to configure their own meanings and create the connective tissue. (There is also a group of artists, including Jenny Holzer, Barbara Kruger, Matt Mullican, and Richard Prince, who use the graphic conventions of advertising to critique its intentions. They are analyzing the content of advertising and graphic design, tapping its power and associations, rather than aestheticizing the page or surface.)

But designers such as Greiman and those experimenting with graphic Deconstruction — whose work has expanded the boundaries of the field — have also emerged as role models for graphic designers who want to think of themselves as "artists," rather than "service" designers. Working within tight printing schedules, many of them hastily appropriate the forms of some very thoughtful work — they view the elements on a page as visual objects rather than as meanings. Their goal is not to be a sensitive servant of the text but an expressive and experimental artist. One student beginning a graphic design program, for example, refused to design a text in sedate Baskerville type because, he said, "I'm a high-energy guy."[10] Helene Silverman articulates the reasoning: "A magazine's design is personal and expressive, yet you're working on something that has a life of its own."[11]

Silverman started her career as the art director of the music-and-teen-culture tabloid *The Rocket* and then became senior designer at *Mademoiselle*. Her career represents the manner in which unconventional graphic design has found its way into mainstream publications, or at least has served to challenge them. "There are the regular magazines; tasteful, successful, dependable, perfect — *New York, Texas*

10. The student was a member of a class taught by the Los Angeles graphic designer Sheila Levrant de Bretteville. De Bretteville in a conversation with the author, Spring 1987.
11. Supra, note 1.

Monthly, New England Monthly, etc.," she writes in a 1988 issue of the magazine *ID*. "Then there are the others, from the almost incredible ones to the almost awful ones. And those, for me, are the fun ones. They leave me energized and hopeful that in this era of scary concepts like magazine marketing, there are designers and editors and publishers who are not afraid to challenge and surprise and even shock their readers."[12] She goes on to review several periodicals, revealing in the process her own attitudes and values as a designer:

> ***Actuel*** From France comes this glossy social and political exposé magazine with overkill photos, lots of collage, red circles around heads, and fake blood spots. *Actuel* was a big influence on Condé Nast design, especially *Vanity Fair*.
>
> ***Ryuko Tsushin*** From Japan, this is known as Fashion News. Sophisticated and naive, it's the ultimate fusion of design/ads/content. Surreal photo essays and fresh approach to Western type.
>
> ***Paper*** The black & white New York monthly bible of hip nerddom is ultra-bold, with a sense of humor that's definitely not up tight. It's designed with the big picture in mind; shapes, blacks, whites, spaces — very Japanese.
>
> ***i-D*** An encyclopedia of experimental design of the eighties, it was the first to use computer generated type and images and then to destroy it all with a xerox machine.[13]

Clearly, for Silverman design is the object of the exercise and not simply a way to structure and clarify content.

Although graphic design may have its origins in the word, it no longer resides in it. Its independence from the word has even led it to thrive off the page, entirely free of both words and pictures. A recent American Institute of Graphic Arts annual contained pictures of bedsheets that are bold, solid, and graphic. There are buildings with graphic surfaces, and there are even graphic cities. During the 1984 summer Olympics, Los Angeles was "illustrated" by graphically conceived stars, columns, hot-air balloons, tents, and platforms, all painted in vibrant pastels. Corridors of long, thin balloon streamers embellished the backlot entrance to a Hollywood studio, for example, illuminating the doors, like the elaborated B in *Beatus* — only the word had disappeared and become a building.

As in film, a dominantly visual medium in which writing plays a

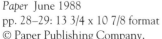

Richard Pandiscio, Art Director
Paper June 1988
pp. 28–29: 13 3/4 x 10 7/8 format
© Paper Publishing Company,
New York

12. Supra, note 1: 50–53.
13. Ibid.

contributory role, the writing in a graphically aggressive publication fades. Writing becomes the servant art. Writers and even photographers have become wary of graphics. One author, Tracy Kidder, who wrote *House*, deliberately chose not to have photographs in this book about the construction of a Massachusetts dwelling because he felt they would compete unfairly with the writing. Instead, the building was illustrated by unprepossessing drawings done by the contractor.[14]

Some writers would rather appear in newspapers or newsprint publications than in magazines precisely because, by and large, these are still dominantly oriented toward the word. Papers may have large photo displays in certain features and visually aggressive ads, but they are generally not slick to the point of distraction. The basic reading unit — the column — remains intact; articles may jump a page, but most are self-contained. Each newspaper, of course, has several graphic environments, and while the new layout of the "Arts and Leisure" section of *The New York Times* challenges text, *The New York Times Magazine*, despite its abundant use of color and many advertisements, is still basically committed to reading.

Sometimes, the pages that now catch the reader's attention are the classic designs — not unlike Nathanael West, who attracted a great deal of attention in his New York Bohemian circles by wearing conservative suits. The pinstripes are unexpected.

Certain mainstream magazines, such as *Harper's*, have not thrown out text for pizzazz but retain a balance among words, photographs, and design and maintain a clear separation between ads and editorial material. But even within the graphically calm pages of this magazine, where a column of ads might be juxtaposed to two of text, there are spreads that are arresting because they are composed of text alone. On these spreads words are presented in regular columns with generous margins and clear heads; the layouts have a presence that lends a sense of importance to the text. In the November 1988 issue of *Harper's* the design clarity of "Think about It: Ways We Know, and Don't," an essay by Frank Conroy, establishes a visual environment that quiets the page and the reader, allowing the measured thought and textual progressions of the essay to stand. No feats of mind-eye coordination are necessary to read the page. Each of the article's three pages is organized into two readably wide columns; one simply turns the second page and reads to an end marked by a square bullet. The text is broken only when the text calls for a pause. Conroy writes of two black shoeshine men who have the habit of looking beyond their own dreary working environment in a New York subway to avoid seeing the immediate detail. The designer of the page seems to

14. The author in an interview with Kidder, *The New York Times*, 3 October 1985: 21. For the drawings themselves, see *House* (New York: Houghton Mifflin, 1985).

The Last Time Emmett Modeled Nude, *by Sally Mann. From an exhibition of her photographs at the Marcuse Pfeifer Gallery in New York City, this fall.*

MY SINGING

There were probably a lot of songs that got sung to me when I was little because people will always sing to babies. Especially ones whose nerve problems you think it's going to help. When you get older, you may never have anyone sing to you personally again, but go all over the world and I bet you can't find one baby that has never been sung to.

Take my cousin Ellen's baby for example. I'm always singing to him. And I'm probably not even going to like him when he grows up.

I don't sing to him only because I'm stuck up about my singing talents. It turns out I'm a rotten singer. I've been tested. I know it for a fact.

And I don't sing to him because I have to watch him all of the time and I think he wants to hear a bunch of songs. If it was only songs, then why should I sing? Why not just play the radio for him? But when I am alone with him and I touch him or especially when I open up one of his midget little hands, all of a sudden I feel something moving inside of me, this natural message for him, and how am I supposed to say it to a baby who can't even talk yet if I don't sing it?

When I was little I used to imagine that I was a great singer, the best singer of all time, and that my singing was a secret power that could make anyone who heard it cry from its beauty. It could make anyone cry, anyone in the world, even Bonna Willis my ex–best friend who used to chase me down the alley on my way home from school so she could beat my ass, shouting at me in front of everybody, "Run honky bitch! Run!"

I imagined my singing could make Bonna cry, only it would make her cry for a different reason. When she saw me on TV leaning over our President who had just been shot in the head and whose last request was to hear me sing in order to perform a miracle on him and bring him back to life, then she would be sorry. Then she would be sorry for ever having been mean to me, for ever having pushed me into the corner of the girls' bathroom and slapping me across the face in front of her stupid idiot new friends, I don't care what the reason was for it. She'd cry so hard she couldn't stand it anymore and she'd climb up onto the roof of the school and jump off and bust her head wide open. ∎

have understood the message and has suppressed close-up, eye-catching details on the page, so that the reader sees beyond its physicality into the meaning of the text. The words are thoughts, not visual blocks.

Harper's is, of course, a literary magazine, predisposed to the word rather than to the image. However, it treats photographs with the same graphic respect. Also to be found in the November 1988 issue is a black-and-white photograph by Sally Mann of a young boy. Entitled *The Last Time Emmett Modeled Nude*, it is encased in a frame of blank space with a visually supporting text below that acts like a pedestal. The texts and photos appear in a publication that is visually uncrowded. The climate is thoughtful, not commercial; articles rather than ads comprise the body and look of the magazine. Within that kind of context, a reader can settle more easily into a text and its argument or story.

Establishing graphic quiet around an article is, of course, difficult in a more commercially based publication. *Esquire*, which, like *Harper's*, has a strong literary tradition, is also a major advertising vehicle, and the line dividing its articles from its ads is usually blurred. Still, the designer of an article on the Democratic and Republican conventions, which appeared in the November 1988 issue, isolated the piece by taking it out of the body of the magazine: the article was printed on heavy matte stock; there were no photographs, only illustrations, and no ads. It was a graphic time-out. Other articles in this issue are visually jumpy or fragmented or mix with ads in a way that encourages scanning. The dominant impression is that, literary or not, *Esquire* is a magazine to flip through, a way of reading that is rewarded by large, luscious images on which the eye lands at random. Flipping, however, sets up a superficializing pace.

One of the most graphically responsible American publications is one that needs to be responsible, the bimonthly professional journal *Communication Arts*. Its balance of word, image, and graphics is carefully weighed; design is tailored to subject. The magazine does not, however, present the Renaissance page that existed through the nineteenth century but offers instead a twentieth-century page with a mixture of photographs, illustrations, ads, and papers on diverse topics. The layout of *Communication Arts* has a very strong physical presence.

Proponents of an expanded role for bold graphics speak of visual literacy, of stretching literacy beyond strictly verbal messages to visual ones. In this view all the world is a text, on and off the page, for anyone who can read it. But in the pursuit of visual literacy, literacy of the plain old verbal kind is being eroded by small graphic detonations that disrupt the flow on which meaning, rather than sensation, is built. It is true that screen culture — embodied by television, movies, video, and the computer — has heightened our visual expectations, expanded our appetite for surprise, and placed demands on the printed page to be entertaining. But the need to retain the attention of

Deborah Rust, Art Director
Harper's Magazine
November 1988
p. 41: 11 x 8 1/2 format
Sally Mann photograph
© Harper's Magazine Foundation,
New York

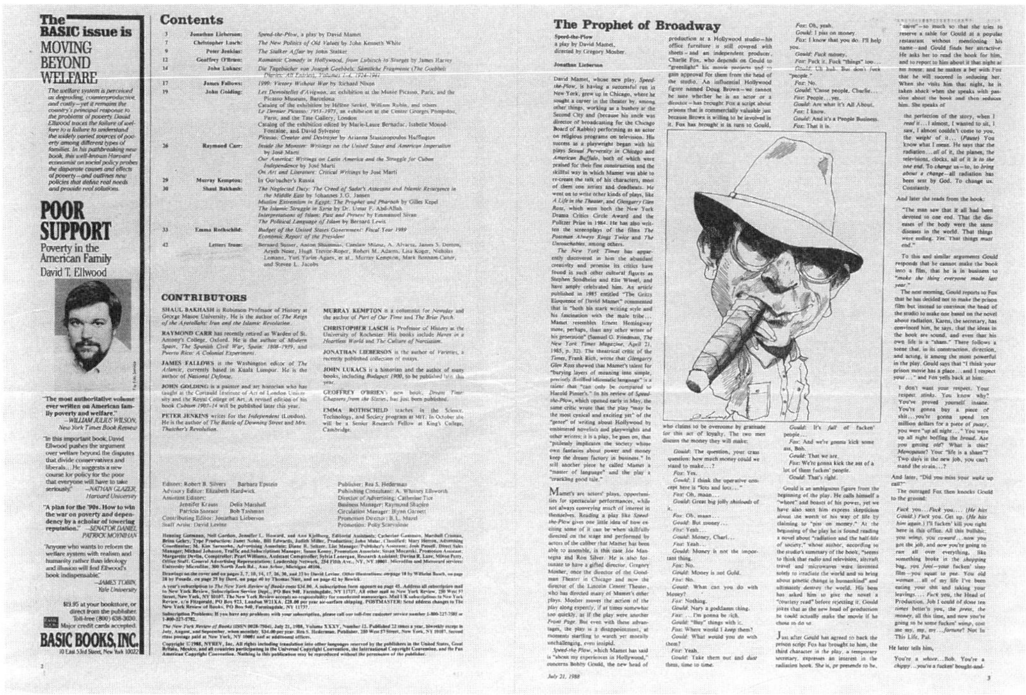

The BASIC issue is MOVING BEYOND WELFARE

The welfare system is perceived as degrading, counterproductive and costly—yet it remains the country's principal response to the problems of poverty. David Ellwood traces the failure of welfare to a failure to understand the widely varied sources of poverty among different types of families. In his pathbreaking new book, this well-known Harvard economist on social policy probes the disparate causes and effects of poverty—and outlines new policies that define real needs and provide real solutions.

POOR SUPPORT
Poverty in the American Family
David T. Ellwood

"The most authoritative volume ever written on American family poverty and welfare."
—WILLIAM JULIUS WILSON
New York Times Book Review

"In this important book, David Ellwood pushes the argument over welfare beyond the disputes that divide conservatives and liberals... He suggests a new course for policy for the poor that everyone will have to take seriously."
—NATHAN GLAZER
Harvard University

"A plan for the '90s. How to win the war on poverty and dependency by a scholar of towering reputation."
—SENATOR DANIEL PATRICK MOYNIHAN

Anyone who wants to reform the welfare system with realism and humanity rather than ideology and illusion will find Ellwood's book indispensable."
—JAMES TOBIN
Yale University

$19.95 at your bookstore, or direct from the publisher. Toll-free (800) 638-3030. Major credit cards accepted.

BASIC BOOKS, INC.
10 East 53rd Street, New York 10022

Contents

CONTRIBUTORS

SHAUL BAKHASH is Robinson Professor of History at George Mason University. He is the author of *The Reign of the Ayatollahs: Iran and the Islamic Revolution.*

RAYMOND CARR has recently retired as Warden of St. Antony's College, Oxford. He is the author of *Modern Spain*, *The Spanish Civil War*, *Spain 1808-1939*, and *Puerto Rico: A Colonial Experiment.*

JAMES FALLOWS is the Washington editor of *The Atlantic*, currently based in Kuala Lumpur. He is the author of *National Defense.*

JOHN GOLDING is a painter and art historian who has taught at the Courtauld Institute of Art of London University and the Royal College of Art. A revised edition of his book *Cubism 1907-14* will be published late this year.

PETER JENKINS writes for the *Independent* (London). He is the author of *The Battle of Downing Street* and *Mrs. Thatcher's Revolution.*

MURRAY KEMPTON is a columnist for *Newsday* and the author of *Part of Our Time* and *The Briar Patch.*

CHRISTOPHER LASCH is Professor of History at the University of Rochester. His books include *Haven in a Heartless World* and *The Culture of Narcissism.*

JONATHAN LIEBERSON is the author of *Varieties*, a recently published collection of essays.

JOHN LUKACS is a historian and the author of many books, including *Budapest 1900*, to be published this fall.

GEOFFREY O'BRIEN's new book, *Dream Time: Chapters from the Sixties*, has just been published.

EMMA ROTHSCHILD teaches in the Science, Technology, and Society program at MIT. In October she will be a Senior Research Fellow at King's College, Cambridge.

The Prophet of Broadway

Speed-the-Plow
a play by David Mamet,
directed by Gregory Mosher.

Jonathan Lieberson

David Mamet, whose new play, *Speed-the-Plow*, is having a successful run in New York, grew up in Chicago, where he sought a career in the theater by, among other things, working as a busboy at the Second City and (because his uncle was director of broadcasting for the Chicago Board of Rabbis) performing as an actor on religious programs on television. His success as a playwright began with his plays *Sexual Perversity in Chicago* and *American Buffalo*, both of which were praised for their fine construction and the skillful way in which Mamet was able to re-create the talk of his characters, most of them con artists and deadbeats. Mamet went on to write other kinds of plays, like *A Life in the Theater*, and *Glengarry Glen Ross*, which won both the New York Drama Critics Circle Award and the Pulitzer Prize in 1984. He has also written the screenplay of *The Verdict*, *The Postman Always Rings Twice* and *The Untouchables*, among others.

TONY SCHWARTZ

service time. That's the worst time you can get: time they can't sell. Buying media is cheaper in many cases even than sending out all the ads, hoping to get on public service time." Of course, he adds, focused media selection, targeted precisely to the group one wants to reach, is critical. He strongly favors local radio, and suggests that there are even situations where a prerecorded message on a telephone answering machine would be the most effective.

Schwartz calls this approach "Guerrilla Media," which he advocates as a way for individuals and groups with a public agenda to get their message across by co-opting the power of the established media. Outlined in a two-hour videotape he prepared in conjunction with a TV producer associate named David Hoffman (produced by Hoffman's firm, Varied Directions Inc. of Camden, Me.), are techniques for the making of effective radio and TV spots at bargain-basement costs, and getting them exposed, via paid and unpaid media placements, in ways that deliver results.

None of this is pure theory; he's proved it in action. With radio commercials—some of which were never even aired, but just played over the phone to public officials who hastened to correct an offending condition to avert their being broadcast—he's shamed the police into closing up a notorious drug hangout in his neighborhood, and defeated proposed state legislation that would have banned Sunday shopping, in one instance, and built a prison next to a Girl Scout camp, in another. A radio commercial got McDonald's to switch from beef tallow to vegetable shortening; it ran only in Chicago, where corporate headquarters are located. A Schwartz radio campaign was credited, by the policemen's union, with helping avert a threatened New York City police strike, another produced a major revision in the Massachusetts state budget.

"Today's tools for today's fight," Tony calls this craft.

Alongside the public service area—some of it on retainer and some on a volunteer basis, which apparently depends both on Tony's level of interest and the organization's ability to pay—he's experimenting with radio as an effective medium for employment advertising. Print employment ads, he says, reach people who are looking for work, while properly placed radio ads can reach out and attract the attention of better prospective employees elsewhere. He cites successes he's had, along these lines, recruiting specialized engineers for high-tech companies, and was amused when a furniture store used radio to advertise for salespeople with degrees in interior decorating, and experienced a vigorous pickup in business because customers liked the idea of that kind of sales assistance.

"Be aware of the side effects of what you do," he counsels.

Kodak Film (4 seconds)
Annc: As long as you've been taking pictures, you've trusted them to one film. Kodak.

Kodak Film (3 seconds)
Annc: Kodak Film. Would you trust your pictures to anything else?

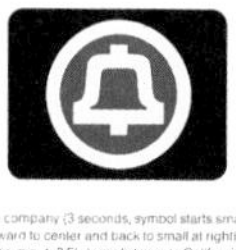

Telephone company (3 seconds, symbol starts small so will end moves forward to center and back to small at right)
Annc: Got a minute? Fly long-distance to California.

Telephone company (2 seconds)
Annc: For Valentine's Day, give her a ring.

"Many times you're more effective when your real goal appears as a side effect of what you're ostensibly after."

Another area he's experimenting with, on behalf of the Cable News Network, are 2-, 3- and 5-second commercials. He sees these fitting between news items where, he says, their brevity does not create any sense of disturbance in the viewer. Cable, he notes, sidesteps the limits on spot frequency with which open-broadcast must deal. What's more, these short commercials go by too fast to zap.

You zap a commercial when you switch channels, he points out. Today, when so much TV is watched in VCR replay, zipping, or fast-forwarding, is a bigger problem. Tony has made zip-proof spots.

He makes the visual simple: a product shot with minimum or slow movement, often with a meaningful or exciting sound track. Then, when the commercial is speeded up four or five times, it becomes what he calls a video motion poster. As for the sound, he demonstrates that closing in the spaces between thoughts, overlapping a new phrase before the prior one has been completed, actually enhances attention and absorption.

"We hear about four times faster than we can talk. People do a lot with this extra time—they accept, they reject, they associate and they react to the material they're hearing. By designing copy that uses more of the listener's time, we can actually cut down their rejection and increase their involvement."

Thus, especially when the product is readily recognized and the sound evokes feelings and ideas already in the viewer's mental storehouse, the combination of a video poster and an involving soundtrack can be incredibly effective, he feels. "In full length, it's a live commercial, with full sound. In the mini-version, it's a motion poster."

Through the forty-odd years of extraordinary achievement since he first took his primitive wire recorder into the New York City streets, Tony Schwartz's work and life have been characterized by a restless impatience with commonly accepted wisdom or limitations, and by a unique, highly individual angle of vision that combines exceptional sophistication with the kind of seamless sincerity that can be taken—and mistaken—for naivete. His approach, with its enormously successful accomplishments, may indeed by based on the simple logic of facing directly into a problem in order to discover its solution.

Simple as the answer to the question: That mysterious notice posted on your front door—what does it say?

The answer: "Please do not put any menus into our vestibule."

Written in Chinese, of course.

GUERRILLA MEDIA
A Citizen's Guide to Using Electronic Media for Social Change

"Don't use the old tools for today's fight," said Tony Schwartz. That's what this two-hour video tape is all about. It is possible for the citizen-activist to have access to the media, to fight city hall, or a mammoth corporation, or anyone else that is doing or proposing something that you truly believe is not in the best public interest.

It's not that expensive, and not nearly as difficult as you might have thought. It can be very effective, as Schwartz points out and demonstrates. It has to be a much more productive use of time and expenses than staging a rally or demonstration in the hope that it will result in a newspaper photo and caption, or twenty seconds on the evening news that may, or may not, be an accurate statement of your point of view.

The introduction, and a most unusual one, is by Mayor Edward Koch. Tony's other guests include: David Hoffman, film and TV producer and president of Varied Directions; Kathleen Jamieson, Chair, of the Communications Dept., University of Texas; Michael Pertschuk, co-director of the Advocacy Institute; Joe Napolitan, founder, International Association of Political Consultants; and Bob Landers.

I've heard two other tapes in the series: *Secrets of Effective Radio Advertising* and *How I Use Media in Politics*. Lacking space here, I'll discuss those tapes further in my editor's column.

If you would like information about how to get *Guerrilla Media* or other tapes in the series, contact:

David Hoffman
Varied Directions
69 Elm Street
Camden, Maine 04843
Phone: (207) 236-8506

the reader on the page has altered the quality of the attention itself.

The difficulty with hyperactive pages is that they eventually exhaust the eye: readers come off the graphic high to realize that they have consumed very little of substance. These hyperactive designs are becoming clichéd. The irony is that pages designed not to be boring, are. The shock disappears.

The case can be made for a zero degree of graphics, that is, for neutralized designs that de-aestheticize the page and serve the thoughts conveyed by the words. The notion of a return to the Renaissance page is a tempting but hardly practical one in what has overwhelmingly become an advertising culture. One looks almost longingly to the Soviet Union, not for the politics of its publications but for the general absence of aggressive advertisements on their pages. These publications do not have the hard visual sell that distorts editorial content and unsettles concentration.

Short of the Renaissance and short of Russia, there are a few graphic models in contemporary American commercial publications that synthesize the often conflicting demands of advertisements, photographs, and editorial content into a reasonable whole — transforming the traditional page into a contemporary one yet retaining the message in an articulate graphic context. But their quietness generally makes them faint presences in what is otherwise a visually competitive arena. The mind all too often tends to follow the eye, and the eye, all too often, seeks the publications that pulse with conspicuous visual energy.

Trained as an architect at Harvard University, Joseph Giovannini has served as an architectural writer and critic for the Los Angeles Herald Examiner *and* The New York Times. *He is currently practicing architecture and completing the book* On Graphics, *to be published by Alfred A. Knopf in 1990, on which this essay is based.*

The New York Review of Books
21 July 1988
pp. 2–3: 15 x 11 5/8 format
Sam Antupit original format design
David Levine drawing
© NYREV, Inc.

Richard Coyne, Art Director
Communication Arts
September–October 1988
pp. 48–49: 10 7/8 x 8 5/8 format
© Coyne & Blanchard, Palo Alto, California

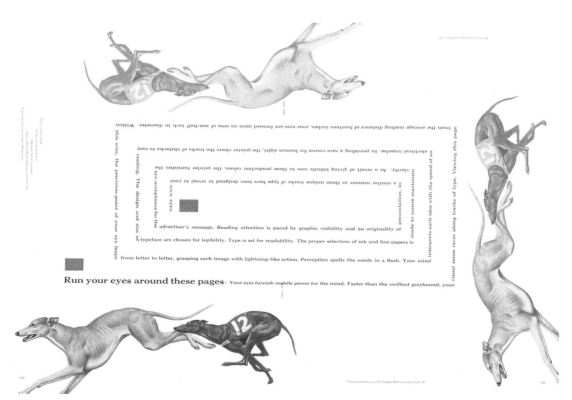

Run your eyes around these pages: Your eyes furnish mobile power for the mind. Faster than the swiftest greyhound, your visual sense races along tracks of type. Viewing this page from the average reading distance of fourteen inches, your eyes are focused upon an area of one-half inch in diameter. Within this area, the precision-point of your eye leaps from letter to letter, grasping each image with lightning-like action. Perception spells the words in a flash. Your mind interprets each idea with the speed of an electrical impulse. In providing a race-course for human sight, the printer clears the tracks of obstacles to easy reading. The design and size of typeface are chosen for legibility. Type is set for readability. The proper selection of ink and fine papers is made to assure maximum eye-acceptance for the advertiser's message. Reading attention is paced by graphic visibility and an originality of presentation, in a similar manner as these unique tracks of type have been designed to reveal to your own eyes.

214

Bradbury Thompson

[born 1911]

These spreads from *Westvaco Inspirations* exemplify two areas of graphic design in which Bradbury Thompson has been a major innovator: photographic reproduction and typography. In a 1954 piece photographer Ben Somoroff's self-portrait is reproduced using three colors of ink in a split fountain on a one-color press. The eye, opposite, looks through the die-cut hole of a camera lens from the page that follows.

A typographic game, "Run your eyes around these pages," is played to show how rapidly our eyes respond to the unexpected. The greyhounds also dash around the page in two, three, and four colors, reinforcing the movement of the typography.

Westvaco Inspirations 198 1954
letterpress
frontispiece: 12 x 9 format
and
Westvaco Inspirations 177 1949
"Run Your Eyes"
letterpress
pp. 3530–3531: 12 x 9 format
Published by Westvaco Corporation,
New York

Topeka, Kansas, is not the first place one would expect to find a modernist designer. Yet in the mid-1930s, as a student who coveted copies of the urbane magazines *Vanity Fair, Vogue,* and *Harper's Bazaar,* Bradbury Thompson knew that his life's work would be committed to printing and the design of type and image. What he could not predict was that so many of his designs for magazines and books in the years that followed would be valued for what they taught the profession. One of his major contributions was as a designer and an editor of *Westvaco Inspirations* from 1938 to 1962, a paper and printing periodical sent to educators and art directors in all disciplines; it featured alternatives to conventional design and was a showcase for new illustration, typography, and posters. Yet *Westvaco Inspirations* was more than just a periodic report on the state of the art. It was a vehicle for Thompson to experiment with printing, type, and color. Allowing his typography to be playful or to mirror content with dynamic juxtapositions using both modern and historical references, Thompson sought to achieve clarity without forsaking vitality. Throughout the many issues of *Westvaco Inspirations* his approach was decidedly eclectic, giving equal weight to modern and historical references. Thompson was also art director of *Mademoiselle* and design director of *ArtNews* in the decades following World War II; and he designed the formats for three dozen magazines, including *Smithsonian.* Thompson has designed over one hundred United States postage stamps. In these he has distilled history and emotion in a visual form of haiku.

In the late 1950s I was asked to provide Westvaco an idea for a gift which they could present to their clients at Christmastime. I thought, here is a paper company that produces the products on which books are printed; and I offered to assist them with the publication of classic books. Therefore, the first book, *The Legend of Sleepy Hollow* by Washington Irving, was designed with classic restraint, centered type, and margins. For the next, *The Celebrated Jumping Frog of Calaveras County, and Other Sketches* by Mark Twain, I gained the courage to do it in a modern spirit, like the design I had been using in *Westvaco Inspirations.* I wanted to break from the traditional characteristics of the 1867 first edition, justified spacing and the use of cap letters, so I went to a flush left-ragged right type arrangement. Although my book design was based on classic models, there was no reason why one should be forever tied to tradition, and this method brought new vitality to a classic text. Tradition and new ideas can be reconciled on the basis of appropriate typefaces and illustrations.

In 1963 I really broke free from traditional book restraints with the design for *American Cookery,* by Amelia Simmons. The type is all flush left-ragged right, with overhanging heads on the left and asymmetrical placement of other design elements. I used

Genesis

1:1 In the beginning
God created the heaven and the earth.
2 And the earth was without form, and void;
and darkness was upon the face of the deep.
And the Spirit of God
moved upon the face of the waters.

3 And God said,
Let there be light:
and there was light.
4 And God saw the light, that it was good:
and God divided the light from the darkness.
5 And God called the light Day,
and the darkness he called Night.
And the evening and the morning
were the first day.

6 And God said,
Let there be a firmament
in the midst of the waters,
and let it divide the waters from the waters.
7 And God made the firmament,
and divided the waters
which were under the firmament
from the waters
which were above the firmament:
and it was so.

8 And God called the firmament Heaven.
And the evening and the morning
were the second day.

9 And God said,
Let the waters under the heaven
be gathered together unto one place,
and let the dry land appear:
and it was so.
10 And God called the dry land Earth;
and the gathering together of the waters
called he Seas:
and God saw that it was good.
11 And God said,
Let the earth bring forth grass,
the herb yielding seed,
and the fruit tree yielding fruit after his kind,
whose seed is in itself, upon the earth:
and it was so.
12 And the earth brought forth grass,
and herb yielding seed after his kind,
and the tree yielding fruit,
whose seed was in itself, after his kind:
and God saw that it was good.

STEPHEN CRANE.

THE RED BADGE
OF COURAGE.

*An episode of the
American Civil War.*

WESTVACO.

As demonstrated in the opening spread from the Book of Genesis in Thompson's *Washburn College Bible*, setting the type for its prose-poetry in phrases clarifies the meaning of the text. Sixty-six works of art are illustrated in this Bible, which was commissioned by a college in Topeka, Kansas. *Adam and Eve in the Garden of Eden*, from the collection of the Mauritshuis, The Hague, was painted in 1620 by Peter Paul Rubens and Jan Bruegel the Elder.

The Washburn College Bible 1979
three volumes
pp. 2–3: 14 x 10 format
Published by Washburn College,
Topeka, Kansas

The Red Badge of Courage
by Stephen Crane
frontispiece: 8 1/2 x 5 1/2 format
Published by Westvaco Corporation
as part of the American Classic Book
Series, 1968

Since 1969 Bradbury Thompson has not only designed a number of United States postage stamps, but he has influenced the work of many others in this field. In his 1982 commemorative stamp for America's libraries (shown actual size) he uses letter forms from a 1523 alphabet drawn by the French aesthetician Geofroy Tory for *Champ Fleury*, a treatise on Roman lettering.

classical illustrations but deployed them the way one might in a magazine. In a different vein, for an Edgar Allan Poe story called "The Balloon Hoax" I researched a copy of *The Sun* newspaper from 1844 and designed the format in the fashion of old newspapers, using engravings of the period. Unlike a purely classical rendering, this approach was imbued with a modern, eclectic spirit.

For the design of Stephen Crane's *The Red Badge of Courage* we die-cut a bullet hole through the book, and printed what appear to be splatters of blood on random pages. This idea came from stories about Bibles and other objects saving the lives of men in battle during the Civil War. This was a way of bringing realism to the design. I made the outside of the book look like an old cartridge case, and instead of printing the title on the spine, I put "Stephen Crane," as if that case were a diary. For the interior I retained the classic book design of that time, centered heading and justified type, to provide realism.

The Washburn College Bible project came about because I had been a consultant to the Field Enterprises Educational Corporation, which asked me if I would like to design a Bible. Of course I wanted to, but it needed to be on my aesthetic and typographic terms.

First, I set the type flush left-ragged right, which would be a completely modern interpretation of Gutenberg's original. Then, I realized that once set this way the short verses would often come up too short. I often had one word left over in the last line, so I made some adjustments. I found that by setting it in phrases I could emphasize the rhythm of the human voice, and help make the archaic English of the King James Version of 1611 perfectly clear. If one reads this version in its original justified form, it's hard to comprehend. When I put it into phrases beautiful things happened. At first I made them too long, and they weren't effective. So I shortened them, starting with "In the beginning" or "God created the Heavens and the Earth" as one line. In the

early Bibles typographers did not use quotation marks because they had not been invented, so the editors of 1611 began a sentence wherever there was a quotation by writing "And God said" or "Behold." As short phrases these were functional and vital aids to understanding. But my approach seems appropriate when one recalls that the King James Version was written during the time of Shakespeare, when eloquent dialogues were made on stage.

I was also determined to bring great art into this book: here was a chance to have works of art begin each chapter. The caption on the verso side of each picture not only gives all the practical information, including artist, date, and collection, but it also provides the verse from the Bible that inspired the artist to paint the picture in the first place. This was actually a modern publishing technique, for it was my hope that the reader would be persuaded to turn to that text.

If the job of a designer is to make material more understandable, the Bible is the ultimate challenge. I was pleased because I was able to include in this English, or Protestant, textual version many great works of art from the Catholic Italian Renaissance. And more important, I came to realize that three-fourths of the Bible is the Hebrew Old Testament. So I was happy to be joining all of these related, but disassociated, religions and eras into one homogeneous entity.

Plates

The exhibition *Graphic Design in America: A Visual Language History* is organized in a series of case studies related to specific design genres. The plates reproduced on the following pages provide a brief review of the categories that are explored in depth in the exhibition.

Design in the Environment, including signs and symbols, maps and charts, events and exhibitions, posters and broadsides, and various ephemera;

Design for the Mass Media, encompassing newspapers, magazines, books, and graphics in motion; and

Design for Government and Commerce, which includes designs for business such as packaging and advertising, and designs for public institutions such as the Works Progress Administration and the National Park Service.

The printed broadside, which served
the slow-moving traffic of the early
1900s, has been replaced today with
neon and computerized electronic
signage designed to keep pace with
the automobile.

Photographer unknown
The Metropole Hotel building,
New York 1909
Collection The Bettmann Archive,
New York

Audrey Bernstein
Times Square, New York 1989
Collection Walker Art Center

Some trademarks and logotypes, designed to identify products and develop company "image," are often used unchanged for many years, while others go through a subtle evolution over time. Designed by Rudolph Ruzicka, the mark for Borzoi Books, a division of Alfred A. Knopf, which first appeared in 1922, is found in countless Knopf books in a variety of iterations.

In 1901 the Victor Talking Machine Company introduced the dog and Victrola. Taken over by the Radio Corporation of America (RCA) in 1929, this mark continues in use today with modest changes.

Herbert Matter's livery for the New Haven Railroad was developed in 1954–1955 and applied in a variety of forms and colors to everything from railroad cars and engines to stationery.

Oct o ber °

In these calendars, using the simplest means, Barbara Solomon has created small masterworks of typographic invention.

Barbara Stauffacher Solomon
Monthly calendars for the
San Francisco Museum of Modern
Art 1965–1971
7 x 7 format
Collection the designer

FREEDOM PAVILION

GERMANY YESTERDAY — GERMANY TOMORROW

This broadside was designed for the New York World's Fair's proposed Freedom Pavilion, a pointedly anti-Nazi hall conceived for the conquered peoples of the world. However, the pavilion was never realized as the promised site was withdrawn and American thoughts of war were superseded at the Fair by the promise of material wealth inherent in its "World of Tomorrow" theme.

Lester Beall
Germany Yesterday — Germany Tomorrow 1939
letterpress
10 1/16 x 7
Collection Lester Beall Archive, Rochester Institute of Technology

The XXIII Olympiad, held in Los Angeles in the summer of 1984, presented an environmental-design problem of enormous proportions. Given the task of providing continuity and recognizable symbols that would direct a diverse, multilingual audience to the many athletic sites, the forty-two cultural venues, and the athletes' three residential villages were The Jerde Partnership, Inc., architects, and the design team at Sussman/Prejza & Co. Together with a small-town-size staff of consultants, designers, architects, and artists, these two offices produced a remarkable pattern language, a color palette, and a "kit of parts" using materials and programs geared to work for the two weeks of the games and suitable for worldwide television transmission.

Sussman/Prejza & Co. and The Jerde Partnership, Inc.
Environmental design for the
XXIII Olympiad
Los Angeles, California 1984
Photography directed by
Annette Del Zoppo Productions,
Los Angeles

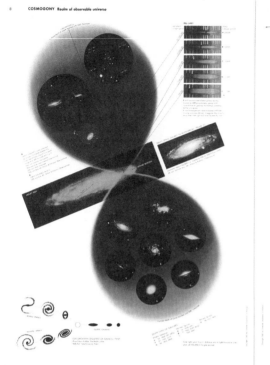

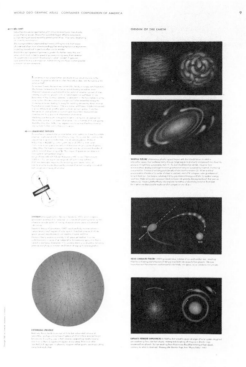

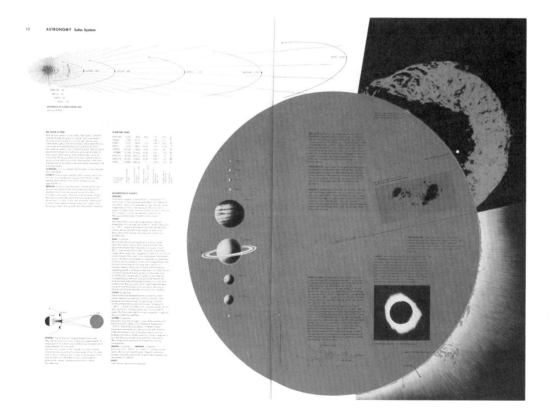

A labor of love by Herbert Bayer, an early environmentalist, this extraordinary atlas includes geology, economics, demography, astronomy, and climatology, in addition to the geographic data basic to the genre.

Herbert Bayer
World Geo-Graphic Atlas 1953
pp. 8–9, 10–11: 15 1/2 x
10 3/4 format
Published by Container Corporation
of America, Chicago

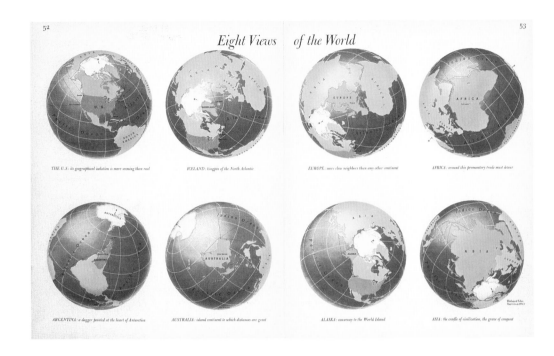

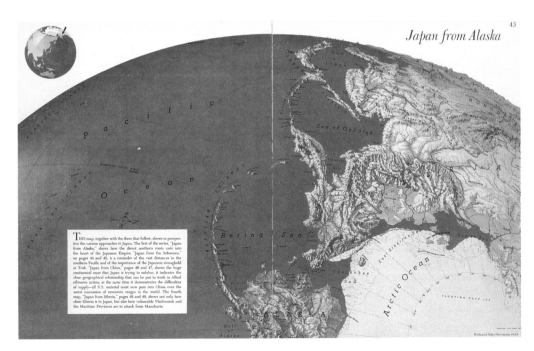

Many of these remarkable views of the globe were first published in *Fortune* magazine and later brought together in this volume. Created between 1940 and 1944, these visionary drawings actually "look at the world" as a geographic sphere; they prefigure the startlingly beautiful photographs of the Earth from outer space that were first made in the 1960s.

Richard Edes Harrison
Look at the World 1944
pp. 52–53, 42–43: 14 x 10 3/4 format
Published by Alfred A. Knopf,
New York

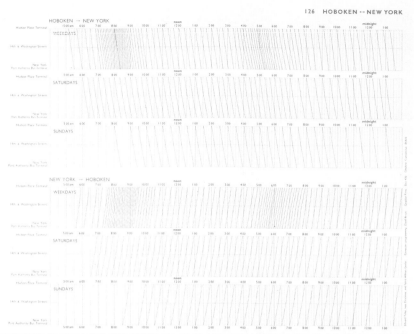

Edward Tufte's Manhattan-to-Hoboken bus schedule combines a graphical timetable and a route map overlaid on an aerial photograph. Hourly, daily, and weekly patterns of the bus line's route are clearly revealed, and the aerial map has such fine resolution that bus riders can find their own houses on it.

Edward Tufte, Inge Druckrey, Nora Hillman Goeler
Visual Timetable and Aerial Map, Bus Schedule, Manhattan to Hoboken, New Jersey 1987
24 x 12 format
Computer programming:
David Bruce
Aerial photographs: U.S. Geological Survey
Published by Graphics Press, Cheshire, Connecticut

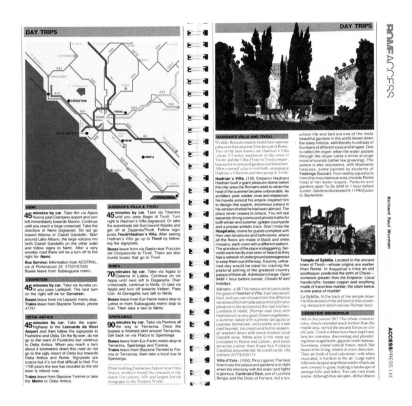

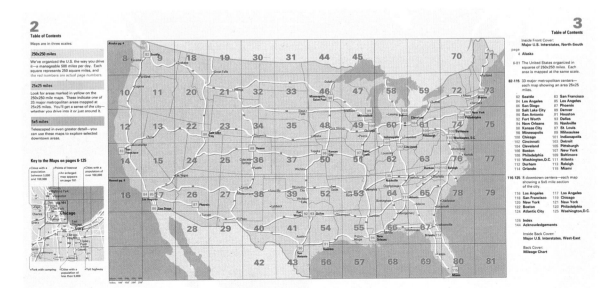

Richard Saul Wurman has been a practicing architect and teacher, but those activities have always been related to an intense interest in the communication of information — especially data about cities — both verbally and visually. So for the last ten years he has devoted himself to the writing, designing, and publishing of guides to cities, such as New York, Los Angeles, Washington, D.C., Paris, and Rome, as well as guides to such diverse topics and events as *The Wall Street Journal*, medicine, dogs, and the Olympics.

Richard Saul Wurman
Rome Access 1987
pp. 118–119: 10 3/8 x 5 1/2 format
Published by Access Press, Ltd.,
New York

In the San Francisco office of Access Press, which is called The Understanding Business (TUB), Wurman has developed a new United States road atlas that allows the traveler to look at its maps the way one drives across country — from state to state. The maps are at three scales: 250 square miles; twenty-five square miles; and five square miles. Like his city guides, the atlas includes marginalia about the places that appear along the way.

Richard Saul Wurman and the staff of Access Press
US Road Atlas 1990
pp. 2–3, proof: 10 1/4 square format
© 1989 by Access Press, Ltd.,
New York

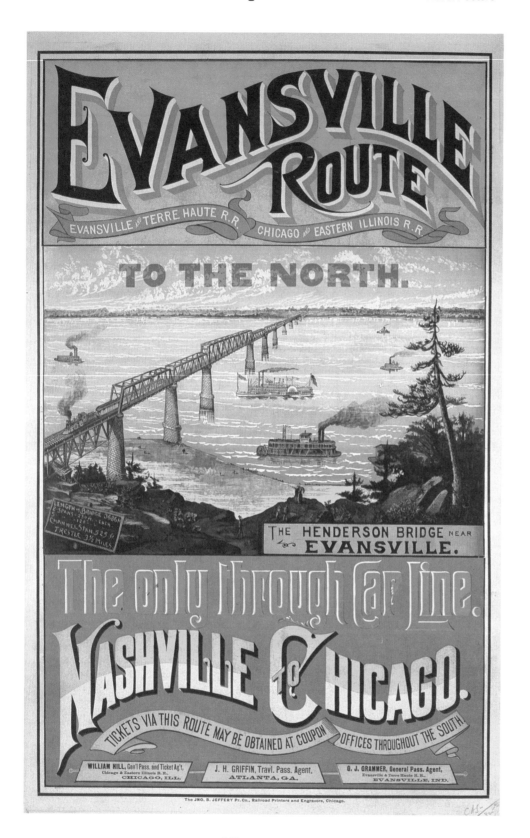

Railroad company advertisements in the form of lithographic posters were produced by printing companies in the latter half of the nineteenth century. Rarely credited to the designers who created them, these images celebrated the opening of the American West. The Evansville and Terre Haute Railroad and the Chicago and Eastern Illinois Railroad crossed the Henderson Bridge near Evansville, Indiana.

Designer unknown
Evansville Route n.d.
chromolithograph
22 3/4 x 14 1/2
Published by JNO. B. Jeffrey
Printing Co., Chicago
Collection Merrill Berman

Cranbrook Ceramics

Graham Marks
Artist in Residence,
Head of Ceramics
Roy Slade, President,
CAA

Recent Visiting Artists
and Scholars

The Department strives
to be an environment
in which one can work
toward a vision of
the thing one does not
quite yet know.

We seek to support a
breadth of inquiry,
from the poetics of un-
apologetic function to
speculative, expansive,
unnamed form.

Ceramic history is seen as
a rich resource in which
one can test precedent
and transcend the purely
subjective. We are
committed to enlisting
the evocative potential
of ceramic materials
and value the dialogue
between maker and
process.

A two year graduate
program of advanced
study.

For information write to
Office of Admissions
Cranbrook Academy of Art
500 Lone Pine Road
Box 801
Bloomfield Hills
Michigan 48013 USA

313.645.3303

Philip Rawson
Goldsmith's College,
University of London
Author Ceramics

Wayne Higby
New York State College
of Ceramics at
Alfred University

Betty Woodman
University of Colorado

Robert Turner
Alfred, New York

William Daley
Philadelphia College
of Art

Jacquie Rice
Rhode Island School of
Design

Judy Moonelis
New York City

Walter Ostrom
Nova Scotia College of
Art and Design

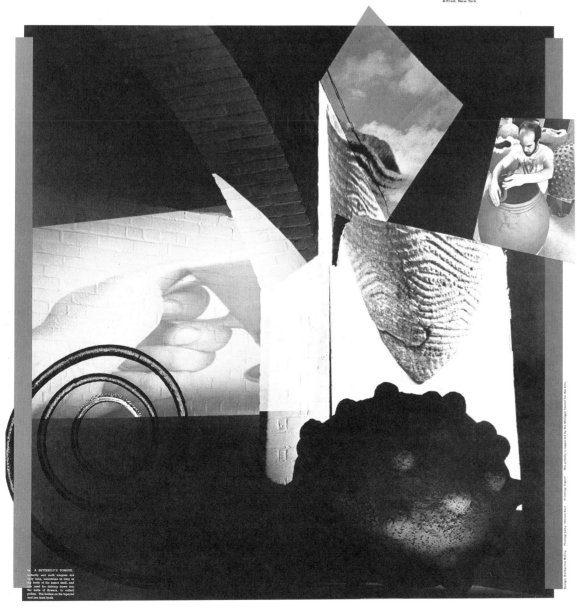

The appointment of Graham Marks as the new head of the ceramics department at the Cranbrook Academy of Art, Bloomfield Hills, Michigan, is announced with this poster. Images referring to influences and themes that recur in his work are included.

Katherine McCoy
Cranbrook Ceramics Poster 1986
28 x 22
Steven Rost photographs
Collection the designer

Strange case of
Dr. J E K Y L L and Mr.
H Y D E. *Robert Louis*
Stevenson. With illustrations
by W. A. D W I G G I N S.

RANDOM HOUSE · NEW YORK 1929

DYNAMIC DISSONANCE IN NATURE AND THE ARTS

splendour is the prosperty of a nation more efficaciously asserted than by the measure of how far forward may have progressed the tribute of its solicitude for that proliferent continuance which of evils the original if it be absent when fortunately present constitutes the certain sign of omnipollent nature's incorrupted benefaction. For who is there who anything of some significance has apprehended but is conscious that that exterior splendour may be the surface of a downwardtending lutulent reality or on the contrary anyone so is there inilluminated as not to perceive that as no nature's boon can contend against the bounty of increase so it behoves every most just citizen to become the exhortator and admonisher of his semblables and to tremble lest what had in the past been by the nation excellently commenced might be in the future not with similar excellence accomplished if an inverecund habit shall have gradually traduced the honourable by ancestors transmitted customs to that thither of profoundity that that one was audacious excessively who would have the hardihood to rise affirming that no more odious offence can for anyone be than to oblivious neglect to consign that evangel simultaneously command and promise which on all mortals with prophecy of abundance or with diminution's menace that exalted of reiteratedly procreating

JAMES
JOYCE

ULYSSES

Two of America's most inventive designers are represented here with brilliant examples of their ability to take book design in new directions. Using a combination of hand-drawn calligraphy, illustration, and typeset letter forms, William Addison Dwiggins created a new design standard for the trade book in his years of work with the publisher Alfred A. Knopf. While Dwiggins made the initial leap from traditional to modern book design, Merle Armitage brought a new elegance and sophistication to the form with daring typography, as in his use of transparent red ink over the black text in this 1952 edition of Joyce's *Ulysses*.

William Addison Dwiggins
Strange Case of Dr. Jekyll and Mr. Hyde
by Robert Louis Stevenson
letterpress
title page: 8 x 5 1/2 format
Published by Random House, New York, 1929

Merle Armitage
Dynamic Dissonance in Nature and the Arts 1952
by Louis Danz
spread from "title page" sequence: 9 1/4 x 6 format
Published by Farrar Straus and Young, New York

Native Arts

of the Pacific Northwest

From the Rasmussen Collection of the Portland Art Museum

Introductory text by ROBERT TYLER DAVIS

Stanford University Press

GEOMETRIC FIGURES & COLOR SOL LEWITT

This volume devoted to the art of the Pacific Northwest Coast Indians was one of Alvin Lustig's many distinguished book designs of the 1940s and 1950s. Lustig brought extraordinary imagination, understanding, and knowledge to the design of the printed page.

Alvin Lustig
Native Arts of the Pacific Northwest
1949
by Robert Tyler Davis
title page: 11 x 9 format
Published by Stanford University Press, Stanford, California

The American painter, printmaker, and sculptor Sol LeWitt is also recognized as one of America's most distinguished book designers. He has produced a number of remarkable volumes of graphic works.

Sol LeWitt
Geometric Figures & Color 1979
8 x 8 format
Published by Harry N. Abrams, Inc., New York

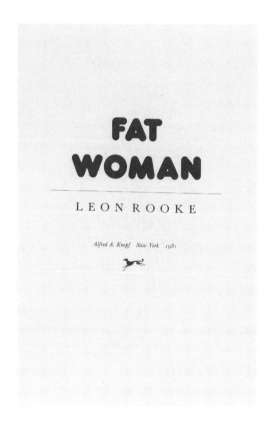

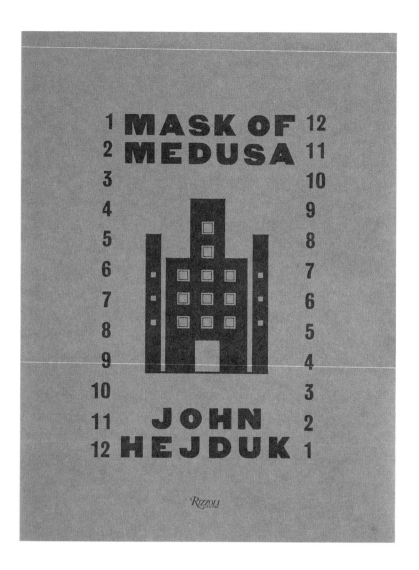

These two trade books demonstrate how perfectly design can reflect content when it is carried out by assiduous designers and publishers.

Judith Henry
Fat Woman 1981
by Leon Rooke
title page: 8 1/4 x 5 1/2 format
Published by Alfred A. Knopf,
New York

Lorraine Wild
Mask of Medusa 1985
by John Hejduk
cover: 12 x 9 format
Published by Rizzoli International
Publications, Inc., New York

Mehemed Fehmy Agha,
Art Director
Vanity Fair May 1934
"Trapping the Magical Waves of
Sound"
letterpress
pp. 26–27: 12 3/4 x 9 3/4 format
Margaret Bourke-White
photographs
Courtesy *Vanity Fair*
© 1934 (renewed 1962)
The Condé Nast Publications, Inc.,
New York

Mehemed Fehmy Agha,
Art Director
Vanity Fair April 1933
"Rainy Days Are Here Again"
letterpress
pp. 34–35: 12 3/4 x 9 3/4 format
Courtesy *Vanity Fair*
© 1933 (renewed 1961)
The Condé Nast Publications, Inc.,
New York

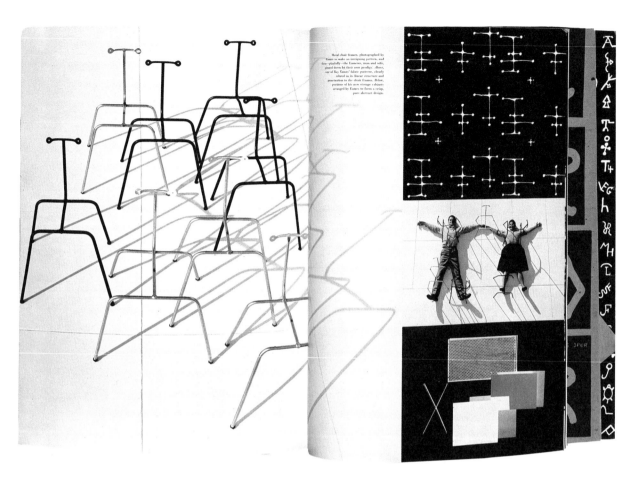

Alexey Brodovitch was art director of the short-lived (only three issues were published) *Portfolio Magazine*. This embossed cover, illustrating a design for a kite by Charles Eames, was reproduced from his original tissue-paper collage. The double-page spread shows the designers Charles and Ray Eames "pinned down" by their metal chair frames. A fabric design by Ray and the elements from an Eames storage unit are included on the right-hand page.

Alexey Brodovitch, Art Director
Portfolio Magazine
Summer 1950
cover and unpaginated spread:
13 x 10 format
Courtesy Ex Libris, New York

John Lennon and Yoko Ono, New York City, November 1980

Rolling Stone and *Emigré*, both aimed at a young, design-wise, pop culture-wise audience, nevertheless provide two distinct views of publication design in the late 1980s. Despite its content, *Rolling Stone*'s design is lively but relatively traditional, while *Emigré*'s is openly experimental and risky.

Derek Ungless, Art Director
Rolling Stone October 1982
pp. 38–39: 12 1/2 x 10 1/4 format
Allan Tannenbaum, photographer
© 1982 Straight Arrow Publishers,
Inc., New York

Published "no more than four times a year," *Emigré* magazine appears with new typefaces created for every issue on a Macintosh computer. These digitized faces reflect the inventive attitude toward periodical design of its typographer, Zuzana Licko, and its art director, Rudy VanderLans. An emigrant from the Netherlands, VanderLans started the publication with the idea that there should "be no boundaries" in the freedom to design.

**Rudy VanderLans and
Zuzana Licko**
Emigré 4 1986
cover: 16 1/2 x 11 3/8 format
Published by Emigré Graphics,
Berkeley, California

One of innumerable American newspapers that have come and gone, the *New York American* devoted a great deal of space to sports. The design of this page is remarkable on several counts: the scale and disposition of the central image; the headline above the nameplate; and the high first column all combine to create a design more akin to that of avant-garde magazines of the period than to the conservative tradition of newspapers.

Designer unknown
New York American
27 October 1933
p. 21: 22 x 17 format

The juxtaposition of these two pages from *The New York Times* and *USA Today* demonstrates the profound philosophical chasm that divides classical newspaper design from the growing tendency toward fewer words and more colorful images, which are appearing not only in Sunday magazine supplements but throughout the pages of American daily newspapers.

Louis Silverstein, Art Director
The Week in Review
9 November 1969
section 4, p. 1: 22 x 13 3/4 format
Courtesy *The New York Times*

America's Cup
14 January 1987
section C, p. 12:
22 3/4 x 13 1/2 format
Courtesy *USA Today*
© Gannett Company, Inc.,
Arlington, Virginia

The New York Times

Editorials, Letters,
Science, Religion,
Education, Law,

© 1969 The New York Times Company

THE WEEK IN REVIEW

Section **4**

Sunday, November 9, 1969

Lindsay's Victory
Page 2

Guerrillas in Mideast
Page 4

Indian Party Split
Page 7

Apollo 12's Mission
Page 8

Nixon and the War

The Plan: To Let Saigon Take Over Fighting

WASHINGTON—After a substantial buildup that started before the Oct. 15 moratorium and lasted through nearly three weeks of it up and down the nation, President Nixon exposed himself to the nation last week. In an effort to gain in detail than ever before his strategy for ending the war in Vietnam.

Following his Vietnam speech last week, President Nixon pointed to piles of telegrams he received, above, as evidence of what he called "silent majority" support for his policy. His plan calls for withdrawal of American troops, such as those below.

The Critics: It Is Not A Plan to End U.S. Involvement

WASHINGTON—The reaction to President Nixon's long and anxiously awaited Vietnam address last week was a peculiar unexpected muttering among critics, like a fuse that had been lit but was not yet ready to detonate.

To Get Them Home

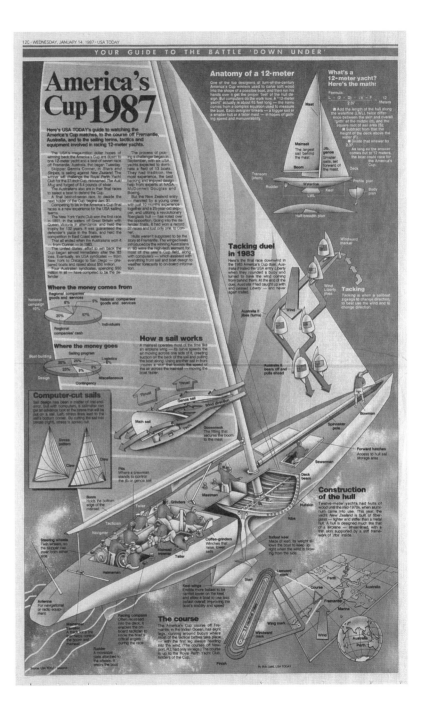

Anonymous

legibility

pantographic

EPHEMERAL

refinement

DISPLAY

Advertising Europe

innovation

technology

new idiom

translate (bits)

digital

wood display type

Century

Goudy Old Style

Cheltenham

Centaur

Franklin Gothic

Cooper Black

Metroblack

Electra

Caledonia

Tempo Bold

Bell Centennial

Charter

In 1828 Darius Wells, inventor of mass-produced **wood display type**, published the first known wood-type catalogue, helping to launch an era of job printing and advertising. Wood type was widely used, announcing ship sailings, auctions, theatrical events, and wanted criminals. The designers of wood type were largely anonymous artists and engravers who embellished fat-face versions of European typefaces. In the latter part of the century competition among the wood-type manufacturers created a golden age of wood engraving, with new American styles, elaborate decorative devices, and marked individuality.

Century typeface was designed by L.B. Benton for *Century Magazine* in 1894. The magazine's publisher, Theodore Low De Vinne, wanted a typeface that was heavier than existing faces and was therefore better able to withstand the pressure of the new high-speed presses. In this way, **Century** represents the earliest example of what were later called legibility types (advanced by Mergenthaler Linotype in the 1930s): these are specialized fonts designed to meet the standards of high-speed quality printing for newspapers and magazines.

Frederic W. Goudy designed Camelot in 1896, the first of more than one hundred typefaces he created in his lifetime. Goudy came into the field at a time when pantographic engraving machines were beginning to replace hand punchcutting. Not all of Goudy's types are admired today; many are similar to one another, differing only in the most subtle variations of letter shape and thickness. Among his most distinguished are Kennerley Old Style, designed in 1911, and **Goudy Old Style**, commissioned by the American Type Founders Company (ATF) in 1915.

In 1896 **Cheltenham** was designed by Bertram Goodhue for use by the Cheltenham Press. During this period fine typography and presswork were the marks of several private presses, influenced by William Morris's work at the Kelmscott Press. The typeface was originally cut by ATF for hand-setting, but ATF and Mergenthaler Linotype later issued it to the printing trade, making it the first face to be available in both hand-set type and Linotype. The face became extremely popular; for the next ten years, **Cheltenham** dominated ephemeral printing as Mission-style furniture dominated the domestic scene.

Bruce Rogers designed his first typeface, Montaigne, for the Riverside Press publication of *The Essays of Montaigne* in 1901. Montaigne was a handsome refinement of the fifteenth-century Jenson type, but Rogers resolved to improve upon it at a later time. The result was **Centaur** (1915), which has been praised as the most elegant version of the much-copied Jenson. Rogers recaptured the spirit of the early type and pared away the accidents of punch-cutting.

M.F. Benton designed **Franklin Gothic** in 1903, one of a program of Gothics he developed between 1900 and 1908. In America the first nineteenth-century Gothic faces were experiments to simplify solid, square-serif letters. These early sans-serif types were called Gothic because of their heavy weights and black letters. They were thought of as suitable only for display lines, although many typefounders tried to improve the weight, width, and size. Following the sweep of popularity of the **Cheltenham** design, the use of Gothics declined. Only after the impact of European geometric sans serifs did the typeface seem acceptable for text.

Cooper Black (1920) was derived from the early nineteenth-century fat-face style of lettering that had been popular for advertising and broadsides by Oswald Cooper. It was not uniformly admired in design circles, but the advertising world accepted it wholeheartedly as the "telling and selling type supreme." Lanston Monotype, needing to compete, asked Goudy for a similar design, which was called Goudy Heavy Face. In the 1960s heavy black faces were used by the designer Herb Lubalin, who exploited their bold and emotional qualities with contemporary phototypesetting technologies.

Robert Hunter Middleton of Ludlow Typograph Company developed two sans-serif families, Record Gothic and **Tempo**, which followed current fashion. Record, a successful version of earlier German Gothic faces, was begun in 1927. The cutting of the series was interrupted by the design of **Tempo** (1930), when Ludlow wanted a typeface modeled on the newer geometric sans serifs such as Futura. After World War II the Record family was completed. Ludlow was, like many typefounders, aware of the introduction of new European sans-serif styles, and he tried to develop comparable designs in the new idiom.

William Addison Dwiggins was commissioned by Mergenthaler Linotype to design **Metroblack** (1929–1930), a modern sans-serif face. Dwiggins introduced unusual features in his lowercase letters, such as a varied stroke thickness and letters sheared at an angle; these set his design apart from the geometric sans serifs of the time. While several different weights were introduced, **Metroblack** lost much of its popularity when the German typeface Futura became available for Linotype composition.

In 1935 Dwiggins designed **Electra** and introduced a new innovation: an italic that appears more as simple, slanted romans than as flowing, calligraphic italics. Dwiggins was thinking of a type that reflected the modern age of speed yet resembled his own drawing of letters. In this way, he is an interesting link between the classical and the modern. While he had sharp criticism for modern schools, such as the Bauhaus, his own approach was often unorthodox and distinctively new.

In 1938 Dwiggins cut **Caledonia**. The design grew from his liking for the Scottish faces of the nineteenth century, when, however, there was a need to strike every curve with a compass and suffer through many recuttings. Dwiggins designed his face with the twentieth-century technology of Linotype in view, adding a lively curve and a calligraphic flick. He often distinguished himself in this way, accepting the limitations of manufacturing type for mechanical composition and making use of its possibilities.

Mergenthaler Linotype's Matthew Carter introduced **Bell Centennial**, which was commissioned by AT&T, in 1978. Replacing Bell Gothic of 1938, the new design was intended to be compatible with AT&T's corporate graphic style and technically functional for the high-speed cathode ray tube typesetters used in composing phone directories. The design of the small, individual characters had to be legible under different inking conditions and within strict spacing limitations. Once the design concept was approved, Carter painstakingly translated each character into individual digital elements (bits), first in pencil sketches on a grid, then as finished bitmaps.

Charter was developed by Matthew Carter on a computer-based design system in 1987. In addition to original type designs, Carter translates contemporary and historical typeface designs into digital form, using a more economical technique than that of bitmaps: each letter is stored in the computer as a control point; these points define the curves and straight lines of the character's outline.

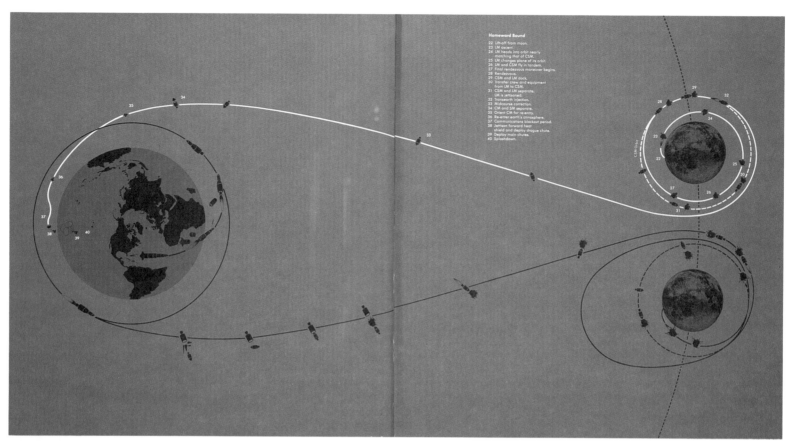

Homeward Bound
22 Lift-off from moon.
23 LM ascent.
24 LM heads into orbit nearly
     matching that of CSM.
25 LM changes plane of its orbit.
26 LM and CSM fly in tandem.
27 Final rendezvous maneuver begins.
28 Rendezvous.
29 CSM and LM dock.
30 Transfer crew and equipment
     from LM to CSM.
31 CSM and LM separate;
     LM is jettisoned.
32 Transearth injection.
33 Midcourse correction.
34 CM and SM separate.
35 Orient CM for re-entry.
36 Re-enter earth's atmosphere.
37 Communications blackout period.
38 Jettison forward heat
     shield and deploy drogue chute.
39 Deploy main chutes.
40 Splashdown.

The ubiquitous CBS "eye," with
and without the letters CBS in the
Didot Bodoni typeface that is the
company's standard, has appeared
throughout the years in a variety of
guises: on occasion the "pupil" has
become a camera lens, a ball for
sports, or a globe for world affairs.

William Golden
CBS logo 1951

Lou Dorfsman was named creative
director of CBS television after the
untimely death of William Golden in
1959. He spent the following thirty
years with the expanding network,
creating some of its most sophisticated print and motion graphics.
Among them is an extraordinary
book commemorating man's historic
landing on the moon. Its last spread
contains a diagram of the astronauts'
return voyage to Earth indicating all
stages of the journey, from lift-off to
splashdown.

Lou Dorfsman
10:56:20PM, EDT 7/20/69
pp. 47–48: 11 x 10 1/4 format
Published by CBS, New York

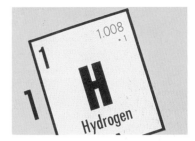

The images of this five-second station identification popped on the screen in time with the announcer's voice saying, "WGBH-TV Boston." The 3D-2 is used for program promotions, seasonal IDs, special occasions, and holidays.

Christopher Pullman and the design staff at WGBH
Television spots 1975–1980
Designers: Gaye Korbet, John Kane, Paul Souza, Doug Scott, Tom Sumida
WGBH Educational Foundation, Boston

241

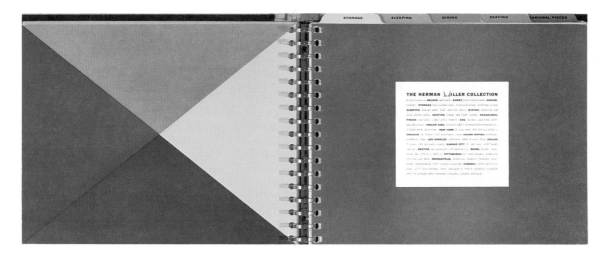

From the early 1950s until the late 1970s the Herman Miller furniture company had an astonishing group of brilliant consultants — George Nelson, Charles and Ray Eames, and Alexander Girard — who created the high design standards that still obtain at this company today.

George Nelson Associates
The Herman Miller Collection 1955
frontispiece: 9 1/2 x 12 format
Designers: Charles and Ray Eames, Irving Harper, Carl Ramirez, and Deborah Sussman
Courtesy Herman Miller, Inc., Zeeland, Michigan

The Office of Charles and Ray Eames
Advertisement for Herman Miller, 1963
12 x 8 3/4 format
Deborah Sussman design
Courtesy Herman Miller, Inc., Zeeland, Michigan

FROM THE COLLECTION OF MOLDED PLASTIC CHAIRS DESIGNED BY EERO SAARINEN ● KNOLL ASSOCIATES, INC., 575 MADISON AVENUE, NEW YORK 22, N. Y.

Herbert Matter was design consultant to Knoll Associates from 1946 to
1966. In those years he created a
series of memorable advertisements.
Matter expresses the formal,
sculptural qualities of the molded
plastic chairs of Eero Saarinen
through his unique use of photomontage.

Herbert Matter
Advertisement for
Knoll Associates, Inc. 1948
various formats
Courtesy Knoll International,
New York

The first Great Ideas of Western Man advertisement by the Container Corporation of America appeared in 1950 as a result of the desire on the part of the company's founder, Walter Paepcke, publicly to express a concern for issues beyond the immediate one of sales generally dealt with in print advertising. To provide material for the series, Mortimer Adler, who had worked on the Encyclopedia Britannica's Great Books program, was hired to develop a list of significant statements by philosophers, scientists, and political leaders from which a company committee could choose. Designers were asked to submit ideas that would give visual expression to the text. Institutional advertising, for which the Great Ideas series was the prototype, has since been undertaken by many American corporations.

Will Burtin
John Milton on the Purpose of Education
and
Gene Federico
Disraeli on Education and the Future
from the series Great Ideas of Western Man
13 x 10 1/2 each
Published by Container Corporation of America, Chicago, 1950–1962

244

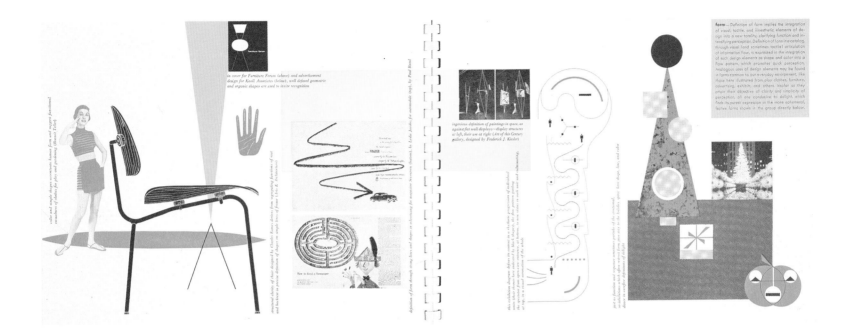

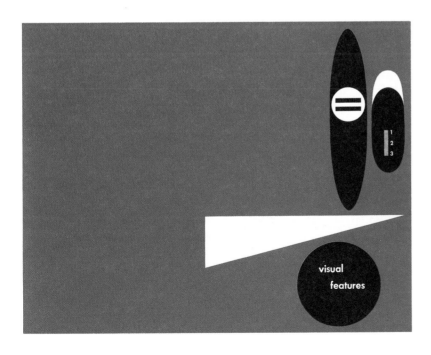

Sweet's, the venerable architectural resources catalogue company, published *Catalog Design Progress* to assist manufacturers in the development of information design. In it the authors analyze the application of typography and imagery designed to convey data to architects and builders.

K. Lönberg-Holm and Ladislav Sutnar
Catalog Design Progress 1950
unpaginated: 9 1/2 x 12 1/2 format
Published by Sweet's Catalog Service, New York

The National Biscuit Company (currently Nabisco Brands) has been producing food products since 1898 and in that time has created some of America's most engaging package designs, including two from the 1930s illustrated here: a 1934 store ad for Ritz crackers, and the flat carton label for "Uneeda Bakers" Oreo Creme Sandwich.

Courtesy Nabisco Brands, Inc., Parsippany, New Jersey

The advertising agency Doyle Dane Bernbach created a series of remarkable ads for Volkswagen in the 1960s. These represent, in a sense, the quintessential ad campaign, as their wordplay and design respond so directly and frankly to the character of that unique automobile.

Helmut Krone, Art Director
various formats
Courtesy Volkswagen United States, Inc., New York

American paper companies have, over the last forty years, produced printed materials for the trade that are more than ads. These publications, in addition to demonstrating the ways various papers may be used, often contain beautifully produced designs and useful documentary information.

Henry Wolf
Imagination 11 1968
"Circus"
10 3/4 x 12 format
Published by Champion International, Stamford, Connecticut

Seymour Chwast
Design & Style 2 1987
12 x 10 1/8 format
© The Pushpin Group
Published by Mohawk Paper Mills, Inc., New York

Yosemite

National Park
California

National Park Service
U.S. Department of the Interior

From Glacier Point the scenery spreads out in all directions, giving you a breathtaking view no matter which way you look. Looking east, you see Half Dome.

Yosemite National Park embraces a vast tract of scenic wildlands set aside in 1890 to preserve a portion of the Sierra Nevada mountains that stretches along California's eastern flank. The park ranges from 610 meters (2,000 feet) above sea level to more than 3,960 meters (13,000 feet) and offers three major features: alpine wilderness, groves of Giant Sequoias, and Yosemite Valley. The 325 kilometers (200 miles) of roads give access to all of these features either by car or by free shuttlebus in some areas. To get to know the real Yosemite, however, you must

leave your car and take a few steps on a trail. You don't have to walk far to discover the grandeur that can be found here and the values this special place offers. Thousands of people have come to Yosemite and left refreshed and relaxed and perhaps a bit more knowledgeable about what they want out of life. See what you can find.

The story of Yosemite began about 500 million years ago when the Sierra Nevada region lay beneath an ancient sea. Thick layers of sediment lay

on the sea bed, which eventually was folded and twisted and thrust above sea level. Simultaneously molten rock welled up from deep within the earth and cooled slowly beneath the layers of sediment to form granite. Erosion gradually wore away almost all the overlying rock and exposed the granite. And even as uplifts continued to form the Sierra, water and then glaciers went to work to carve the face of Yosemite. Weathering and erosion continue to shape it today.

Visiting the Park

Tuolumne Meadows and the High Country

This section of Yosemite has some of the most rugged, sublime scenery in the Sierra. In summer the meadows, lakes, and exposed granite slopes teem with life.

Giant Sequoia Groves

Glacier Point

Wawona

Yosemite Valley

Backcountry

IN CASE OF EMERGENCIES CALL 911

Activities, Services, General Information

Protecting Yourself

The National Park Service publishes some five hundred brochures, guides, and ephemera of all kinds each year. The expansion of the park system and the need for publication guidelines led the Park Service to consult with the designer Massimo Vignelli in the mid-1970s. Vignelli created the "Unigrid System," an elegantly simple framework for Park Service publications that allows people with diverse backgrounds and abilities to create materials that have consistency while retaining individuality.

Massimo Vignelli,
System Designer
Yosemite
23 1/2 x 16 5/8
Art Director: Vincent Gleason
Published by the National Park Service, U.S. Department of the Interior, Washington, D.C.

From 1935 to 1943 the Works Progress Administration printed two million posters dealing with significant public issues such as education, health, and trade — a government effort unequaled before or after that eight-year period. Long overlooked in histories of American graphics, those posters and the designers responsible for them have been reevaluated in a 1987 book, *Posters of the WPA*, by Christopher DeNoon.

Martin Weitzman
Foreign Trade Zone No 1 1937
silkscreen
28 x 22
Collection Library of Congress

Among the most arresting and posteresque of the WPA images — with their flat color and simplified form — was the series of eight designed by Lester Beall from 1937 to 1941 for the Rural Electrification Administration. The messages they convey are as direct and unequivocal as their designs.

Lester Beall
Posters for the *Rural Electrification Administration* 1937
silkscreen
40 x 30 each
Collection Lester Beall Archive, Rochester Institute of Technology

Mehemed Fehmy Agha (1896–1978) was instrumental in making design an integral part of the modern magazine. Born in the Ukraine to Turkish parents, he studied art in Kiev and received advanced degrees in languages in Paris. In 1928, while working on the German *Vogue* in Berlin, he met Condé Nast, who recognized in Agha a versatile and brilliant designer and invited him to become art director of *Vogue* in the United States. Eventually Agha would direct the design of *Vanity Fair* and *House & Garden* as well. Employed by Nast from 1929 to 1943, he changed the face of *Vogue*, making bold use of negative space, altering the shape of headlines, and introducing European sans-serif type styles. He transformed photographic presentation in magazines, hiring innovators such as Edward Steichen and Cecil Beaton and placing images asymmetrically on a page. Agha is also credited with introducing color photographs and full-bleed pages to the modern magazine.

Herbert Bayer (1900–1985) was a pioneer in applying European avant-garde design principles in the United States. He studied at the Bauhaus from 1921 to 1923 and, as a professor there later in the 1920s, was a leader of the modernist revolution in typography and graphic design. He gave the Bauhaus publications their unique appearance by using geometric compositions, a sans-serif alphabet, and an entirely lowercase alphabet. In 1938 Bayer emigrated to America, becoming the self-appointed spokesman for the Bauhaus movement, lecturing, writing, and designing exhibitions. Beginning in 1946 he played a seminal role as designer and educator at the Aspen Institute for Humanistic Studies. Bayer worked for the Container Corporation of America for many years and, in 1956, was made chairman of its design department.

Lester Beall (1903–1969) was a self-taught graphic designer who was experimenting with European avant-garde ideas well before European designers began emigrating to the United States, just prior to World War II. He earned a doctorate in art history at the University of Chicago and worked as a free-lance designer in Chicago (1927–1935); in New York (beginning in 1935); and in Brookfield Center, Connecticut (1951 until his death). Among his main clients were the *Chicago Tribune*, *Collier's* and *Time* magazines, the Rural Electrification Administration, the International Paper Company, and the Connecticut General Life Insurance Company. His posters for the Rural Electrification Administration of the late 1930s made bold use of everyday scenes and objects to create memorable images. In 1937 Beall became the first American commercial artist to be honored with a one-man show at The Museum of Modern Art, New York. His notions about the expressive use of typography and photography were adopted by some sectors of the American advertising community. As an author and lecturer, he was an outspoken proponent of design as a force for social change.

Will Bradley (1868–1962) was a self-taught designer whose work marked the beginning of Art Nouveau in America. He began as an errand boy and apprentice in the printing business. Bradley did his first important work in 1894, for *The Inland Printer*, a print-trade journal published in Chicago. The eighteen covers he created for that periodical from 1894 to 1896, as well as his series of covers for *The Chap-Book* magazine, reflect his interest in the heavily ornamented Arts and Crafts books of William Morris and the sinuous drawings of Aubrey Beardsley. In contrast to Morris's love for heavy Gothic typefaces, however, Bradley advocated simpler forms, sometimes designing his own lettering. Carrying on the Arts and Crafts philosophy, he established The Wayside Press in 1895 and during 1896 published a literary and art journal, *Bradley: His Book*. After the turn of the century he was a consultant to the American Type Founders

Company (ATF), designing typefaces and ornaments. He became art editor of *Collier's* magazine in 1907 and in the early 1920s was art and typography supervisor for the Hearst chain of newspapers, magazines, and motion pictures.

Alexey Brodovitch (1898–1971), as art director of *Harper's Bazaar* for twenty-five years, had a transforming impact upon modern magazine design. He was born and educated in Russia and worked at various illustration, advertising, and department store jobs in Paris before emigrating to the United States in 1930. Brodovitch joined *Harper's Bazaar* in 1934 and remained there until he retired in 1958. His unconventional cropping of photographs, use of negative space, and layouts brought an almost musical feeling to the magazine's pages. He was especially gifted in his use of photography — relating the composition and tone of an image to the type that accompanied it — and hiring such innovators as Henri Cartier-Bresson, Man Ray, and Richard Avedon. As a teacher, Brodovitch influenced a generation of designers and photographers. He led informal classes in his home in the 1930s and taught at the New School for Social Research, New York, from 1941 to 1949.

Will Burtin (1908–1972) was a pioneer in the use of graphic design to convey scientific information. He was trained as a typographer and designer in his native Germany and taught at the Werkschule in Cologne. Burtin came to the United States in 1938 and designed training manuals and graphic presentations for the Office of Strategic Services, as well as gunnery manuals for the U.S. Army Air Corps, during World War II. He served as art director of *Fortune* magazine from 1945 to 1949 and there began exploring innovative graphics to portray complex scientific material. His most significant work was for the Upjohn pharmaceutical company, notably a 1958 cell exhibition and the design of *Scope*, Upjohn's magazine

for physicians. By using photomontage, models, cutaway views, geometric diagrams, photographic blowups of microscopic forms, and overprinting, Burtin was able to make cell structures, molecular construction, and natural processes visible.

Louis Danziger (b. 1923) creates designs that are widely admired for their discipline, restraint, and visual order. He studied graphics under Alvin Lustig at the Art Center College of Design, Los Angeles (1947–1948), and magazine design briefly under Alexey Brodovitch at the New School for Social Research, New York (1948). In 1949 he established his own practice in Los Angeles. He was corporate design consultant to the Atlantic Richfield Company (1978–1986) and has created advertising graphics for the Container Corporation of America, Clinton Laboratories, and the Champion Paper Company. He has also distinguished himself with the design of exhibition catalogues for the Los Angeles County Museum of Art, notably *The Avant-Garde in Russia, 1910–1930: New Perspectives* (1980) and *Art in Los Angeles: Seventeen Artists in the Sixties* (1981). Well versed in the history of his field, Danziger has also taught at a number of schools, including the California Institute of the Arts, Valencia (1972–1978).

Sheila Levrant de Bretteville (b. 1940) has used her graphic skills in nontraditional projects dealing with community issues and women in society. De Bretteville received her B.A. in art history from Barnard College, New York, in 1962 and her M.F.A. from the Yale University School of Art in 1964. In 1971 she created the first women's design program at the California Institute of the Arts, Valencia, and in 1973 founded the Women's Graphic Center at the Woman's Building, Los Angeles. Since 1981 she has chaired the department of communication design and illustration at Otis Art Institute of Parsons School of Design, Los Angeles. She also maintains a design studio in Los Angeles and has numbered among her clients Warner

Bros. Records, *American Cinematographer* magazine, and the *Los Angeles Times*. Her publication designs include *Chrysalis*, a quarterly magazine of women's culture (1977–1979) and the periodical *Art Coast: Contemporary Art West and East* (1989).

Lou Dorfsman (b. 1918) exerted a great deal of influence on design for radio and television during his forty-two years with CBS. While a student at The Cooper Union for the Advancement of Science and Art, New York, he created exhibition designs for the 1939 New York World's Fair. Dorfsman joined CBS in 1946, served as the radio division's art and creative director, and became creative director of the television network in 1960 following the sudden death of William Golden. In 1964 he was named director of design for the entire CBS Corporation, a post he held until his resignation in 1988. His early years at the network coincided with a challenging period in design — when television came of age, when radio was brought back from its decline, and when the corporate approach to advertising was emerging. Dorfsman broke new ground by combining simple ideas with a provocative, well-ordered visual presentation. As the corporation's design director, he created a luminous reputation for CBS in advertising and design, keeping tight control over the integrity of everything that bore the company's trademark.

William Addison Dwiggins (1880–1956) was an original and prolific book and type designer best known for his work for Alfred A. Knopf and the Mergenthaler Linotype company, although his early graphic work was in advertising. He studied at the Frank Holme School of Illustration in Chicago with designer Frederic W. Goudy. In 1903 and 1904 he operated his own press in Cambridge, Ohio, and thereafter was a free-lance designer based in Hingham, Massachusetts. His work as a calligrapher and lettering artist helped revive respect for classic letter forms. In 1923 Dwiggins met the publisher Alfred Knopf, for whom he was to design more than three hundred books.

Given the freedom to experiment with paper covers, two-column formats, and stencil ornaments, he was largely responsible for establishing that firm's reputation for design excellence. Dwiggins also designed a number of private-press and limited-edition books, many for the Limited Editions Club. His most celebrated edition was H.G. Wells's *The Time Machine* (Random House, 1931). Two of the eighteen typefaces he created for Mergenthaler between 1928 and 1956, Electra (1935) and Caledonia (1938), are among the outstanding type designs of this century.

William Golden (1911–1959) was a gifted art director at CBS. The pioneering work he did there in the 1950s remains to this day a benchmark of excellence in communications. Golden was educated at the Vocational School for Boys in New York City, where he was taught photoengraving and the rudiments of commercial design. He learned ad layout at the *Los Angeles Examiner* and spent a year under Mehemed Fehmy Agha at Condé Nast Publications. Agha's goal of unceasing artistic development stayed with Golden throughout his career. He joined CBS in 1937 and ultimately gave the network a distinctive, and pervasive, house style long before the concept of corporate image took hold. As art director, and eventually as creative director of advertising and sales promotion for CBS television, he shaped the company's visual identity, devising the classic "eye" logo, advertisements, exhibitions, corporate materials, promotional graphics, and more. He also proved to be an effective speaker and writer on behalf of responsible design.

Frederic W. Goudy (1865–1947) was one of the great innovative type designers of the century, able skillfully to select models that could be adapted to our times. While still in his twenties, he

and a friend began a small printing business, the Booklet Press, which was later renamed the Camelot Press. In 1896 he sold his first type designs to the Dickinson Typefoundry in Boston, part of the recently formed American Type Founders Company (ATF) group. After a brief spell as a cashier, Goudy decided to become a free-lance lettering artist. At first he sent his drawings to foundries for a fee. Later, however, he became increasingly involved in the manufacture of his types: he supervised the engraving of matrices by a craftsman, commissioned the casting, and marketed the fonts himself. Eventually he also took up his own matrix engraving and casting. Among the best of his more than one hundred typefaces are Goudy Modern (1918); Italian Old Style (1924); and University of California Old Style (1938), created for the University of California Press.

E. McKnight Kauffer (1890–1954), who was born in America but grew up artistically in Europe, helped establish advertising design as a serious art form. He was almost entirely self-taught. In 1913 he saw the groundbreaking Armory Show, was profoundly affected by the Cubist works included in it, and soon afterward moved to Europe. Kauffer began his career as an advertising artist in England in 1915, remaining there until 1940. His first poster commission was for the London Underground Railway Company, and, with that organization's encouragement, he persevered to make design his life's work. His designs of the early 1920s were some of the first to show the influence of painters such as Picasso and Braque. This is demonstrated particularly in his use of emphatic angular forms. From 1924 to 1940 he did poster series for the London Underground and for the Shell and B.P. Ethyl oil companies. He also produced book illustrations for Nonesuch Press and for Faber and Gwyer. After Kauffer returned to his homeland he created posters for the New York Subway Advertising Co., Inc. (1949) and American Airlines (1947–1948), as well as book jackets for Alfred A. Knopf.

Gyorgy Kepes (b. 1906) is important as a designer and teacher and also as an advocate of the use of design to serve human values. He studied at the Royal Academy of Arts, Budapest (1924–1928), and worked in Berlin and in the London studio of fellow-Hungarian László Moholy-Nagy before emigrating to the United States in 1937. Influenced by Moholy-Nagy and Walter Gropius, Kepes recalls these Bauhaus masters in his experimental approach and interest in the links between design and architecture. His book *Language of Vision* (1944), a basic text in design schools for nearly forty years, was based on classes he taught at the Institute of Design, Chicago. Outstanding among his graphic designs are advertisements for the Container Corporation of America (1938–1944). His exhibitions, which explored ways of involving and educating the viewer, included *The New Landscape* (1951) and *Light as a Creative Medium* (1965). Kepes has also collaborated with numerous architects, designing installations that made creative use of natural and artificial light. Interdisciplinary collaboration is at the heart of the Center for Advanced Visual Studies, a workshop Kepes founded at the Massachusetts Institute of Technology, Cambridge, in 1967.

Herb Lubalin (1918–1981) entered The Cooper Union for the Advancement of Science and Art in 1935 and quickly grew enamored of typography. After working sporadically for small firms Lubalin became art director at Sudler and Hennessey. He remained with that agency until 1964. In his most innovative work he united concept and visual form into what has been called a typogram — a brief, visual typographic poem. He favored overlapping, compressed type and intense layouts. From 1964 until his death, under numerous partnerships and associations, he influenced editorial design with his work for the magazines *Eros*, *Fact*, and *Avant*

Garde. In 1970 he cofounded with Aaron Burns the International Typeface Corporation (ITC), an organization formed to secure royalties for typeface designers. ITC's bimonthly journal, *U&lc.*, established a complex, dynamic layout that had a great impact during the 1970s.

Alvin Lustig (1915–1955) was a prominent designer in the 1940s and 1950s. He studied at the Art Center College of Design, Los Angeles (1934–1935), and briefly with Frank Lloyd Wright. At age twenty-one Lustig was operating his own typographic and printing shop in Los Angeles. From 1940 until his early death he worked as a free-lance designer, alternating between New York City and Los Angeles. Extremely versatile, he created book designs, interior designs, identity programs, trademarks, and even designed a small helicopter. He is best known for his book jackets for New Directions and Noonday Press, which reflect his belief in the power and beauty of type. Lustig was also visual-research director for *Look* magazine (1944–1946). In all his work Lustig saw form and content as one, and he searched for symbols to capture the essence of the contents. As a teacher he sought to open his students to all the arts and technology.

Herbert Matter (1907–1984) was a designer and photographer responsible for some of this century's most inventive and beguiling advertisements. He studied under the painter Fernand Léger at the Académie Moderne, Paris (1928–1929), and later worked with the architect Le Corbusier and the great French poster artist A.M. Cassandre. Beginning in 1932, Matter designed a series of now-famous posters for the Swiss National Tourist Office that demonstrate his flair for dramatic montages and bold figure-ground contrasts. He settled in New York City in 1936 and worked as a free-lance photographer for *Vogue* and *Harper's Bazaar.* He was later a staff photographer for Condé

Nast Publications (1946–1957). His abstract, innovative advertisements of the 1950s for the Knoll Associates furniture design and manufacturing firm were widely emulated. He also made films on Alexander Calder and Buckminster Fuller and wrote a book about Alberto Giacometti.

Katherine McCoy (b. 1945) holds a position of leadership in the graphic design field as cochair (with her husband, Michael McCoy) of the design department at the Cranbrook Academy of Art, Bloomfield Hills, Michigan. Under their influence the department has become a center for the development of new trends in graphics. McCoy was educated at Michigan State University. In 1967 she became a junior designer with Unimark International, Chicago. She took up her current position at Cranbrook in 1971. McCoy contends that designers interpret and communicate cultural values through the forms they create. She believes that designers must do more than simply present information clearly and impartially, that they must also have a role in creating symbolic meanings. Her own work has evolved to become increasingly animated and complex. Her clients have included the Chrysler Corporation, MIT Press, and the Formica Corporation.

László Moholy-Nagy (1895–1946) was among the European émigrés who helped make postwar American art and design decidedly abstract. A gifted and enthusiastic experimenter, he explored various media and expanded the definitions of both photography and design. While a young law student at the University of Budapest, Moholy-Nagy was already painting, writing, and publishing an art review. He went to Berlin in the early 1920s, where he became associated with the Constructivists and earned a reputation among European avant-garde circles for his "photograms." These were created by arranging paper, cut and shaped to reflect and defract light, into abstract patterns. In 1923 Walter Gropius invited him to teach the foundation course at the Bauhaus, and the two collaborated closely on the school's publications.

After leaving the Bauhaus he worked as a graphic and exhibition designer, photographer, and filmmaker in Europe. In 1937 he was invited to establish the New Bauhaus in Chicago, which later became the Institute of Design. Moholy-Nagy's most important legacy was his impact on the students and teachers with whom he worked. His books, *The New Vision* (1932) and *Vision in Motion* (1947), influenced a generation of design teachers, photographers, and artists.

Christopher Pullman (b. 1941) is design manager of WGBH, Boston's public broadcasting television station. He received a B.A. in history from Princeton University in 1963 and an M.F.A. from Yale University in 1966. Before joining WGBH, in 1973, he had a free-lance practice in New Haven, Connecticut, and was a graphic design consultant. At WGBH Pullman is in the unusual position of being able to oversee all aspects of the station's visual communications. Among his department's projects have been the titles segments of the "Masterpiece Theatre," "American Short Story," and "Evening at Pops" series. He also directs the design of books, promotional materials, and set designs for the station itself as well as promotional slides, advertisements, and press kits accompanying programs that WGBH distributes nationally through the Public Broadcasting System (PBS).

Bruce Rogers (1870–1957), one of the most important book and type designers of the early twentieth century, brought the ideal of the elegantly designed book to commercial publishing. At Purdue University in Indiana he studied illustration but was inspired to design books by the publications of the Kelmscott Press, which were just beginning to appear. In 1896 he joined the Riverside Press of the Houghton Mifflin Company, where he helped establish a special department for limited editions. From 1900 to 1912 he completed sixty

editions that reflected the evolution of a new approach to book design. Each volume was different in design, format, type, paper, printing, and binding. In 1912 he became a free-lance designer, working for the Metropolitan Museum of Art, Cambridge University Press, and Harvard University Press. Among his seven hundred books, several, including T.E. Lawrence's translation of Homer's *Odyssey* (1932) and the *Oxford Lectern Bible* (1935), are classics of design. Rogers also designed his own typefaces; one of these, Centaur (1915), is among the half-dozen great American typefaces.

Nancy Skolos (b. 1955), with her partners, Tom Wedell and Kenneth Raynor, creates illusory compositions incorporating elements of design and photography. Skolos received her B.F.A. from the Cranbrook Academy of Art, Bloomfield Hills, Michigan, in 1977 and her M.F.A. from Yale University's School of Art and Architecture in 1979. She began collaborating with Wedell and Raynor at Cranbrook, where both were pursuing graduate degrees in photography. The three established their practice in Boston in 1980. The group integrates techniques of graphic collage, multiple exposures, and gradated papers to create three-dimensional, often surreal images. Some of their work is inspired by the illusory spaces of early modern artists such as Giorgio de Chirico. Their clients include the Boston Acoustics stereo speaker company and Digital Equipment Corporation. In 1988 Skolos designed an issue of *Design Quarterly* that was devoted to the Minneapolis Sculpture Garden.

Barbara Stauffacher Solomon pioneered the development of the large-scale graphic works called supergraphics. She studied at the San Francisco Art Institute and the Basle School of Design in Switzerland (1957–1961). Her supergraphics, created during the 1960s, employed bold geometric shapes of bright color, giant Helvetica letter forms, and large diagonals and arcs that alter perspective and add vitality to a given architectural space.

Biographies

From 1962 to 1972 she created several signing and supergraphics projects, most notably for the architect Charles Moore's Sea Ranch housing development in northern California and for Ghirardelli Square in San Francisco. After receiving degrees in history and architecture from the University of California, Berkeley, she worked as a landscape designer with the SWA Group; Williams, Roberts and Todd; and Michael Van Valkenburgh. Among her writings are *Green Architecture and Agrarian Gardens* (1988), in which she discusses gardens where architecture and nature meet.

Deborah Sussman (b. 1931) has advanced the field of environmental design, creating visual images and applying them to a variety of architectural and public spaces. Her work has been informed by a unique amalgam of folk art, regional styles and colors, and cross-disciplinary experience. Sussman attended Bard College, Annandale-on-Hudson, New York (1948–1950), and the Institute of Design, Chicago (1950–1953). For periods in the 1950s and 1960s she was an art director in the office of Charles and Ray Eames in Los Angeles, working on films, advertisements, fair pavilions, packaging, and toys. She studied and worked in Europe from 1957 to 1960. In 1968 she opened her own office and in 1980 incorporated as Sussman/Prejza & Co. with her husband, Paul Prejza. The firm developed the environmental design of the 1984 summer Olympics, held in Los Angeles, creating an array of signing systems and related banners and decorative objects. The firm has also developed graphics for mixed-use building complexes such as the Crocker (now the Wells Fargo) Center, Los Angeles, and South Street Seaport, New York.

Ladislav Sutnar (1897–1976) was a pioneering designer whose work prefigured by many years what is now called "information design." In Prague he trained at the Academy of Applied Arts and at the Technical University. He then worked as a painter and stage designer and served as the director of the State School for Graphic Arts, also in Prague. In the 1930s he emerged as one of Europe's leading exhibition designers. Arriving in the United States in 1939, he embarked upon a prolific career comprising typography, packaging, and advertising and exhibition design. As art director of *Sweet's Files* (1941–1960), a set of annually updated catalogues of industrial and architectural products, Sutnar showed designers how to cope with complex information, using visual articulation of type — underlining, type-size and weight contrasts, spacing, color, and reversing — to facilitate searching, scanning, and reading. He opened his own design firm in 1951 and was art director of *Theatre Arts* magazine. Sutnar also wrote articles and books in which he discussed his notion of design as a systematic, problem-solving process.

George Tscherny (b. 1924) is a native of Budapest, but he spent his childhood in Berlin. In 1941 he emigrated to the United States, attending Pratt Institute, Brooklyn, from 1947 to 1950. In the early 1950s he worked in the offices of the industrial designers Donald Deskey and George Nelson and in 1955 opened his own office. His designs have included corporate identity programs, advertising, posters, displays, stamps, and annual reports. Tscherny aims at formal effects in keeping with the specific occasion, letting the message logically determine the graphic means. He sometimes presents the essence of the subject simply and dramatically, as in his advertisements for the Herman Miller furniture-manufacturing firm, but can also lean toward richness and experimentation, as his book cover designs demonstrate. He has numbered Air Canada, IBM, RCA, and the Public Broadcasting System (PBS) among his clients.

Rudy VanderLans (b. 1955) and **Zuzana Licko** (b. 1961) design and publish the avant-garde magazine *Emigré*. Born in The Hague, VanderLans received a B.A. in graphic design from the Dutch Royal Academy of Fine Arts in 1979. He worked as an apprentice designer in the Netherlands for three years, coming to California in 1982 to study photography at the University of California, Berkeley. He founded *Emigré* that year. Since the third issue he has produced the magazine with Zuzana Licko, who was born in Czechoslovakia and received her B.A. in graphic communication from the University of California, Berkeley, in 1984. The experimental, stripped-down look of the publication largely derives from its computer-designed typefaces. The magazine also showcases inventive layouts and startling images. VanderLans does all layout, design, and production, and Licko is responsible for typesetting and type design. The two also do free-lance graphic design work for clients such as Esprit, Apple Computer, the *San Francisco Chronicle*, and *Mother Jones* magazine.

Massimo Vignelli (b. 1931) and his wife, Lella, create designs whose hallmarks are clean and simple forms, clear bright colors, and a sense of vitality and drama. Vignelli studied architecture in Milan (1950–1953) and Venice (1953–1957). He and his wife, who is also an architect, moved to the United States in 1965. In New York City in 1971 the couple established Vignelli Associates, a design practice whose work has included furniture, tableware, showrooms, interiors, posters, and corporate identity programs. In his graphic work Vignelli makes lettering itself a means of expression by using contrasts of scale, type size and weight, color, texture, and spacing. He has designed numerous books for Chanticleer Press and for Rizzoli International Publications. Among his major graphic designs are logos for American Airlines (1967) and Bloomingdale's department store (1972); corporate identity programs for Knoll International (1966); subway graphics for the Washington, D.C. Metro (1970); and the development of a graphics program for the National Park Service (1977).

Henry Wolf (b. 1925) emerged as a force in the magazine publishing field in 1960s. He was born in Vienna, emigrated to the United States in 1941, and attended the School of Industrial Art and the New School for Social Research, both in New York City. Beginning in 1946, he worked successively for Arnold Studios, a design firm; the Geer, duBois and Company advertising agency; and the U.S. Department of State. He became art director of *Esquire* magazine in 1952 and soon began commissioning work by artists such as Ben Shahn and Richard Lindner. He succeeded Alexey Brodovitch as art director of *Harper's Bazaar* in 1958, and in 1961 he became the first art director of *Show*, an arts magazine that proved to be well ahead of its time in both form and content. He left *Show* in 1964 to embark on a career in advertising. Since 1971 he has been head of his own advertising design firm and has taught at The Cooper Union for the Advancement of Science and Art and the School of Visual Arts, both in New York City.

Richard Saul Wurman (b. 1936) has devoted his career to making various kinds of visual information understandable through his inventive design of maps and guides. In 1959 he received his M.A. from the University of Pennsylvania, Philadelphia, where he studied with and worked for the architect Louis Kahn. From 1963 to 1976 he was a partner in the Philadelphia architecture and urban-planning firm of Murphy Levy Wurman. At the same time, Wurman became well known for his writing, teaching, and exhibition development. In 1981 he founded Access Press, which has produced guidebooks for Los Angeles, New York City, Washington, D.C., San Francisco, and Paris, among other cities, as well as a 1990 United States road atlas. In addition, Wurman's San Francisco office has designed Pacific Bell's new *Smart Yellow Pages* (1988).

Selected Bibliography

Note: Listed here are the major works that were used extensively in the preparation of this book and exhibition. Numerous other important references are cited in the essays.

Ades, Dawn. *The 20th-Century Poster: Design of the Avant-Garde.* New York: Abbeville Press, 1984.

Aldersey-Williams, Hugh. *New American Design: Products and Graphics for a Post-Industrial Age.* New York: Rizzoli, 1988.

Allen, James Sloan. *The Romance of Commerce and Culture: Capitalism, Modernism, and the Chicago-Aspen Crusade for Cultural Reform.* Chicago: University of Chicago Press, 1983.

American Institute of Graphic Arts. *Symbol Signs.* Washington, D.C.: United States Department of Transportation, 1976.

American Institute of Graphic Arts. *Graphic Design USA,* vols. 1–9. New York: Watson-Guptill, 1980–1988.

Art Directors Club. *Art Directors Annual,* vols. 1–67. New York: ADC Publications, 1921–1988.

Blumenthal, Joseph. *The Printed Book in America.* Hanover, N.H.: University Press of New England, 1989.

Burns, Aaron. *typography.* New York: Reinhold, 1961.

Carter, Rob, Ben Day, and Philip B. Meggs. *Typographic Design: Form and Communication.* New York: Van Nostrand Reinhold, 1985.

Cohen, Arthur. *Herbert Bayer: The Complete Work.* Cambridge, Mass.: MIT Press, 1984.

Cohen, Barbara, Steven Heller, and Seymour Chwast. *Trylon and Perisphere: The 1939 New York World's Fair.* New York: Harry N. Abrams, 1989.

DeNoon, Christopher. *Posters of the WPA.* Los Angeles: Wheatley, 1987.

Davis, Alec. *Package and Print: The Development of Container and Label Design.* New York: Faber and Faber, 1967.

Day, Kenneth. *Book Typography, 1815–1965, in Europe and the United States of America.* Chicago: University of Chicago Press, 1965.

Dreyfuss, Henry. *Symbol Sourcebook: An Authoritative Guide to International Graphic Symbols.* New York: McGraw-Hill, 1972.

Dwiggins, William Addison. *Layout in Advertising.* New York: Harper and Brothers, 1928.

Forty, Adrian. *Objects of Desire: Design and Society from Wedgwood to IBM.* New York: Pantheon Books, 1986.

Golden, Cipe Pineles, Kurt Weihs, and Robert Strunsky, eds. *The Visual Craft of William Golden.* New York: George Braziller, 1962.

Goudy, Frederic W. *A Half-Century of Type Design and Typography, 1895–1945.* 2 vols. New York: The Typophiles, 1946.

Grannis, Chandler B. *Heritage of Graphic Arts.* New York: R.R. Bowker, 1972.

Harris, Neil. *Designs on Demand: Art in the Modern Corporation.* Washington, D.C.: Smithsonian Institution, 1985.

Harrison, Richard Edes. *Look at the World.* New York: Alfred A. Knopf, 1944.

Heller, Steven and Seymour Chwast. *Graphic Style: From Victorian to Post-Modern.* New York: Harry N. Abrams, 1988.

Jacobson, Egbert, ed. *Seven Designers Look at Trademark Design.* Chicago: Paul Theobald and Company, 1952.

Jussim, Estelle. *Visual Communication and the Graphic Arts: Photographic Technologies in the Nineteenth Century.* New York: R.R. Bowker, 1974.

Kelly, Rob Roy. *American Wood Type: 1828–1900.* New York: Van Nostrand Reinhold, 1969.

Kepes, Gyorgy. *Language of Vision.* Chicago: Paul Theobald and Company, 1944.

Kepes, Gyorgy. *Sign, Image, Symbol.* New York: George Braziller, 1966.

Lönberg-Holm, K. and Ladislav Sutnar. *Catalog Design Progress.* New York: Sweet's Catalog Service, 1950.

Lustig, Alvin. *The Collected Writings of Alvin Lustig.* Edited by Holland R. Melson. New York: Thistle Press, 1958.

Marchand, Roland. *Advertising the American Dream: Making Way for Modernity, 1920–1940.* Berkeley: University of California Press, 1985.

Massey, John, ed. *Great Ideas.* Chicago: Container Corporation of America, 1976.

Meggs, Philip B. *A History of Graphic Design.* New York: Van Nostrand Reinhold, 1983.

Moholy-Nagy, László. *Vision in Motion.* Chicago: Paul Theobald and Company, 1947.

Mott, Frank Luther. *A History of American Magazines.* Cambridge, Mass.: Belknap Press of Harvard University Press, 1957.

Neurath, Otto. *Modern Man in the Making.* New York: Alfred A. Knopf, 1939.

Pope, Daniel. *The Making of Modern Advertising.* New York: Basic Books, 1983.

Pulos, Arthur. *American Design Ethic.* Cambridge, Mass.: MIT Press, 1983.

Rand, Paul. *Thoughts on Design.* New York: Wittenborn, Schultz, 1947.

Rand, Paul. *Paul Rand, A Designer's Art.* New Haven, Conn.: Yale University Press, 1985.

Remington, R. Roger and Barbara J. Hodik. *Nine Pioneers in American Graphic Design.* Cambridge, Mass.: MIT Press, 1989.

Sutnar, Ladislav. *Visual Design in Action: Principles, Purposes.* New York: Hastings House, 1961.

Thompson, Bradbury. *Bradbury Thompson: The Art of Graphic Design.* New Haven, Conn.: Yale University Press, 1988.

Tracy, Walter. *Letters of Credit: A View of Type Design.* Boston: David R. Godine, 1986.

Tufte, Edward R. *The Visual Display of Quantitative Information.* Cheshire, Conn.: Graphics Press, 1983.

Updike, Daniel Berkeley. *Printing Types: Their History, Forms and Use.* Cambridge, Mass.: Harvard University Press, 1937.

Wilson, Richard Guy, Dianne H. Pilgrim, and Dickran Tashjian. *The Machine Age in America, 1918–1941.* New York: Harry N. Abrams, 1986.

Word and Image: Posters from the Collection of the Museum of Modern Art. Edited and selected by Mildred Constantine. Text by Alan M. Fern. Greenwich, Conn.: New York Graphic Society, 1968.

Zim, Larry, Mel Lerner, and Herbert Rolfes. *The World of Tomorrow: The 1939 New York World's Fair.* New York: Harper and Row, 1988.

The following periodicals have been used extensively in research for this book and exhibition:

AIGA Journal of Graphic Design (New York: American Institute of Graphic Arts)

Communication Arts (Palo Alto, Calif.: Coyne and Blanchard)

Graphis (New York: Graphis U.S.)

ID: Magazine of International Design (New York: Design Publications)

PM (New York: PM Publishing)

Print (New York: RC Publications)

Lenders to the Exhibition

ABC Broadcast Graphics, New York

Access Press Ltd., New York and San Francisco

Alfred A. and Blanch Knopf Library, Harry Ransom Humanities Research Center The University of Texas at Austin

Alfred A. Knopf, New York

American Institute of Graphic Arts, New York

Governor Elmer Andersen

David Anderson

Apple Computer, Inc., Cupertino, California

Saul Bass

Merrill C. Berman

Tom Bonauro

Champion International Corporation, Stamford, Connecticut

Art Chantry

Chermayeff & Geismar Associates, New York

Children's Television Workshop, New York

Seymour Chwast

Coca-Cola Archive, Atlanta

Elaine Lustig Cohen

College of St. Scholastica Library, Duluth, Minnesota

Columbia University Library, New York

Muriel Cooper

Louis Danziger

DDB Needham Worldwide Inc., New York

Sheila Levrant de Bretteville

Lou Dorfsman

Emigré Graphics, Berkeley, California

Ex Libris, New York

Farleigh Dickinson University Library, Madison, New Jersey

Fashion Institute of Technology, New York

Dan Friedman

The Getty Center for the History of Art and the Humanities, Santa Monica, California

Milton Glaser

April Greiman

H.J. Heinz Company, Pittsburgh

Clifford L. Helbert

Helen Farr Sloan Library, Delaware Art Museum, Wilmington

Steven Heller

The Henry Francis Du Pont Winterthur Museum Library, Winterthur, Delaware

Herb Lubalin Study Center of Design and Typography, The Cooper Union for the Advancement of Science and Art, New York

The Herbert Matter Archive, Yale University, New Haven, Connecticut

Herman Miller, Inc., Zeeland, Michigan

IBM, Stamford, Connecticut

Indianapolis Electrotype Service Company, Indianapolis, Indiana

Knoll International, New York

David Kunzle

Landor Associates, San Francisco

Leo Lionni

Library of Congress, Washington, D.C.

Linotype Company, Hauppauge, New York

M&Co., New York

Richard Martin

Katherine McCoy

McGraw-Hill Information Systems Company, Sweet's Group, New York

The Metropolitan Museum of Art, New York

Melissa Meyer

Minnesota Historical Society, St. Paul

Minneapolis Institute of Arts

Minneapolis Public Library

Minnesota Center for Book Arts, Minneapolis

Mohawk Paper Mills, Inc., New York

Victor Moscoso

The Museum of Modern Art, New York

Nabisco Brands Inc., Parsippany, New Jersey

National Museum of American History, Smithsonian Institution, Washington, D.C.

National Park Service, Harper's Ferry, West Virginia

The New York Times

Norwest Corporation, Minneapolis

Cipe Pineles

The Queens Museum, Flushing, New York

R.W. Smith, Bookseller, New Haven, Connecticut

R/Greenberg Associates, Inc., New York

Paul Rand

Rochester Institute of Technology, Graphic Design Archive, Rochester, New York

St. Cloud State University, Learning Resource Center, St. Cloud, Minnesota

Douglass Scott

Siegel & Gale, New York

James Sitter

Nancy Skolos

Barbara Stauffacher Solomon

Sumner Stone

Sussman/Prejza & Co., Culver City, California

Edward Tufte

Type House + Duragraph, Inc., Minneapolis

University of Iowa Library, Iowa City

United States Postal Service, Washington, D.C.

USA Today, Arlington, Virginia

Vignelli Associates, New York

Douglas Wadden

Westvaco Corporation, New York

WGBH Educational Foundation, Boston

Whitney Museum of American Art, New York

Henry Weiland

Lorraine Wild

Elliot Willensky

Wilson Library, University of Minnesota, Minneapolis

Wm. Wrigley Jr. Company, Chicago

Henry Wolf

The Wolfsonian Foundation, Miami

Acknowledgments

The exhibition *Graphic Design in America: A Visual Language History* is the first effort by a museum to examine the full range of work that falls within the realm of American graphic design. The overwhelming quantity of this material in all of its manifestations has led us to describe the breadth of it in terms of genres of design and to present these in selective "case studies" that exemplify specific design directions. For that reason, and because of the fugitive materials and ephemeral nature of so much graphic design, a great deal of the more than one hundred years of this history does not appear in this volume nor in the exhibition: much remains for subsequent explorations.

It is not possible to include here the names of all of the extraordinarily knowledgeable people who have given advice and assistance in the development of this book and exhibition, but some of them must be mentioned. Over the past three years I have worked closely with the American Institute of Graphic Arts staff, particularly with its director, Caroline Hightower. Significant contributions to the organization of the exhibition have been made by a number of remarkable designers, writers, and critics, including: Elaine Lustig Cohen, Hugh Dubberly, Lorraine Ferguson, Robert Greenberg, April Greiman, Tom Hardy, Steven Heller, Tom Hewitt, Ellen Lupton, Eric Martin, J. Abbott Miller, Chris Myers, Douglass Scott, and Louis Silverstein. The authors who have contributed essays to this book — Joseph Giovannini, Neil Harris, Estelle Jussim, David Kunzle, Maud Lavin, Ellen Lupton, J. Abbott Miller, and Lorraine Wild — deserve particular thanks, as in many instances they have courageously tackled uncharted territory with skill and grace. And special thanks to those sixteen brave designers whose interviews with Steven Heller bring us to the heart of the matter.

There is an unusually long list of generous lenders on page 257; I am extremely grateful to them for making their treasures available for public view. Two especially devoted collectors must be acknowledged: Merrill Berman, whose Presidential ephemera and early graphics have provided the framework for the time line and a large part of the nineteenth-century material; and Roger Remington, whose superb Rochester Institute of Technology Graphic Design Archive was a primary source of information and loans. And for making computers available for use in the exhibition I am indebted to Apple Computer, Inc.

My thanks to Paul Gottlieb, Margaret Kaplan, and Gertrud Brehme of Harry N. Abrams, Inc. for their enthusiastic collaboration with the Walker Art Center in the publication of this book. Thanks also to Steve Katz of Champion International Corporation for his advice and printing expertise. For many hours spent in negotiating permissions for the use of film clips in this book and in the exhibition, I am indebted to Wendy Reilly and Marion McLusky. And particular thanks to Naegele Outdoor Advertising and Metromedia Technologies, companies that have generously provided the billboard announcing the exhibition, which was designed by April Greiman.

The members of the Walker Art Center staff who have contributed their time and energy to this endeavor are listed opposite. Particular appreciation is due our chief graphic designer, Glenn Suokko, whose care and knowledge gave this book its visual quality and character. For editorial diligence and expertise I thank Phil Freshman and Linda Krenzin. To Mark Kramer and Stephen Ecklund, who with their usual proficiency supervised the installation of the exhibition, my admiration. And my thanks to Martin Friedman, whose support of this project has been vital to its realization.

Two people who are not members of the Walker staff have given countless hours to this project: Jennifer Tobias, who joined us in the early stages as a summer research intern; and Deborah Karasov, who has contributed a great deal to the research and writing of the didactic materials during the final year of organization, have both earned my gratitude.

And kudos to Audrey Bernstein, whose extraordinary photographs of New York City signage were commissioned for the exhibition.

On behalf of the Walker Art Center Board of Directors and staff I want to thank Champion International Corporation for its generous funding of this exhibition, and to Marian Jill Sendor and John Hildenbiddle of Champion who provided encouragement and commitment throughout the development of the exhibition and this book, our special thanks. We are grateful for their support and that of the National Endowment for the Arts.

Mildred Friedman
Design Curator

Staff for the Exhibition

Walker Art Center Director
Martin Friedman

Administrator
David M. Galligan

Curator
Mildred Friedman

Registrar
Sharon Howell

Graphic Designer
Glenn Suokko

Publication Editors
Mildred Friedman
Phil Freshman

Editorial Assistant
Linda Krenzin

Publication Indexer
Michelle Piranio

Education Director
Margaret O'Neill-Ligon

Budget Supervisor
Mary Polta

Librarians
Rosemary Furtak
Susan Lambert-Smith

Public Information Director
Deborah Blakeley

Slide-Tape Producer
Charles Helm

Photographer
Glenn Halvorson

Installation Supervisors
Mark Kramer
Stephen Ecklund

Reproduction Credits

All photographs not otherwise credited, Walker Art Center

pp. 8, 219 (right): Audrey Bernstein
p. 15: Venturi, Rauch and Scott Brown, Philadelphia
pp. 16, 18: Bass/Yager and Associates, Los Angeles
pp. 20, 22, 23: Aaron Burns
All Presidential-election material pp. 25–65 and pp. 28 (right), 32 (right), 76, 228: Jim Frank, courtesy Merrill Berman
pp. 26, 30: The New-York Historical Society, New York
p. 27 (left): Clarence P. Hornung and George Braziller, Inc., New York
p. 28 (left): University of Michigan Press, Ann Arbor
p. 29 (left): Amon Carter Museum, Fort Worth, Texas
p. 29 (right): Earl F. Lundgren
p. 31 (left and center): Louis A. Warren Lincoln Library and Museum, Fort Wayne, Indiana
pp. 31 (right), 36 (right), 46 (left), 94, 102 (top), 250: Library of Congress, Washington, D.C.
pp. 32 (left), 219 (left): The Bettmann Archive, New York
p. 33: The Quaker Oats Company, Chicago
p. 34: General Research Division, The New York Public Library, Astor, Lenox and Tilden Foundations, New York
pp. 35 (right), 80: Chicago Historical Society
pp. 36 (left), 108: Norwest Corporation, Minneapolis
p. 37 (left and center): H.J. Heinz Company, Pittsburgh
pp. 37 (right), 38: Trefoil Publications, Ltd., London
p. 39 (left): The Saturday Evening Post, ©1920 The Curtis Publishing Co., Indianapolis
p. 39 (center): Rare Book and Manuscript Division, The New York Public Library, Astor, Lenox and Tilden Foundations, New York
p. 39 (right): The Schlesinger Library, Radcliffe College, Cambridge
p. 40: American Red Cross, Washington, D.C.
p. 41: Yale Collection of American Literature, The Beinecke Rare Book and Manuscript Library, Yale University, New Haven, Connecticut
p. 42: Art Directors Club, Inc., New York
p. 43 (right): Philadelphia Museum of Art

pp. 45, 162: Harper's Bazaar, ©The Hearst Corporation, New York
pp. 46 (right), 50, 51, 58 (right): The Museum of Modern Art, New York
pp. 47, 49, 166 (left): The Denver Art Museum, Herbert Bayer Collection and Archive
p. 48 (left): National Museum of American Art, Smithsonian Institution, Washington, D.C.
p. 48 (center): Container Corporation of America, an affiliate of Jefferson Smurfit Corporation, St. Louis
p. 48 (right): Bauhaus-Archiv, Museum für Gestaltung, Berlin, West Germany, ©Hin Bredendieck
p. 53: Esquire Magazine, New York
pp. 54 (left), 110, 214, 216: Westvaco Corporation, New York
pp. 54 (right), 247: ©Volkswagen United States, Inc., Troy, Michigan
p. 56 (left): Whitney Museum of American Art, New York
p. 56 (right): Ebony Magazine and Johnson Publishing Company, Inc., Chicago
pp. 57, 136, 240: CBS Inc., New York
p. 58 (left): ©1978 Matt Herron
pp. 58 (center), 178, 181, 182, 184, 185, 186, 188, 190: David Kunzle
p. 59 (left): Ray Frieden
pp. 59 (right), 100, 102 (bottom): Milton Glaser
p. 60 (left): Seymour Chwast
p. 60 (center): Herb Lubalin Study Center of Design and Typography, The Cooper Union for the Advancement of Science and Art, New York
pp. 62 (left), 196, 198, 237 (left): Louis Silverstein
pp. 62 (right), 124, 125: April Greiman
p. 64: Emigré Graphics, Berkeley, California
pp. 66, 68, 69: Matthew Carter
pp. 70, 72, 73: Chermayeff & Geismar Associates, New York
p. 74: Metropolitan Life Insurance Company Archives, New York
p. 78: The Wolfsonian Foundation, Miami
p. 84: American Lung Association, New York
pp. 86 (top), 92: Minnesota Historical Society, St. Paul
p. 86 (bottom): The Art Institute of Chicago
p. 90 (left): Metro Decatur Chamber of Commerce, Decatur, Illinois
p. 90 (right): Broome County Historical Society, Binghamton, New York
p. 96 (top): reprinted from The Bauhaus by Hans M. Wingler, published by

The MIT Press, English adaptation ©1969 The Massachusetts Institute of Technology, Cambridge
p. 96 (bottom): reprinted from Learning from Las Vegas by Robert Venturi, Denise Scott Brown, and Steven Izenour, published by The MIT Press, ©1972 The Massachusetts Institute of Technology, Cambridge
pp. 104, 115: Superman is a trademark of DC Comics Inc. Used with permission.
pp. 116, 144, 146: M&Co., New York
p. 126: Landor Associates, San Francisco
p. 129: Steve Hayden
pp. 131 (bottom), 132 (left): The New York Public Library, New York
p. 132 (right): DDB Needham Worldwide Inc., Chicago
p. 134: Dan Friedman
p. 140: Sheila Levrant de Bretteville
p. 142 (top): Barbara Kruger
p. 142 (bottom): Leslie Sharpe
p. 154 (bottom): Steam Press, New York
p. 155: Musei Civici di Rovereto, Galleria Museo Depero, Italy
p. 156: Art and Architecture Library, Yale University, New Haven, Connecticut
pp. 164, 222, 251: Rochester Institute of Technology, Graphic Design Archive, Rochester, New York
pp. 166 (right), 243: The Herbert Matter Archive, Yale University, New Haven, Connecticut
p. 168: Institute of Design Collection, Special Collections, The University Library, University of Illinois, Chicago
pp. 192, 194: Paul Rand
p. 210 "My Singing" text: reprinted from The Good Times Are Killing Me, ©1988 Lynda Barry; The Real Comet Press, Seattle
p. 220 (bottom): Mercedes Matter
p. 231 (top): reprinted from Native Arts of the Pacific Northwest, introductory text by Robert Tyler Davis, with the permission of the publishers, Stanford University Press, © 1949 the Board of Trustees of the Leland Stanford Junior University
p. 223: Sussman/Prejza & Co., Culver City, California
p. 242: Herman Miller, Inc., Zeeland, Michigan
p. 246: Nabisco Brands Inc., Parsippany, New Jersey

Index

Index

Colophon

The text for this book was composed in four American typefaces. Franklin Gothic was designed by M.F. Benton in 1903 for the American Type Founders Company; Goudy Old Style was designed by Frederic W. Goudy in 1915 for the American Type Founders Company; the original of New Caledonia, called Caledonia, was designed by William Addison Dwiggins in 1938 for the Mergenthaler Linotype company; News Gothic was designed by M.F. Benton circa 1908 for the American Type Founders Company. Updated versions of these typefaces by Linotype were composed with Aldus's PageMaker on a Macintosh II computer at the Walker Art Center, Minneapolis, and output on Linotronic's L300.

The title page was composed in Goudy Old Style, New Caledonia, News Gothic, Gothic, and Gothic Round; the latter two, introduced by George F. Nesbitt in 1838, were among the first wood types to be cut in the United States.

The book was printed at The Village Craftsmen/ Princeton Polychrome Press, Princeton, New Jersey, on 100 lb. Pageantry® Text paper produced by Champion International Corporation, Stamford, Connecticut; and was bound by Horowitz/Rae Book Manufacturer, Fairfield, New Jersey.